PRODUCTION

AND

INVENTORY CONTROL:

PRINCIPLES AND TECHNIQUES

Second Edition

George W. Plossl
(First edition coauthored with Oliver W. Wight)

Prentice-Hall, Inc., Englewood Cliffs, NJ 07632

Library of Congress Cataloging in Publication Data

PLOSSL, GEORGE W. (date)
    Production and inventory control.

    Bibliography: p.
    Includes index.
    1. Inventory control.   2. Production control.
I. Title.
TS160.P55   1985   658.7'87   85–517
ISBN 0–13–725144–0

© 1985, 1967 by **Prentice-Hall, Inc.**, Englewood Cliffs, New Jersey 07632

Printed in the United States of America

10   9   8   7

ISBN   0-13-725144-0   01

Prentice-Hall International, Inc., *London*
Prentice-Hall of Australia Pty. Limited, *Sydney*
Editora Prentice-Hall do Brasil, Ltda., *Rio de Janeiro*
Prentice-Hall Canada Inc., *Toronto*
Prentice-Hall Hispanoamericana, S. A., *Mexico*
Prentice-Hall of India Private Limited, *New Delhi*
Prentice-Hall of Japan, Inc., *Tokyo*
Prentice-Hall of Southeast Asia Pte. Ltd., *Singapore*
Whitehall Books Limited, *Wellington, New Zealand*

To Marion, my partner in life and in business.

We have achieved much together and have
enjoyed it. Nowhere has her help been so
needed as in writing books. From the first—
the first edition of this book, the five
that followed and now this second edition—
she has been the "woman behind the man." She's
still there, supporting and pushing me—what a
tremendous teammate!

THE PRODUCTION-CONTROL EXPERTS

(with apologies to "The Blind Men and the Elephant,"
by John Godfrey Saxe)

It was six men of management
To learning much inclined
Who discoursed on production control
And the answers they did find
—from experience, and the lessons
That reward an inquiring mind.

"Order to mins and maximums,"
The first was heard to say,
"You'll have neither too much nor too little
When production's controlled this way."

"But the answer lies in a forecast,"
Said the second man in line,
"Just anticipate your sales,
And everything will be fine."

"I doubt it" said the third one,
"You've forgotten the EOQ.
With balanced setups and inventories,
What problems can ensue?"

The fourth one said: "Use order points
To get the desired control.
When you order materials soon enough,
You'll never be 'in the hole.' "

"But you really need a computer."
Said the fifth— "P.C.'s a dream
With loads run from last week's payroll cards
And exception reports by the ream."

Said the sixth, "Materials management
Is a concept to which I'm devoted—
Instead of learning production control,
I've escaped by getting promoted!"

So study each book and seminar,
Attend every one you can, sir!
You'll find a thousand experts
—most with PART of the answer.

O. W. Wight

CONTENTS

CHAPTER THREE   THE ECONOMIC LOT-SIZE, 33

CHAPTER FOUR   DEMAND MANAGEMENT, 62

CHAPTER FIVE   MATERIALS CONTROL: INDEPENDENT DEMAND, 96

CHAPTER SIX   MATERIALS CONTROL: DEPENDENT DEMAND, 133

CHAPTER SEVEN   MASTER PLANNING, 168

CHAPTER TWELVE   FEEDBACK AND CORRECTIVE ACTION, 320

PROBLEMS, 350

CASE STUDIES, 361

BIBLIOGRAPHY, 374

APPENDICES, 381

LIST OF PRINCIPLES
AND ILLUSTRATIONS

List of Principles

CHAPTER ONE

1 The system framework needed for effective planning and control is common to all manufacturing industries.
2 A manufacturing plant is a single entity and needs an integrated system and teamwork to manage it.
3 Shorter lead time is the most important factor in making a plan more valid.

CHAPTER TWO

4 Manufacturing control requires effective management of all three classes of inventory.
5 Control requires numbers that really count, not just those numbers easy to count.

CHAPTER THREE

6 Distributing setups to cut inventories of high-value items easily offsets increases in those of low value items.
7 The right EOQ is good but shorter setups are far better.
8 EOQ calculations are only a starting point; modify them for practical results.

CHAPTER FOUR

 9 A forecast is a set of numbers to work from, not to.
10 Give each user a forecast suitable for his or her needs.
11 Forecast only what you must; calculate whatever you can.
12 Track forecasts regularly and do it often; find and fix the bad ones.
13 Agree in advance when forecasts will be revised; don't play games with moving goal lines.
14 Don't commit stocked items to any specific location until the last possible moment.

CHAPTER FIVE

15 Correctly answering the question about when an item is needed is far more important than determining how much to order.
16 Order points require reserve stocks because of uncertainties that cannot be eliminated.
17 Apply statistical techniques for setting reserve stocks only where their assumptions are valid and only after testing.
18 Rules of thumb for setting reserve stock levels fail because they ignore the reasons it is needed.
19 Simple physical techniques may provide more economical control of inventories.
20 Time-phasing order point data greatly increases the power of this technique.
21 Orlicky's independent/dependent demand rule provides a good guide to select ordering techniques.

CHAPTER SIX

22 MRP logic applies to all types of products and processes involving multiple components.
23 The ideal part number is short, numerical and unique.
24 Bills of material form the framework of modern systems; they must be highly accurate and properly structured.
25 Control of engineering design changes to bills of material are as vital to a company's success as the new designs.
26 MRP simply mechanizes the fundamental logic of manufacturing.
27 Materials planning simply initiates the procurement process; execution completes it.
28 The logic of MRP is universally applicable; the way it is applied depends on the environment.

CHAPTER SEVEN

29 Data farther out in the planning horizon can and should be in less detail, more aggregated.

30 Stand-alone, independent and multipurpose plans are worse than useless; they are dangerous.
31 The MPS drives the planning, not the execution, process.
32 The best MPS has the least number of items and serves the needs of adequate material and capacity plans.
33 Structuring bills of material properly is a vital part of master production scheduling.
34 The MPS must be well managed, complete and capable of being executed.

CHAPTER EIGHT

35 Inventories must first be managed in aggregate before they can be controlled in detail.
36 EOQ theory should be used to draw trade-off curves for management decision making.
37 Studying alternatives using trade-off curves results in better decisions than calculating reserve stocks for a given level of customer service.
38 Inventory is a liability; less is better.

CHAPTER NINE

39 Managing work center lead times requires managing capacity.
40 Managing order lead times requires managing both priority and capacity.
41 Capacity plans should use the broadest possible product groups that go through similar manufacturing operations.
42 Production plans, even though rough-cut, provide effective means for capacity management.
43 A capacity requirements plan cannot be deferred; rough-cut approaches are very practical.
44 Capacity must be adequate to support the MPS and handle additional unplanned demands.
45 Detailed capacity requirements plans may look highly precise and still be very inaccurate.
46 Capacity is wasted when used to make unneeded items.

CHAPTER TEN

47 Ordering techniques should be used simply to rank orders in priority sequence before selection for release.
48 Backlogs can be controlled better in the office than on the factory floor.
49 Input should be less than or equal to—but never more than—output.
50 Scheduling rules must develop allowances for all elements of lead time.
51 Loading is a priority control technique, useful only if the data represent reality.
52 For on-time deliveries, treat vendors exactly like plant work centers.
53 The more input is controlled, the less output has to be controlled.

CHAPTER ELEVEN

54 Output control must cover both capacity and priority.
55 Effective capacity control is a prerequisite for priority control.
56 The less expediting there is, the more effective it will be.
57 The best method of controlling work on plant floors is to prevent it from getting there too soon.

CHAPTER TWELVE

58 Getting back on plan is tougher—but far better—than replanning.
59 Sound planning and effective control involve information, not data.
60 For control, timeliness is more important than accuracy, although both are necessary.
61 Operations control involves picking the least worst choice from available alternatives.
62 On-time vendor deliveries depend on adequate capacity and short lead times, not on customer ownership, closeness or clout.
63 Select performance measures carefully; people perform to look good on them.
64 The difference between excuses and control information is simply timing.
65 Problems interfering with planned operations can and must be solved.
66 Significant cuts in inventory come only from finding and fixing the causes of excess.

List of Illustrations

PREFACE

The first edition of this book was an astounding success. Written originally for practitioners, it found widespread acceptance and use by data-processing, accounting, manufacturing and industrial engineering managers, consultants, students, and professors. Although never formally translated into other languages, an unauthorized edition appeared in Taiwan in Chinese. I was amazed in my travels around the world at how many offices had copies, which I saw during counseling visits to companies in the industrial countries.

Sales never really dropped off, but it seemed that a new edition was due. Some techniques, like the MPS and MRP, needed more coverage. There was also too little on the integrated system. While the principles were there, they were buried in the text and needed to be highlighted. Very little was obsolete and could be eliminated, so the real problem was to find the best way to organize the material for maximum use by readers.

The solution was two volumes: the original, *Principles and Techniques,* to focus on the fundamentals, the mechanics and the tools of the trade, and a sequel, *Applications,* to cover how these tools should be used in companies. The second volume was completed first and published by George Plossl Educational Services, Inc., in Atlanta, Georgia. This book, published by Prentice-Hall, was completed a few months later.

Together, these volumes contain more complete, authoritative, tested, practical coverage of the field of manufacturing control than any other source except perhaps the APICS Handbook. They are far more readable and better integrated than the Handbook and at least as good as a reference source. The problems and cases in the original text have been retained for those using and familiar with them. New problems have been added to match the additional materials included. Bibliographies have been updated and expanded.

As first chairman of the APICS Certification Council, I was priviledged to lead this outstanding group toward three objectives:

1. Codify the body of knowledge; this was completed successfully.
2. Prepare examinations to test peoples' understanding of this knowledge; this is in place and growing.
3. Improve the dialogue between academicians and practitioners; they are talking but too little and about the wrong subjects.

The widespread use of the first edition of this book in colleges and universities was as gratifying as it was unexpected. It is my hope that the second edition, coupled with the second volume, will speed the development of the mutual assistance programs so urgently needed by both industry and academia.

This second edition was produced after the coauthor of the first edition, Oliver W. Wight, had died. Without him, it was not as much fun, but it took much less time and, I am sure, is at least as good as if we both worked on it. My confidence in this is based on the lack of significant technical differences between us during our long careers and the material in his publications. I welcome the readers' comparisons.

As in the first edition, mathematical and data-processing subjects are treated lightly; I wanted to allocate the maximum space to the other topics of primary importance not so well covered in the literature. Success in any field comes from knowing the trade, not the tricks.

GEORGE W. PLOSSL

CHAPTER ONE

PERSPECTIVE

The Objectives of Production and Inventory Control

Three of the major objectives in most manufacturing firms intent upon earning profit are:

1. Maximum customer service
2. Minimum inventory investment
3. Efficient (low-cost) plant operation

The major problem in meeting these objectives is that they are basically in conflict. Maximum customer service can be provided if inventories are raised to very high levels and the plant is kept flexible by altering production levels and varying production schedules to meet the customers' changing demands. The second and third objectives thus suffer in meeting the first. Efficient plant operation can be maintained if production levels are seldom changed, no overtime is incurred and machines are run for long periods once they are set up on a particular product; however, this results in large inventories and poor customer service while meeting the objective of maximum plant efficiency. Inventories can be kept low if customers are made to wait and if the plant is forced to react rapidly to changes in customer requirements and interruptions in production. In the business world, few companies can afford to work toward one of these objectives to the exclusion of the others, since all are about equally important for sustained success.

Production and inventory control is concerned basically with providing the information needed for the day-to-day decisions required to reconcile these objectives in plant operations. The fact that these objectives are in basic conflict was readily apparent to the manager who owned his own small manufacturing company. He had invested his money in the machines and equipment in the plant, controlled his own manufacturing schedules, and was his own sales representative. When a customer demanded immediate delivery, his alternatives were clear—either spend money on breaking into machine setups and working overtime or let the customer wait. He also had the alternative of carrying inventory in the future—finished products, parts or raw materials—so that he would be able to give his customer better service. The basic conflicts among the objectives existed in this one-manager company and they were not easy to resolve, but at least the manager could see the conflict and weigh the alternatives.

In a large manufacturing company today, the responsibility for customer service rests with one organizational group, the sales department, which seldom recognizes much responsibility for either plant efficiency or for the levels of inventory. On the other hand, manufacturing people usually feel little responsibility for inventories and perhaps little more for customer service. In fact, many plant managers and supervisors have probably never thought of their activities from a customer's point of view. Frequently, the performance of these people is measured not on their contributions to overall company objectives but only on their abilities to meet their assigned, limited goals. Very few first-line supervisors, for example, are rated on their abilities to control lead times and keep items in stock, but they know that their careers depend greatly on how well they get out production, work well with the union and meet their budgeted expense goals. By the same token, very few sales personnel are judged by their contributions to profit; they are rated instead solely on their abilities to sell more products. One of the overworked cliches in business today is: It is healthy to have managers within a company competing against one another. There is truth to this statement when managers are competing for the *same goals*—such competition can produce excellent results—but when they start competing for *different goals*, the results will be waste, conflict and frustration.

Reconciling these conflicting objectives in a modern company, where responsibilities have been sharply divided and where managers have been encouraged to suboptimize by their performance measures, becomes a challenging problem; attempting to solve this problem is the primary function of production and inventory planning and control. Working through an information system, planning, measuring actual performance against the plan and then presenting information to line managers who must take corrective action, the function of production and inventory control is to reconcile these objectives to meet the overall profit goals of the company. There is no other group to do this job.

The Evolution of Production and Inventory Control

Production control and inventory control developed separately. In its very beginnings, production control was only one of the many functions performed by the line foreman. He ordered material, set the size of the work force and the level of production by hiring and releasing people, expedited work through his department and controlled customer service through the inventories that resulted from his efforts. As his workload increased, the foreman was assisted by a clerk, who was added to take care of such functions as timekeeping, other miscellaneous record-keeping and answering the telephone in his department. This brought the clerk into frequent contact with the sales department while answering requests for the status of jobs and queries about delivery promises; the clerk also began reordering material and planning other preparations needed for production in addition to following progress of the work. The clerk was really the beginning of the production control function.

Eventually, as record-keeping activities were transferred into the main office, this clerk developed into a stock-chaser. One prominent New England company had a department in the 1890s known as the "Hurry-up Department"—it is easy to imagine the responsibilities and activities of these people. There were a few attempts at a more organized and scientific approach to production control; there was evidently a fairly comprehensive production control system installed at the Watertown Arsenal in the 1880s (5) but general application did not develop prior to World War II.

By World War II, the position of stock-chaser had fallen into disrepute because of its association (in the minds of co-workers) with crises, upsets, pressure and trouble. Henry Kaiser gave the stock-chasers in his shipbuilding company the name expediters and, with the aid of a *Reader's Digest* article, popularized the concept of the expediter as an action-oriented go-getter, who made a vital contribution to meeting production schedules. By the 1950s, the term *expediting* was often used in books defining production control; one practitioner about that time characterized his activities as ordering the necessary parts to make an assembly after receiving a customer's order and then, when the customer asked why it was not delivered on time, following up to find out where these parts were and putting *RUSH* tags on them. Even today, the expediter is an integral, necessary part of most production control systems.

Inventory control, on the other hand, developed—at least in theory—along more scientific lines. The basic concept of the economic lot-size was first published in 1915 (1) and the statistical approach to determining order points was presented by R. H. Wilson in 1934 (8). However, these fairly sophisticated techniques of inventory management had very little application. Perhaps this was because the 1930s and 1940s were not years that encouraged scientific management. For most companies during the depression of the 1930s, the most important objective was survival. Much as people in a damaged airplane over the ocean throw food and valuables overboard in order to keep the plane aloft long enough to reach land, long-term profit and growth became subordinate during the Great Depression. During the late 1940s, when pent-up demand provided a ready market for every article that could be produced, the objectives of inventory control—leveling workload or competing on the basis of customer service—were not important in most business operations.

The scientific management movement from the early 1900s to World War II, under Taylor, Emerson, Gantt, the Gilbreths and others, had helped to provide recognition that the work of planning and controlling production should be a staff activity; as a result, production and inventory control existed as distinct functions in most companies—but were usually very crude. Production control, with the exception of some simple machine-loading techniques, still consisted basically of expediting in most companies and, while inventory control had developed some scientific theories, these had seen very little real application.

Out of World War II came operations research, the application of scientific techniques to solving the problems of war, where the allocation of limited resources was a matter of victory or defeat. The techniques of operations research were quite effective in World War II. When the scientists who did this work got back to the problems of a peacetime world, their attention focused on production and inventory control, where elements of the problem can be expressed numerically, where statistical probability theories can be applied and where so many of the decisions are the result of balancing alternative solutions. Some notable results were produced in forecasting, inventory control, and mathematical programming. While operations research solved very few of the business problems it set out to solve, it did generate new interest in a more rational approach to production and inventory control.

Probably the biggest problem in applying scientific techniques in industry was the fact that companies were not ready for them. They had not even begun to solve many of their basic problems in controlling manufacturing. Many companies did not even have reasonably accurate lists of the parts that made up their products or route sheets to show the sequences of operations; they depended instead upon the memories of the people in the factory who had made the product for years. Before scientific techniques could be applied, basic information had to be accurate and readily available. In addition, the volume of calculations required for applying such techniques as the statistical determination of forecasts and order points, both highly developed by operations research, was considerably beyond the capabilities of manual systems.

By the late 1950s electronic computers were being used widely in industry but, as with most new technologies, there were as many failures as successes in applying these powerful tools. The information processed had to be complete and accurate because the personal interference that even a reasonably good clerk could give was no longer available to correct obviously ridiculous errors and compensate for missing information. While computers offered almost unlimited capacity in computation, they focused attention on the need for disciplines in information-handling that many companies had failed to develop in the past. Efforts to apply computers were often attempts to install a mechanized system in companies that had never taken manual systems seriously enough to make them work satisfactorily.

In 1957 a group of 27 men working in production and inventory control met in Cleveland and formed the American Production and Inventory Control Society

(APICS). Its objectives were the development of a body of knowledge, dissemination of information on language, principles and techniques and education of its members and others in the field. APICS, through its journal, training aids, special reports, chapter meetings and seminars, regional conferences and an annual international conference, has been a potent force in the evolution of production and inventory control. In its first 25 years, the Society grew to almost 200 chapters—some in every industrial country in the world—and over 50,000 members.

Along the way, the language of the field was defined in a dictionary, the literature was catalogued in a series of bibliographies, a Crusade was conducted introducing the MRP (material-requirements planning) technique (see Chapter 5), an Education and Research Foundation was established to expand the body of knowledge, an Academic Liaison Committee was formed to improve communications between practitioners and academia and the Society's financial strength was evidenced by the purchase of its headquarters' building in Falls Church, Virginia.

Probably the most significant development, however, was the Certification Program. Like CPA's, engineers, doctors and other professionals, people could now demonstrate their understanding of the field by passing examinations. Started in 1973, over 70,000 tests were administered and over 7300 individuals certified, more than 1100 of them at the prestigious Fellow level by the Society's 25th birthday. The roles of the practitioners enlarged also, along with their positions in the organization and their salaries. From stock-chaser and clerk, production- and inventory-control people moved steadily upward through planner, supervisor and manager to the level of vice-president overseeing all functions related to the field, including data processing in many cases. Women played increasing roles and now hold jobs at all levels of their organizations. The name of the field changed to Materials Control and then Manufacturing Control.

Although education, the body of knowledge and the practitioners' roles expanded dramatically, on-the-job performance was disappointing. Inventories that were essentially out of control continued to aggravate the business cycles which became more severe and occurred at shorter intervals. On-time deliveries of products to customers were still more the exception than the rule and unmoving inventories still cluttered the floors of most manufacturing plants and tied up billions in capital urgently needed for other uses. Productivity growth slowed to a stop in the late 1970s. *We knew how to do the job, but we were not doing it.*

Also during this period many U.S. manufacturers lost their dominant positions in their domestic markets as well as internationally. The list of products for which foreign suppliers, principally the Japanese, set the pace was staggering—from automobiles through wristwatches, with almost every letter of the alphabet in between represented at least once. Many (irrelevant) reasons were advanced for this situation, including lower wages, cultural differences, cartels, cooperative unions, paternalistic governments and trade restrictions but professionals in production and inventory control knew better. We had certainly developed our ability to plan better and we could replan at blinding speeds. *But we failed to execute the plans as well as competitors did.*

Manufacturing Control Today

Improved planning and control of operations are recognized today as vital needs in recouping or maintaining a company's strength. Starting in the mid-1970s, projects to achieve this via modern, computerized, integrated systems were common. The organization structure called *Materials Management* was applied in many companies. In its classic form, the materials manager is responsible for traffic, purchasing, inventory and production planning and control, receiving, shipping, branch warehouses, storerooms and interplant trucking, although many variations are practiced. The materials-management concept was the subject of magazine articles and caused much animated discussion and competition among purchasing agents, inventory and production control managers and materials-handling managers. They disagreed about which activity provided the best preparation for the materials manager position—usually overlooking the fact that choosing a person for such a newly created position should depend a great deal more on the individual's knowledge of the profession and managing talents than upon previous experience.

Materials management offers some solid benefits as a form of organization but, unfortunately, it is rarely the cure-all that many expect it to be. This organization format does not of itself improve the use of planning and control systems, procedures or techniques. All can be used well without it. The principal benefit to be derived from this form or organization, in which all the people concerned with the flow of materials through the plant report to one person, is that this person can direct activities to get the most cooperation and effectiveness from these people working together. If the only way to get the supervisors and the people under them who are responsible for handling materials, traffic, purchasing, and production control to work together effectively is to have them report to the same boss, then the materials management concept offers real potential benefits. It suffers from myopia; materials are only one factor important in manufacturing control. Money, workers and machinery are at least as important.

Should a company adopt the materials management concept? If it has an organizational problem or if a revision in organization will bring more expert talent to help solve some of the problems, materials management should be adopted. If, on the other hand, the real problems lies in faulty systems design, poor quality and timeliness of information or bad execution, an organizational change will not solve these problems. It would be unfortunate to divert attention from or delay action in solving the real problems by reorganizing.

The real challenge in manufacturing control has been in proper application of known tools and techniques. The paradox has been that practioners know that their company is "different," yet they are continually searching for a technique someone else has used successfully, hoping it will solve their problems. Blind transplanting of techniques fails when basic principles are unknown or ignored. As long as the emphasis remains on techniques and principles remain subsidiary to these techniques, good techniques will be misused and results will be disappointing.

Professionals understand basic principles and know the useful techniques and how to apply them to the elements that make up a manufacturing-control system.

These elements are shown in Figure 1-1. This diagram shows the principal activities (boxes), the way they are interlocked in the system (arrows) and the foundations and overall control (bars). The foundations are, of course, the data on such factors as orders, materials, products, costs and times, the capability to process the masses of data involved in reasonable time and the people to operate the system and use it to manage the business. Performance measures (covered in detail in the second volume of this series) are applied throughout the system and the operations to aid in control.

Planning and control are, of course, an ongoing, iterative series of activities.

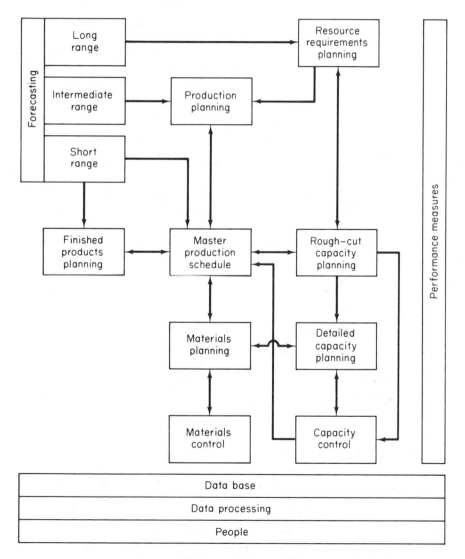

Figure 1-1 MANUFACTURING CONTROL SYSTEM FRAMEWORK.

It is convenient, however, to think of the process beginning with forecasting, discussed in Chapter 2. Long-range projections are used to develop resource requirements, such as plant, equipment, machinery, capital, technology and skills. A discussion of these is beyond the scope of this book. Intermediate-range forecasts are converted to production plans and master production schedules in the near term, as covered in Chapter 2. Short-range forecasts are the principal ingredients in finished goods planning of stocked products and also provide information directly to master scheduling for products made to order or comprised of many customer options.

Rough-cut capacity data, derived partly from resource requirements planning and partly from the master schedule, test the validity of the latter *before* the formal planning system is activated. When the master production schedule is deemed realistic (achievable), the system goes to work. Plans for material and capacity requirements are generated in detail or updated, feedback during execution detects significant deviations from plan and corrective actions are initiated. Chapters 3 through 9 cover these activities and Chapter 10 discusses the techniques of designing and implementing such formal systems.

Careful study of Figure 1-1 reveals some interesting aspects:

1. Most interactions between elements are "two-way streets" (two-headed arrows), indicating that direct linkages are needed in the system to keep them in step.

2. Forecasting and rough-cut capacity planning are exceptions. Forecasts are made unilaterally—they should not be influenced by constraints on producing the required materials. (Note that the master schedule must be so constrained). Rough-cut capacity planning is locked to the master schedule but can be used to drive capacity control or detailed capacity planning when this is the only alternative (other input is lacking).

3. The left half of the chart deals primarily with priority information—making the right things.

4. The right half deals with capacity data—making enough.

5. Effective control of capacity is essential to execution of the plan expressed in the master production schedule, as shown by the arrow linking them. The master schedule must be revised if the capacity requirements of the formal plan cannot be met.

Once complete plans are made via such an integrated system, control is required to insure that they are met in the execution phase. This involves feedback after execution to report the actual status in relation to the plan and the determination of *significant* deviations, showing where corrective action is required to get back to the original plan. Materials control involves the priority planning system that generates orders on vendors for purchased items or on the plant for manufactured components and finished goods. Capacity control governs the flow from the producing facility, whether it be the vendor or the company's own manufacturing plant. The intimate, inseparable relationship between priority and capacity control must be recognized in any successful system.

The design of sophisticated software on powerful computers, unfortunately, has beguiled many companies into frequent replanning. Instead of working back to the schedule, they give up and replan after such problems as unexpected scrap, job delays, or record errors. Many have found it impossible to resist the lure of more precise data—in the mistaken belief that it will make a better plan. More precise is not the same as more accurate, however, when planning future activities.

The system elements do not have equal weight in every inventory management and manufacturing-control system. Distributors, for example, are not very concerned with planning manufacturing capacity, since they merely place orders on suppliers and depend on them being able to deliver to meet their requirements. On the other hand, a make-to-order plant will not maintain a finished goods inventory; most of the emphasis in this type of plant will be reaction—control of production rates, input and output, and open orders. Make-to-stock plants must be deeply concerned with all elements and problems of both inventory and manufacturing control.

The conviction of uniqueness was a major deterrent to progress in several different industries—aerospace, defense, process and repetitive manufacturing. Until the early 1980s they thought they could learn little from the job shop and intermittent manufacturing people who represented the great bulk of APICS membership. In 1981, those within APICS interested in the process industries and others they enlisted conducted the first seminar solely on their type of manufacturing and published the first articles directed at their problems. One of these (7) contained a system framework suitable for their needs—it is essentially Figure 1-1. Shortly thereafter another subgroup of APICS members was organized to focus on repetitive manufacturing (mass production). Several other special interests groups (SIG's) have been organized.

The truth is contained in the first principle.

Principle 1. The system framework needed for effective planning and control is common to all manufacturing industries.

Only the emphasis on various elements and the way the techniques are applied are different. We have a full set of tools in our tool box; there are fundamental principles that apply anywhere; by applying these principles and using the tools properly we can do the job of *managing manufacturing as it should and must be done*.

I can tell success stories about companies in practically every industry, proving we are on sound ground. Few companies in the Western industrial world, (the United States, Canada, and Europe) can match the performance of the Japanese. What is their secret? is a question asked frequently. As I mentioned earlier in this chapter, many "experts" give the wrong answers. The truth is simple and elegant— the Japanese do the fundamentals right and they strive constantly to find better ways to *execute the plan*, viewing the total operation as a single process and *working together as a team* to improve it.

This book focuses on the usable, workable techniques and the principles under which they work effectively. The Japanese have invented no new techniques—they

Preproduction:
    Research and development
    Application design
    Prototype production
    Methods, tooling, and standards
    Equipment procurement
    Plant layout

Operations planning and control:
    Master scheduling
    Capacity
    Priorities

Execution:
    Vendor deliveries
    Plant centers output
    Maintenance of machines and equipment
    Problem-solving

Figure 1-2 BASIC FUNCTIONS.

just use them better. They understand the same principles as the rest of the world—but they apply them more effectively.

Principle 2. A manufacturing plant is a single entity and needs an integrated system and teamwork to manage it.

The system is diagramed in Figure 1-1. The functions to be planned and controlled by it are listed in Figure 1-2. Planning and control cannot be complete and, obviously, will not be effective unless preproduction and execution functions are handled at least as well as operations planning and control. The contrast between Western and Japanese practices with these functions is striking.

All the techniques needed to do the job are now available. Figure 1-3 shows the useful techniques for each of the activities in Figure 1-1. These will be described in this volume, together with their strengths and weaknesses; the application of the techniques is the subject of the second volume in this series, *Production and Inventory Control: Applications* (4).

The Relationship Between Inventory Control and Production Control

One common misconception in industry is that production and inventory control are separate functions. Inventory control writes the orders; production control gets them made in the plant. However, the basic truth is that inventories in a manufacturing plant are maintained to support production or are themselves the result of production. Only where inventories are purchased and then resold without requiring further work can inventory control have meaning apart from production control.

Much of the literature written on the subject of order quantities, order points and MRP, for example, assumes inventory control in a manufacturing plant to be an independent function. However, MRP, order points and economic order quantities (EOQ's) cannot be used successfully to control finished goods inventories without considering how they affect plant production rates and component

Economic Lot-Sizing:

Square root	Part-period balancing	Least total cost
Welch families	Least unit cost	Lot-for-lot
Major/minor setups	Period order quantity	LIMIT

Forecasting:

Delphi	First-order exponential smoothing
Judgment	Second-order exponential smoothing
Running average	Base index (seasonal)
Weighted average	S-curves
Focus	

Materials Planning:

General:
    ABC Classification, aggregate trade-off curves.
Order point:

Classical	Reserve stock (normal distribution)
Time-phased	Reserve stock (Poisson distribution)
Two-bin	Periodic review
	Visual review

Material requirements planning:

Explosion chart	Structuring bills of material
Conventional	Engineering change control
Regeneration	Allocations
Net change	Pegging

Capacity Planning:

Production planning	Detailed CRP
Rough-cut CRP	Graphical

Input Control:

Selecting orders	Block scheduling	CPM
Forward scheduling	Infinite loading	CPS
Backward scheduling	Finite loading	PERT

Output Control:

Input/output control	Expediting	Critical Ratio
Dispatching	Feedback	Flow control

Figure 1-3 POPULAR TECHNIQUES.

schedules. By the same token, production scheduling techniques cannot be developed apart from the inventory control system that generates the orders which make up the schedules. The backlogs that build up ahead of operations in the plant are very real inventories and have a very real effect on the ordering technique through their influence on lead times. The scheduling system must control these inventories if it is to control production properly.

Since purchasing is usually separate from both inventory and production control, it seems natural to run all three as independent activities. However, when inventory control is functionally separated from production control, it is typical for the inventory controller to issue orders to the plant as individual items reach their order points or order release dates and then for the production controller to try to expedite these orders through the manufacturing operations, exerting intense pressure on the plant people to work overtime, making extra setups, shifting the working force or taking other extraordinary—and expensive—actions to cope with the peaks and valleys of work that result. In practice, this usually results in fluctuating backlogs of manufacturing orders and large amounts of in-process material ahead of the manufacturing facilities as plant operating people strive to keep production going at a level rate. Using backlogs to level the workload, of course, means high inventories, long lead times and poor service. In many companies, the reaction of inventory control to this problem is simply to assert that they put the right dates on the orders and manufacturing must get the orders through on time. The major philosophical point of operations research—that people tend to work toward minor goals, or to "suboptimize" can find no clearer illustration than in these circumstances.

Perhaps the most important result of this division of responsibility and the consequent ineffectiveness of both functions is that production control and manufacturing almost inevitably become the whipping boys for most of the ills of the plant. Production control people view line people as shortsighted and uncooperative. Plant people feel that production control personnel are irresponsible and demanding and that they contribute little or nothing to help operate the plant efficiently, but rather interfere with such efforts and cause upset and confusion. Sales people see the plant as "a millstone around our necks."

Effective manufacturing control requires all functions to work together to satisfy all three objectives. It would be pleasant if the control system could be broken into independent elements so that each might handle its own area of responsibility without regard to the others. Unfortunately, the elements of a manufacturing control system are so interrelated that they cannot be isolated from one another in practice without impairing their effectiveness.

Management Policy and Manufacturing Control

The actions taken to meet the goals of customer service, inventory turnover, and efficient plant operation should be conducted in accordance with well-defined management policy but two breakdowns frequently occur. Management establish policy without having the salient facts needed to enable them to make the correct decisions, or management fail to set important policies needed to control their operations properly. The first situation can best be illustrated by policies set by many managements for inventory turnover rates based only on industry averages. Built into the acceptance of an industry average turnover rate as a company's own goal are two basic assumptions: first, that other companies in the industry are managing their operations properly and, second, that such operations are comparable. Both of these are highly questionable. In addition, they neglect "par for the course"; Most managers set turnover goals far too low.

On the other hand, when policies are not defined, management yields its decision-making rights to clerical personnel by default. Material planners can establish company policy by the manner in which they place inventory replenishment orders, for example. These clerks do not have the information required to decide which inventory levels best fit the company's overall requirements. They characteristically react to immediate pressures—increase inventories just when the plant is having the most difficulty meeting its production goals or decrease inventories when the plant is able to produce products at a higher rate.

The absence of intelligent policies relating to inventory levels also leads to a panic reaction to overweight inventories in times of falling business activity. The usual reaction is to issue a decree that inventories must be cut by some specific amount, without regard to the requirements of the business and without full realization of the impact such cuts may have on customer service, costs and employment levels. Not only is customer service hurt, but production rate changes caused initially by falling demand are amplified greatly by untimely and excessive inventory reductions. The reverse sequence (with the same amplification effect) occurs when business picks up again and crash programs are initiated to rebuild depleted inventories. Poor inventory management and production planning aggravate the effects of the business cycle. Modern society, as well as professional management, should expect and demand better performance.

In a well-run modern company, the management policies concerning inventories, customer service, and plant hiring and layoff are developed rationally from information supplied by the manufacturing planning and control function. The effective manager identifies the real alternatives in each problem situation, recognizing that many seemingly impregnable companies have foundered because their managements did not recognize and face up to the unpleasant alternatives and make the necessary decisions in time to avert real crises.

The master production schedule provides the mechanism by which policies are converted to plans. The process of translating policies to numbers (called **master scheduling**) requires teamwork among all functions. The set of numbers developed by this process is used to drive the formal system. Once policy has been established, the manufacturing planning and control manager develops plans to suit these policies and follows up to see that the plans are executed properly. The manager needs no direct authority over supervisors or workers in the plant or over toolroom, maintenance or engineering people; his or her primary role is to generate *information* to show other managers what must be done to meet common objectives. To some extent, the manager must act as a catalyst, urging others to take proper action in order to satisfy the overall objectives of the company. To do this job, the manager has no need for the authority to tell a supervisor when people must work overtime or be assigned to more urgent jobs—this authority must rest with the line personnel, the plant manager, superintendents and department supervisors. Perhaps the distinction can be better understood by using the six basic question words of the English language: what, when, who, how, where, and why. Planning and control determines *what* items and quantities should be made and *when* they should be made, taking into account management policies and the three basic objectives. It is up to the manufacturing people and their supporting staffs to decide *how* and *where* the product should be made and *who* should make it. When, as is so frequently the case, actual performance does not meet the plan, the answer to *why* will depend on whether the cause was a bad plan or poor execution.

The Future

Manufacturing control has evolved from a set of simple clerical chores to a position close to the focus of management attention. Progressive top-level executives recognize the need for a sound function to plan and control plant operations. The advent of the computer has made fully integrated systems with powerful techniques practical, yet many companies have found it difficult to take full advantage of these. The principal reason is that they do not handle information in the disciplined manner required by any real control system. At the same time, they have found that increasing product complexity and pressures of competition on costs and service have made it impossible to manage their operations with manual and fragmented systems. The old ways must go.

During the 1960s, manufacturing planning and control struggled to break out of the "order-launching and expedite" mode of operation. Computer programs were designed to keep inventory records and to recalculate EOQ's and safety stocks as necessary. Practitioners worked valiantly to get the right lot-sizes and safety stocks to buffer their operations against the inevitable variations in demand and lead time. They were thankful for the help of mathematicians, statisticians and computer wizards.

In the 1970s, however, it became clear that the real need was valid due dates on orders. This required a replanning capability, an integrated schedule linking parents and components in bills of material and the management of lead times by controlling order priorities. The prayers of thanksgiving now went to MRP on powerful computers.

Early in the 1980s the big picture came into full focus. To manage any manufacturing operation requires *a sound, integrated, well-executed plan*. The plan is not improved by revising it more frequently.

Principle 3. Shorter lead time is the most important factor in making a plan more valid.

Execution requires solving the problems that interfere with production, not covering them up with inventory or compensating with time buffers. Teamwork among all those invovled in the total manufacturing process is needed to solve these problems. There are no panaceas, no prayers, no incantations, no magic—just hard work on the fundamentals.

Manufacturing control is an integrated concept, not a loose collection of techniques. It is focusing new attention on presenting timely, objective decison alternatives to all managers. These managers, in turn, are recognizing a basic truth in a competitive business world: At the heart of any company that is going to take advantage of its marketing opportunities, control its financial investment and run its manufacturing facilities to make a profit is an effective planning and control system—but the muscles must be present to execute the plan. Manufacturing can be controlled and the rewards are enormous. The successful company will balance planning and execution.

## CHAPTER TWO

FUNDAMENTALS
OF
INVENTORY MANAGEMENT

Definition of Inventory

Ask any group of people associated with manufacturing what inventory is and you will get two types of answers.

1. Those people concerned primarily with costs and finance will answer money, an asset or cash in material form.

2. Those involved with operations will say finished goods, raw materials, work-in-process or materials used in the products.

The financial view is a real paradox. No doubt inventories have value, particularly in buying or selling companies and their value is always shown on the asset side of the balance sheet. Yet few managers can identify specifically *how* inventory earns a return (as any asset should) or, at least as important, how much return is being earned. Practically without exception, people who view inventories financially believe strongly that less is better—the right conclusion for the wrong reasons and a strange way to treat a true asset. They talk about inventories as if they were pure liabilities.

Those who look on inventory as production materials have similar myopia. Generally they believe more is better. It provides cushions against "the slings and arrows of outrageous fortune" in manufacturing—capricious customers, poor vendors, cranky machinery and Murphy's Law. It's good to have extra, just in case. They, too, don't think in terms of return on the investment. Both limit their thinking to *product inventory*—materials related to the goods produced and sold.

The true professional recognizes two other classes of inventory: preproduction and maintenance materials. Both require significant investments (although some accountants write off substantial items as expense), both are essential to manufacturing and both can be managed more effectively using information in the formal planning and control system and good techniques of inventory control. The procurement and replenishment of these two classes of inventory are beyond the scope of this book. The need is recognized in the fourth principle.

Principle 4. Manufacturing control requires effective management of all three classes of inventory.

Three cliches are frequently heard in business:

1. You can't sell from an empty wagon.
2. Inventories are the graveyard of American business.
3. Why don't you make plenty of them—we can always use them.

These comments illustrate the problems involved in reaching rational inventory decisions. Inventories usually represent a sizable portion of a company's total assets but few other business topics are subject to such partisan attitudes. The sales department sees inventory as fundamental to good customer service and feels that manufacturing has failed if any item is not available when an order for it is due to be shipped. The financial people believe that inventories are a necessary evil that tie up capital which could be used better elsewhere. Factory people have difficulty understanding the costs associated with carrying inventories and frequently look upon inventory-control measures with dismay because of the apparent inefficiency forced on the plant. From the factory point of view, inventories should be an unlimited resource. Obviously, the problem is simply that inventories are viewed from a limited point of view rather than from an overall company standpoint.

What, then, are inventories from the overall company viewpoint? Inventories in a business serve much as the suspension system of an automobile. Ups and downs in sales can be absorbed by inventory, just as the car springs absorb bumps in the road. Without inventories, production would have to respond directly to sales if service to customers were not to suffer. Inventories also disengage manufacturing operations with different production rates. Lot-size inventories make possible fewer machine setups and higher machine utilization. Work-in-process guards against idle time of people and downtime of equipment resulting from erratic flow.

It was stated in Chapter 1 that the three conflicting objectives in manufacturing are good customer service, minimum inventory investment and efficient plant operation and that it is the job of manufacturing control to reconcile these three objectives in the best interests of the company. Inventories are necessary to give good customer service, to run the plant more efficiently by keeping production at fairly level rates and to run reasonably sized manufacturing lots. Inventories are not a necessary evil but are instead a very useful shock absorber.

Nevertheless, while some inventory investment is necessary and useful, too much of it is harmful. In most companies, resources are limited: Money that is used for inventories is also needed for plant improvement, for paying dividends to stockholders, for developing new products and for all the other uses a vigorous business has for capital. Excess inventory serves no purpose and simply ties up capital uselessly.

From an overall company point of view, then, it is important to balance inventory investment against other demands for capital, considering the benefits and costs related to both. This balancing requires decisions that fall into four major categories.

1. **What balance is desired between inventory investment and customer service?**

   Where effective manufacturing control exists to execute management policy and where unexpected demands or interruptions in supply occur, there is a definite relationship between the amount of inventory carried and the service that results. The lower the inventory, the more back orders and stockouts; the higher the inventory, the better the service.

2. **What balance is desired between inventory investment and costs associated with changes in the production level?**

   Excess equipment capacity, overtime, idle time, hiring, training and laying off employees and related costs will be higher if production must fluctuate in response to changing sales rates. Inventory can dampen these fluctuations.

3. **What balance is desired between inventory investment and the cost of placing inventory-replenishment orders?**

   Low inventories can be maintained by running jobs frequently or by placing a great many purchase orders for small quantities. These practices result in high setup and purchasing costs, lost quantity discounts and other excessive operating expenses.

4. **What balance is desired between inventory investment and transportation costs?**

   Providing the labor and materials handling equipment so that jobs in production can be moved hourly, for example, requires a greater expenditure than if jobs were moved daily. The faster the mode of transportation, the higher the cost.

Functions of Inventories

There are five basic inventory types defined by function:

1. Fluctuation (demand and supply)
2. Anticipation
3. Lot-size
4. Transportation
5. Hedge

Fluctuation Inventories: These are inventories carried because the quantity and timing of sales and production cannot be predicted accurately. Orders may average 100 units per week for a given item but there will be weeks when sales are as high as 300 or 400 units. Material may usually be received in stock 3 weeks after it was ordered from the factory but it may occasionally take 6 weeks. These fluctuations in demand and supply may be covered by *reserve stock* or *safety stock,* the common names for fluctuation inventories. Fluctuation inventories exist in work centers when the flow of work through these centers cannot be completely balanced. Fluctuation inventories, called *stabilization stocks,* may be provided in the production plan so that production levels do not have to change in order to meet *random* variations in demand.

Anticipation Inventories: These are inventories built up in advance of a peak selling season, a marketing promotion program or a plant shutdown period. Basically, anticipation inventories store worker- and machine-hours for future needs and limit changes in production rates.

Lot-Size Inventories: It is frequently impossible or impractical to manufacture or purchase items at the same rate at which they will be sold. The items, therefore, are obtained in larger quantities than are needed at the moment; the resulting inventory is the **lot-size inventory.** The setup time is a major factor in determining the amount of such inventory.

Transportation Inventories: These exist because material must be moved from one place to another. Inventory on a truck being delivered to a warehouse may be in transit as long as 10 days. While the inventory is in transit, it cannot serve a useful function for plants or customers—it exists solely because of transportation time.

Hedge (or Speculative) Inventories: Companies using large quantities of basic minerals (such as coal, petroleum, silver, or cement) or commodities (such as wool, grains, or animal products) that are characterized by fluctuating prices can realize significant savings by purchasing large quantities, called **hedge inventories,** when prices are low. Also, buying extra quantities at an existing lower price will reduce material costs of items scheduled for a price rise later. The important factors in such transactions, including price trends, obsolescence risks and handling commodity futures, are beyond the scope of this book. Obviously, the saving realized is the true return on the added investment.

As an example, a typical finished product may be manufactured in 12 lots per year of 1000 units apiece. Each month, 1000 units will be received in inventory. If used up uniformly, there will be an average of 500 units on hand—the average lot-size inventory will be 500 units. To cover fluctuations in demand, 250 extra units may be carried as reserve or safety stock. This item would therefore have an average total inventory (equal to the average lot-size inventory plus the reserve stock) of 750 units. To cover a coming vacation period when the plant is shut down, another 250 units might be added to the inventory; this is anticipation inventory. If this product were distributed through branch warehouses in distant locations, additional transportation inventory would exist between the main plant and the warehouses in trucks, trains or planes en route.

The relationships between investment and return for each type of inventory based on the functions it performs are illustrated in Figure 2-1, which details the potential benefits.

Note that there are overlapping functions performed by inventories. Seasonal anticipation inventory will act like safety stock to provide better customer service, for example, as well as reducing the need to react to minor variations in the total demand rate. Thorough consideration of the interrelationships shared by these inventories is necessary to take advantage of such dual roles that can be played by inventory.

Classes of Inventory

In addition to grouping by functions, inventories can also be classified according to their condition during processing.

1. **Raw materials:**
   These are steel, flour, wood, cloth or other materials used to make the components of the finished product.

2. **Components:**
   These are parts or subassemblies ready to go into the final assembly of the product.

3. **Work-in-process:**
   These are materials and components being worked on or waiting between operations in the factory.

4. **Finished products:**
   These are finished items carried in inventory in a make-to-stock plant or finished goods ready to ship to a customer against an order in a make-to-order plant.

These classes are the groupings in which total inventory values are presented in accounting reports. Every company gets such data; the only use is to show *whether* inventory grew or shrunk. *Why* it did so, how much a plant should have and what return the inventory is earning are legitimate questions. Unfortunately, the best that can be said for these classes is that they make the accounting job easy.

Principle 5. Control requires numbers that really count, not just those numbers easy to count.

Details of cost accounting practices are beyond the scope of this book. An analysis of an inventory according to its functions, using techniques to be described in the following chapters, can usually result in very substantial inventory reduc-

Type	Function	Benefits
Lot–size	Uncouple manufacturing operations (i.e., screw machines vs. assembly; supplier vs. user)	Purchased discounts; reduced setup, freight, material handling, paperwork and inspection expense, and so on
Demand– fluctuation	Insurance against unexpected demand (safety stock)	Increased sales; reduced outgoing freight, substitution of higher value product, customer service, clerical, telephone, telegraph, packaging costs, and so on
Supply– fluctuation	Insurance against interrupted supply (i.e., strikes, vendor lead time variations)	Reduced downtime and overtime, substitute materials and incoming freight; increased sales
Anticipation	Level out production (i.e., to meet seasonal sales, marketing promotions)	Reduced overtime, subcontract, hiring, layoff, unemployment insurance, training, scrap and rework expense, and so on. Less excess capacity in equipment needed
Transportation	Fill distribution pipeline (i.e., in-transit, branch warehouse and consigned material)	Increased sales; reduced freight, handling and packaging costs
Hedge	Provide hedge against price increases (i.e., copper, silver)	Lower material costs

Figure 2-1 TYPES OF INVENTORY: FUNCTIONS AND BENEFITS.

tions with no lessening of return or in very substantial increases in return with no additional increase in inventory.

Costs in Inventory

The costs that are affected by each specific decision must be determined when deciding how much inventory to carry. The following classes of costs are involved in inventory decisions.

1. **Ordering costs:**
   The **costs of ordering** can be either those of placing purchase orders to buy material from a vendor or those associated with ordering a manufactured lot from the plant. When material is purchased, material requisitions and purchase orders must be written, invoices must be processed to pay the vendor and the lots received must be inspected and delivered to stores or process areas. When a manufactured lot is ordered from the

plant, costs are incurred for paperwork, machine setup, normal start-up scrap that results from the first production of the new setup and other one-time costs that are a function of the number of lots ordered or produced. The sum of all these costs is the ordering cost for the lot.

2. **Inventory-carrying costs:**
    These costs include all expenses incurred by the company because of the volume of inventory carried. The following elements are usually included in inventory-carrying cost:
    a. *Obsolescence.* These costs are incurred because inventory is no longer salable due to changing sales patterns and customer desires. This problem is acute in style goods, high technology and defense industries.
    b. *Deterioration.* Material carried in inventory may get damp, dried out, dirty from handling, or deteriorate in many other ways so that it is no longer salable or usable.
    c. *Taxes.* Many states and municipalities have inventory taxes. Some are based on the inventory investment at a particular time of the year, while others are based on the average inventory investment for the entire year.
    d. *Insurance.* Inventories, like most other assets, are covered by insurance usually carried as a part of other company insurance policies.
    e. *Storage.* To store inventory requires a storeroom with supervisory and operating personnel, material handling equipment, necessary records, and so on. The costs of these facilities would not be incurred if there were no inventory.
    f. *Capital.* Money invested in inventory is not available for use in other activities of the company and, in fact, may have to be borrowed from banks. The cost of borrowing the money or the cost of *foregone investment opportunity* from using this capital in other areas of the company must be charged against the inventory investment as the cost of capital.

3. **Out-of-Stock Costs:**
    If material is not available to ship when customers order it, sales may be lost or extra costs, called **out-of-stock costs,** may be incurred. The work of processing a back order (shipping, invoicing and perhaps inventory control paperwork and extra time) can be considerable. The cost of back orders results not only from extra paperwork but also from the time spent by personnel in the various departments who handle the back-order paper, pick and pack the actual shipment and answer customer inquiries. The cost may include such factors as high freight premiums because of the small quantity of material being shipped.

4. **Capacity-Associated Costs:**
    The costs that are related to **capacity** include overtime, subcontracting, hiring, training, layoff and idle time costs. These costs are incurred when

it is necessary to increase or decrease capacity or when too much or too little capacity exists temporarily.

Many difficult problems arise in determining and using costs to make inventory decisions. Even when the specific factors to be considered are recognized, the accounting records for most companies will not yield the cost data required in immediately usable and meaningful form. Two basic rules apply to these costs:

1. They should be actual out-of-pocket costs, not standard accounting costs.
2. They should be costs that are actually affected by the specific decision being made.

Before using cost data in an inventory decision problem, the questions, *From where will the savings come?* and *How much will be saved?* must be answered specifically to be certain that the calculation actually represents the real-life situation. Consider each of the four cost classes in turn.

Ordering Costs: The basic problem with ordering costs is in isolating those cost elements that vary with the number of orders placed. A simple example illustrates the problem for purchased material.

A purchasing agent makes $16,000 a year in a very small company, placing 2000 purchase orders a year, principally with local merchants like the hardware store in town. No paperwork is involved; the P.A. simply turns around and puts a quarter in the adjacent pay telephone each time an order is to be placed. Invoices are paid from a cashbox in the desk drawer.

The cost for each purchase order can then be calculated:

$$\text{Salary of agent} = \$16,000$$
$$\text{Telephone bill} = \underline{\quad 500}$$
$$\text{Total} = \$16,500$$

$$\text{Cost per order} = \frac{\$16,500}{2000} = \$8.25$$

Obviously the company will save money by placing fewer purchase orders per year. Suppose larger lots were purchased, so that only 1500 purchase orders per year were required. The savings to the company might appear to be: $(2000 - 1500) \times \$8.25 = 500 \times \$8.25$, or $4125 per year.

However, the only savings that will be realized are the phone calls, since the purchasing agent's salary would not be cut nor would time be used effectively for additional work. In fact, the company would only save $125.00 per year, which is the telephone cost for the 500 orders not placed. In this case, a purchase order does not cost $8.25, but only $0.25. Only if all purchases could be eliminated (or reduced to such a low level that someone else could handle them at no additional cost to the company, thus eliminating the purchasing agent's job) could a cost of $8.25 be assigned to each purchase order when making inventory decisions.

Similar analyses must be made of setup costs when studying manufactured lot-sizes and ordering costs. Reducing the number of setups by running larger lots through a machine will save the company nothing if the work of the setup person is simply made easier. Likewise, overhead portions of ordering paperwork charges should not be included unless fewer orders permit reductions to be made in these expenses.

Inventory-Carrying Cost: The inventory carrying cost is a useful concept (albeit an artificial one) required by the mathematical formulas used in lot-sizing calculations. As listed earlier, many separate elements are assumed to make up this cost. Obsolescence is a reality in any inventory but this cost element in the inventory carrying cost varies widely with time and is not the same for different items in an inventory (that is, it is highest for style items). This would indicate that a different carrying cost might be used for each item in the stock list. This is obviously impractical and an average figure is usually chosen, either for all products or for each major type of product. Identical reasoning applies to deterioration costs.

Taxes are usually handled more easily, particularly if the tax rate is based on the average value of the inventory. Taxes, at least up to the present time, have represented a very minor part of the total inventory carrying cost.

As shown by the derivation of the EOQ formula in Appendix III, storage and related handling costs can be handled as a separate element in lot-size decisions. For simplicity and convenience, however, these costs are usually assumed to be part of the inventory-carrying cost. The storage charge portion of inventory carrying cost, like other elements, is assumed to vary directly with the size of the inventory. Unless storage space freed up by inventory reductions can be put to use, however, there is no saving. Conversely, unless additional storage space must be purchased by leasing or building more warehouse capacity, there is no increase in storage costs by increasing inventory.

One of the most important and most controversial elements of the inventory carrying cost is the *capital cost*, covering the value of capital tied up in inventory. Two alternative choices were indicated earlier:

1. If inventory has to be increased, money may have to be borrowed from a bank or other source of capital. If existing loans can be reduced by reducing inventory, it would seem reasonable to assume that the interest on such loans would be the proper cost of inventory capital.

2. Many practitioners believe the proper cost to be the return on investment that management expects to realize on the total capital in the business, regardless of whether the source is sale of stock, accrued surplus or borrowed money.

This second alternative will charge inventory with much higher costs than the first. Its use also raises the question of which return rate to use—the actual rate being earned at present or the rate that the management plans to earn on the net worth in the future.

The proper choice can also vary with time. At one time management may wish to reduce inventories to raise capital from within rather than from outside sources or to improve the return on net worth of the company, so that its stock is more attractive to investors or in merger transactions. Expressing such objectives as a cost is hardly worthwhile.

The whole discussion is purely academic. The inventory carrying cost has practical use only as a management policy variable which, rather than being a fixed, magic number, is one that should be manipulated to attain the overall objectives of the company. Additional discussion of this concept and of ways of using it in managing inventories is given in Chapter 8.

Out-of-Stock Costs: An equally difficult problem arises when an attempt is made to determine *out-of-stock costs*. Customer dissatisfaction with back orders may be very costly, but it is difficult—if not impossible—to assign a specific value to it with any degree of accuracy. One back order may cause little or no customer inconvenience, while the next may be the reason that the customer buys elsewhere in the future. The stock out cost, like the inventory carrying cost, is an artificial concept demanded by the mathematical formulas which have been derived to assist in making inventory decisions. We should not, however, be so "beguiled by the mathematical convenience" (1) of having such a number that we lose sight of the real implications of such decisions or their aggregate effects.

Capacity-Associated Costs: Such costs as overtime and idle time, can often be calculated by using accounting data; however, hiring, training and layoff costs, like ordering costs, are not linear. While unemployment compensation taxes, for example, vary visibly with any changes in the employment level, other costs associated with hiring, training and layoff are hidden in the total costs of such areas as supervision or operating costs of the personnel department and change only when a change in activity is such that it results in increased or reduced clerical labor in the personnel department. These costs are discussed again in Chapter 9.

Distribution by Value

For any given group, a small number of items in the group will account for the bulk of the total value. About 20% of the people in this country have 80% of the wealth; about 20% of the various makes of cars account for 80% of the annual automobile sales; 20% of the items in the family budget account for 80% of the dollar expenditures. This is a very useful concept in business, where it can be applied to inventory control, production control, quality control and many other management problems. This is one of the most applicable and effective, yet least exploited, of the basic principles of production control.

When applied to inventories, this concept is called the **ABC classification.** Any inventory can be separated into three distinct parts:

1. **A items:**
    High value—those relatively few items whose value accounts for 70 to 80% of the total value of the inventory. These will usually make up 15 to 20% of the items.

2. **B items:**

   Medium value—a larger number in the middle of the list, usually about 30 to 40% of the items, whose total value accounts for 15 to 20% of the total.

3. **C items:**

   Low value—the bulk of the items, usually 60 to 70%, whose total inventory value is almost negligible, accounting for only 5 to 10% of the value.

The breakdown into A, B and C items is, of course, an arbitrary one; many companies make further divisions, such as adding a D group or breaking down the A group into AAA, AA and A items. Each group of items, of course, has an ABC distribution within the group. There are some items that justify the plant manager's personal attention just because of the large amount of money they represent.

This concept has wide application in many other manufacturing control activities:

1. A few customers give a company most of its orders.

2. A few departments perform the bulk of the work of the manufacturing operations.

3. A few operations produce most of the scrap.

4. A few vendors cause most of the delays in procuring purchased materials.

5. A few items hold up most of the back orders for customers.

Figure 2-2 shows a typical ABC distribution for a group of items. The horizontal scale represents the percentage of total items while the vertical scale represents the percentage of total annual usage dollars. Note that a very small number of items accounts for the great bulk of the usage value. These, of course, are the A items so indicated on the curve. In the B section of the curve, it is typical to find that the percentage of B items is almost equal to the percentage of dollars represented by these B items. The C items occupy the opposite end of the scale—a very large number of items accounts for a very small fraction of the total usage dollars.

An oversimplified example using only ten items illustrates how to make an ABC analysis. The first step is to list the items and their annual usages, then multiply the annual usages by the unit costs and finally assign a number to rank the items in order, starting with the highest dollar value of annual usage. This listing is shown in Figure 2-3.

Next, these items are listed in ranked order and the cumulative annual usage plus the cumulative percentage calculated. Step 2 in this ABC analysis is shown in Figure 2-4. If it is decided arbitrarily that the A items will be the first 20% of the items, this A group would include the first and second items. The next three in ranking order would be B items and would account for 30% of the total items. The remaining 50% of the items would be designated C items.

This ABC analysis can be summarized as in Figure 2-5. If by concentrating maximum efforts on the A items, this inventory could be reduced by 25%, a very

Distribution of Inventory Dollars

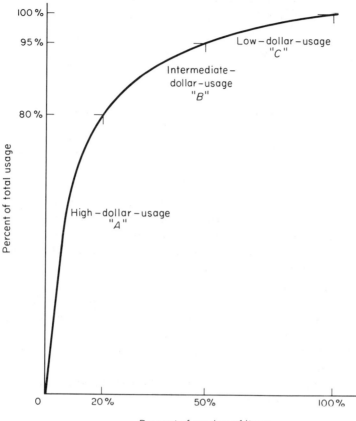

Percent of number of items

Figure 2-2 ABC CURVE.

substantial reduction in total inventory would result, even if the C-item inventory increased by 50% because of reduced attention and looser controls.

There are two general rules to remember about the ABC approach:

1. *Have plenty* of the low value items; these must be available when needed.

2. *Use the control effort saved* to reduce the inventory of high value items.

The following examples are typical of the applications of the ABC concept:

1. **Degree of Control:**
   a. For the *A items,* exert the tightest possible control, including most complete, accurate records, regular review by top-level supervision, blanket orders with frequent deliveries from vendors, close follow-up through the factory to reduce lead time, and so on.
   b. For the *B items,* exert normal controls involving good records and regular attention.

Item	Pcs. annual usage	$ unit cost	Annual $ usage	Rank
F-11	40,000	0.07	$2,800	5
F-20	195,000	0.11	21,450	1
F-31	4,000	0.10	400	9
L-45	100,000	0.05	5,000	3
L-51	2,000	0.14	280	10
L-16	240,000	0.07	16,800	2
L-17	16,000	0.08	1,280	6
N-8	80,000	0.06	4,800	4
N-91	10,000	0.07	700	7
N-100	5,000	0.09	450	8

Figure 2-3 RANKING ANNUAL USAGE.

    c. For the *C items,* use the simplest possible controls, such as periodic visual review of physical inventory with simplified records or only the simplest notations that replenishment stocks have been ordered, large inventories and order quantities to avoid stockouts and low priority in scheduling in the factory are adequate.

2. **Inventory records:**
    a. The *A items* require the most accurate, complete and detailed records with frequent even real-time updating. Tight control of transaction documents, scrap losses, receipts, and issues, is essential.
    b. The *B items* need only normal handling of records, batch updating, and so on.
    c. For the *C items,* use no records (or only the simplest), batch updating, simplified bulk counting and the like.

3. **Priority:**
    a. *A items* have high priority in all activities to reduce lead time and inventory.

Item	Annual $ usage	Cumulative annual $ usage	Cumulative percentage	Class
F-20	$21,450	$21,450	39.8%	A
L-16	16,800	38,250	71.0%	A
L-45	5,000	43,250	80.2%	B
N-8	4,800	48,050	89.3%	B
F-11	2,800	50,850	94.4%	B
L-17	1,280	52,130	96.7%	C
N-91	700	52,830	97.9%	C
N-100	450	53,280	98.9%	C
F-31	400	53,680	99.6%	C
L-51	280	53,960	100.0%	C

Figure 2-4 ASSIGNING ABC CLASSES.

Classification	% of items	Annual usage $ per group	% of $
A = F-20, L-16	20%	$38,250	71.0%
B = L-45, N-8, F-11	30%	12,600	23.4%
C = All others	50%	3,110	5.6%
Totals	100%	$53,960	$100.0

Figure 2-5 SUMMARY ABC ANALYSIS.

    b. *B items* require only normal processing with high priority only when critical.

    c. *C items* are lowest priority.

4. **Ordering procedures:**

    a. For *A items,* provide careful, accurate determination of order quantities, order points and MRP data. Manual check of computer data is needed, along with frequent review to reduce inventory.

    b. For *B items,* review EOQ and order points quarterly or when major changes occur. MRP output is handled routinely.

    c. For *C items* require no EOQ or order-point calculations. The orders frequently are not planned via MRP. Order 1 year's supply while there still is plenty of stock on hand. Use visual review, bank stock and so on.

Further applications of specific techniques to take advantage of the ABC relationship are discussed in later chapters. It is the most universally applicable concept in production and inventory control.

How Well Are Inventories Managed?

The role of industrial inventories in the drama of business cycles has been of great topical interest to economists, politicians and business leaders. While there is little agreement among these people on the best solution, there is a common recognition that the problem is how inventory can be controlled to minimize or eliminate the amplifying effect on business cycles.

When sales rates change at the consumer level, production rates must also change. The time interval between these changes depends on

1. How quickly the new trend is identified as a trend, not a random fluctuation

2. Whether inventories should increase or decrease

3. How much change in inventory is desired

When sales rates increase, well-controlled inventory levels must also generally increase to maintain the same level of customer service. Therefore production is called on to increase to meet

1. The increase in sales rate

2. The additional inventory desired

The second factor is, of course, a temporary one existing only until the necessary additional inventory is provided. Because of it, however, a moderate increase in sales can generate a very substantial increase in production, particularly if management moves quickly to maintain customer service. The opposite effect causes production to drop drastically when sales fall off even moderately. Control over such fluctuations must be established to ease the impact of unemployment and the other economic ills of depression-boom cycles.

Many illustrations, such as the following, have been given:

. . . in automotive manufacture, a 5% variation in retail sales may be amplified to a 10% variation at the vehicle assembly plant, to a 20% variation at the first level of component manufacture below the assembly plants and to perhaps a 40% variation at the third level below. If we compare the retail automotive sales trend with the procurement of steel sheets for automotive use, we find that the sharp increases or decreases in automotive steel procurement are due more to inventory correction than they are in changes in the true demand for automobiles. This is not only an automotive problem, because most of American industry works on the same principle (4).

This is particularly significant since the automobile industry is probably more advanced in control techniques than many other industries. Another article suggested that changes in retail sales will be magnified six to ten times in the effect they have on factory output (7).

Figure 2-6, illustrating the 60-day ordering rule, shows how this type of inflated inventory building and reduction can occur when we employ "common sense" inventory control techniques. The 60-day ordering rule is a very simple technique which can be stated as follows: *Each time a reorder is placed, order enough material so that the total on hand and on order is equal to sales for the past 60 days.* This rule embodies the sales idea of how inventories should be managed and has had wide application in branch warehouses.

In the example shown, sales increase very substantially from March to May and decrease from June through August. The **target inventory**, or the "order-up-to" level, is always equal to the sales for the previous 2 months. For example, February's target is 120 units, equal to sales for January and February. The amount on hand is the balance from the previous month plus the receipt of the previous month's factory order less the current month's sales. The new factory order for the month is derived by deducting the amount on hand from the target inventory.

Notice the substantial amplification effect that results from this "common sense" technique. Sales increase from a minimum of 60 to a maximum of 100 and the factory orders increase to 120. When sales decrease to 60 units in August, factory orders actually decrease to 30 units. This type of irrational ordering technique adopted by amateurs has contributed substantially to serious inventory buildup and inventory reduction problems that amplify business cycles.

There is no question that some inventory increase may be required when

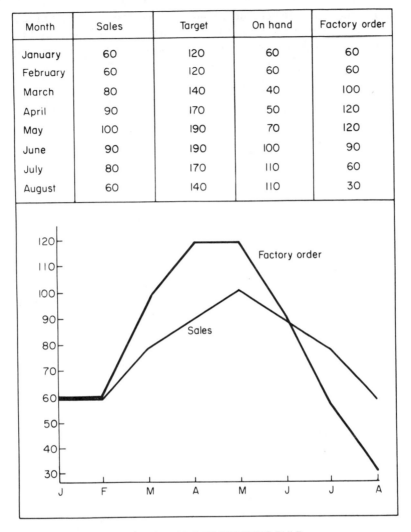

Month	Sales	Target	On hand	Factory order
January	60	120	60	60
February	60	120	60	60
March	80	140	40	100
April	90	170	50	120
May	100	190	70	120
June	90	190	100	90
July	80	170	110	60
August	60	140	110	30

Figure 2-6 60-DAY ORDERING RULE.

business goes up if the same level of service is to be provided, but those with only the most elementary knowledge of sound inventory-control principles recognize that the increase in inventory should not be proportional to the increase in sales. Actually, for short-term sales buildups, inventories may decrease without harming customer service if the inventories are being managed properly.

Moreover, manufactured inventories can seldom be controlled by inventory-control techniques alone, since the high cost and difficulty of changing production rates makes it essential to use inventories to help stabilize production, particularly in repetitive and process industries. The effective use of inventories to help keep costs down and provide competitive customer service without excessive in-

ventory investment requires an understanding of the basic principles of manufacturing control. These principles and the techniques for implementing them will
be the subject of the following chapters. Successful application of the techniques
is covered in the second volume (5).

CHAPTER THREE

THE ECONOMIC LOT SIZE

The Value of the Concept
of Economic Ordering Quantity

In manufacturing control analyses, it is usually convenient and practical to study together those items that fall into natural groups. These groups may be made up of parts processed by common manufacturing equipment, purchased items handled by the same buyer or material ordered from the same vendor. This is particularly true in determining the sizes of lots in which material is procured. Costs, capital requirements, space needs, operating conditions and other factors that must be considered in setting lot-sizes are most meaningful when families of related parts are considered.

In the first example of lot-size calculations to be used, five items have been chosen. These items can be imagined as products made on the same manufacturing equipment. Figure 3-1 shows the present situation, with lot-sizes determined by the rule-of-thumb, run-once-a-quarter, representative of intuitive rules used frequently by nonprofessionals.

Four setups, or orders, per year are being placed for each item, giving a total of 20 orders per year; the resulting average lot-size inventory is $2430, which is half the toal of all lot-sizes. It is assumed that each lot is received in one total batch and then is used up uniformly over a period of time so that the inventory is reduced to zero. The average lot-size inventory is then one-half the lot-size. It is apparent that if some of the setups being used on item 5 were used instead on item 1, the total inventory could be reduced significantly. Even if a year's supply of

Item	Annual use	Present orders/yr	Present order quantities
1	$10,000	4	$2,500
2	6,400	4	1,600
3	2,500	4	625
4	400	4	100
5	144	4	36
Totals		20	$4,861

Average lot-size inventory = $2,430

Figure 3-1 RULE-OF-THUMB LOT-SIZES.

item 5 were to be run, it would not affect the inventory investment very much, while each additional setup that could be made on item 1 would result in a very substantial reduction in inventory. Figure 3-2 shows a redistribution of the 20 setups made simply by inspection. The result is a very substantial reduction in average total inventory from $2430 to $1828 without changing the number of orders placed per year.

Item	Annual use	Proposed orders/yr	Proposed order quantities
1	$10,000	10	$1,000
2	6,400	5	1,280
3	2,500	3	833
4	400	1	400
5	144	1	144
Totals		20	$3,657

Average lot-size inventory = $1,828

Figure 3-2 ECONOMICAL USE OF SETUPS.

Principle 6. Distributing setups to cut inventories of high value items easily offsets increases in those items of low value.

The use of inspection to make this type of analysis is practical only for a very few items. Sometimes a significant improvement can be made in practice using such a common approach on the key items made in some critical work center. While the resulting order quantities are not economic order quantities (since they were arrived at without considering the costs of carrying inventory, setting up or ordering), they are more reasonable than the original order quantities. Their use will lower any costs associated with carrying inventory without affecting costs related to ordering.

In many companies—particularly distributor warehouses that purchase from a manufacturing firm and sell to a retailer—the system of reviewing all products every 2 or 3 months and reordering all at the same time and in equivalent time supplies (such as a 2-month supply of each item) was common for many years. When a discount for joint purchase of all items was offered, this practice had some justification, but this type of reordering system was more frequently used just because it seemed to make sense. The example of the 60-day ordering rule in Chapter 2 and the changes made by inspection in the lot-sizes in Figure 3-2 illustrates non-professional approaches. The latter is not an economical solution; substantial improvements in the use of the company's resources can be made by a better redistribution of setup or reordering effort.

Does the example show the best possible distribution of 20 setups per year? Actually, it does not. There is a simple mathematical approach that will result in a better distribution of orders. Before looking at this calculation, however, it is important to understand the concept of EOQ.

There are many situations where the EOQ concept has no value. There is no reason to calculate an EOQ when

1. The customer specifies the quantity (that is, on make-to-order items).
2. The production run lot is limited by equipment capacity (for instance, fine chemicals).
3. The shelf life of the product is short.
4. Tool life or the need for sharpening, dressing, and so on limits the run length.
5. Raw material batches fix the order quantity.

The Basic Concept of EOQ

One of the basic decisions that must be made in inventory management is that of balancing the costs of inventory investment against those of placing inventory replenishment orders. The question to be answered is, How much should be ordered? The right quantity to order is that which best balances the costs related to the *number* of orders placed against the costs related to the *size* of the orders placed. When these costs have been balanced properly, the total cost is minimized. The resulting ordering quantity is called the **economic lot-size**, or **economic ordering quantity** (EOQ).

The EOQ concept applies under the following conditions:

1. The item is replenished in lots or batches, either by purchasing or manufacturing, and is not produced continuously.
2. Sales or usage rates are uniform and are low compared to the rate at which the item is normally produced, so that a significant amount of inventory results.

The EOQ concept does *not* apply to all items produced for inventory. In a refinery or on an assembly line, for example, production is continuous and there are no lot-sizes as such. The bulk of the jobs in a make-to-order plant are made in lot-sizes ordered by the customer. Limited tool life, short shelf life, economical use of raw material and other constraints override the application of EOQ techniques. Nevertheless, the concept has broad application in industry, since most production is not continuous and individual lots of material are being taken from one inventory, processed and then delivered to another inventory.

It is important to distinguish in a manufacturing organization between economic *manufacturing* lot-sizes and *movement* lot-sizes. Where a large steel blanking press, for example, feeds subsequent piercing and trimming operations, there is no need to wait until the entire EOQ has been blanked before moving part of the lot to the subsequent operations. This portion of the EOQ is the **movement lot-size**. The movement lot-size is usually determined by container sizes or pallet capacities and may be a small fraction of the economic lot-size.

It is essential to manage both manufactured and purchased lot-sizes because they often represent the largest single functional segment of the inventory. Lot-sizing techniques are good tools to aid in such managing efforts but the professional practitioner recognizes that their application is literally just making the best of a bad situation. When setups or ordering costs are high, EOQ's introduce a balance with inventory carrying costs to minimize the total. Better results, plus some great additional benefits (covered in later chapters in this volume and in the second volume), can be realized *if setup and ordering costs are reduced.*

Principle 7. The right EOQ is good but shorter setups are far better.

Working independently, materials control people can select lot-sizing techniques and apply them to make some gains for their companies. Working as a team with supervisors, tool designers, manufacturing and design engineers and workers, these people can generate many times these benefits by reducing setup times. The Japanese have proved this without a shadow of doubt.

Trial-and-Error Approach

What are the alternatives available in choosing a lot-size? Assume that a standard stock item is being ordered from the factory by manufacturing orders authorizing the factory workers to make the item. One replenishment order could be placed for the total annual requirements. This would mean that the factory would only have to set up to manufacture this item once during the year. It would mean also that the average lot-size inventory would be very large, equal to $\frac{1}{2}$-year's requirement if usage were uniform.

This average lot-size inventory could be reduced very substantially by ordering 50 times during the year—approximately once a week. This would place a very heavy burden on the factory since the job would have to be set up 50 times to manufacture the annual requirements. These alternatives are shown in Figure 3-3, which shows the basic dilemma that must be faced in determining an economic lot-size: Ordering or setup cost can be kept down by ordering infrequently but the resulting inventory investment will be very high; inventory investment can be kept low by ordering frequently but the resulting ordering costs will be very high. Determining the economic lot-size requires finding the quantity that results in the lowest *total* cost, the sum of the two.

For example, assume the cost of placing a replenishment order to be $10,

Annual Requirements = $1,000 Worth

Replenishment orders/yr	Lot-size	Average lot-size inventory
1	$1,000	$500
50	20	10

Figure 3-3 ORDERING EXTREMES.

(If only out-of-pocket costs were being considered, this cost could be realistic; the costs in this example are not intended to be representative of real costs but are used simply to make the calculations clear and the relationships obvious.) Also assume the inventory-carrying cost to be equal to 20% of the average dollar inventory investment per year. An economic lot-size can be determined by trial and error, as shown in Figure 3-4. If this item has $1000 worth of annual usage and is ordered in ordering quantities of $50, the average lot-size inventory would be $25; the annual carrying cost at 20% would be $5. A total of 20 orders would be placed per year at $10 each, giving an annual ordering cost of $200. The total annual cost associated with an ordering quantity of $50 would be $205, equal to the sum of the $200 ordering cost and the $5 carrying cost.

Ordering cost = $10 Annual usage = $1,000 Inventory carrying cost = 20%					
Order quantity	Average inventory	Carrying costs	Orders yr	Order cost	Total cost
$ 50	25	$ 5	20	$200	$205
100	50	10	10	100	110
200	100	20	5	50	70
250	125	25	4	40	65
500	250	50	2	20	70

Figure 3-4 TRIAL-AND-ERROR CALCULATION.

As the ordering quantity is increased, the average inventory is larger and, consequently, the inventory carrying cost increases. With the larger ordering quantity, the number of orders placed per year decreases and the resulting order cost decreases. Looking at the far right-hand column, headed "Total Cost," it can be seen that the lowest total cost would result from an ordering quantity of $250. This is the ordering quantity that "balances" the cost of ordering with the cost of carrying inventory; it is the EOQ for this item.

Figure 3-5 shows these costs plotted on a graph. As ordering quantities are increased, it can be seen that carrying costs go up and ordering costs go down. The upper curve, the total cost curve, decreases with increasing ordering quantities to a minimum at the $250 ordering quantity; from there the total costs increase

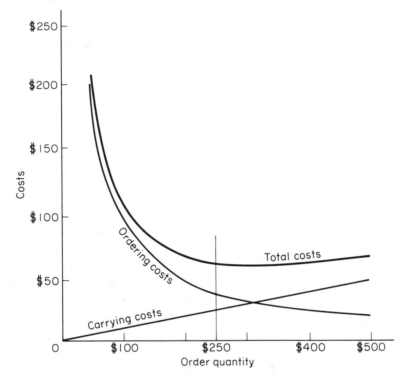

Figure 3-5 ORDER SIZE VERSUS TOTAL COST.

with larger lot-sizes. Note, however, that the increases are relatively small. The penalty from ordering lots larger than the EOQ is much less than for smaller batches. Remember, however, that *only ordering and carrying costs* are being considered.

This is a useful concept in inventory control leading to substantial savings over intuitive "guesstimates." The total costs associated with an ordering quantity of $250 are much less than half of those resulting from the ordering quantity of $50.

EOQ with Imprecise Costs

In the simple example just shown, it was assumed that precise values of the ordering cost and inventory carrying cost were known. These are assumed by every formula for EOQ to be available. In actual practice these costs are difficult to determine accurately (for reasons discussed later in this chapter). The practitioner should not be discouraged from seeking the economies possible through use of EOQ by lack of precise cost data. Nevertheless, use of the concept of economic lot-sizes results in practical benefits to production control for two reasons:

1. Ordering quantities set by a consistent, orderly method gives far superior results to orders determined by rule of thumb or guess. Improvements over intuitive lot-sizes can almost always be made.

2. The total cost curve (Figure 3-5) is flat for a fairly broad range on each side of the EOQ. This means that reasonably economic ordering quantities can be found using cost data which are considerably short of perfection. It also means that adjustments can be made to the ordering quantity arrived at by formula (such as rounding a formula EOQ of 1910 units to a more practical figure of 2000 units) without sacrificing significant savings.

Square Root EOQ

In industry it is not practical to use a trial-and-error method to arrive at economic lot-sizes for thousands of items in inventory. Several EOQ formulas are available to calculate the EOQ for any item in one step. The oldest form of this formula is:

$$EOQ = \sqrt{\frac{2AS}{I}} \tag{3-1}$$

where

A = the annual usage, in dollars

S = the setup or ordering cost, in dollars

I = the inventory carrying cost, as a decimal fraction per dollar of average inventory

Substituting the data used in our trial-and-error calculation, Figure 3-4, the EOQ can be calculated directly from formula (3-1) as follows:

$$EOQ = \sqrt{\frac{2 \times 1000 \times 10}{0.20}}$$
$$= \sqrt{100,000}$$
$$= \$316$$

Note that the formula gives a more precise answer than the trial-and-error calculation. Is it more economical? Calculations with this formula are greatly simplified by the use of a table of square roots (such as the one in Appendix I). The mathematical derivation of this formula is included in Appendix II. The EOQ formula is derived by solving the separate equations for inventory-carrying cost and ordering cost to find the lowest total cost; in other words, the formula finds the lowest point on the total cost curve of Figure 3-5 and shows it is slightly different from the value selected in Figure 3-4.

The EOQ formula expressed in (3-1) contained two cost factors:

S = setup or ordering cost, in dollars

I = inventory-carrying cost, as a decimal fraction

For a family of items such as the one discussed in the first section of this chapter, the inventory carrying cost is generally assumed to be the same for all items and the setup or ordering cost for the group is often practically the same. If this is true, formula (3-1) can be written as:

$$\text{EOQ} = \sqrt{\frac{2S}{I}} \times \sqrt{A} = K \times \sqrt{A} \qquad (3\text{-}2)$$

where

$$K = \sqrt{\frac{2S}{I}} \qquad (3\text{-}3)$$

Formula (3-2) points out a very useful relationship: The most economic lot-sizes are functions of the square root of the annual usages of the items expressed in dollars.

Returning to the five items in Figure 3-1, whose lot-sizes were adjusted in Figure 3-2, the best possible distribution of the 20 annual setups can now be calculated. The results of the calculation, based on formula (3-2), are shown in Figure 3-6: The value of K used in these calculations for the 20 orders was obtained without knowing the cost factors by using the relation derived from formula (3-3):

$$K = \frac{\Sigma\sqrt{A}}{\Sigma N} = \frac{262}{20} = 13.1 \qquad (3\text{-}4)$$

(The symbol Σ is the mathematical notation for sum.) In this formula, the sum of the square roots of the annual usages ($\Sigma\sqrt{A}$) of all items is divided by the present total of orders (ΣN) per year.

Item	Annual use	$\sqrt{A}$	N present orders/yr	Present O.Q.'s	Calculated orders/yr	Calculated O.Q.'s
1	$10,000	$100	4	$2,500	7.6	$1,310
2	6,400	80	4	1,600	6.2	1,050
3	2,500	50	4	625	3.8	655
4	400	20	4	100	1.5	262
5	144	12	4	36	0.9	157
		$262	20	$4,861	20.0	$3,434
Average lot–size inventory				$2,430		$1,717

Figure 3-6 LOWEST INVENTORY FOR NUMBER OF ORDERS.

Using formula (3-2), new lot-sizes were then calculated for each item by multiplying 13.1 by the square root of A for each item. These lot-sizes are shown in the last column of Figure 3-6. The average lot-size inventory of $1717 is the *lowest possible total lot-size inventory* for this group of items when only 20 orders per year are issued. This value was obtained without knowing specific values of the ordering or inventory carrying costs.

To the practical-minded, the concept of 7.6 orders per year may be somewhat disturbing because 0.7 of a setup has no real meaning. Nevertheless, the order quantity of $1310—which would probably be rounded to $1300—for item 1 is valid.

In an actual factory, it would result in 7 orders some years and 8 in others. While fractional setups are not real, they are a convenient concept in making lot-size calculations because they make it possible to use the period of 1 year as a consistent period over which costs can be compared.

This approach could also be used to calculate the lowest total number of orders that could be written for the same average lot-size inventory of $2430. The resulting lot-sizes are shown in Figure 3-7. These are calculated using the formula:

$$K = \frac{\Sigma\, Q}{\Sigma\sqrt{A}} = \frac{4861}{262} = 18.55 \tag{3-5}$$

Here, the sum of the present order quantities ($\Sigma\, Q$) is divided by the sum of the square roots of the annual usages ($\Sigma\, A$).

Item	Annual use	$\sqrt{A}$	N present orders/yr	Present O.Q.'s	Calculated orders/yr	Calculated O.Q.'s
1	$10,000	$100	4	$2,500	5.4	$1,855
2	6,400	80	4	1,600	4.4	1,484
3	2,500	50	4	625	2.7	928
4	400	20	4	100	1.1	371
5	144	12	4	36	0.7	223
		$262	20	$4,861	14.3	$4,861
Average lot-size inventory				$2,430		$2,430

Figure 3-7 SMALLEST NUMBER OF ORDERS FOR INVENTORY.

Using formula (3-2) again, new lot-sizes were calculated for each item, without using specific values of the ordering or inventory carrying costs. For this family, 14.3 orders per year are the fewest that can be written for an average lot-size inventory of $2430.

Formulas (3-4) and (3-5) for finding the value of K were first suggested by W. Evert Welch and are derived in his book (9). This was the first attempt by anyone to calculate *aggregate* lot-size inventories. This approach to EOQ calculations has five significant advantages:

1. For a family of items where setup (or ordering) and inventory carrying costs are about the same for all items, it provides a much-simplified method of calculating EOQ's. The value of K is calculated once for all items and is then multiplied by the square root of the annual usage dollars to determine the EOQ for each item. This is illustrated by a sample problem is the next section.

2. If there is a restriction on the number of orders that can be handled by the present organization, this approach can be used to obtain the least total lot-size inventory for the family of items subject to the restriction. This is illustrated by Figure 3-6.

3. If the amount of inventory cannot be increased to the full extent required by EOQ's, the technique can be used to set lot-sizes that result in the

least total orders with this restriction and, hence, the lowest ordering cost, as illustrated in Figure 3-7.

4. The approach illustrates a method of obtaining some immediate benefits from applying the EOQ concept where intuitive means have previously been used to set order quantities. As shown in the examples, inventory can be reduced while keeping ordering costs the same—or ordering costs can be reduced while keeping inventory the same.

5. This calculation illustrates a very important point that is often overlooked: *The application of EOQ's is much more effective when items are grouped together.*

While it is not necessary to know the specific costs of ordering and carrying inventory to apply the Welch method, the basic assumption must be made that these are the same for all items in the family. In addition, the results may not be most economical when *actual* costs are considered and further improvements might be made if representative cost figures can be obtained.

In actual applications, other limitations may make it impractical to attain the full benefits from EOQ's immediately. Among these are shortage of capital for investment in inventory, restricted space to store inventory, too few skilled setup people and limited machine capacity available for setting up.

A technique called *LIMIT* (lot-size inventory management interpolation technique) makes it possible to attain the full economies of the EOQ concept within the limits of such restrictions and to study the alternatives available in balancing ordering and inventory carrying costs. This technique is discussed in Chapter 8, *Aggregate Inventory Management.*

Costs in the EOQ Formulas

Undoubtedly, the most difficult problem to deal with in applying the EOQ concept is the assumption in the formula that there is a proportional relationship between the amount of inventory carried and the actual out-of-pocket inventory costs and also between the number of orders placed and the actual total ordering cost. In practice, reducing the number of purchase orders, for example, does not result in a proportional reduction in ordering cost. The truth is that the relationship between costs and ordering quantities is not directly proportional but is stepped. These steps are controlled by the aggregate effects—such as total number of orders to be placed and total storage space needed—not by the size of individual item lots; hence the need for studying the whole inventory.

Two rules given in Chapter 2 to be used in determining costs in inventory decisions apply specifically to costs used in the economic ordering formulas:

1. Costs should be actual out-of-pocket costs that will result from the ordering quantities chosen.

2. Costs should be those that are actually affected by changes in the size of the ordering quantity.

Unfortunately, the costs shown by the accounting records of most companies are seldom suitable for immediate use in economic lot-size calculations. The unit cost in the EOQ formula is a good example of this type of problem. In many companies, the unit cost of an item is most readily available as a "standard cost," which consists of labor, material and overhead elements for all manufacturing operations, including some allowance for setup. There are two apparent choices for determining the unit cost to be used in the EOQ formula:

1. Use the standard cost.
2. Use only the labor and material portions of the standard cost plus some overhead, which varies with the lot-size.

If the full standard cost is used, the two rules regarding costs will be violated (since the overhead portion of the standard cost does not result from and will be affected very little by changes in lot-sizes). An increase in the lot-size inventory, for example, will not actually require any substantial increase in out-of-pocket expense for most of the overhead factors, such as factory clerical expense, supervisory expense, depreciation on equipment, inspection, etc. If the standard cost is used in projecting the dollars that will be spent to increase the inventory, an inflated figure will result, since proportionately more will be spent in labor and material but not on overhead. Furthermore, the standard cost usually includes setup, which is a separate cost element in the formulas and should not be included in the unit cost used.

On the other hand, the accounting records will charge overhead to inventory at the rate indicated in the standard costs. Use of only labor, material and the variable portion of overhead costs in the unit cost will mean that total inventory dollar projections based on the EOQ calculations will not agree with the accounting figures. For example, a predicted inventory increase of $100,000 based on costs used in the EOQ formula could result in some real surprises for the manager involved, since the accounting records would probably charge this material to inventory at full standard cost, including all overhead. The book figures might then show an inventory increase of $150,000 rather than the predicted $100,000.

Another common problem in using costs occurs on low-volume items. When a large supply of a low-volume item with high setup cost is run, it is put into the dollar inventory records at standard cost. If double this quantity were run on the same machine setup, the inventory value subject to obsolescence risk would undoubtedly be increased but usually not by the amount indicated by the accounting records. Running an extra supply on the same setup would really result only in a proportional increase in cost of material, labor and a portion of the overhead. Sometimes, even labor costs are not increased proportionately on some semiautomatic equipment. Yet the full standard cost will usually be charged to—and will eventually be written off—the inventory records.

How can this dilemma be handled? Only by speaking two languages of cost. One is the real out-of-pocket cost actually affecting decisions—this is used in the calculations. The management of the company must also be aware of the effect a given change in inventory will have on the accounting records, which uses another language, since their performance will usually be evaluated based on these records.

In many companies, operating and accounting people are working to devise mutually satisfactory costing techniques. In the meantime, it is essential for people making operating decisions to do the following:

1. Understand the company's costing system and work closely with the company financial people, so that costs are used intelligently in making decisions and presenting alternatives to management.

2. Always make trial applications and predict the results of EOQ application for the total inventory based on the sample results before using EOQ's on a large scale.

Square Root EOQ Formula Variations

Shortcut: The use of K in Formula (3-2) for simplifying EOQ calculations for groups of items where each item in the group has the same setup or ordering cost and the same inventory-carrying cost was covered in the preceding section. Using Formula (3-3), $K = \sqrt{2S/I}$, the constant K is calculated once. Economic ordering quantities are then calculated by using Formula (3-2), EOQ = $K \times \sqrt{A}$, multiplying this constant by the square root of the annual usage (in dollars) for each item. Here is a simple example with three items.

	Item 1	Item 2	Item 3
Annual usage (A)	$10,000.00	$20,000.00	$30,000.00
Ordering cost (S)	5.00	5.00	5.00
Inventory-carrying cost (I)	0.20	0.20	0.20

We can then calculate K and EOQ.

$$K = \sqrt{\frac{2S}{I}}$$

$$= \sqrt{\frac{2 \times 5.00}{0.20}} = \sqrt{\$50.00} = 7.07$$

$$\text{EOQ} = K \times \sqrt{A}$$

$$= 7.07 \times \sqrt{A}$$

For item 1, EOQ = $7.07 \times \sqrt{\$10,000} = \$ 707$

For item 2, EOQ = $7.07 \times \sqrt{\$20,000} = \$1000$

For item 3, EOQ = $7.07 \times \sqrt{\$30,000} = \$1225$

This type of shortcut can speed up EOQ calculations very substantially, particularly when square root tables are used or when curves or nomographs are available (9).

In formula (3-1), the annual usage and the EOQ's calculated were expressed in dollars. This is sometimes inconvenient; some practitioners prefer to calculate EOQ's in pieces. The formula for this is as follows:

$$EOQ = \sqrt{\frac{2US}{IC}} \qquad (3\text{-}6)$$

where

U = annual usage, in pieces

S = ordering or setup cost, in dollars

I = inventory-carrying cost, as a decimal fraction per dollar of average inventory

C = Unit cost, in dollars per piece

Using the example of the preceding section, where the annual usage in dollars was $1000, and assuming that this represents 2000 pieces at $0.50 each, this formula gives an answer in pieces.

$$EOQ = \sqrt{\frac{2US}{IC}} \quad = \sqrt{\frac{(2 \times 2000 \times 10)}{(0.20 \times 0.50)}}$$

$$= \sqrt{\frac{40,000}{0.10}} \quad = \quad \sqrt{400,000} = 630 \text{ pieces}$$

which is equivalent to a $315 order quantity of pieces worth $0.50 each.

This formula can also be used for material ordered in pounds, feet or other units. The EOQ calculated by Formula (3-6) will always have the same units as the annual usage *if* the cost, C, is the value of one such unit (either a pound, a foot or any other unit).

There are times when the form in which the inventory record has been kept makes it convenient to calculate the EOQ based upon the monthly usage of the item. The formula for doing this where usage is in dollars is:

$$EOQ = \sqrt{\frac{24MS}{I}}$$

where

M = monthly usage, in dollars

S = setup or ordering cost, in dollars

I = inventory carrying cost, as a decimal fraction per dollar of average inventory

Using the same example, but now expressing the $1000 annual usage as a monthly usage of $83.30, gives the same EOQ:

$$\text{EOQ} = \sqrt{\frac{24MS}{I}} = \sqrt{\frac{24 \times 83.30 \times 10}{0.20}}$$

$$= \sqrt{100,000} = \$315$$

This monthly usage formula can also be applied where it is more convenient to deal with pieces or other units. In this case, the formula is expressed as follows:

$$\text{EOQ} = \sqrt{\frac{24MuS}{IC}} \qquad (3\text{-}8)$$

where

Mu = monthly usage, in pieces or other units

S = setup or ordering cost, in dollars

I = inventory-carrying cost, as a decimal fraction per dollar of average inventory

C = unit cost, in dollars per piece

Calculating the EOQ once again with the demand for the item now expressed in pieces per month, the same answer results:

$$\text{EOQ} = \sqrt{\frac{24MuS}{IC}} = \sqrt{\frac{24 \times 167 \times 10}{0.20 \times 0.50}}$$

$$= \sqrt{400,000} = 630 \text{ pieces}$$

In many companies, the forecasts for individual items are made on a quarterly basis. When forecasts are available by the quarter, the EOQ calculation can be made directly using the formula

$$\text{EOQ} = \sqrt{\frac{8QS}{I}} \qquad (3\text{-}9)$$

where

Q = quarterly usage, in dollars

S = setup or ordering cost, in dollars

I = inventory-carrying cost, as a decimal fraction per dollar of average inventory

Calculating the EOQ once again, using Formula (3-9); gives

$$\text{EOQ} = \sqrt{\frac{8QS}{I}} = \sqrt{\frac{8 \times 250 \times 10}{0.20}}$$

$$= \sqrt{100,000} = \$315$$

There are many more variations of the EOQ formula to facilitate the use of available data. See the bibliography for references that discuss formula variations in more depth.

Noninstantaneous Receipt

In additon to variations enabling simple EOQ formulas to handle different units, there are other adjustments to the formula that can be made to get more accurate answers in special circumstances. Frequently, for example, the entire lot-size is not received into stock at once. The manufacturing rate may be such that it takes several days or even weeks for the complete lot to be made and delivered into stock. While production is going on, partial deliveries to stock are made, but withdrawals are also made during this period. Consequently, the average lot-size inventory will not equal one-half of the lot-size, as it does where all the lot is received once.

This situation, given the rather formidable name of **noninstantaneous receipt**, can be handled by using the following modification of the basic EOQ formula:

$$EOQ = \sqrt{\frac{2AS}{I(1 - s/p)}} \qquad (3\text{-}10)$$

where

A = annual usage, in dollars

S = setup or ordering cost, in dollars

I = inventory carrying cost, as a decimal fraction per dollar of average inventory

s = usage rate, in the same units as production rate

p = production rate, in the same units as usage rate

Using the same example, with sales at the rate of $4.00 per day ($1000 annual usage divided by 250 working days) and production assumed to be at the rate of $16.00 per day, the calculation is then:

$$EOQ = \sqrt{\frac{2AS}{I(1 - s/p)}} = \sqrt{\frac{2 \times 1000 \times 10}{0.20(1 - 4/16)}}$$

$$= \sqrt{133,333} = \$365$$

The answer of $365 is higher than the $315 that was calculated by formula (3-1), in which instantaneous receipt is assumed. The size of the manufactured lot is increased by formula (3-10), but the average lot-size inventory is not increased because material will be withdrawn while the balance of the lot is being produced. It can be demonstrated easily that the higher ordering quantity with noninstantaneous receipt will give the same average lot-size inventory as that for a lot received instantaneously.

Figure 3-8 shows a line diagram of the behavior of the lot-size inventory of one item as ordering quantities are received and used up. When the material is received all at once, the quantity in inventory immediately increases to the total of the lot-size that was ordered. This quantity is then decreased as material is withdrawn over a period of time until a new lot-size is once again received. In Figure 3-8, this is shown by the dashed line as a right triangle. When the entire lot is

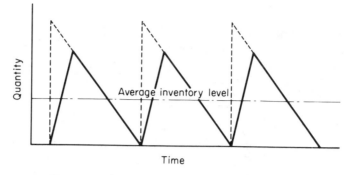

Figure 3-8 EOQ—NONINSTANTANEOUS RECEIPT.

not received instantaneously, the highest inventory point is not reached until the complete lot has been delivered and the saw-toothed inventory diagram triangles, the solid lines, are no longer right triangles.

Major and Minor Setup

A situation frequently encountered in industrial applications of EOQ is **major and minor setup**, where it is most economical to run groups of items in a definite sequence. When producing items on a screw machine, for example, it is often economical to run several similar items consecutively, so that only minor changes have to be made in the basic setup to change from one item to the next in the sequence.

Similar parts that can be made with only a minor setup modification in a sheet metal press can also be grouped together economically. In paper, chemical, paint, cosmetics and other similar processing industries where it is time-consuming and expensive to clean out equipment, the light colors are run first, followed by darker and darker colors; then the whole process line is shut down, cleaned and changed over after the darkest batch is completed.

The basic approach to EOQ applies to these situations but will necessitate special handling of the data. Figure 3-9 shows a simple example of five items which can be made in one major setup. In this example, it is assumed that inventory

Item	Annual usage (A)	Setup cost (S)
1	$ 2,000	$2.00
2	4,000	3.00
3	800	3.00
4	10,000	2.00
5	900	2.00
		$12.00 Minor total
		$50.00 Major total
Family totals	$17,700	$62.00

Figure 3-9 MAJOR AND MINOR SETUPS.

costs 20% and that annual usage and setup costs for each item are as shown in the figure.

There is a major setup cost of $50.00 in addition to the cost S for each item, which represents only the changeover cost for the items within the group. The total setup cost thus equals $62.00. The standard EOQ formula can be revised to handle this problem by writing it as

$$EOQ = \sqrt{\frac{2 \times \Sigma A \times \Sigma S}{I}} \qquad (3\text{-}11)$$

where

$$\Sigma A = \text{sum of the annual usages for all items}$$

$$\Sigma S = \text{sum of the setup costs for all items}$$

Other factors are the same as in formula (3-1). From this;

$$EOQ = \sqrt{\frac{2 \times 17,700 \times 62}{0.20}} = \sqrt{10,970,000} = \$3300$$

Each time a setup is made, $3300 worth of *all* items should be run. Individual lot-sizes for the items can be calculated using formula (3-1) but would have no practical value. The principal objective is to run enough of each item to equalize the time period covered by the inventory, so that new lots of all will be needed when the major setup is made again. It would be highly undesirable to have the inventory so badly balanced among the items that one was required much sooner than the rest, particularly one of the low-usage items (3 or 5).

EOQ's calculated individually vary as the square root of the usage, and the popular items would run out of stock before the slow-moving ones. The proper solution is to run a quantity of each item that will result in a balanced inventory having an equal number of days' supply of each item. This is known as **equal runout time**. This is assumed to be an equal number of days' supply based on average usage for each item in the examples that follow. A more refined calculation would take into account the probable forecast error to improve the chances of all items running out of stock simultaneously.

The present inventory for each item is tabulated as shown in Figure 3-10, together with the average daily usage rate obtained by dividing the annual usage by the number of working days per year.

Item	Present inventory	Daily usage rate (250 days/year)
1	$336	$ 8.00
2	320	16.00
3	100	3.20
4	600	40.00
5	97	3.60
Totals	$1,453	$70.80

Figure 3-10 FAMILY ITEMS PRESENT INVENTORY.

The procedure for making the proper distribution is first to calculate the total inventory that will result after the new run is added to the present supply. After running the calculated $3300 family lot-size, the total inventory will be $3300 + $1453 = $4753. If all items were in perfect balance, there would be $4753/$70.80 = 67 days' supply of each.

Therefore, a quantity of each item should be run to increase its present inventory to 67 days' supply. This is calculated as shown in Figure 3-11 by subtracting the present inventory from the 67-day total for each item. The quantity to be run is shown in the right-hand column.

Item	67 days supply	Present inventory	Run quantity
1	$ 536	$336	$ 200
2	1,072	320	752
3	214	100	114
4	2,690	600	2,090
5	241	97	144
Totals	$4,753	$1,453	$3,300

Figure 3-11 FAMILY ITEM LOT SIZES—INSTANTANEOUS RECEIPT.

In this example, the basic EOQ formula (3-11) was used with the annual usages and the setup cost totaled for all items in the group. When a group of items such as this is being run, the production run might require a considerable period of time. If it did, the noninstantaneous receipt formula (3-10) would be more applicable. When applied to a group of items, this is

$$EOQ = \sqrt{\frac{2 \times A \times S}{I(1 - s/p)}} \tag{3-12}$$

Item	A	S	Daily usage rate (250 days/yr)	Daily production rate
1	$ 2,000	$ 2.00	$ 8.00	$ 60
2	4,000	3.00	16.00	80
3	800	3.00	3.20	75
4	10,000	2.00	40.00	70
5	900	2.00	3.60	69
Major setup:		50.00		
Totals:	$17,700	$62.00	$70.80	$354

Figure 3-12 FAMILY ITEM LOT SIZES—NONINSTANTANEOUS RECEIPT.

The production and usage rates are shown in Figure 3-12 for each of the items. The calculations are

$$EOQ = \sqrt{\frac{2 \times 17,700 \times 62.00}{0.20(1 - 70.80/354)}}$$

$$= \quad \sqrt{2,194,000/0.20(1 - 0.2)}$$

$$= \quad \sqrt{2,194,000/0.16} = \quad \sqrt{13,700,000}$$

$$= \quad \$3700$$

Once again, the use of the noninstantaneous receipt adjuster resulted in a larger lot-size. When this group of items is run, the total of the individual lot-sizes should equal $3700. The lot-sizes of the individual items should balance the inventory to give an equal number of days' supply in inventory for each item after the new lot is added to the current inventory of the item.

Note that it may not matter *what sequence is followed* in running the items in the family. The first items to run should be those in greatest danger of being used up and causing shortages if there are no overriding considerations like color sequencing.

Quantity Discounts

When material is purchased, vendors frequently give the buyer some of the advantages of running larger manufacturing lots by offering a discount schedule. The following example shows the EOQ calculation for an item where

$$\text{Annual usage} \ = \ \$10,000$$

$$\text{Ordering cost} \ = \ \$5.00$$

$$\text{Inventory-carrying cost} \ = \ 20\%$$

Using Formula (3–1), the EOQ equals $707. If the vendor offered a 1% discount on lots of $2000 or more, the economics of this offer could be shown by setting up a table to determine the total cost of 1 year's supply in each case as shown in Figure 3-13.

EOQ (no discount)				Large lot (with discount)	
$707		Lot-size	($2,000 –1% =)	$1,980	
$353		Average lot-size inventory		990	
	$70.60	Inventory carrying cost (20%)			$198
14.1		Number of orders/yr		5.0	
	$70.50	Cost of orders ($5.00 each)			+ 25
		Savings from discount	(1% X 10,000 =)		− 100
	$141.10	Total cost of one year's supply			$123

Figure 3-13 EOQ FOR PURCHASE DISCOUNT.

In this figure the average inventory value was determined with and without the discount and the inventory carrying cost was calculated for each case. The total cost of ordering was then determined by calculating the number of orders to be placed in a year and multiplying this by the ordering cost. The left-hand column of the figure shows that the total cost for the calculated EOQ is $141.10.

The calculation of these inventory carrying and ordering costs for the discounted quantity shows a total of $223, made up of $198 carrying cost for the higher inventory and only $25 ordering cost, since fewer orders have to be placed. On this basis, it would not appear to be economical to order the larger quantity. However, the discount reduces the unit cost of the item and the cost of 1 year's requirement would be $100 less if the discount were accepted. This factor is not considered in the standard EOQ formula. It is worthwhile to accept this discount, since the total annual cost would be only $123 instead of $141.10 for the calculated EOQ.

The following are characteristic of discount problems:

1. In order to obtain the discount, a larger quantity will have to be purchased; consequently, the inventory investment will go up and carrying costs will increase (usually by a substantial amount).

2. Ordering in larger quantities reduces the number of orders per year and the total cost of ordering consequently goes down. This is not usually a large factor in the total. (Note that the larger lot also reduces exposures to stockouts and thus the need for safety stock.)

3. The discount reduces the unit cost of the total annual volume, which is usually a significant savings.

In order to simplify the discount calculation, the first step of calculating the inventory investment based on the discounted value of the lot-size is often omitted. In the example just given, for instance, the lot-size with the discount would have been shown as $2000 if this first step had been omitted. This is not significant enough to change the results in most practical instances.

Least Total Cost

The square root EOQ formulas calculate a lot-size for each item to which they are applied, based on the costs and other factors in the particular formula chosen. No consideration is given, however, to the way items are related in bills of materials. An assembly A (EOQ = 200) could be made from components B (EOQ = 450), C (EOQ = 675) and D (EOQ = 940). Obviously, there should be a balance between an item's EOQ and the way it is used in its parent items; the alternative is to make and carry in inventory some of the component which is never used (called a *remnant*). The square root formula assumes uniform usage; actual usage for all components in batch manufacturing is nonuniform, occurring in "lumps" equal to the lots in which its parents are made, sometimes with several occurring simultaneously in one time period.

Computerized MRP (see Chapter 6 for a full description of MRP) projects future time-phased requirements of each item so that these can be used in lot-sizing decisions to eliminate or minimize both remnants and the need to assume uniform demand. **Least Total Cost** is one technique used to do this. Its basic assumption is the same as that for the square root formula: The total cost will be a minimum when the carrying and ordering costs are equal. It does not assume uniform usage, instead using future requirements, as shown in Figure 3-14.

Item cost = $4.00
Carrying cost = 30%/yr. = 0.6%/wk.

Future net requirements	Week no. required	Cumulative lot-size	Excess inventory	Weeks carried	$ Carrying cost This lot	$ Carrying cost Cumulative	$ Ordering cost	$ Total cost
93	4	93	0	0	0	0	30.00	30.00
233	5	326	233	1	5.59	5.59	30.00	35.59
194	6	520	194	2	9.31	14.90	30.00	44.90
219	7	739*	219	3	15.77	30.67	30.00	60.67
87	8							
448	9							

*Recommended lot-size

Figure 3-14 LEAST TOTAL COST.

The mechanics of the technique involve a series of iterations; Figure 3-14 shows these. If the lot-size were set at 93, equal to the first requirement in week 4, no excess inventory would be carried (it would be used up in the same week) and one setup would be necessary. Another setup would then be needed to meet future requirements.

If the needs of weeks 4 and 5 were run together, the lot-size would be 326; 233 units would be carried in stock for 1 week but the cost ($5.59) would be much less than that of another setup. This is, therefore, a better decision. Adding successive weeks' requirements increases the lot-size, as shown in the third column, and the cumulative carrying cost. A lot of 739 units has a cumulative carrying cost of $30.67, very nearly equal to the setup cost. An addition to the lot-size would increase this cost; it would be better to make another setup to meet requirements in week 8 and beyond.

The name *Least Total Cost* refers to a long time period—such as several weeks—and not to any one period's total. The recommended lot-size in this example would be 739 units.

Part-Period Balancing

This is simply another name and another set of calculations for essentially the same technique. This variant was developed for IBM's software packages and is simpler to program. The term *Part-Period* refers to 1 unit carried for 1 period, usually a week. An assumption is made that one unit carried 20 periods, for example, would be the same as 20 units carried 1 period. Figure 3-15 illustrates the mechanics, using the same data as Figure 3-14.

The first step is to calculate an *economic part-period* using the formula at the top of Figure (3-15) relating the ordering and carrying costs for 1 unit and 1 period. The iterative calculations, as in Least Total Cost, determine cumulative part-periods by increasing the lot-size to cover successively more periods. For a lot-size of 739, the cumulative part-periods *are closest to the economic part-period* calculated first, and this is the recommended order quantity. Note that Least Total Cost and Part-Period Balancing give the same answer.

$$\text{Economic Part-Period} = \frac{\text{Ordering cost}}{\text{Carrying cost 1 part 1 period}} = \frac{\$30.00}{\$4.00 \times 0.006} = 1{,}250$$

Future net requirements	Week no. required	Cumulative lot–size	Excess inventory	Weeks carried	Part–periods This lot	Part–periods Cumulative
93	4	93	0	0	0	0
233	5	326	233	1	233	233
194	6	520	194	2	388	621
219	7	(739*)	219	3	657	1,278

*Recommended lot–size

Figure 3-15 PART-PERIOD BALANCING.

Look Ahead/Look Back

With the ubiquitous human ability to make more and more refinements in techniques, IBM added two features—called *Look Ahead* and *Look Back*—to part-period balancing. Figure 3-16 illustrates how the **Look-Ahead feature** works. After Part-Period Balancing has developed a recommended lot-size of 739 pieces, as in Figure 3-15, the program explores another alternative: whether or not the next requirement (for period 8) should be included in the lot-size just calculated. Notice the large requirement for 448 in period 9. Alternative 1 would start the calculations for the next batch with the 87 in period 8, followed by 448 in period 9, involving 448 part-periods. As shown in alternative 2 in Figure 3-16, by including the relatively small requirement for 87 in period 8, the previously calculated lot would increase to 826 from the original 739. The next lot would then begin with the large requirement of 448 in period 9. The program would select alternative 2 as the preferred one because it involves only 348 part-periods, whereas alternative 1 requires 448 part-periods. Notice particularly the significant change this makes in the calculated lot-sizes; think about the effects this may have on component availability and work center loads.

Future net requirements	Week no. required	Cumulative lot – size	Excess inventory	Weeks carried	Part–periods This lot	Cumulative
219	7	739	219	3	657	1,278
Alternate #1						
87	8	87	0	0	0	0
448	9	535	448	1	448	
Alternate #2						
87	8	(826*)	87	4	348	
448	9	448	0	0	0	

*Recommended lot–size

Figure 3-16 LOOK-AHEAD FEATURE.

The **Look-Back feature** is another enhancement intended to improve the economics or ordering; it is illustrated in Figure 3-17. Following the normal sequence of Part-Period Balancing, alternative 1, the technique determines that a lot size of 990 pieces will be best to fill requirements from weeks 9 through 13. First looking ahead to investigate alternatives for week 14 and 15, the technique finds no significant benefits. It then looks backward at the requirements in weeks 9 through 13. With the relatively large requirement in week 12 compared to that in week 13, alternative 2 shows in Figure 3-17 that it would be better to run a total of 677 pieces in the first batch and start the next lot with the 226 required in week 12. This would involve a much smaller total of part-periods than alternative 1. The recommended lot-size would be 677, not 990. Note the very large changes in order quantities developed by both looking ahead and looking back.

Future net requirements	Week no. required	Cumulative lot – size	Excess inventory	Weeks carried	Part–periods This lot	Cumulative
Alternate #1						
448	9	448	0	0	0	0
153	10	601	153	1	153	153
76	11	677	76	2	152	305
226	12	903	226	3	678	983
87	13	(990)	87	4	348	1,331
175	14					
98	15					
Alternate #2						
448	9	448	0	0	0	0
153	10	601	153	1	153	153
76	11	(677)	76	2	152	305
226	12	226	0	0	0	0
87	13	313	87	1	87	87

Figure 3-17 LOOK-BACK FEATURE.

Here is another example of how a good idea can be carried to a ridiculous extreme from the user's point of view.

Least Unit Cost

Still another example is the technique of **Least Unit Cost**, which calculates a unit cost for each step of the iteration. Using the same data as in the discussion for Least Total Cost, Figure 3-18 shows how the total cost (fourth column) is calculated by adding the carrying and ordering costs and dividing this sum by the cumulative lot-size at this step in the iteration. The choice of names is confusing. Normally unit cost means the total of the material, labor and factory overhead per unit of the item; in this technique, however, it means only carrying and ordering costs per unit.

In the example in Figure 3-18, the technique arrives at the same recommended

$ Carrying cost This lot	Cumulative	$ Ordering cost	Total cost	Cumulative lot – size	Unit cost
0	0	30.00	30.00	93	0.323
5.59	5.59	30.00	35.59	326	0.109
9.31	14.90	30.00	44.90	520	0.086
15.77	30.67	30.00	60.67	(739)	0.082
8.26	38.93	30.00	68.93	826	0.084

Figure 3-18 LEAST UNIT COST.

order quantity, 739 pieces, as Least Total Cost and Part-Period Balancing. Several large-scale simulations by IBM and other companies have shown that Least Unit Cost will sometimes recommend lot-sizes different from and—more important-ly—*not as economical as these other methods.* Writing in the APICS Quarterly, Production & Inventory Management, First Quarter, 1968, Thomas Gorham, then with Outboard Marine Corporation, compared the methods of Least Unit and Least Total Cost and concluded in his article, "Dynamic Order Quantities," that the method of Least Unit Cost was erratic, developing lower setup and higher inventory costs on one set of data and higher setup and lower inventory costs on another, but not achieving total costs as low. There is no reason to use Least Unit Cost; why make more calculations to get poorer results?

Period Order Quantity

This is one of the simplest techniques to use with time-phased requirements data. It expresses the order quantity as equal to the total future net requirements over a number of time periods (such as 6 weeks). The time periods used for the period order quantity should be "economical," based on balancing ordering and carrying costs.

The simplest approach uses the square root formula to calculate an EOQ and then converts this to the equivalent time periods of supply, called the POQ, based on the average rate of usage. For example:

$$POQ = \frac{EOQ}{(\text{average weekly usage})}$$

$$\text{Annual usage} = 15{,}600 \text{ pieces}$$

$$\text{Item EOQ} = 2100 \text{ pieces}$$

$$POQ = \frac{2100}{(15{,}600/50)} = 7 \text{ weeks}$$

Note that this calculation is approximate; 50 weeks in a year is employed to get average usage and the POQ is rounded to the nearest whole number of weeks. There is no need for precision in these calculations.

Calculation of period order quantities in an MRP program are illustrated in Figure 3-19. Gross requirements on this component are generated by planned orders to make parent items. An open order for 925 (probably the balance of a partially completed order) is due this week and will cover all requirements for the next 2 weeks and part of the third. The technique then adds net requirements for 7 weeks, based on the POQ just calculated. The order is due, of course, in the first week there is a need (week 3) and should be released in the current week to provide the necessary lead time. The next order, due in week 10, is somewhat smaller; the 7 weeks that it covers have lower requirements.

The technique has several good features. It generates orders at regular intervals and can help smooth input to starting work centers. It matches projected requirements and should leave no residues or remnants of unused lot-size inventory.

On hand = 0   Safety stock = 0   Lead time = 2 wks.

Weeks	1	2	3	4	5	6	7	8	9	10	11
Gross req'ts	510	115	320	400	270	190	605	360	180	410	335
Open order	925										
Net req'ts	–	–	20	400	270	190	605	360	180	410	335
Order due			2025							1960	
Order start	2025							1960			

Figure 3-19 PERIOD ORDER QUANTITY.

In the example in Figure 3-19, had the square root EOQ of 2100 been used, a balance of 75 would have remained in stock in week 9. This amount would be too small to cover week 10 requirements and another order would still be needed then. Changes in requirements will alter this match, of course; this could be what happened in week 3, where the open order falls 20 short of meeting the week's requirements. Another possibility, of course, is that 20 units may have been scrapped on the order.

Lot-for-Lot

A definition of the ideal lot-size is an amount that is just what is really needed today or this week. The name **Lot-for-Lot** has been applied to the technique of matching order quantities to the requirements for the planning period, usually a week. This is easily programmed in MRP. Very little inventory is carried and the flow of work into and through work centers is smoother and more reliable. Material handling costs could be large. Setup costs would also be high *unless* setup times were shortened. Principle 7 highlights this need.

Practical Considerations

There are several other techniques, including Wagner-Whitin's Algorithm, for determining EOQ's. Since these have little or no practical application, they will not be covered in this book. In the language of mathematicians, the various EOQ formulas are very simple models. It is important to understand the basic concept of EOQ and to be sure that the model used is the best available for the particular circumstances being studied. The EOQ formulas contain many assumptions that must be understood by the practitioner if he or she is to use them properly.

These formulas assume, for example, that the amount of inventory carried is a direct result of the number of orders placed and that this inventory will be withdrawn at a fairly uniform rate. They further assume that the only factors significant in the calculation of the most economical lot are those included in the formula and that costs relating to ordering and to carrying inventory vary uniformly and continuously with the size of the lot ordered. Other costs and related factors are presented in the second volume. (7) The balance of this section deals with some practical situations in which common sense must be used in applying the EOQ formula.

Many products have a seasonal sales pattern. It is not unusual to see most of the anticipated product requirements produced well before the peak season in order to keep production fairly level throughout the year. During this period of inventory building, the inventory that is being added is *anticipation inventory, not lot-size inventory,* and the regular EOQ model does not apply. Instead of balancing ordering costs against inventory, the company is now trying to store work-hours in inventory most economically. If the peak season is very short—like Christmas—the sales forecast is the only real information available to the inventory manager, since information about actual sales will come too late for him or her to react. For this reason, many seasonal items are produced in one lot during the year. The question of what lot to run next involves comparing labor versus material costs for all items, ranking them so that the item with the highest ratio of labor to material will be run farthest in advance of the selling season and will therefore be carried in inventory longest. For a product line with less pronounced seasonal demand, where anticipation inventory is built only during a brief part of the year, the economic lot-size concept would apply—but during the inventory building period, some lots could be combined to reduce setups.

Another common situation encountered is the problem of determining lot-sizes for assemblies and their components and once again the extreme situations present the clearest examples. For an assembly composed of unique components not used on other assemblies, the lot-size should be calculated by taking into account all setup costs for the components and the assembly, and most of the components should be manufactured in the same lot-sizes as the assembly. Some components with extremely high setup costs could be manufactured in quantities that are multiples of the assembly lot; a simple calculation of the inventory that would be generated versus setups saved will show the economics of the decision.

There is no specific allowance in most EOQ formulas for the fact that the space cost for different items can be very different indeed. Shipping cartons usually have a low unit value, a very attractive discount schedule and take up great amounts of storage space. On the other hand, electronic components have a very high unit value and take up very little storage space. Using the same inventory carrying cost for both items (where the storage cost is assumed to be included in the inventory carrying cost) would charge the latter more for storage than the former and make little sense. Particularly with bulky items, an estimate of total space requirements resulting from EOQ calculations is essential; storage costs can then be applied to similar groups of items in order to obtain practical results.

The ordering quantities indicated on the records and the ordering quantities actually used in the factory are frequently quite different. For example, in an assembly plant, where components are chronically in short supply, assembly orders may be put out for quantities of 2000 to 3000 units, yet the assembly line may never run quantities of more than 500 or 600 units for lack of an adequate supply

of components. Any comparisons of new lot-sizes with the present order quantities to determine the effects and economies of change should be based on the actual lot quantity being processed in the plant, not the quantity ordered by the
materials control department.

Many items are processed through a sequence of operations. The ordering
cost must then include the sum of the setup costs for all operations. If setup on
one of the early operations is an extremely large proportion of total setup cost,
it may be economical to establish an inventory called a **hold point** beyond this high
setup operation and then do further processing in smaller lots. The decision to have
this hold point should be based on the alternatives of processing the lot through
to completion with the resulting inventory of finished part or of carrying the inventory as a semifinished part further back in the process sequence in a less expensive form. Here are a few points to keep in mind regarding this type of calculation:

1. When choosing between alternatives of carrying an item in a semifinished
    state or processing it through to completion, only that portion of the unit
    cost actually affected should be used in the calculations. By carrying an
    item as a finished part rather than in a semifinished state, only the labor
    and material of operations beyond the semifinished point (certainly very
    little or no overhead) are actually added to the inventory investment,
    although the accounting records will seldom recognize this.

2. The lead time required to replenish the finished-item inventory will be
    reduced and lower inventories can often be carried at this more expensive
    stage. This is of even greater benefit when several finished items can be
    made from one semifinished item. This occurs, for example, where the
    semifinished item is unpainted and can be painted one of four different
    ways to make four different finished items. Note, however, that *total* lead
    time will probably increase because larger lots are processed and time will
    be added moving the inventory into and out of the hold point.

3. In general, semifinished hold points should seldom be established on the
    basis of differentials in setup alone. Semifinished inventories are extreme-
    ly difficult to control and the processing of excessively large lot-sizes
    through the primary operations often makes mix control to meet chang-
    ing needs for finished goods very difficult. This is especially true when
    business is increasing and finished goods requirements cannot be satis-
    fied completely from the hold point. The increasing withdrawals from
    the hold point will generate a large number of replenishment orders that
    may very well—since the lot-sizes are typically large for these compo-
    nents—create bottlenecks in primary operations that soon cause serious
    shortages because it becomes impossible to get some of everything through.

4. Hold point inventories will require more control effort, more record-keep-
    ing and more paperwork. Both their advantages and disadvantages should
    be clearly recognized when the establishment of hold points is being con-
    sidered.

5. The best all-around solution is to reduce setup times.

Principle 8: EOQ calculations are only a starting point; modify them for practical results.

One of the best means of checking the reasonableness of calculated EOQ's is a detailed review by those familiar with the practical situations involved. After the EOQ's have been calculated, someone familiar with the manufacturing equipment should review them with the supervisor responsible for the area in which these lot-sizes apply or with the setup person working on the machine and round the calculated EOQ's to usable figures. Because of the flatness of the EOQ curve, reasonable rounding will not result in any serious loss of the economies of EOQ. Such review, however, will insure that practical limitations in applying the lot-sizes have not been overlooked. The experienced practitioner will check each EOQ application to be sure that the model is valid. With a thorough understanding of the EOQ formula and its applications, the technique can be used to yield large benefits, but if the technique is applied blindly by rote, it may result in actual increased costs to the company.

There are many reasons for modifying the results of EOQ calculations. *Scrap losses* can be offset by inflating the lot-size by the percentage of average loss expected. *Minimum quantities* can be established to place a floor under the calculated EOQ's to reflect a vendor's minimum purchase of quantities or batches of items made from one unit of raw material (bar, sheet, or barrel). *Maximum figures* are set as a ceiling on calculations for bulky items where space limitations exist. Calculated EOQ's are also adjusted to even multiples of packaged lots (such as dozens, pallet loads, or drums), container batches in which the item is moved or units of raw material (coils, bundles, drums, etc.) from which the item is made.

Calculations of EOQ's can be worthwhile in generating tangible benefits and can also be a source of real problems. Mathematical calculations can present an aura of great precision (note the unit-cost figures in Figure 3-18), but this should not be confused with accuracy. Different techniques develop different answers but time spent trying to find the "best" is an exercise in trivia and could be used better elsewhere. Frequent recalculations of EOQ's generate troublesome nervousness in planning systems, as discussed fully in the second volume. (7) The formulas also work on *one item at a time;* the impact on capacity, total capital invested and family relationships is usually far greater than the savings on individual items. These effects are discussed in Chapter 8, *Aggregate Inventory Management,* and in Appendix II of both this and the second volume (7).

CHAPTER
FOUR

DEMAND MANAGEMENT

Scope of Demand Management

As defined in my Glossary, (9) demand management is the modern term covering all the activities involved in planning for and handling all types of demand on a manufacturing facility. This would include demand from the following:

1. Customers, domestic and foreign
2. Other plants in the same corporate family
3. Branch warehouses in other locations
4. Consigned stocks in customers' locations

It would embrace the activities of the following:

1. Forecasting such demand
2. Handling order entry
3. Making delivery promises
4. Interfacing with master planning

Demands would involve all classes of materials, including

1. Finished products
2. Components furnished as products
3. Repair parts

In its broadest sense, demand management includes planning for warehouse locations, alternate methods of shipping from manufacturing source to warehouses and warehouse layout, materials handling, and operation. Generally called *distribution,* these topics are beyond the scope of this book. Chapter 5 includes the time-phased order point and Appendix VII covers other techniques employed in ordering replenishment materials and the principles of effective inventory management in such warehouses. Chapter 6 discusses the blending of warehouse demand with other types of demand in materials planning. Order entry activities are concerned primarily with data handling and processing and will not be covered in this book or the applications volume. The principal subject of this chapter is forecasting demand from customers.

The Importance of the Forecast

Manufacturing planning and control are concerned basically with the future. The past is beyond control—it is necessary to start from the present situation and prepare for the future. To do this, it is necessary to guess, assume or otherwise estimate what is going to happen from now on. All other things being equal, a company can survive only be preparing itself to meet its customers' needs at least as quickly as its competitors. The word *forecast* covers estimates of such future customer needs. *Plans* and *budgets* are the names given to projections of data related to plant operations.

Since all the planning activity in a company deals with meeting future needs of customers, much of the organization must work with sales forecasts. Figure 4-1 shows a summary of the various forecasts made by a typical company and the uses of these forecasts. Household formations, for example, are used by marketing departments to determine total potential market growth. Plant managers and plant engineering departments want to know 5-year production requirements, since plans for land acquisition, development of new production processes based on changing volumes and technology, and the procurement of additional manufacturing facilities require long lead times. Figure 4-1 shows only the major requirements; there are many more ways of using the forecasts.

The materials control department, frequently called the planning department, is assigned the responsibility for planning to meet the future needs for manufacturing the product. The demand forecast is the vital element in this preparation. The material control people need this forecast for planning how many components to purchase, how much raw material to buy, what rate to machine or assemble and—most important—when to order.

There are conflicting requirements for forecasts. The general manager, for example, is concerned with a forecast of shipments, since these generate the dollars the company receives from its customers. He or she may be at odds with the marketing manager, who is more concerned with incoming business, since this measures customers' demands on the company that require servicing. Shipments really repre-

Forecast	Required by
1. Household formations	Marketing: determine total potential market growth
2. Total production required next five years	Manufacturing: plant expansion program
3. Number of equipment hours (by type) required next two years	Manufacturing: next year's capital budget
4. Next year's sales of individual products in family groupings	Sales: quotas Finance: expense budgets Manufacturing: worker and machine capacities Material control: seasonal inventory requirements and blanket purchase orders
5. Sales for next quarter of individual products	Material control: work center capacities, manufactured and purchased components
6. Sales for next week of individuaul products	Material control: assembly schedules and dispatching priorities

Figure 4-1 TYPES OF FORECASTS AND THEIR USES.

sent incoming business modified by the company's ability to respond to demand. The sales manager is typically interested in setting optimistic goals as a challenge to sales personnel, while the controller would rather have a more conservative forecast on which to estimate profits. The material control department wants the forecast in terms that are meaningful to the manufacturing departments (in product groups that go through similar manufacturing facilities, for example). The groups that are meaningful to marketing are those sold in similar channels and are not necessarily the same as the manufacturing product groups.

Several forecasts are needed in most companies. These can be classified in many ways, one being the time period involved:

Long-range forecasts:
Used for plant expansion and acquisition of new machines and equipment, in order to plan capital investment 5 years or more in advance.

Intermediate-range forecasts:
Used for procurement of long-lead-time materials or planning of operating rates, taking into account seasonal or cyclical products 1 to 2 years in advance.

Short-range forecasts:
Used to determine the proper order quantities and order timing for purchasing or manufacturing components and to plan the proper manufacturing capacity, taking into consideration the desirability of leveling workload 3 to 6 months in advance.

Immediate-future demands:
Used for assembly schedules and finished-goods inventory distribution on a weekly or daily basis.

Long-range forecasting involves complex considerations beyond the scope of this book. It covers the range of 2 to 5 or more years ahead. It requires an understanding of economic factors, competitive and technological influences and capital expansion plans made by top management. Development of such forecasts includes consideration of market strategies, employment policies and governmental regulations. Increasing attention is being given in larger corporations to this type of forecasting but medium-sized and smaller companies largely ignore the need. There is real value, however, in making a serious effort to chart a course for any company. Of greatest benefit may be the definition of the charter of the company: What business is it really in? Many industries, particularly railroads and steel, could have avoided serious problems had they seen more clearly that their real businesses were furnishing transportation and production of basic materials, not operating railroads and steel mills, respectively.

The shorter-range forecast, in general, requires greater accuracy. A medium-range forecast of capacity, for example, may indicate a certain number of hours required in a work center. When the time comes to utilize these hours, they may be used on a job that was not even considered when the original capacity forecast was made. (The total forecast hours are likely to be quite accurate if there are many items going through the department.) On the other hand, this week's forecast establishes a schedule for final assembly or packaging of a particular mix of products. Since these products will determine the specific finished goods inventory available for shipment, it is important that this forecast be as accurate as possible.

Another way to classify forecasts is by the type of item covered, such as individual products, families or subgroups. The specific forecasts needed by a company depend on the relationship between the length of its manufacturing cycle and the lead time allowed by its customers, as illustrated in Figure 4-2. If customers will wait while the company determines what materials are needed, procures these materials, processes them and finally delivers the product, there is really no need for any type of forecast. Of course, few customers of any business will wait for their vendor to build or enlarge the plant or to get additional machine tools or other equipment, so all companies need long-range forecasts for capital investment in production facilities.

Marketing people like to say that nothing really happens until a company gets a customer's order. It sounds good, but it simply is not true. Many things had better have happened *before* the order is received. If a company's competitors can furnish products to the customers in slightly more than the required shipping time, it will be necessary for the company to maintain a finished goods inventory in order to fill orders as rapidly as everyone else. This means that the company will have to forecast raw material needs, purchase and manufacture parts and schedule production of the necessary finished goods based on forecasts.

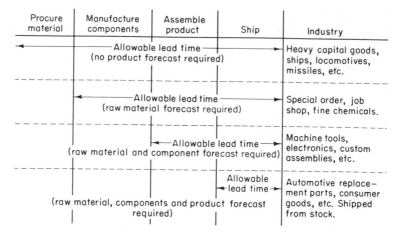

Figure 4-2 ALLOWABLE LEAD TIMES VERSUS FORECASTS REQUIRED.

Figure 4-2 also indicates the major elements of lead times for some typical industries. Undoubtedly, this picture has now changed dramatically; many companies found their competitors shipping products in shorter lead times without *maintaining higher inventory investments.*

Many factors influence the demand for a company's products and services and it is never possible to identify all these factors and measure their impact or predict their effects. Nevertheless, it is helpful in forecasting to identify broad, major influences and attempt to predict the changes they are likely to cause. These can be external or internal. **External factors** include general business conditions and the state of the nation's economy, which influence almost every company's customers and thus affect demand for its products. All long-range forecasts—and many intermediate-range ones—must include some evaluation of the effect of a changing economic climate. Competitive factors are another external force to be considered. Competition comes indirectly from other demands on the customer's money as well as directly from similar or identical products. No company can afford to neglect an evaluation of what competitors are doing and the probable effects of this on its own business. Trends in the marketplace, including changing desires of customers, growing demand, styles, fashions, etc., must also be considered to affect a company's sales. Occasionally, these forces can be influenced to some extent by advertising but in any case they are most difficult to control.

Internal factors, such as a company's plans for advertising, sales promotion, selling effort, pricing and quality improvement, can have a major effect in creating or boosting demand. No forecast can be valid without an effort to include these factors. On-time deliveries, lower costs and shorter manufacturing cycles are other internal actions that can have significant effects on demand for a company's products.

The Evolution of Forecasting

In the early days, formal procedures for the preparation of forecasts were not developed in most companies. Where they were, clear responsibility was not assigned to any individual or any segment of the organization. A forecast was rarely recognized as a real need. The need was usually filled unconsciously and intuitively by an owner-manager who decided to buy more material because he or she had confidence that it could be processed and sold in the future, by a supervisor who decided to hire an individual because he or she believed the work load would continue to stay high or by a stock clerk who wrote out a new order to replenish a dwindling supply of bolts in the stock room.

Some years prior to World War II, many companies began to recognize the potential benefits of preparing forecasts in a formal manner. They set up a separate group responsible for preparing the data, outlined the procedures for approval of the forecast by those in the organization who were vitally concerned and frequently restricted distribution to those eligible to receive such confidential information. In many cases, large sums of money were spent to develop forecasts using statistical techniques, market research or other sophisticated methods. During this period, the basic assumption seemed to be that forecasting problems could be solved if only enough money, effort and intelligence were put into making them. This could well be termed the *rose-colored-glasses era* of forecasting.

When perfect forecasts were not forthcoming, the inevitable period of disillusionment began. Planning and control systems based upon this premise excused their failures with the explanation that all would have been well if only there had been a good forecast. As a result of this reaction, many companies ceased all organized attempts to forecast and returned to intuitive guesses, stung by the failures and high costs of the methods that had let them down. This could be called the *backlash era*. Most companies have now recovered completely from this reaction. Naive attitudes toward forecasting are rare in industry; only a very few companies still believe they should expect more accurate forecasts and could get them if only they could find the right technique.

Most people recognize two distinct problems in forecasting: making a more accurate forecast and making better use of inexact forecasts.

Principle 9. A forecast is a set of numbers to work from, not to.

Any forecast, however derived, provides starting data with which to begin planning via an integrated formal system. As changes are made to the forecast based on better knowledge or new opinions or when actual demand does not match the forecast, the plan can be updated to indicate specific corrective actions needed. The second problem of forecasting, making better use of the forecasts, provides far more potential benefits than striving for more accurate projections.

The present trend is to a more rational point of view recognizing that forecasts must and will be made and, therefore, that they might better be made by those most capable; it recognizes the value of using one formal forecast as a basis for all other forecasts rather than having many operating departments making their own guesses about the future.

Forecasting Characteristics

Before discussing the techniques of forecasting, it is important that the general characteristics of forecasts be understood. The most important of these can be stated briefly:

1. Forecasts will be wrong.
2. Forecasts are most useful with an estimate of error.
3. Forecasts are more accurate for larger groups of items.
4. Forecasts are more accurate for shorter periods of time.

The present rational approach recognizes that forecasts will always be subject to error and that, while there are tools available to improve the art of forecasting, the amount of money and effort put into applying such tools rapidly reaches a point of diminishing return. Beyond this point, it is far more profitable to develop flexibility to cope with forecast inaccuracy instead of trying to improve the forecast. The best solution is to develop a formal forecasting program and a system that detects and measures forecast errors and then to react quickly to correct for such errors. This solution is covered in this chapter in detail.

An estimate of the error, based on previous actual versus forecast data or on personal opinions of knowledgeable people, can be used to develop contingency plans. These will speed up and make more effective the corrective actions taken in response to forecast errors. Every forecast should include an estimate of forecast error—the forecaster's expression of *how wrong* the forecast might be. This estimate can be expressed as a percentage (plus or minus) of the forecast or as a range between maximum and minimum values. In establishing order points, as described in Chapter 5, it is necessary to know both the estimated average usage during the lead time and the maximum anticipated usage during the lead time. The latter, of course, is a function of the accuracy of the demand forecast during the lead time. Estimates of forecast error provide the basis needed to set up decision rules to determine when to take actions (such as recalculating EOQ's or changing the production rate of a department). When actual demand falls outside the forecast range, it is probable that more than random influences are present and that action is required.

Although new items reaching the market are the most unpredictable, there are few situations where the estimate of forecast error can be used more profitably than in the new-product forecast. The new product may be quite similar to something fairly stable already in the product line. In this case, where the sales department has some experience selling similar items and the marketing department has forecast similar products in the past, the anticipated forecast error may be low. On the other hand, for an entirely new product in a market where the company has had no experience, the forecast might be off by as much as 300%. Later sections of this book treat in detail the use of the forecast error in making decisions in production and inventory control.

A fundamental statistical observation is that the behavior of individuals in a population is random even where the population as a whole has very stable characteristics. For example, it is extremely difficult to forecast the life expectancy of an individual, but insurance companies predict the average life expectancy of large groups of individuals with great accuracy. Likewise, it is possible to make a forecast for a large family of manufactured products with a fairly high degree of accuracy, although forecasts of individual items within the family are subject to a high degree of error.

Figure 4-3 shows an example of this fundamental observation for a group of ten items. The individual items were forecast for the third quarter of the year.

Third Quarter				
Item	Forecast*	Actual	Difference	% Change from forecast
#7147–Lamp	47,600	42,784	−4816	− 10.1
#8014–Tongs	12,800	9125	−3675	−28.7
#8663–File	1505	1157	− 348	−23.1
#8726–Stapler	22,500	28,392	+5892	+26.1
#8933–Screwdriver	10,100	11,934	+1834	+18.1
#9250–Shears	17,450	14,860	−2590	−14.8
#9261–Scissors	28,500	27,733	− 767	− 2.7
#9337–Rake	68,000	68,105	+ 105	+ 0.2
#9604–Hoe	27,200	17,556	−9644	−35.4
#9638–Shovel	3320	4638	+1318	+39.8
Average forecast error for items =				19.9
Group totals	238,975	226,284	−12,691	− 5.3

*Forecast made at end of the second quarter

Figure 4-3 FORECAST ERROR FOR ITEMS VERSUS GROUPS.

At the end of that period, the actual sales totals were compared with the forecasts and the percent of change from the forecast noted. These forecast errors for the items averaged 19.9%, ranging from almost 30% high to about 40% low. The product group containing all items showed a forecast error of only 5.3%, while only two items had errors this small.

Figure 4-4 shows the comparison of a typical item forecast with the actual demand over a long period. This item was originally forecast to sell at 900 units per week and the forecast was not revised over a 50-week period. The cumulative forecast demand is simply the weekly forecast rate extended by the number of weeks,

| | | Item #9 | | |
Week no.	Cumulative forecast demand	Cumulative actual demand	Approximate deviation from forecast	Deviation as a multiple of weekly forecast
2	1800	2004	200	0.2
5	4500	5230	700	0.8
10	9000	10,224	1200	1.3
15	13,500	15,465	2000	2.2
20	18,000	19,912	1900	2.1
25	22,500	24,472	2000	2.2
30	27,000	28,712	1700	1.9
35	31,500	33,312	1800	2.0
40	36,000	39,120	3100	3.5
45	40,500	46,785	6300	6.9
50	45,000	54,242	9200	10.2

Forecast = 900 units per week

Figure 4-4 FORECAST ERROR OVER THE FORECAST HORIZON.

while the cumulative actual demand is the sum of the totals of actual sales through the number of weeks shown. The deviation tended to increase as the forecast was extended. For example, at the end of the second week, the actual deviation from forecast was approximately 200 units, representing about $\frac{2}{10}$ of 1 week's supply, while at the end of the 35th week, this had gone up to 1800 units—representing approximately a 2-week supply. At the end of the 50th week, this increased further to approximately a 10-week supply. In general, forecast error will tend to increase as the length of the forecast horizon increases.

A good forecasting system will always be in a state of flux as the forecaster learns more about the art of forecasting. The forecaster may develop new techniques and wish to test them against actual company data. If the forecaster wants to determine whether or not a new forecasting technique is effective, he or she does not have to wait for sales to materialize before learning whether this technique is or is not valid. The forecaster can pretend that the forecast is being made a year or two earlier and then test the forecasting method against what really happened.

Figure 4-5 shows a very simple example. In this case, a seasonal sales index for each quarter was developed based on the average of 5 years' actual sales prior to the last year. The last year's actual sales were omitted from this calculation. They were used to test the method by comparing the percentage of sales forecasted in each quarter with actual quarterly sales percentages for the test year. This very simple test indicates that, for the past year, the forecasting technique for determining quarterly sales percentages would have been reasonably accurate. This technique would not be valid if the test year were one of the 5 years used to establish the

Estimating quarterly sales percentages	
Estimated quarterly sales percentages (based on average of five years actual sales prior to last year)	Actual quarterly sales percentages last year
1st quarter – 21.00%	20.50%
2nd quarter – 29.00%	30.30%
3rd quarter – 29.00%	28.90%
4th quarter – 21.00%	20.30%
Total 100.00%	100.00%

Figure 4-5 TESTING THE FORECAST TECHNIQUE.

original percentages, since these indices would obviously be very likely to correlate well with the history used in developing them.

The important advantage of testing is that the forecaster is able to make inexpensive mistakes by simulating his or her forecasting technique. If the forecasting system is shown to be good by the testing, then it is likely to be good in practice. This is the basic data behind *focus forecasting* (10), in which a computer program performs such a simulation using a number of preselected forecasting models and uses the one performing best on recent data to project future demand.

Making a Forecast

There are five essential steps in forecasting:

1. Defining the purposes
2. Preparing the data
3. Selecting the techniques
4. Making the forecasts (and the estimates of forecast error)
5. Tracking the forecasts

Every function in a company has a need for information on its sales forecast. No function can operate effectively without knowledge of future demand for its products. It is also true that no single forecast can serve all these needs. For best results, every company should produce *a set of related forecasts* designed to meet the users' needs.

Principle 10. Give each user a forecast suitable for his or her needs.

If Principle 10 is not followed, users will be forced to interpret the forecast themselves to produce the data they need. On occasion, manufacturing, materials, engineering, purchasing and finance departments in a company have had to do this with the "official" marketing forecast; it was not evident that these groups were all working for the same company.

Some of the various uses of forecasts are indicated in Figure 4-1; there are many more. It would be trite to attempt to list them all. Various uses, however, have distinct differences in

1. The horizon—short, medium and long

2. The period—weekly, monthly, quarterly, annually

3. The frequency of review—daily, weekly, monthly, or longer.

4. The unit of measure—money, pieces, hours, gallons, dozens, etc.

Each purpose should be identified and its requirements for each of these four factors specified. The individual or group responsible for issuing the official forecast should then restructure the data for groups of users with similar requirements. Only in this way will a consistent, integrated planning approach be possible.

For many companies, the basic problem of preparing sound data can often be formidable. Finding sales figures for a long-enough period to develop a good forecasting method and test it requires more than a set of historical sales figures. Without related information, looking at past sales history would not show when strikes, price increases, inventory tax dates, changes in the accounting calendar, special sales promotions and the like may have introduced elements into the data that make them unreliable as a basis for forecasting.

In preparing the data, the forecaster must also determine just what is to be forecasted. A factory that sells most of its goods to customers through branch warehouses must gear its production to warehouse requirements as well as customer requirements, since the warehouses will undoubtedly require some inventory in anticipation of peak customer demands. This will generate requirements on the factory in excess of actual customer sales during such periods. If the forecaster merely predicts the increase in incoming business from customers, the factory will not be ready to produce enough goods at the proper time to fill the distribution pipeline.

The forecaster must determine whether to use the data to forecast shipments or incoming business. Data on shipments reflect what the production facility has been able to do in response to incoming orders. For example, a popular product that has been in short supply for 4 or 5 months will show a history of low shipments in spite of a high rate of incoming business. The forecaster who bases his or her estimates of future requirements on past shipments will prolong the shortage period by not reflecting true demand for the product. Very few companies, even with adequate inventories, can respond rapidly enough to sudden surges in demand to keep shipments equal to incoming business. In Figure 4-6, a typical example of shipments versus demand, it can be seen that the sudden increase of business in April and May resulted in an increase in the shipping rate but the shipping room was not able to overcome the resulting backlog until November. This does not mean that a large number of May orders did not get shipped until November, but it does show that the delay in customer shipments increased greatly during the peak season. The forecaster who used shipments as a basis for deter-

Month	Shipments	Incoming orders	Order backlog
Jan.	302	305	31
Feb.	373	372	30
Mar.	465	471	36
Apr.	530	562	68
May	591	681	158
June	626	615	147
July	603	664	208
Aug.	687	675	196
Sept.	731	658	123
Oct.	642	570	51
Nov.	372	340	19
Dec.	254	269	34
Total	6176	6182	

Figure 4-6 SHIPMENTS VERSUS INCOMING ORDERS.

mining seasonal activity would forecast a later and higher peak. As a result, the factory would be manufacturing products too late to meet actual customer demand.

It is also important to separate **streams of demand** in forecasting. The same factory mentioned above might well be shipping 45% of its goods directly to customers and 55% to them indirectly via warehouses. This will mean two separate types of forecasts for orders on the factory, one representing actual customer demand directly on the factory and the other representing customer demand on warehouses plus increases or minus decreases in the warehouse inventories.

Many companies have products that are sold to different classes of trade. For example, a company may make a hardware item normally sold to wholesalers in small quantities ordered frequently—but occasionally purchased by an original-equipment manufacturer to be used in manufacturing furniture in two lots per year. Twice a year there would be extremely large demands upon the inventory in addition to the great number of small demands from wholesalers; these two streams of demand would require different forecasts. The average demand would be meaningless.

It is extremely important for the forecaster to use the proper period in analyzing historical data as well as making forecasts. Figure 4-7 shows the deceptive picture that monthly sales can give. Looking only at this column, it appears that sales in February have dropped substantially from January levels and that sales in March increased over both January and February. When the number of working days per month is taken into account, it can be seen that the sales per working day actually increased from January to February and were lower in March than in the previous two months.

Some of the literature on forecasting divides techniques into objective (based

Month	Monthly sales	Working days per month	Sales per working day
January	334,000	22	15,200
February	310,000	20	15,500
March	338,000	23	14,700

Figure 4-7 MONTHLY VERSUS DAILY SALES.

on "cold" statistical or mathematical analyses) and subjective methods (based on "warm" human judgment). This is useful for discussion but every good forecast is a combination of both. All statistical techniques are based on the assumption that *the future will continue to be like the past.* Patterns, trends and cycles in past data are assumed to continue and forecast models are selected to project or extrapolate them into future periods.

Managers in every business strive to make the future different from the past— better, it is to be hoped. Before any objective forecast becomes official, therefore, it should be subjected to the tests of human judgment on how it will be affected by these differences. Consideration must be given to two factors:

1. *Internal:* Within the company, what effect will such factors as price changes, market promotions, quality improvements, better on-time deliveries, shorter manufacturing time, etc. have?

2. *External:* Outside the company, how will competitors, the general economy, government laws, etc. affect them?

Statistical forecasts are only a starting point, a way to handle a large number of items in a consistent, orderly way and in a reasonable time via computers. The follow-up review by people is properly an important part of master scheduling, covered in Chapter 7.

The question, Who should make the forecasts? is asked frequently; the usual answer is, marketing or sales. It is obvious from this discussion of evaluating effects of internal and external factors, however, that forecasting is a team sport. Material control, data processing and market analysis people will select some forecasting techniques and generate "first-cut" forecasts. These will be reviewed by marketing, sales, manufacturing, engineering and other people able to help evaluate the impact of these other factors.

Judgment Forecasts

The most important point to make here is that both approaches to forecasting, *judgment forecasts* and *statistical forecasts* (using the term *statistics* in its broadest sense) are used together. **Judgment forecasts**, sometimes called *predictions*, include those based on the expert opinions of individuals with "a feel for the business," surveys of salespeople to determine the amount of product they think or have been told that their accounts will be ordering during the coming forecast period, and market surveys, in which an interviewer goes out to the marketplace, perhaps with sample products, and either interviews the potential customers directly or the wholesalers or retailers who have close contact with these customers.

There are many pitfalls in the judgment approach to forecasting. While many executives know the marketplace and have the ability to foresee future developments, it is wrong to assume that simply because a person holds an executive position, he or she is automatically a good sales forecaster. Salespeople, by their very natures, are not oriented toward analytical thinking and tend to be either optimistic or pessimistic, depending on recent trends. Salespeople might believe that survey results would be used to increase their quotas, so they would give pessimistic estimates. Getting an objective forecast from a salesperson is extremely difficult. Many companies have discarded this method.

Market surveys—whether by mail, telephone, or personal interview—are expensive means of gathering information and their reliability depends upon the accuracy with which a small sample represents the total market. In some cases surveys have proven unreliable because people did not really do what they told the interviewer they would. Companies selling consumer products frequently use a test-market approach, picking a small section of the country thought to be representative and selling their product only in that area in order to determine public reaction. This is a fairly expensive method which has proven highly successful in many instances. As a means of forecasting the whole market, its success depends upon the marketer's ability to pick a representative sample area.

Perhaps the greatest problem with judgment forecasts is the fact that human beings are most intensely affected by recent occurrences. Judgment forecasts normally tend to overreact to immediate circumstances. The human forecaster who uses nothing but judgment can make some very serious mistakes. Figure 4-9, shown later in this chapter, shows a trend line fitted to 12 years of actual sales. An individual making a judgment forecast at the end of year 5, following very little growth over 3 years, would be unlikely to recognize the long-range trend and would probably make a forecast that is much too low. A serious practical limitation of judgment forecasts is the relatively small number of forecasts an individual can make in comparison to the hundreds of items most companies must handle.

An extremely difficult task is forecasting the effects or results of entirely new technologies or products like personal computers, space exploration and fiber optics. Some success has been achieved in asking the right questions, if not in obtaining answers, through the Delphi technique. A panel of "experts," people familiar with the technology and the areas of application, are asked a series of questions, and each member gives his or her estimates. These are then reviewed by all members and a second round of forecasts is developed. The procedure continues until no panel member revises the figures. The user then applies the results as seems suitable.

Subjective forecasts are nevertheless invaluable. They are the only means by which human judgment can be brought to bear on the forecasting problem. Very few companies use judgment forecasts alone, however, since they are expensive, tend to overreact to recent events and are limited to a few items.

Statistical Forecasts

The other basic approach to forecasting—the use of statistical techniques—can involve the use of a product's own demand history to determine a forecast of future sales (using intrinsic factors such as averages or historical trends), or it can be based on multiple correlation analysis (using extrinsic factors such as carloadings, gross national product, housing starts, gasoline consumption and other related activities) to forecast sales of products not directly related to these activities.

Statistical forecasts treat the basic elements in a demand series separately. The 7-year record of motor fuel consumption in New Jersey (Figure 4-8) shows that sales are increasing yearly and that there is a definite seasonal pattern. This series can be separated into three major components—trend, seasonal, and randomness—and each component can be expressed mathematically.

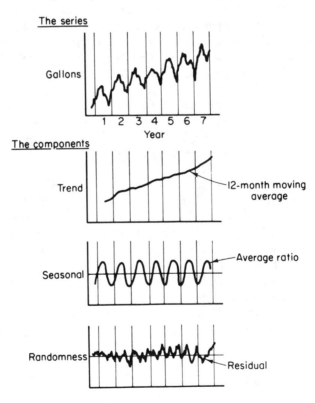

Figure 4-8 ANALYSIS OF DEMAND SERIES.

Trend extrapolation is one of the simplest and best-known techniques of forecasting. Figure 4-9 shows 12 years of actual sales with a long-range trend line visually fitted to these data. Having this long-range trend line helps the forecaster to stabilize his or her forecasts without overreacting to short-term occurrences. There are much more accurate methods than visually establishing trend lines; the mathematical tech-

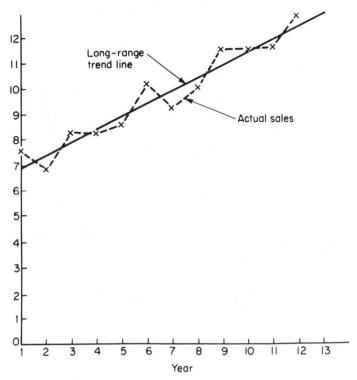

Figure 4-9 FITTING A TREND LINE.

nique of *least squares*, described in most standard texts on statistics (6), is an important tool of the forecaster's trade. Moving averages, covered in detail later in this chapter, can be used to develop the long-range trend of the series and to project this trend into the future. The **seasonal** pattern, when consistent year after year, can be represented by ratios of actual monthly sales to average monthly sales, as will be described later.

What remains after the trend and seasonal components have been removed is **randomness**. There is no way to forecast randomness, but the range of randomness can be expressed as an error percentage, so that maximum and minimum expected demand can be determined from forecast averages. If this random element is large, then production plans and individual product reorder points, for example, will have to include large safety stocks. If, on the other hand, the randomness experienced in the past tends to be small, the forecast can be expected to be more accurate, and smaller inventory reserves may be adequate.

Overall Business Forecasts

Before detailed product or group forecasts can be useful, an overall business forecast for the company is necessary. This type of forecast is also needed for developing the Production Plan (see Figure 1-1). There are many methods of making this

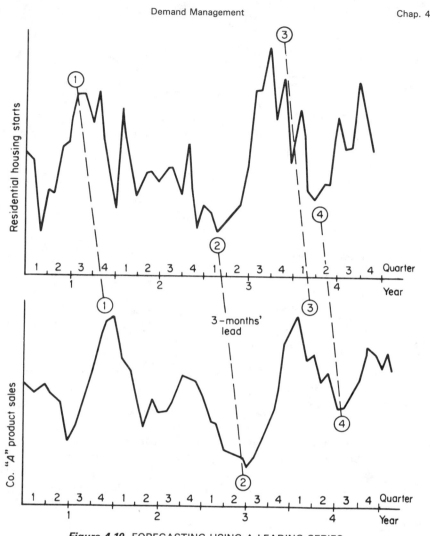

Figure 4-10 FORECASTING USING A LEADING SERIES.

type of forecast, including some very useful statistical techniques. Figure 4-10 shows one such technique based on using a leading series. In this case, analysis of past demand has shown that residential housing starts lead the sales of the products of Company A by approximately 3 months. There are some businesses where this fortunate type of relationship exists. It is important to determine that there is a consistent reliable relationship, not just a brief coincidence, and to track the relationship continuously in order to detect changes. When this type of relationship is available, however, a fairly accurate forecast can be made. Information on activities such as residential housing starts is published regularly in trade magazines. Government agencies (such as the Bureau of Labor Statistics) and private research groups (such as the National Bureau of Economic Research) regularly publish data on many economic series which can form the basis for forecasting various industrial products.

Even if a leading series cannot be found, a company's sales can frequently be forecast using a related series whose movement is found to coincide or even lag in time, since many other rather sophisticated forecasts of these series are made by government or private research agencies. A small company in the automotive replacement parts business might not be able to afford much effort in forecasting but could use forecasts or data on actual sales generated by larger companies. It does not necessarily follow that forecasts will be accurate just because they are made by large companies or prestigious government economists. The user of such forecasts should be prepared to detect significant errors and initiate action promptly to respond to changing demand.

One of the more complex mathematical techniques for forecasting consists of establishing the correlation between a number of extrinsic elements and a company's sales, called **multiple correlation**. The result of this type of analysis is a formula giving relative weights to the various factors included in the development of the forecast. Figure 4-11 shows a simplified example of an extrinsic forecast for packaging material based on retail sales, steel ingot production and carloadings. These figures, available weekly and monthly from many of the business publications, are used to develop weighting factors by means of multiple correlation. Multiplying the weighting factor by the current activity rate of each element establishes a new total index of 1.14, indicating that the forecast for this company's product will now be 14% higher than the base forecast period. Multiple correlation, while beyond the scope of this text, is described in advanced texts on statistical analysis. Computer programs are able to handle multiple correlation rapidly and accurately—this type of forecast will undoubtedly be applied more widely in the future for estimating *total market* demand. Companies will still have to estimate *their shares* of such markets as well as the breakdown into product families.

The salesperson's estimate definitely has a place in making the overall business forecast. It can be extremely valuable if reconciled with a statistical forecast base. For example, statistical techniques could be used to establish a forecast indicating that the total market potential for a company's product should be 10% higher next year. The salespeople could then be polled to determine whether or not the

Element	Current activity rate	Weight*	Index
Retail sales	$24.3 (billions/mo.)	0.023	0.56
Steel ingot prod.	2700 (tons/week)	0.0001	0.27
Carloadings	62 (thousand cars/day)	0.005	0.31

New index = 1.14

*Developed by multiple correlation

Figure 4-11 EXTRINSIC FORECAST FOR PACKAGING MATERIAL

company's market share would remain constant. The salespeople, knowing the competitive climate, would be in a position to say better than others in the company whether or not market penetration would be likely to go up or down from the overall trend indicated by the statistical forecast.

Product-Group Forecasts

Once the overall business forecast is made, it must be broken down into more detailed product group forecasts. These product groups, as previously mentioned, must be meaningful to both marketing and manufacturing. A farm-implement manufacturer, for example, might make an overall business forecast in dollars, relating it to the government estimate of disposable farm income. The overall dollar total would then be broken down into dollars for each major product line (such as tractors, combines, or balers) by farm groups (i.e., wheat, corn, soybean, etc.). This could be done using a percentage based on past experience, modified by any sales department or marketing department knowledge of trends in demand for a particular product line in a particular market. There would be indicators that relate directly to a particular product, such as the number of acres of wheat under cultivation or a change in the subsidy being awarded for soybeans.

The next step would be to apply known seasonal indices peculiar to the product lines, particularly in a business such as the manufacture of farm implements. Figure 4-12 shows the development of such a seasonal index for each month, stating it as a percent of the year's sales of combines. In this hypothetical case, 5 years of history have been analyzed and the monthly sales are shown as a percentage of each annual total. An overall average for each month is calculated, using the

Month	Y-1	Y-2	Y-3	Y-4	Y-5	Average %
January	7.48%	5.46%	6.36%	6.56%	6.54%	6.50
February	8.24	4.70	6.68	7.35	5.78	6.55
March	8.27	7.30	8.84	7.90	8.03	8.05
April	7.95	9.34	9.40	8.79	9.29	8.95
May	9.66	9.65	10.50	11.11	10.44	10.30
June	10.00	11.30	10.60	8.79	9.71	10.10
July	9.06	8.70	7.66	9.01	9.96	8.90
August	9.85	11.10	10.80	10.12	11.00	10.60
September	9.71	9.50	8.15	9.70	7.90	9.00
October	6.65	8.72	8.09	8.78	8.95	8.25
November	7.80	8.08	7.64	7.34	7.72	7.70
December	5.12	6.15	5.13	4.54	4.64	5.10
Total	99.79	100.00	99.85	99.99	99.96	100.00

Figure 4-12 DEVELOPING A SEASONAL INDEX FOR COMBINES (Monthly sales as a percent of annual total).

data for the 5 years. A good forecaster would want to have 1 or 2 additional years of data, which could be used in a simulation to test the validity of the seasonal percentage. Using the annual forecast of sales for this product line, the average percentages in Figure 4-12 for each month could be used to come up with a monthly forecast. A major problem might arise in expressing this forecast in terms (such as worker-hours) meaningful to manufacturing, since it is possible that one specific type of farm implement is built in one manufacturing plant, while a second type is built in another. In addition, each plant would need to differentiate between small and large models of this implement if the production-hour requirements varied greatly. The forecaster should know such details so that data useful to manufacturing users can be produced.

Product-group forecasts are used to make capacity plans; they should not be used to schedule model mix. They are used to determine the worker and machine capacity requirements for each major production facility. The important purpose of product group forecasts is to *establish production levels*. This application makes use of the principle that group forecasts are more accurate than item forecasts.

Chapter 9 discusses production level planning and control and the use of measures of forecast error to establish decision rules for determining when to change production levels. This is probably the most important use of a forecast and a primary function of manufacturing control. There is no chance of providing good service and keeping inventories in balance if the level of production is not planned and controlled effectively.

Item Forecasts

Item forecasts are needed for determining order points, order quantities and master scheduling. They are best made using simple intrinsic statistical techniques based on their own demand histories. The sum of individual item forecasts for each group should equal the group forecast prepared (as discussed earlier) for planning production levels. They usually do not and will have to be adjusted (as explained later in this chapter) to make these totals equal.

The key to successful use of statistical forecasts is selecting those techniques suitable for use with the demand patterns experienced by the items being forecast. These fall into four general categories, illustrated by the data in Figure 4-13. Hori-

	Jan.	Feb.	Mar.	Apr.	May	June	July	Aug.	Sept.	Oct.	Nov.	Dec.
Horizontal	45	55	35	55	60	40	65	50	45	60	40	50
Intermittent	6	0	5	0	0	7	3	0	1	4	0	2
Trending	10	15	20	15	20	30	25	25	30	35	30	40
Seasonal	65	60	50	40	25	30	35	50	60	70	75	70

Figure 4-13 DEMAND PATTERNS.

zontal demand typifies mature products with stable demand. Intermittent demand is experienced by low volume products in the very early or very late stages of their life cycles and by most repair parts. Trending demand shows rather steady growth or decline and seasonal items experience peaks and valleys each calendar year. In addition to these, there are some special cases of demand, which will not be covered in this book, such as regular periodic demand and cyclical demands longer than a year.

Forecasting Techniques

Averages: **Averages** provide a very useful technique. Two types are common in forecasting: running and weighted. **Running averages** can be calculated over any number of periods of data—the larger the number, the more stable but less sensitive the forecast developed. The rule for updating the average is

$$F = \frac{D_1 + D_2 + D_3 + \cdots + D_n + D_{n+1} - D_1}{n}$$

where:

$$D = \text{actual demand in each period} \qquad (4\text{-}1)$$
$$n = \text{number of periods in the average}$$
$$F = \text{forecast}$$

This simply develops a new average each period by adding the latest actual demand and subtracting the oldest. The new average is projected as the forecast as far into the future as the forecaster believes is reasonable or necessary.

Figure 4-14 shows forecasts calculated using this technique for the horizontal and intermittent demand patterns of Figure 4-13. Note that the forecasts change as they are affected by differences between demands added and subtracted. The running average is a simple calculation but it requires storing large amounts of data (demand in each period). It is easy to change to a smaller number of periods but much more difficult to increase to a larger number, since historical figures must be found and loaded. Obviously this technique would have no use with trending or seasonal patterns since it projects the same number in all future periods.

Figure 4-15 shows how weighted averages are used in forecasting item demand. In this particular example, a weekly forecast made previously (called the *old forecast*) indicated that sales would run at 100 units per week; actual sales the

	Jan.		Feb.		Mar.		Apr.
	Forecast	Actual	Forecast	Actual	Forecast	Actual	Forecast
Horizontal	50	60	51	35	50	55	51
Intermittent	2.3	0	1.8	0	1.8	6	1.9

Figure 4-14 12-MONTH RUNNING AVERAGE FORECAST.

First week		
	Weight	Weight
Old forecast = 100 (per wk. avg.)	x 0.5 = 50	x 0.9 = 90
Sales = 70 (latest week)	x 0.5 = 35	x 0.1 = 7
New forecast =	85	97
Second week		
Old forecast = 97*		x 0.9 = 87
Sales = 105		x 0.1 = 11
New forecast =		98

General formula:

$$\text{New forecast} = \alpha \times \text{sales} + (1 - \alpha) \times \text{old forecast} \qquad (4-2)$$
$$\alpha \text{ (alpha) is the term for the weighting factor}$$

*This was the "new forecast" last week

Figure 4-15 WEIGHTED AVERAGE FORECAST.

first week afterward amounted to 70 units. Using a straight arithmetical average, a new weekly forecast of 85 units would then be made. This, in effect, gives equal weight (50% = 0.5) to the old forecast and the latest week's sales and most people would agree that this is improper.

Using a weighted average, it would be possible (as shown in the example) to give 90% of the weight to the old forecast and 10% to the actual sales and thus to calculate a new forecast of 97. In this case, the forecast would decline only slightly because of the drop in sales. Most people would agree that something like this is more reasonable. Note that the sum of the weighting factors must always equal 1.0 (or 100%).

Figure 4-14 also shows how the forecast for the second week is calculated using the same weighted-average approach. The old forecast is now the 97 pieces forecast the first week and actual sales the second week amounted to 105; the new forecast is therefore 98. It has gone up slightly since sales increased. This technique is called *exponential smoothing* and is based upon the work done by R. G. Brown (1). It provides a routine method for updating forecasts regularly. With computers, a simple program can do this for several thousand items on a regular basis in a very short time.

The exponential-smoothing equation in Figure 4-14 is called **first-order smoothing;** there are more-advanced exponential smoothing formulas, which include adjustments for trends and seasonal changes. The first-order smoothing equation can be rearranged to simplify the calculations as follows:

$$\text{New forecast} = \text{old forecast plus } \alpha \text{ (sales} - \text{old forecast)} \qquad (4-3)$$

This form requires only one multiplication. Using the data for the second week from Figure 4-14 (how to determine α will be discussed later).

$$\text{New forecast} = 97 + 0.1(105 - 97) = 98$$

The forecasts for the two items in Figure 4-13 are essentially the same using this technique as they are using running averages.

Both formulas (4-2) and (4-3) are classified as first-order exponential-smoothing formulas. They work very well when dealing with fairly stable items and they will detect trends quite readily, although the *forecast will lag behind actual demand if a significant trend exists*. However, where such a trend is believed to exist (when a new product has been introduced, for example), **second-order smoothing** can be used. With second-order smoothing, the forecast is made up of two parts, A and B:

$$A_{new} = \text{old forecast} + \alpha(\text{sales} - \text{old forecast}) \tag{4-4}$$

$$B_{new} = B_{old} + \alpha(A_{new} - B_{old}) \tag{4-5}$$

The first part, A_{new}, is simple first-order smoothing. The second part, B_{new}, provides a factor to adjust the forecast for a trend in order to eliminate the lagging effect of first-order smoothing. In other words, A_{new} lags the actual demand pattern based on sales orders. The B forecast, using A *as if it were the actual demand*, will lag behind the A forecast by a like amount. The correction is made by adjusting the first-order forecast (A_{new}) by the difference between the two ($A_{new} - B_{new}$):

$$\begin{aligned} \text{New forecast} &= A_{new} + (A_{new} - B_{new}) \\ &= 2A_{new} - B_{new} \end{aligned} \tag{4-6}$$

To apply this technique to the trending demand pattern in Figure 4-13 requires figures for A_{old} and B_{old}. Any reasonable data could be used; the effects of bad guesses would become insignificant in the calculations after a number of periods, depending on the α-factor used. Inspection of the data indicates that $A_{old} = 35$ and $B_{old} = 32$ seem reasonable and $\alpha = 0.2$ is quite common. With actual sales in January equal to 45, the forecast for February is:

$$A = 35 + 0.2(45 - 35) = 37$$

$$B = 32 + 0.2(37 - 32) = 33$$

$$\text{New forecast} = (2 \times 37) - 33 = 41$$

A decision on whether or not second-order smoothing is required can be confirmed by taking real data on a few items and simulating results. In general, it has been found by practitioners that first-order smoothing gives quite satisfactory results for most items—particularly for short-range forecasts. The exponential-smoothing techniques are not satisfactory where demand is very low or with no demand at all in some forecast periods. A quick test of first- or second-order smoothing on the intermittant-pattern data on Figure 4-13 shows how poorly these techniques perform on the wrong types of data.

Assuming simulation demonstrates that exponential smoothing will give satis-factory results, the problem is to determine the proper weighting factor (α). In Figure 4-15, a low α-factor of 0.1 results in the old forecast being the controlling factor in the new forecast with sales exerting little influence. Changing trends will not be picked up as quickly as might be desirable. If a high α-factor, such as 0.3, is used, the forecast will react sharply to changes in sales and will, in fact, be high-ly erratic if there are sizeable random fluctuations in demand. Any α-factor is a compromise between being too sluggish and too erratic. The proper α-factor for a given set of data can be determined by simulation, which will show how a particu-lar α-factor will work as long as demand patterns are the same in the future. It is usually quite satisfactory to use a factor in the range of 0.1 to 0.2 in order to get moving quickly and to let actual experience show those exceptions where a dif-ferent α-factor is necessary.

Where a company has been using a moving average of several weeks and wishes to substitute exponential smoothing in order to gain the advantages of storing less data and being more flexible for change, the formula (4-7) can be used to deter-mine the α-factor that will give results approximately equivalent to the number of periods in the previously used average:

$$\alpha = \frac{2}{(n + 1)} \qquad (4\text{-}7)$$

For example, if the previously used forecast were a 12-period moving average, the α-factor would be

$$\alpha = \frac{2}{(12 + 1)} = 0.15$$

Using this formula, it can be seen that an α-factor of 0.2 is approximately equivalent to a 9-period moving average and a 0.1 α-factor is approximately equiva-lent to a 19-period moving average. After these periods of time, any effects of poor starting values will disappear using exponential smoothing.

Seasonal forecasts: Sophisticated mathematicians seem to be unable to resist the temptation of trying to fit elaborate curves to seasonal data. The effort is not only largely unnecessary, it won't produce results as good as those using the period base indices illustrated in Figure 4-12. This will do as good a job if the seasonal pattern is repetitive and will do much better if the pattern is skewed and jagged.

Using the data from Figure 4-13 for the seasonal pattern, the indices for each month are as shown in Figure 4-16. Each index is simply the ratio of that month's actual demand to the average month for that year. Good practice in developing the indices would require using several years' data, as was done in Figure 4-12. The indices are used to deseasonalize and seasonalize data when updating forecasts.

Seasonal forecasting requires some method of projecting a new average-month figure. This could be done by any of the methods already discussed in this chapter. Before using the actual demand, regardless of the techniques used, it should be

Month	Demand	Base index
Jan.	65	1.2
Feb.	60	1.1
Mar.	50	1.0
Apr.	40	0.8
May	25	0.5
June	30	0.6
July	35	0.7
Aug.	50	1.0
Sept.	60	1.1
Oct.	70	1.3
Nov.	75	1.4
Dec.	70	1.3
Total	630	
Avg.	52.5	

Figure 4-16 SEASONAL INDICES.

normalized to an average month by dividing actual data by the index. After the forecast for the average month is updated, the new forecast is then seasonalized by multiplying it by the index for all months for which forecasts are desired. Figure 4-17 shows how well this technique works on a very skewed pattern when the average is forecasted accurately and the indices are valid.

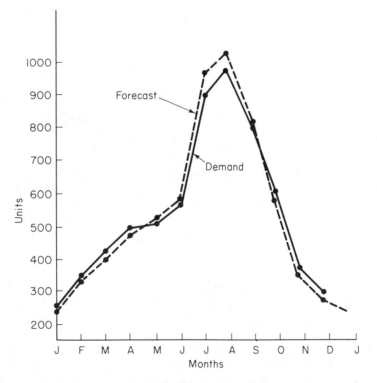

Figure 4-17 SEASONAL FORECAST.

Special Forecasts

Forecasts for promotions and new products are much more difficult to make than those for stable items. Since few new products are truly original, such forecasts can frequently be based upon past experience with a similar product. A television manufacturer, for example, can use experience with 24-inch black-and-white and 21-inch color television sets that have been marketed in the past to estimate sales for a new 24-inch color television set. A company manufacturing a new product unlike any thing now on the market would probably have to use some type of market survey. Many companies manufacturing toiletries or foods, where personal preference and consumer acceptance are extremely difficult to predict, generally use market surveys or test markets in order to determine product acceptance before manufacturing the items on a large scale.

Sales promotions conducted on a repetitive basis can develop data useful in forecasting the demand they generate. The *S*-curve shown in Figure 4-18 was drawn after analyzing the results of several such promotions. In the first quarter of the life of the program, only 15% of the total demand had been booked in customer orders. Halfway through, 70% had come in, and the last quarter generated only 10% more business. Use of the *S*-curve requires careful, timely tracking of sales as they materialize and fast response by the plant and its suppliers to react to the changes in projected total demand.

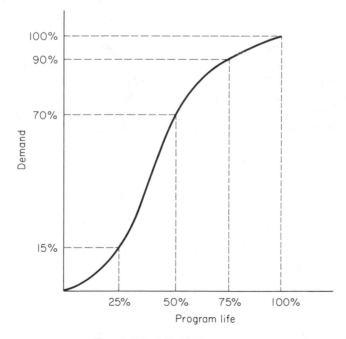

Figure 4-18 SALES PROMOTIONS.

Like seasonal base indices, the success of the technique of *S*-curves depends on successive promotions having closely similar characteristics. A tough management choice to make would be between a series of similar promotions with good *repeatability* of results (and hence better planning potential) and radical changes that might produce much higher sales but introduce significant production problems.

For new products and promotion items, the estimate of forecast error is essential. The management of the company should be shown the effects of planning to meet a forecast of 100,000 units when actual sales could be as low as 20,000 units or as high as 500,000 units. If such wide variations in sales are believed possible when the forecast is made, intelligent planning of high-value items will minimize the risk of excess inventory, while shrewd handling of tooling designs and components with long lead times will make it possible for production to respond quickly to increased demands. Such realistic planning will be possible only if an effort is made to estimate the forecast error.

Forecasting demand for promotion items and new products must also consider the **pipeline-filling** pattern. When a new program or product is announced to which salespeople react enthusiastically, most salespeople will be able to call their important customers and convince them over the telephone to buy at least a token supply. On their regular sales calls in the following days, their enthusiasm will sell more of this new product. Back at the factory, an initial surge of orders will be received, followed by a steady influx of orders—all of which merely reflects the demand of the distributor, wholesaler or other class of customer who is stocking up. Most products pass from manufacturer to distributor to ultimate consumer, so that very few initial orders represent actual consumer demand. Once the shelves have been stocked, there is a drop-off in demand until actual consumer sales are felt—and these determine what the real demand will be. A knowledge of this pipeline-filling pattern will prevent a forecaster from overreacting to the surge due to the salespeople's initial enthusiasm, to the sales drop-off when stocking orders are completed and, finally, to the initial consumer response. Steady nerves and this knowledge will help the forecaster to interpret new product sales properly.

Using the Forecast

All people have their own biases, prejudices, preconceptions, strengths and weaknesses; forecasters are no exception. Four steps essential in using forecasts well are to

1. Select the proper technique
2. Manage the updating carefully
3. Track actual versus forecast sales closely
4. React promptly to correct significant deviations

Prior discussion of individual techniques cited their strong points and limitations. The primary factor in selecting the right technique is the demand pattern. The following is a summary of the way popular techniques relate to these patterns.

1. **Horizontal demand** (some variation)
   a. *Running average:* Good; insensitive with too many periods, nervous with too few; large storage of data; inflexible.
   b. *Exponential Smoothing*
      First-order: Good; insensitive with low α; nervous with high; little storage; flexible.
      Second-order: poor; interprets variation as trend.
2. **Intermittent demand** (frequently none, wide variation)
   a. *Running average:* Good; better if periods of no demand are ignored.
   b. *Exponential smoothing*
      First-order: Poor unless zero demand ignored.
      Second-order: Never use here.
3. **Trending demand** (steadily up or down, some variation):
   a. *Running average*: Never use here.
   b. *Exponential smoothing*
      First-order: Poor unless slight trend, must use very high α then very nervous.
      Second-order: Good, designed for this.
4. **Seasonal demand** (annual cycle, some variation, some shift):
   a. *Base index:* Good, designed for this. Combine several periods if peak and valley shift with weather. Requires good history to develop useful indices.

During its life cycle, every product goes through several of these demand patterns. When first introduced, lack of history and the pipeline-filling phase dictates the use of judgment forecasts, which are subjective. Moderate or fast growth means shifting to techniques capable of handling trends. Mature products are easiest to predict with several usable techniques, but the forecaster must stay alert to the onset of decay, when demand trends downward. Old age brings intermittent demand, which is very difficult to handle and should initiate policy decisions to cease stocking and make only to order. This minimizes the need for forecasts.

These considerations require careful managemant of forecasting. Techniques must be changed when necessary. **Focus forecasting** (10) is designed to do this mechanically for many items. Unusual demands (selling in new areas, adding a new, big customer) must not be allowed to distort the forecasts. Filters can alert forecasters to this type of demand by highlighting individual orders larger than a specified percentage of totals or from new sources. Frank MacCombie (5) stated the next principle:

Principle 11. Forecast only what you must; calculate whatever you can.

He pointed out that bills of material (see Chapter 6) can be used to calculate requirements for components and bills of labor (see Chapter 9) to calculate direct labor and machine hour needs, making forecasting unnecessary for such "dependent" demands.

Forecasting must be a continuous process, not an annual rite. The performance of the forecasting techniques must be monitored frequently by comparing actual demand to forecast. To manage by exception, a tolerance range must be established; the primary factor in setting such limits is the range of past errors. It is unrealistic to expect forecasts to improve dramatically and setting tight tolerances simply overloads the reviewers. Don't be too quick to alter forecasts or switch techniques; expect them to be wrong and don't become a victim of nervous prostration.

Principle 12. Track forecasts regularly and do it often; find and fix the bad ones.

When there are many items to handle, tracking signals can be helpful in identifying those to be reviewed manually for change. A simple one is: actual sales this period − average forecast over last three periods. Any item outside a specified range (for instance, 0.8 to 1.2) would be marked for review. The range would be adjusted to yield a *manageable* number of items to be checked; there is no point in picking out more items than can be reviewed intelligently. A more complex tracking signal (available in most computer programs in some similar form) is: *running sum of forecast errors — average error.* This signal highlights an item when its cumulative errors exceed a specified limit. Again, the ratio selected to be the trigger should not overload the reviewers. More sensitive signals and tighter tolerances should be used on group totals and family forecasts because of their high impacts on capacity, common materials and aggregate inventories. Calculations of tracking signals are also included in Chapter 5.

If the market penetration for a product group were expected to increase substantially because of a new pricing policy, this would not show up in the forecasts for individual items, since these are based upon past history. Figure 4-19 shows how the forecasts for each of 10 items in a product group would be revised due to an increase in the product group forecast. In this particular case, a new total product-group forecast has been received from the marketing department, equaling 52,000 units. The individual forecasts total only 48,874 units, and the difference is then prorated across the 10 products, each of them being adjusted upward in proportion to its share of the total, so that the sum of forecasts for the individual products equals 52,000.

Using a computer, this type of forecast adjustment is very readily made, even for hundreds of items. This assumes, of course, that all items will be affected equally by the pricing change. If some items are not involved, these are omitted from the correction. If exponential smoothing is used for the item forecasts, the forecast for item 1 to be used in calculating the next week's forecast is 10,450 before the adjustment; this is discarded and an old forecast of 11,130 is used in its place.

Forecast reviewers walk a fine line between reacting too quickly to errors and failing to act soon enough. Figure 4-20 illustrates the problem. The forecast has been performing reasonably well in the first few periods shown but actual sales at point *A* show a slight "blip." Most reviewers would agree this is too soon to

Item	Exponential smoothing forecast		New pro—rated item forecast *
#1	10,450		11,130
#2	4117		4360
#3	6720		7150
#4	1050	New total product	1120
#5	774	group forecast	825
#6	896	from marketing	955
#7	14,140	department:	15,050
#8	2325	52,000	2480
#9	3734		3960
#10	4668		4970
Total	48,874		52,000

* This will be the "Old forecast" in the exponential–smoothing calculation for the first week of the new quarter

Figure 4-19 RECONCILING INDIVIDUAL-PRODUCT FORECASTS WITH A PRODUCT-GROUP FORECAST.

take any action. Note, however, that the error increased measurably in both of the preceding periods. A sharp reviewer would begin asking questions; a tracking signal might trip on this item because of the increasing cumulative effect of the errors. At point B, a few die-hards might still argue against changes, but everyone would be in agreement at point C that the forecast needs revision. A well-managed fore-

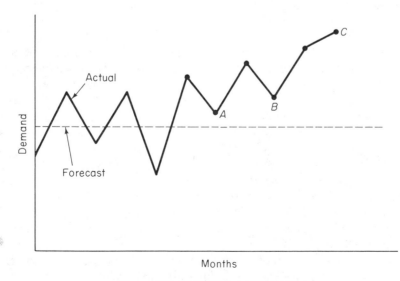

Months

Figure 4-20 TRACKING A FORECAST.

cast effort would set some predetermined, agreed point at which action would be taken to revise the forecast without further debate. Setting such rules is a necessary part of master scheduling.

Principle 13. Agree in advance when forecasts will be revised; don't play games with moving goal lines.

The actions taken are two-fold: Revise the forecast and alter the manufacturing plan. The value of short manufacturing cycles is immediately evident—these changes may be foreseen early enough that real manufacturing or purchased orders are not affected and only planned data are being changed. In most companies, however, some plant activities will probably need changing. The sooner the need to change is detected, the less the corrective action that is needed.

How the forecast will be revised is dependent on the *reasons for the errors.* In Figure 4-20, for example, the *causes* of the increased demand would determine whether simply raising the horizontal forecast is proper or if a significant growth trend were now present, possibly requiring a different technique. Information from order entry, sales and marketing people might be needed to answer this question. Continuous communication should be maintained between the makers and users of forecasts to promote better understanding and insure quick response to changing conditions. This is probably best illustrated in facilities planning, where an engineering group may be given a forecast 5 years in advance on which to plan designs for a new manufacturing plant. The property and building sizes are determined by the overall forecast. This information is needed early in the program in order to establish capital requirements, get approval for the project and begin construction. Specific department areas are determined by subgroups of products, as are major pieces of manufacturing equipment and these breakdowns of the total forecast are needed long after the start of the project, leaving sufficient lead time to have the space and equipment available at start-up time. The original forecast upon which the plant was designed will not be accurate in terms of product mix since it was made so far in advance. As the time for opening up the new plant draws near, constant communication between the forecasters and the engineers will help to avoid starting up a plant with excess capacity in some areas and inadequate capacity in others. Perhaps more important, manufacturing processing equipment is far more likely to be suitable for the volumes of different items to be turned out—and hence more efficient.

Intelligent use of data involving forecast errors can contribute almost as much to profitable operation as an accurate forecast. Raw material, tooling and long lead time components can be procured to meet high estimates, so that successful programs are not hamstrung by a lack of product. Short lead time parts, or those likely to be redesigned as service experience is obtained, can be held to low estimates to minimize the risk of excess and obsolete inventories. Note how all functions in a manufacturing company must become involved as a team in forecasting and planning operations.

In using the forecast, take advantage of forecast characteristics; separate the planning of capacity from actual scheduling within the manufacturing cycle, making a long-term commitment only to capacity and making the shortest possible commitment to the actual production schedule. This permits taking advantage of the greater accuracy with which large product groups can be forecast, as compared to the individual items that make up the production schedule. The shorter the scheduling cycle, the better the reaction to actual changes in sales. For example, a company using a weekly schedule of finished-goods production cannot react to any abrupt changes in demand between schedules except by expediting. Daily schedules can reflect the latest information on actual demand, while firm schedules far into the future are usually highly inaccurate because forecasts become less accurate when they are extended.

Why Forecasts Fail

There is little mystery about the reasons forecasting produces unsatisfactory results. There are six:

1. Forecasting is not a team effort; evaluating the internal and external factors making the future different from the past requires participation of people from all functions. No "expert" can do the job adequately.

2. Disillusionment occurs; unrealized hopes for accuracy cause rejection and failure to use forecasts; strangely, the hope persists and the cycle repeats.

3. The "do-it-ourselves" complex occurs; obviously "their forecast" is wrong so we have to make our own. We didn't do too well yesterday but today's forecast is better.

4. People have different needs; salespeople need to be stretched to meet challenging forecasts, management's financial plans must be conservative and manufacturing must have realism.

5. No one watches; everyone hopes the forecast will be right, knows it will be wrong, and forgets it, thus missing the chance to find out *how wrong* it could be and *when* it obviously needs revision.

6. Unnecessary items are involved; attempting to forecast demand for components in bills of materials describing products or for products that are combinations of options is a waste of time.

Many products offer their users a choice of several options—automobiles, machine tools, computers, radios, bicycles, and home appliances are but a few. Figure 4-21 shows some of the options available in a line of radios. No one could misunderstand the futility of attempting to predict how many of which *specific combination* of choices customers would order in any period, but many people see no alternative. However, it is entirely adequate—in fact, far better—to forecast the *total number* of radios per period and the *percentage* of this total that will have each option. From these data, valid master schedules can be prepared for manufacturing planning. It is not necessary to know which options must be combined into any one radio until final assembly begins; in many cases, this need not occur until the customer order is received. Designing products with this in mind eases

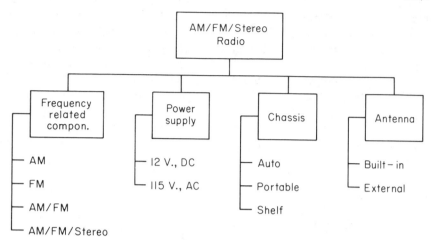

Figure 4-21 FORECASTING OPTIONS.

the forecasting problem, facilitates planning and control and simplifies manufacture. This subject is covered more fully in the second volume with master scheduling and structuring bills of material.

Sources of Demand

A brief reference was made to streams, or sources, of demand earlier in this chapter. All the techniques covered so far have been those used to forecast customer demand. This demand can be divided into three groups: that occurring directly on the factory or main warehouse nearby, that occurring on branch warehouses in other locations in the same country, and that occurring on any of these from other countries. Handling **export**, as it is called, is beyond the scope of this book. There are usually enough differences in market requirements, timing, and product varieties that forecasting export demand must be treated differently from domestic demand.

Customer demand on branch warehouses is essentially the same as that on the main facility except, of course, it is usually lower in volume. Items with very low, intermittent demand are extremely difficult to forecast as has been mentioned. Whether or not such items should even be carried in stock in the branch warehouse is a good question. If they must, it would be better to forecast total demand on the system, schedule replenishment orders to handle it and then distribute to each branch warehouse a portion of each batch produced to provide balanced inventories in all warehouses. The technique for allocating items like this is shown in Appendix VII.

Interplant demand should not be forecast; it should be calculated from the manufacturing plan for the user plant. Master scheduling, discussed thoroughly in Chapter 7 of this book and Chapter 2 of the applications volume, must include consideration of the needs of both the feeder and the user plants for adequate supplies of material and uniform loads. Techniques for doing this are presented in Chapters 5 and 7.

Interwarehouse transfers between branch warehouses should be viewed as problems to be eliminated, not planned. While they are an effective way to handle unexpected or unusually large demands or interruptions in supply, the high costs of handling and shipping such orders make them a last resort, not part of normal operations.

The governing strategy in forecasting, stocking and meeting demands for all classes of materials for all types of customers should be as outlined in Principle 14.

Principle 14. Don't commit stocked items to any specific location until the last possible moment.

## CHAPTER FIVE

MATERIALS CONTROL: INDEPENDENT DEMAND

Replenishing Inventory

The first-time ordering of a new item is a special case of inventory management. The principles and techniques of this type of materials control are covered in Chapter 6. This chapter deals with materials in regular use replenished continuously or periodically in batches.

The EOQ concept of Chapter 3 provides answers to the question of how much should be ordered each time a replenishment order is placed. In answering this question, the costs associated with ordering are balanced against the costs of carrying inventory to give a minimum total cost. In controlling inventories, the other basic question that must be answered is when the replenishment order must be placed. In answering this question, inventory-investment costs must be balanced against a desired customer service level or the costs resulting from shortages. Obviously, if such orders are not placed soon enough, material will not arrive in time and remaining material will be used up before the new lot is received. Conversely, if orders are placed too soon, inventories will be excessively high.

Because the selection of the reorder technique ultimately determines the level of customer service provided, this decision is usually of far more importance to managers than the lot-size decision. Poor customer service usually comes more quickly and forcefully to management's attention than ordering or inventory costs. In practice, this fact results in decisions that are often heavily biased toward customer service at the cost of high inventory investment.

Principle 15. Correctly answering the question about when an item is needed is far more important than determining how much to order.

Any inventory control system, no matter how humble, has some decision rules built into it. The homemaker who shops for groceries once a week makes up a buying list according to intuitive rules that tell him or her when to reorder. Upon examination, some of these rules are quite sensible. The homemaker can probably predict fairly accurately the amount of meat to be used at every meal and will probably be using up the last of last week's meat at the time it is necessary to shop again. Facial tissues, on the other hand, may be subject to a highly erratic demand—depending, perhaps, on whether or not some member of the family contracts a cold. The homemaker may rule that there should always be an extra box of facial tissues in the linen closet and that, whenever this box is opened, he or she will buy another on the weekly shopping trip. Vanilla extract is probably only used occasionally and, when the supply of vanilla runs out, the homemaker may decide not to purchase any more until the next time some baking will be planned. Purchases of sale-priced bargains are limited by available funds and also by the storage space of refrigerator, freezer or pantry shelves.

These are simple rules that can be highly effective in practice even though they may not even be applied consistently. In purchasing groceries the homemaker is usually not aware of balancing the investment in inventory (groceries) against the chance of running out of stock. If he or she should happen to run out of a staple item, the inconvenience is usually minor, since stores are nearby or a neighbor can lend the item.

This is true of most of the inventory decisions that are made in day-to-day living. Such common reorder systems can be very loose simply because of the short lead time, the small amount of inventory investment and the relatively slight inconvenience of being out of stock. There are many inventories in business—such as office supplies—which can be controlled quite satisfactorily using similar simple decision rules.

There are many others, however, that involve very large inventory investment, an extremely high penalty for being out of stock or very long replenishment lead times. In order to control these inventories properly, efficient reorder methods are available. These can take many forms, but are usually related to one of the following:

1. **Two-bin:**
   In this system, a predetermined amount of the stock for a particular item is set aside (frequently in a separate second bin) and not touched until all the main stock of this item has been used. When the reserve supply is opened, notification is then sent to the inventory control office and a replenishment order is placed. (For more, see page 128.)

2. **Visual review:**
   The stock level periodically is checked visually and replenishment orders are placed after each review where needed to restore the stock level to some predetermined maximum of the sum of on hand and on order quantities. (For more, see page 128.)

3. **Order point (Fixed-order quantity—variable-cycle system):**
When withdrawals bring the inventory of an item as shown on perpetual inventory records down to a predetermined level, called the **order point,** a replenishment order (usually in the amount of the precalculated EOQ) is placed. (For more, see page 108.)

4. **Periodic review (Fixed-cycle—variable-order quantity system):**
In **periodic review,** the inventory records are reviewed periodically, perhaps once a week or once a month, and sufficient material is ordered to restore the total on hand plus on order to a predetermined maximum level. (For more, see page 126.)

5. **Material-requirements planning (MRP):**
In **MRP,** material is ordered in amounts and on time schedules to meet a preplanned program of production of the item in which the material is used. (For detailed coverage, see Chapter 6.)

All these are closely related in concept. It is apparent, for example, that the **two-bin method,** although it has no inventory records, is very similar to **order point,** in that the second bin contains the order-point quantity. Likewise, the well-known *minimum and maximum* is merely a variation of order point. The minimum is, in fact, an order point and the maximum is the order point plus the ordering quantity. **Order point,** however, does not have universal application in industrial inventory control. In fact, this technique—and the related techniques just listed through item 4—have excellent application for finished goods inventory and repair parts carried in inventory, for example, where demand for the item tends to be fairly continuous and independent of demand for any other inventory item. Replenishing an inventory of components and subassemblies, however, where demands tend to be intermittent and in variable quantities dependent on a requirement at a higher level of assembly, can usually be handled more effectively with MRP. Each of these reorder techniques will be discussed in more detail, the first four in this chapter.

Order point is discussed in depth because it provides the best example of the methods used to cope with uncertainty in reordering systems. Material-requirements planning will be covered in Chapter 6.

In all these discussions, **demand** is the name given to the total requirement for an item in a given period of time. **Lead time** is the time that elapses from the moment it is determined that a replenishment order must be placed until the material covered by this order has been received into stock and is ready for use. This is the period when an item is most vulnerable to being out of stock, as its inventory is at the lowest point.

Order-Point Basics

Order point, illustrated in Figure 5-1, consists of an estimate of demand during lead time, plus some reserve stock to protect against the fact that neither demand nor lead time can be predicted with certainty. At some point in time, the quantity

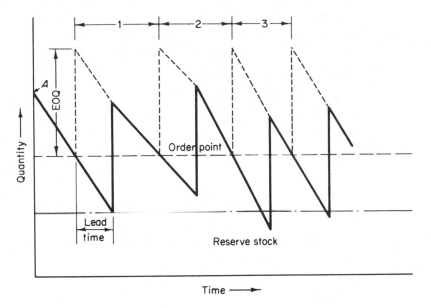

Figure 5-1 ORDER POINT–FIXED ORDER QUANTITY/VARIABLE CYCLE.

of the item in inventory is as shown by A in Figure 5-1. As time passes, the inventory is used up. This is *assumed* to occur at a steady, uniform rate, as shown by the heavy downward-sloping line, until it reaches the predetermined level of the order point. A replenishment order for an EOQ is then placed, as shown by the dashed vertical line. The inventory continues to drop during the lead time, at the end of which the new supply is received; the inventory is then increased by the EOQ, starting the cycle once again. Another assumption is that immediate replenishment is necessary.

Unfortunately, in most real inventory situations, neither the lead time nor the demand can be predicted exactly. Consequently, an order point based simply upon average demand during lead time will not provide enough stock to give even reasonably good protection against running out, since the fluctuating demand will probably *exceed the average half the time.* A major problem, then, is to estimate how much reserve stock will be required in the order point.

This reserve stock is not touched in the first two replenishment cycles shown in Figure 5-1. In the third cycle, however, the rate of usage increases, as indicated by the steeper line. With this higher demand, the inventory drops into the reserve stock before the new supply is received. Should the demand increase even more or the lead time become longer, the inventory might drop to zero—resulting in a stockout.

The following should be noted with this technique:

1. Order quantities (EOQ's) are usually fixed and recalculated only when significant demand changes are expected.

2. In practice, order points are too often fixed and checked only infrequently.

Later in this chapter, techniques will be presented that can be used to update order points at weekly or longer intervals to keep them in tune with expected changes in demand or lead time.

3. Intervals between successive replenishment orders (1-2-3 in Figure 5–1) are *not* constant but vary inversely as the usage rate: the higher the demand, the shorter the interval between orders. (Hence the name *fixed-order quantity—variable cycle.)*

4. The reserve stock portion of the inventory is usually considered to be on hand *on the average* throughout the year.

5. The portion of the inventory or cycle stock corresponding to the full-order quantity will be on hand only immediately after it is received. On the average, only one-half the order quantity will be in inventory throughout the year because of the uniform usage assumption.

6. The planned average total inventory will be equal to one-half the order quantity plus the reserve stock.

Finding Order Points by Inspection

In the case of an item with an average demand of 100 units per week and an anticipated lead time of 6 weeks, it might be found from inspection of past activity—as shown on the inventory records—that demand during the replenishment period was occasionally as high as 800 units because lead times were longer than anticipated or demand was higher than expected. If such inspection indicated that demand during the replenishment lead time seldom exceeded 800 units, satisfactory service might be obtained by setting an order point equal to 800 units. In effect, a reserve stock of 200 units has been established to take care of *both* demand and lead time variations.

The order point is the sum of two elements: anticipated demand during lead time and reserve stock. For the example discussed in the preceeding paragraph;

Order point = 600 units + 200 units = 800 units

While the idea of determining order points by inspection is simple and appealing, there is a major practical problem. In order to determine order points by observation, a large amount of data must be available; yet in the typical business situation, the older data are, the less representative they are of what is going on at the present time and even less so of what might be expected to occur in the future.

Determining an order point requires evaluation of both factors comprising it: demand during lead time and reserve stock. Expected demand in a period of time must be determined by some kind of forecast. Techniques for handling this were discussed in Chapter 4. This demand must then be extended over the lead time period, which usually differs from the forecast period. A technique for doing this is discussed later in this chapter.

The problem of determining the proper reserve stock is a difficult one for which there is no easy solution. Applying rules of thumb will result in excess inventory on many items and insufficient inventory on others. More rigorous approaches can at best reduce only somewhat these excesses and shortages. The amount of reserve stock required is a function consisting principally of the following elements:

1. Ability to forecast *demand* accurately
2. Length of the lead time
3. Ability to forecast or control *lead time* accurately
4. Size of the order quantity
5. Service level desired

Some statistical techniques—applied with a liberal dose of pragmatism—can be used quite effectively in practice to determine useful reserve stocks. The approaches discussed in the following sections of this chapter have had wide application in industry and have been helpful to professional managers.

Principle 16. Order points require reserve stocks because of uncertainties that cannot be eliminated.

Estimating Forecast Error

Figure 5-2 shows the 10-week sales history for 2 items, item T and item V. The data for item T show that, while the forecast is 1000 units per week and an average sales of 1020 is very close to forecast sales, actual sales have been as high as 1400 a week and, on two other occasions, were 1200 units per week. A reasonable order point for item T might be 1200 units, anticipating that it would occasionally go out of stock when the demand during the 1-week replenishment period exceeded 1200 units. The order point would be composed as follows:

$$\text{O.P.} = \text{anticipated demand during lead time} + \text{reserve stock}$$
$$= 1000 + 200 \qquad\qquad (5\text{-}1)$$
$$= 1200$$

If item T should be kept in stock all the time, the order point would have to be set above 1400. Of course, there is no guarantee that sales would not occasionally greatly exceed 1400 in the future—a 10-week sales history is a fairly small sample.

Item V appears to have more erratic demand; in fact, if the order point were set at 1200 for item V, three stockouts would occur, since there are 3 weeks when demand during lead time exceeded the order point. This type of situation occurs frequently in industry; the demand variability is generally higher for low volume items or when fewer customers order the item. Many companies, in addition to selling their products directly to consumers, supply their products with a slightly different configuration to mail-order houses or other large distributors. They usually find that the demand for an item being sold directly to many customers has a more predictable pattern, while the smaller number of large demands tends to be far

Week	Item *T*	Item *V*
1	1200	400
2	1000	600
3	800	1600
4	900	1200
5	1400	200
6	1200	1000
7	1100	1500
8	700	800
9	1000	1400
10	900	1100
Total	10,200	9800

1. Weekly forecast (both items) equals 1000 units
2. Order quantity equals 1000 units
3. Lead time equals one week

Figure 5-2 10-WEEK SALES HISTORY.

less predictable. The order point for item V would obviously have to be higher than that for item T to maintain the same level of service. Equal reserve stocks for these two items would result in carrying excess inventory of item T or in giving poorer service on item V.

The small sample of information available also poses serious problems since there is no assurance that the sales of item V might not occasionally be as high as 2200 units or that item T might not have sales as high as 1900 units. Some reasonably reliable consistent method of determining reserve stocks based on small samples of data is therefore needed in practical applications of the order point concept. A concept that can be very useful in handling this calculation for many items is the *normal distribution*.

The normal distribution is one of the best known statistical relationships—most people are familiar with the bell-shaped curve. Figure 5-3 shows a distribution of the heights of male members of the U. S. population (it is presented for illustration only and is not intended to be statistically correct). If the average male height were 5 feet 9 inches, it would be reasonable to expect that a large number of men would be between 5 feet 4 inches and 6 feet 2 inches, with very few people under 4 feet 6 inches or over 7 feet 0 inches. As illustrated in Figure 5-3, plotting the percentage of the total population against the individual heights would form a bell-shaped curve known to statisticians as the **normal distribution**. This distribution has some general properties that are of great value in drawing conclusions about the population.

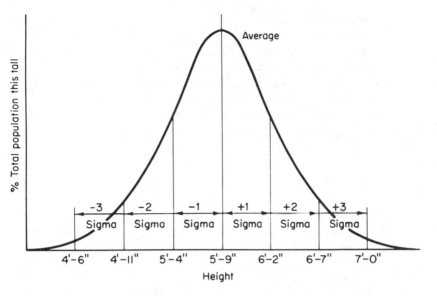

Figure 5-3 THE NORMAL DISTRIBUTION.

The *standard deviation* (σ, or sigma) of the distribution, for example, measures the range of heights that contains a certain percentage of the total population, relative to the average. Referring to Figure 5-3, 1 standard deviation of male heights is 5 inches; approximately 34% of the males would be expected to be between 5 feet 4 inches and 5 feet 9 inches and another 34% would be expected to be between 5 feet 9 inches and 6 feet 2 inches tall. In other words, 68% of all males would be within the range of 5 feet 4 inches to 6 feet 2 inches.

A second standard deviation (2 δ) from the average would add approximately 14% more of the population to each side of the average. For example, it could be expected that somewhat less than 14% of males would be between 4 feet 11 inches and 5 feet 4 inches or, on the higher side of the average, between 6 feet 2 inches and 6 feet 7 inches. For a true normal distribution, only about 4% of the population will be outside the range of ±2 standard deviations from the average.

Two characteristics of normal distributions are of interest in calculating order points:

1. **The mean or average value.**
    This corresponds to the high point of the bell curve and is the value most likely to occur.

2. **The variation or dispersion of the values about the average, measured by the standard deviation.**
    This corresponds to the width of the bell curve and measures how closely the individual values cluster around the average.

The following conditions must be met if the normal distribution is to be applied:

1. **The demand data are unimodal.**

   This merely means that the demands tend to cluster about one average value. If, for example, demand were as likely to be about 500 units per week or approximately 1500 units per week but not very likely to be any value in between, the demand distribution would have two modes of most frequently experienced demands and the normal distribution would not describe the demand data properly.

2. **The demand distribution is assumed to be symmetrical.**

   In other words, the distribution is just as likely to have a demand that is 200 units less than the forecast as one 200 units more than the forecast. This assumption presents some real problems in calculating order points. If the forecast demand is 20 units per week, for example, it can never be less than zero units yet it could be as much as 100 or 150 units. In other words, there is a floor close to the average but the ceiling is far above it. There are two ways of handling this problem:

   a. When the forecast value is so low that the positive variations are likely to be considerably greater than the negative variations, all negative variations can be ignored and only positive variations included in the calculation of the standard or mean absolute deviation.

   b. For certain types of small demand, another special statistical distribution called the *Poisson distribution* frequently gives good results. This is discussed later in this chapter.

3. It is assumed, when using a normal distribution, that the actual average will be the same as the forecast average (that is, the forecast is assumed to be accurate). The best safeguard is to use a technique such as exponential smoothing to update the forecast regularly and to use a tracking signal, discussed later in this chapter, to indicate when this forecast is not performing satisfactorily.

Figure 5-4 shows the calculation of the standard deviation of forecast error for item T, with a weekly forecast of 1000 units and sales as shown in Figure 5-2. The following steps are used to calculate the **standard deviation** of forecast error:

1. Calculate the deviation by subtracting actual sales from the forecast amount for each week.

2. Square each deviation.

3. Add the squares of the deviations.

4. Determine the average of the squares of the deviation.

5. Take the square root of the average of the squares of the deviation. This is the standard deviation.

The precise calculation of the standard deviation requires that the sum of the squares of the deviations be divided by $n-1$, where n is the number of observations. For simplicity, this has been ignored in this chapter. Further information

Item T				
Week	Forecast	Sales	Deviation	D^2
1	1000	1200	−200	40,000
2	1000	1000	− − −	− − −
3	1000	800	200	40,000
4	1000	900	100	10,000
5	1000	1400	−400	160,000
6	1000	1200	−200	40,000
7	1000	1100	−100	10,000
8	1000	700	300	90,000
9	1000	1000	− − −	− − −
10	1000	900	100	10,000
Total	10,000	10,200	1600*	400,000

*Ignoring sign

Average D^2 = 400,000 ÷ 10 = 40,000

Sigma = $\sqrt{40,000}$ = 200 = standard deviation

Alternate method:

Mean Absolute Deviation (MAD) = average D = 1600 ÷ 10 = 160

sigma = MAD x 1.25 = 160 x 1.25 = 200

Figure 5-4 CALCULATING STANDARD DEVIATION.

on the calculation of an unbiased standard deviation is available in almost any text on statistics (5).

In setting an order point, the practitioner is not concerned with lead time periods when demand is less than average. Reserve stocks are needed to cover only those periods *when demand is greater than average.* If the forecast is reasonably accurate and is updated frequently, demand will be less than average approximately 50% of the time over the long run and the practitioner can expect to give 50% service with *no* reserve stock. If he or she then adds 1 standard deviation or 200 units of reserve stock to the forecast average of 1000 (giving an order point of 1200 units), the practitioner will have enough inventory during a replenishment period to cover an additional 34% of the demands (1 standard deviation = 34% of occurrences); thus he or she can expect to give 84% (50% + 34%) service with an order point containing 1 standard deviation of reserve stock. With an order point of 1200 units, the practitioner would experience a stockout during the replenishment period approximately two times out of ten over the long run. Looking at the sales for item T in Figure 5-4, this does not seem too unreasonable.

If two standard deviations or 400 units is now added to the average demand of 1000 units during lead time, the order point becomes 1400 units. The second standard deviation of reserve stock will cover another 14% of the occurrences, giving a total of approximately 98% (84% plus 14%) service. With an order point equal to 1400 units, demand during lead time is likely to exceed it only 2 times out of 100. Again, for the sales data for item T, this looks reasonable.

The standard deviation, although a very useful measure in inventory control, is rather tedious since it involves many calculations. It can be determined in a simpler way via the mean absolute deviation (MAD), as shown on the bottom of Figure 5-4. The MAD is the average (mean) of the differences (deviations) between the forecast and actual sales, taking no account of plus or minus signs (using absolute values). The relationship between the mean absolute deviation and the standard deviation is approximately

$$\sigma = 1.25 \times \text{MAD} \tag{5-2}$$

Figure 5-4 illustrates the alternate method of calculating the standard deviation of 200 by first determining the mean absolute deviation to be 160. While this shortcut result will not always be this close to the results of the direct calculation, it will usually be close enough for most practical inventory control applications. A great deal of computational effort is saved by using the MAD. In addition, the MAD lends itself to periodic updating which is essential in good inventory control; this technique will be described later in this chapter. The MAD also indicates the average amount of a stockout if no safety stock is provided and shows the expected error in the next forecast period.

Figure 5-5 shows the method for calculating the MAD for item V, which obviously had a more variable demand than item T. Here, the MAD is 380 and the

Item V

Week	Forecast	Sales	Deviation
1	1000	400	600
2	1000	600	400
3	1000	1600	−600
4	1000	1200	−200
5	1000	200	800
6	1000	1000	− − −
7	1000	1500	−500
8	1000	800	200
9	1000	1400	−400
10	1000	1100	−100
	Totals	9800	3800*

MAD = 3800 ÷ 10 = 380 units   *Ignoring sign

sigma = 380 x 1.25 = 475 units

Figure 5-5 USING THE MEAN ABSOLUTE DEVIATION.

standard deviation is 475, more than double the value for item T. For item V, an order point for 98% service would be constructed as follows:

Order point = anticipated demand during lead time + reserve stock

Anticipated demand during lead time = 1,000 units forecast

Reserve stock for 98% service = 2σ = 2 × 475 = 950 units

Order point = 1000 + 950 = 1950 units

Approximately 2 times out of 100, demand is likely to exceed 1950 units in a week, which seems reasonable based on the small sample of data available.

For calculating reserve stocks, using MAD is a practical technique that can be tailored to the characteristics of each individual item. Reserve stocks so calculated will be higher for those items that have greater demand variability and lower for those items that have more stable demand. This technique assumes that the actual average demand and the forecast demand are equal, which may not always be true.

This problem is illustrated in Figure 5-6 for item W, which has a weekly fore-

		Item *W*		
Week	Forecast	Sales	Deviation	Running sum (algebraic) of forcast errors
1	1000	1200	−200	−200
2	1000	1000	---	−200
3	1000	1200	−200	−400
4	1000	900	+100	−300
5	1000	1400	−400	−700
6	1000	1200	−200	−900
7	1000	1100	−100	−1000
8	1000	1300	−300	−1300
9	1000	1000	---	−1300
10	1000	900	+100	−1200
	Totals	11,200	1600	

MAD = 1600 ÷ 10 = 160

Tracking signal = RSFE ÷ MAD

$$= \frac{1200}{160}$$

$$= 7.5$$

Figure 5-6 DETERMINING THE TRACKING SIGNAL.

cast of 1000 units and a mean absolute deviation of 160 units (the same as item T in Figure 5-4). Sales of item W, however, have been above the forecast most of the time, indicating that the forecast should be increased to about 1100 units. This would reduce the amount of deviation and, consequently, the amount of reserve stock that would have to be carried in the inventory.

Knowing only the forecast and the MAD for item W, it might be assumed that this item has the same demand characteristics as item T, but a *tracking signal* can be calculated that will promptly flag the fact that the forecast errors are accumulating on one side of the distribution. In this particular case, the forecast is almost always low. By calculating a running sum of the forecast errors algebraically (taking into account the plus and minus signs which are ignored in the absolute deviation) and then dividing the MAD into this sum, a measure of this consistent difference between actual and forecast values, called the **tracking signal**, will be determined. After 10 weeks of history, the tracking signal for item W is 7.5, which is very high, indicating that sales are exceeding the forecast consistently. In an actual inventory system, the forecast would be updated using exponential smoothing and, consequently, the tracking signal would be measuring the effectiveness of this constantly updated forecast. A fixed forecast of 1000 was used in this example to avoid confusing the issue with too many calculations. If the forecast errors tend to balance each other out (as they would for item T, for example), the tracking signal remains low, indicating that the forecast was fairly satisfactory and did not need to be revised.

Acceptable maxima for the tracking signal lie between 4 and 8, depending upon how the signal is to be used. A tracking signal of 4 might be used on a high-value item to trigger an early review of the forecast, thus allowing a possible revision without carrying excess inventory or jeopardizing service by waiting too long. For a low-value item, a fairly high tracking signal (perhaps 7 or 8) would be used, since forecast errors tend to be higher for low-volume items and since most companies place less emphasis on maintaining good service on the less popular items. The use of tracking signals is also covered in Chapter 4.

The weighting factor in the exponential smoothing formula for forecasting described in Chapter 4 is a compromise between reacting too slowly to trends and overreacting to random occurrences; the tracking signal is the same type of tool. A tracking signal set too low might require review of many items for which the system was performing satisfactorily in order to catch those few for which it was not. A tracking signal set too high might delay review and result in poor service or excess inventory. However, having a tracking signal in action does provide an exception technique for indicating that a specific forecast needs to be reviewed and it should be part of every complete system. Ideally, it would call to attention the number of items that people could handle with an effective review.

Calculating the Order Point

Knowing the general statistical properties of the normal distribution and having calculated the standard deviation or MAD of forecast error, the calculation of an order point is straightforward. The fact that adding 1 standard deviation to the anticipated demand during lead time aims at giving 84% service and that adding 2 standard deviations increases the service level to 98% was discussed in the preceding section of this chapter. The service level is directly related to the number of standard deviations provided as reserve or safety stock; this number is usually referred to as the **safety factor**.

Figure 5-7 is a table of safety factors for various service levels for the normal distribution using either the standard deviation or the MAD. Since the MAD is always smaller than a standard deviation, a larger number of MAD's must be used to give the same service level and the safety factor is consequently higher. This does not change the total size of the reserve stock. The table is set up so that the MAD need not be converted to a standard deviation by multiplying it by 1.25—the adjustment is already built into the table. For example, the 84% service level as

Service level (% Order cycles w/o stockout)	Safety factor using:	
	Standard deviation	Mean absolute deviation
50.00%	0.00	0.00
75.00%	0.67	0.84
80.00%	0.84	1.05
84.13%	1.00	1.25
85.00%	1.04	1.30
89.44%	1.25	1.56
90.00%	1.28	1.60
93.32%	1.50	1.88
94.00%	1.56	1.95
94.52%	1.60	2.00
95.00%	1.65	2.06
96.00%	1.75	2.19
97.00%	1.88	2.35
97.72%	2.00	2.50
98.00%	2.05	2.56
98.61%	2.20	2.75
99.00%	2.33	2.91
99.18%	2.40	3.00
99.38%	2.50	3.13
99.50%	2.57	3.20
99.60%	2.65	3.31
99.70%	2.75	3.44
99.80%	2.88	3.60
99.86%	3.00	3.75
99.90%	3.09	3.85
99.93%	3.20	4.00
99.99%	4.00	5.00

Figure 5-7 TABLE OF SAFETY FACTORS FOR NORMAL DISTRIBUTION.

shown in the table would require 1 standard deviation but would require 1.25 MAD's.

This table allows for the computation of reserve stocks for the entire range of service percentages. Assume, for example, that the following data apply to item X:

$$\text{Weekly forecast} = 500 \text{ units}$$

$$\text{Lead time} = 1 \text{ week}$$

$$\text{MAD} = 200 \text{ units}$$

$$\text{Service desired} = 98\%$$

$$\text{Order quantity} = 500$$

Since the weekly demand for this item is 500 units and the lead time is 1 week, then the demand during lead time is equal to 500 units.

The MAD is 200 units. If a 98% service level is desired, Figure 5-7 indicates a safety factor of 2.56 using the mean absolute deviation.

$$\text{Reserve stock} = \text{safety factor} \times \text{MAD}$$
$$= 2.56 \times 200 = 512 \text{ units}$$

and

$$\text{Order point} = \text{demand during lead time} + \text{reserve stock}$$

$$= 500 + 512 = 1012 \text{ units}$$

This order point (according to this table) should give 98% service level—but what does "service" mean in this calculation? It means the percentage of *replenishment periods* during which demand should not exceed the order point quantity. The order point is designed to cover demand during lead time, so that a replenishment order can be placed in time for the material to be delivered into stores before all stock is withdrawn. The end of this replenishment lead time period is the critical time when an item can go out of stock. The number of times that an item is *exposed* to going out of stock is equal to the number of times that a replenishment order is placed and this, of course, depends on the order quantity. An item with a large order quantity will require fewer replenishment orders per year and hence will be exposed to fewer stockouts than one that is ordered more frequently.

Figure 5-8 shows the difference in the number of exposures of an item with an order quantity equivalent to a 1-year supply, in which case there would be one exposure per year versus having an order quantity equivalent to a 2-month supply, which requires six replenishment orders per year. The smaller order quantity would generate six times as many exposures to stockout during the year as the larger order quantity and requires more reserve stock to provide a given level of service. Obviously, if one stockout per year were permissible, the larger order quantity would require no reserve stock. There would be no stockout if actual demand during the replenishment period happened to be below the expected average (as it will about half the time).

This relationship between order quantity and reserve stock can be taken into

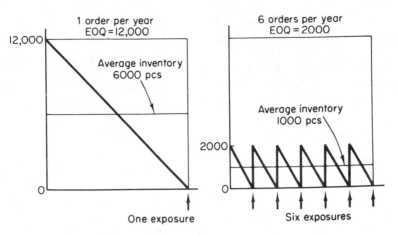

Figure 5-8 EXPOSURES TO STOCKOUT.

consideration by determining the number of replenishment periods that will occur (the number of exposures to stockout) and then calculating the desired service level as the number of replenishment periods during which no stockouts are desired.

The calculation can be illustrated using the data for item X. This item had a weekly forecast of 500 units, 1-week lead time, MAD of 200 units, and a 98% desired service level. If this service level were specified instead as one stockout per year (roughly equivalent to 98% measured weekly, since $\frac{1}{52}$ = 1.9%) and if the order quantity were 2600 units, then:

$$\text{Annual demand} = 500 \times 52 = 26{,}000 \text{ units per year}$$

$$\text{Exposures per year} = \frac{26{,}000}{2600} = 10 \text{ replenishment periods}$$

$$\text{Required service level for one stockout} = \frac{9}{10} \text{ or } 90\%$$

$$\text{Safety factor} = 1.60 \times \text{MAD} \qquad (90\% \text{ service,}$$
$$\text{from Figure 5-7)}$$

$$\text{Order point} = 500 + (1.60 \times 200)$$
$$= 500 + 320 = 820$$

This order point is considerably lower than the previous order point calculated for item X, where the order quantity was only 500 units. Because the 500-unit order quantity resulted in 52 exposures to stockout, a service factor of 2.56 was required, giving an order point of 1012 units.

The straightforward, independent calculation of order points and EOQ's does not necessarily give the most economical total inventory level because of the interaction among order quantities, exposures to stockouts, and reserve stock. Further calculations will frequently reveal that an increase in the order quantity will reduce total inventory investment required for any given service level because it will reduce the number of exposures, and, hence, the required reserve stock. In some cases, the decrease in reserve stock will be greater than the required increase in the lot size. This relationship is shown and explained in an example in Appendix IV. This refinement of statistical technique might very well be worthwhile on the highest value A items, but it probably is not worthwhile on most items; the resulting savings would be too small for the effort exerted to attain them.

Adjusting Forecast and Lead Time Intervals

Another problem frequently encountered in practice when calculating statistical reserve stocks arises because the forecast interval is not the same as the lead time period. The many items involved in the usual inventory have widely different lead times, and it would be very awkward to measure forecast error over each of the lead times for the different items in order to determine variations in demand during the lead time and to calculate reserve stocks. Some other method for adjusting forecast error to compensate for different lead times must be used.

If item X had a lead time of 4 weeks, the demand during lead time would be 4 × 500 units per week = 2000 units. It would be reasonable to expect that there would be a good chance of having more than 1 week with demand considerably above average, so that the reserve stock based on 1 week's demand would have to be increased to give an equivalent level of protection during the longer lead time.

On the other hand, it is equally apparent that the reserve stock for 1-week lead time cannot simply be multiplied by four to determine the reserve stock needed for a 4-week lead time, since it is extremely unlikely that demand would be very high 4 weeks in succession. It is apparent that the reserve stock must increase as lead time increases but that the increase is not directly proportional to the increase in lead time. Some adjustment factor is necessary when the forecast interval is different from the lead time interval, as is so frequently the case in practice.

Figure 5-9 gives a table of factors for adjusting the MAD when lead time is not equal to the forecast interval. This table gives factors for multiplying the MAD for the forecast interval to determine an equivalent deviation for the longer lead time interval to be used in calculating reserve stock. The formula by which these factors were determined is

$$\text{Adjusted MAD} = \text{MAD}\left(\frac{LT}{F}\right)^{\beta} \tag{5-3}$$

where

$$\text{Adjusted MAD} = \text{MAD for lead time interval}$$
$$\text{MAD} = \text{MAD for forecast interval}$$
$$LT = \text{lead time interval}$$
$$F = \text{forecast interval}$$

β = a constant (beta-factor) depending on the demand
patterns of the particular business

The exponent to be used for adjusting a specific company's data should theoretically be determined by simulation, using actual data. In practice, it has been found that a β-factor of 0.7 gives reasonably good results. In fact, a great deal of simulation would be needed to determine a more accurate factor to fit the company's actual demand patterns. The multipliers shown in Figure 5-9 are based on a β-factor of 0.7 and are used as follows:

1. Express the lead time interval as a multiple of the forecast interval.

When forecast interval = 1 and lead time interval is:	Standard deviation or mean absolute deviation should be multiplied by: *
2	1.63
3	2.16
4	2.64
5	3.09
6	3.51
7	3.91
8	4.29
9	4.66
10	5.01
11	5.36
12	5.69
13	6.02
14	6.34
15	6.66
16	6.96
17	7.27
18	7.56
19	7.86
20	8.14

*Assumes beta = 0.7

Figure 5-9 TABLE OF FACTORS FOR ADJUSTING DEVIATION WHEN LEAD TIME DOES NOT EQUAL FORECAST INTERVAL.

2. Find the resulting ratio in the first column of the table in Figure 5-9.

3. Multiply the forecast interval MAD by the corresponding value in the second column to convert it to the lead time MAD.

Using the data for item X and Figure 5-9, the order point is calculated as follows:

1. Assume lead time for item X is 4 weeks (4 times the 1-week forecast interval).

2. When the lead time interval is four times the forecast interval, the adjustment factor from Figure 5-9 is 2.64.

3. The MAD for a 1-week lead time is 200 units.

$$\text{Adjusted MAD} = 2.64 \times 200 = 528 \text{ units}$$

$$\text{Reserve stock required} = 1.60 \times 528 = 845 \text{ units}$$
$$\text{(for OQ} = 2600 \text{ units and 1 stockout per year)}$$

$$\text{Order point} = (4 \times 500) + 845 = 2845 \text{ units}$$

For most items, this type of approximation will be accurate enough. For high-value items, however, results using this table should probably be checked by simulation to determine a more precise adjusting factor or the forecast error should be calculated over the lead time interval.

Forecast weekly demand = 500 units	
Week	Actual demand
1	464
2	330
3	474
4	847
5	618
6	772
7	573
8	432
9	938
10	642
11	750
12	294
13	672
	7806
Average weekly demand = 600	

Figure 5-10 13-WEEK DEMAND HISTORY FOR ITEM X.

   The materials manager must find means for routine updating of the forecast demand during lead time and recalculating reserve stock requirements. Figure 5-10 shows 13 weeks of actual demand for item X, the item discussed in previous examples. The exponential smoothing technique explained in Chapter 4 provides such a method for regular forecast updating; Figure 5-11 shows a new forecast being made each week using this technique and the data in Figure 5-10. In this case, the starting forecast was 500 units per week and the exponential-smoothing calculation has caused this forecast to dip somewhat and then to rise to 526 units for the sixth week. Figure 5-10 shows that the demand for the 13 weeks averaged 600 units and the exponential smoothing calculation, although lagging, is a much better forecast than the original figure of 500 units per week. This demonstrates the usefulness of the technique in correcting a forecast that was obviously too low and making it more responsive to actual sales.

   Figure 5-12 shows the same data used both to calculate and to update the MAD. The updating uses exponential smoothing, substituting MAD for forecast and deviation for demand. In Figure 5-12, for example, the starting MAD is 200. Using the exponential smoothing formula, the old MAD is multiplied by 0.9, the new deviation is multiplied by 0.1, and the new MAD is the sum of the two, as shown in the right-hand column. In practice, the calculations in Figures 5-11 and 5-12 would go on simultaneously and the order point could be recalculated each week. Even for thousands of items, the modern computer can easily handle these calculations.

New forecast = α x actual demand + $(1-\alpha)$ x old forecast where : $\alpha = 0.1$ $(1-\alpha) = 0.9$					
Week	Old forecast	$(1-\alpha)$ x Old forecast	Actual demand	α x actual demand	New forecast
1	500	450.0	464	46.4	496
2	496	446.4	330	33.0	479
3	479	431.1	474	47.4	479
4	479	431.1	847	84.7	516
5	516	464.4	618	61.8	526
6	526	473.4	772	77.2	551
7	551	495.9	573	57.3	553
8	553	497.7	432	43.2	541
9	541	486.9	938	93.8	580
10	580	522.0	642	64.2	586
11	586	527.4	750	75.0	602
12	602	541.8	294	29.4	571
13	571	513.9	672	67.2	581

Figure 5-11 FORECAST USING EXPONENTIAL SMOOTHING.

					Old MAD		New MAD
New MAD = α x deviation + (1−α) old MAD where α = 0.1 (1−α) = 0.9							
Week	Forecast	Sales	Deviation	α x deviation	Old MAD	(1−α) x MAD	New MAD
1	500	464	36	3.6	200	180.0	184
2	496	330	166	16.6	184	165.6	182
3	479	474	5	0.5	182	163.8	164
4	479	847	368	36.8	164	147.6	184
5	516	618	102	10.2	184	165.6	176
6	526	etc.					

Figure 5-12 DEVIATION FROM FORECAST AND MAD.

The full computation of an order point using the techniques covered in this chapter is as follows:

1. Determine the permissible number of stockouts per year (replenishment periods when stock may be exhausted before the order quantity is received). This is a management policy decision, not a calculation.
2. Calculate the number of replenishment orders to be placed (or exposures) per year by dividing the order quantity into the annual demand forecast.
3. Calculate the service fraction, expressed as a percentage. This is the ratio of the number of replenishment periods during which no stockout is desired (total exposures minus the number of permissible stockouts) to the total number of replenishment periods.
4. Use this percentage to find (in Figure 5-7) the safety factor—that is, the number of deviations (standard deviation or MAD) that must be included in the reserve stock.
5. Calculate the standard deviation or MAD as shown in Figure 5-4 or 5-5.
6. Calculate the adjusted deviations (standard deviation or MAD) to account for any difference between the forecast interval and the lead time interval, using the table in Figure 5-9.
7. Multiply the adjusted deviation by the safety factor to calculate the total reserve stock required.
8. Add this reserve stock to the forecast demand over the lead time to get the total order point.

Here is an example using the data for item X:

$$\text{Annual demand } = \text{ 26,000 units}$$
$$\text{Order quantity } = \text{ 500 units}$$

$$\text{Lead time } = 4 \text{ weeks}$$
$$\text{MAD } = 200 \text{ units}$$

Then:

1. Tolerable number of stockouts per year = 1 (set by management)
2. Number of exposures per year = 26,000 ÷ 500 = 52
3. Service fraction = (52 − 1) ÷ 52 = 98%
4. From Figure 5-7, safety factor = 2.56 (using MAD)
5. MAD = 200 units
6. Adjusted MAD = 2.64 × 200 = 528 units
7. Reserve stock = 2.56 × 528 = 1350 units.
8. Order point = DLT + reserve = (4 × 500) + 1350 = 3350 units

The techniques discussed here provide a simple method for generating a revised order point as frequently as once a week. These approaches have had considerable application in industry and have proven to be satisfactory. The advantages come not only from measuring forecast error and determining realistically what the reserve stock level should be but also from having a means for forecasting the demand for thousands of items regularly and for updating both the forecasts and the estimates of forecast error on a routine basis.

These statistical techniques must be used with caution, based on a full understanding of the underlying assumptions and a knowledge of their limitations. All statistical techniques assume that the future will be like the past. Fortunately, this is a reasonably valid assumption for the immediate future in most situations but there will always be changes. Use of techniques such as exponential smoothing, forecast tracking signals and regularly updated measures of forecast error can help to detect these changes promptly and make appropriate corrections.

For the sake of simplicity in the previous calculations, only the forecast error was calculated, and it has been assumed that a constant lead time—usually the average planned lead time—was used. Lead time variations *must not* be added directly to the demand variations, since the longest lead times are not likely to occur simultaneously with the maximum demand. Great care should be taken to avoid changing the planned lead time except under controlled conditions when applying input/output control to reduce work in process. Chapter 5 in the second volume (6) describes the vicious cycle that can result from tinkering with planned lead times.

The techniques of statistics have great value even where applied with some license. Like any other so-called scientific tool, the normal distribution should be used with judgment. If the answers that result do not make sense, the calculations should be reviewed with someone well versed in statistics (the quality control manager, for example) and checked for reasonableness by the practitioner before being applied. Such concepts merely try to describe mathematically the real events that occur in business. It is more important that the practitioner understand their limitations and implications than that he or she understand all the mathematical and statistical theory used in their derivations.

   Principle 17.   Apply statistical techniques for setting reserve stocks only where their assumptions are valid and only after testing.

Using the Poisson Distribution

The **Poisson distribution** is convenient for order-point calculations for certain types of demand because it has the property that the standard deviation is always equal to the square root of the average value. The principal applications of the Poisson distribution have been in quality control and in studies involving random arrivals of customers at supermarket checkout counters or of automobiles at turnpike toll booths. The Poisson distribution has not had wide application in inventory control, although it has been known to practitioners for many years (11). It best fits small, infrequent demands where the quantity of items per order is fairly constant, typical of some low-volume products and repair parts.

   To be used properly in calculating order points, the demand history must be expressed as the *number of orders received* as well as the number of items per order. For example, demand during lead time for an item might average 4000 units; to use the Poisson distribution, further examination of these 4000 units of demand would be necessary to determine that they actually amounted to 40 orders averaging 100 units each.

   The formula for order-point calculation (8) using the Poisson distribution is

$$\text{O.P.} = u \left(a + f \sqrt{a} \right) \tag{5-4}$$

where:

   O.P. = the order point in number of units

   u = the average demand per order in units

   a = the average number of orders arriving during the lead time period

   f = the service factor (similar but not equal to the number of standard deviations used with a normal distribution)

Using the above data, an order point can be calculated for this item

$$\text{O.P.} = 100(40 + 2.1 \sqrt{40})$$
$$= 100(40 + 13.28)$$
$$= 4000 + 1328 = 5328$$

   The service factor of 2.1 was chosen from Figure 5-13, which gives the required values for corresponding service levels using the Poisson distribution. A service factor of 2.1 with the Poisson distribution will give 98% service. This calculation

Min % demand to be met	Max % back orders permitted	f
75	25	0.7
80	20	0.8
85	15	1.0
90	10	1.3
95	5	1.7
98	2	2.1
99	1	2.3
99.9	0.10	3.1

Figure 5-13 POISSON DISTRIBUTION
SERVICE FACTOR f.

shows that a reserve stock of 1328 pieces will be required to give 98% service for this particular item.

If there were another item with the same total number of units demanded during lead time but if this item were sold to a very small number of distributors who ordered infrequently and in large quantities, the answer would be quite different. If the average order size were 1000 units and there were only four orders received during the lead-time period, the calculation would be as follows:

$$\text{O.P.} = 1000 (4 + 2.1 \sqrt{4})$$
$$= 4000 + 4200 = 8200$$

With this more erratic type of demand, a reserve stock of 4200 pieces would be required to give the same degree of customer service as was attained with 1328 pieces in the first example.

The Poisson distribution has been suggested by many authors as a means for calculating order points. It is important to remember one thing: The Poisson distribution *cannot* be used to describe the total *number of units* of demand during the lead time. It *can* be used to approximate the *number of individual orders* that will be received during the lead time.

The accuracy of the results obtained using the Poisson distribution depends directly on how accurately the average quantity of the item included on the orders can be determined. The Poisson distribution accurately predicts the random arrival of orders but not the total unit demand.

The following are the limiting assumptions that must be remembered when using the Poisson distribution for calculating order points:

1. Order arrivals must fit the Poisson frequency distribution curve. The fit is generally better when the number of arrivals per lead time period is relatively small.

2. Order arrivals are random and independent. This would not be true of customer orders filtered through a sales office that accumulates orders for like items over a period of time and releases them in batches.

3. Accurate forecasts can be made of mean order size. Errors in its determination will cause corresponding errors in the order point and reserve stock.

4. Order quantities do not vary widely from the mean. Some research is needed to determine what variation can be tolerated, but it is known that results are poor when the variation is large.

5. Finally, remember the basic assumption of all such statistical methods—the future will resemble the past.

Used in the correct manner, the Poisson formula for calculating order points has two distinct advantages:

1. It gives consistent, useful results far superior to some popular rules of thumb, such as setting reserve stocks equal to 1 month's supply or 10% of the demand during lead time.

2. It does not require the preparation and analysis of a large amount of statistical data. More refined methods of order point calculation will give more accurate results but will require expensive and detailed analyses of data.

The Concept of Service

The measure of service used in the previous discussions—the number of stockouts per year—is a fairly simple one to handle statistically and one that is easy to relate to real business situations. If there are 52 deliveries of stock per year because the order quantity is a 1-week supply, then a service level of one stockout per year would require a delivery ratio of 51/52, or 98%. If the order quantity is a 4-week supply, giving 13 exposures to stockout during the year, then the service level of one stockout per year would require a delivery ratio of 12/13 or 92%. This is merely expressing statistically the obvious fact that the more frequently stock is received and the more frequently the inventory is depleted to the reserve level, the greater the chance of running out of stock.

How would this service measure be used in practice? Stockouts per year do not measure either the amount of the stockout or its *duration*. Nevertheless, this measure is meaningful and can be quite useful. If a product group containing a fairly large number of individual items is checked each week and the number of items out of stock is counted, the result can be correlated fairly well with the statistical concept of stockouts per year per item. Each week, the number of items out of stock could be counted and each of these occurrences would then constitute one stockout.

If, for example, there are 120 items in this product group and the service level goal was one stockout per year per item, average total stockouts for each month should not exceed 10 items. This provides a simple method to verify that safety stocks are adequate or that better control of operations is required.

Another popular statistical measure of customer service specifies the desired percentage of total units of demand that will be filled from goods on the shelf. For example, if total demand for the year is expected to be 26,000 units and it is desired to limit back orders to only 1000 units, the service percentage is then 25/26 = 96%. This measure of customer service must usually be set considerably higher than the service-measure percentage using stockouts per year in order to provide enough reserve stocks to generate a comparable level of service (3). Service measures based on stockouts or on pieces back-ordered do not measure the duration of a stockout period nor do they indicate that important customers are being served or that profitable items are being shipped. If such measures are desired, they can be achieved by adjusting the percent service on individual items in calculating safety stocks. Such measures also involve considerably more expense in tracking actual performance.

Before applying new measures or changing existing measures of customer service, the following should be observed:

1. Simulate the actual functioning of the inventory to be controlled to determine how well the proposed statistical measure of service is currently being used. No statistical measure of service will correlate perfectly, and the statistical service level should always be set *somewhat higher* than the service level actually desired in order to attain the latter in actual day-to-day inventory situations. This simulation can be made manually but most practical applications will require a computer.

2. The service level that actually results is usually somewhat lower than the statistical service level. This is because statistical measures of service usually measure only one characteristic, such as the total quantity back-ordered or number of stockouts; other characteristics (such as the duration of the stockout) also contribute to poor customer service. Also, the basic assumptions of the theory are often violated in practice.

3. Using the statistical service level proposed, start using the control system and reduce reserve stocks as experience shows that fewer reserves are required.

4. Once established and operating, the real power of statistical service measures can be employed to show the economics of changing from one service level to another for families of items. This will be covered in detail in Chapter 8.

5. Statistical measures of customer service deal only with variations in demand over *normal* lead times; they *do not* consider such factors as machine breakdowns, strikes, or quality problems, which affect replenishment lead times drastically. Conversely, since normal lead time is usually assumed in the statistical concept of service, a good supervisor can often make the department perform far better than the statistics indicate it should because it reacts very quickly to changes in customer demand. The supervisor *controls* lead times and thus customer service.

The Value of Statistics

While statistical calculation of order points is simple in concept, it requires the application of considerably more effort than intuitive methods. Is it worth the effort? Emphatically yes, because statistical techniques actually distribute the reserve

				Rule–of–Thumb = 1–wk supply				
Item	Weekly demand forecast	Order quantity	Standard deviation	1-wk reserve	No. std. deviation	Delvy.* service ratio	No. stock-outs
P	500 pcs.	500 pcs.	261 pcs.	500 pcs.	1.92	97.2	2
Y	500 pcs.	500 pcs.	551 pcs.	500 pcs.	0.91	81.9	9
Z	500 pcs.	6500 pcs.	261 pcs.	500 pcs.	1.92	97.2	0
Totals				1500 pcs.			11

		Statistical reserves required for 2 stockouts per yr				
Item	Orders per yr	Delvy. service ratio	No. std.* deviations	Standard deviation	Reserve required	No. stock-outs
P	52	50/52 = 96%	1.75	261 pcs.	460	2
Y	52	50/52 = 96%	1.75	551 pcs.	965	2
Z	4	2/4 = 50%	0	261 pcs.	0	2
Totals					1425	6

*From figure 5–7, table of safety factors

Figure 5-14 VALUE OF STATISTICS IN SETTING RESERVE STOCKS.

stock where it is needed most rather than applying it uniformly across the entire inventory.

Figure 5-14 shows an example of rule-of-thumb application of reserve stocks where the reserve level is set at 1-week's supply for items P, Y, and Z, each of which has the same average weekly demand. Item P is a stock item sold to many customers; its sales history yields a standard deviation of 261 units. Item Y has the same forecast of average weekly demand but is purchased by a small number of customers, so, the demand for it is more erratic. Its standard deviation is found to be 551 units. Item Z has the same weekly demand forecast as items P and Y and the same type of demand variation as P, also with a standard deviation of 261 units. It is a low-value item for which setup costs are high, and, consequently, the order quantity is large, 6500 units. All items are assumed to require 1-week lead time for replenishment.

Setting the reserve-stock level at 1 week's supply for all items would result in approximately 11 stockouts per year, as shown in Figure 5-14. Calculating statistical reserve stocks for these items would reduce this to approximately 6 stockouts per year, at the same time actually reducing the total reserve to 1425 units. The reserve requirements are different for each item from those set by rule of thumb because of the following:

1. Item P has a very small order quantity and, consequently, many exposures to stockout (52 per year).

2. Item Y requires a higher reserve stock because its demands are much more erratic. This greater variation results in the larger standard deviation.

3. Item Z has an order quantity of 6500 units; thus there are only four exposures to stockout during the year. In fact, no reserve stock need be added to the anticipated demand during lead time for Item Z in order to stay within the desired number of stockouts per year.

The reason for the better results is simply that intuitive techniques cannot take into account all of the factors that determine the reserve stocks required. These are

1. Forecast error

2. Lead time

3. Order quantity

4. Desired service level

This example illustrates using statistical approaches to inventory control is worthwhile despite the difficulty and expense. It is not uncommon for improvements from these techniques to result in inventory reductions of one-third or more with no increase in the number of stockouts or to yield reductions in stockouts to one-third the previous level with no increase in inventory as a result of better distribution of reserve stocks.

Modern computers and software programs to make the calculations required to apply statistical techniques to thousands of items are readily available and are relatively inexpensive. Excess inventory and poor customer service, which result from failure to apply them properly, are far more costly.

Principle 18. Rules of thumb for setting reserve stock levels fail because they ignore the reasons it is needed.

While statistical ordering techniques can generate substantial improvements in companies' operations, they should be applied with discretion and common sense, always keeping in mind the principles of ABC inventory classification. The high value items should receive the closest attention. It is sometimes even practical to segregate the A items into "Top A" items, which will receive the frequent personal attention of the materials control manager. These items should probably have **floating** order points calculated periodically using statistical techniques; in some cases, it may be worthwhile to employ even more sophisticated techniques to obtain the greatest economy in control of their inventories. On the other hand, statistical techniques might not be used to control low-value items even with a computer available; simpler techniques applied with discipline can be very effective.

Statistical concepts not only help practitioners to reduce inventories, but an understanding of these concepts can give them a better grasp of the day-to-day workings of inventory systems. One of the problems that constantly faces most material-control people is the ever-increasing number of items that must be kept in inventory. Better knowledge of the behavior characteristics of inventory certainly is not going to eliminate this trend but better knowledge of the functioning of the inventory system can help the practitioner to cope with it. A simple example illustrates the point.

A characteristic of demand in most businesses is that the more active items have more stable demand, while less active items have more variable demand. Stock records usually show that the item that averages 10 units of demand per month typically has few months during which demand is very close to 10 units—it is as likely to be 0 or 30 as it is to be 10, even though the total demand for the year averages 10 units per month. On the other hand, if demand averages 2000 units per month, there will probably be very few months when demand exceeds 3000 or—at most—4000 units. For the popular item, demand will rarely be more than twice as much as the average demand, while the demand for the low-activity item may frequently be three to four times the average demand.

When more kinds of items are added to the inventory, it is almost always necessary to increase the total inventory level. This point is not readily understood by people unfamiliar with inventory control and the question frequently asked is, If we sold 1000 red widgets a month for the last year and we are now going to make them in red, white and blue but still only sell a total of 1000 a month, why should your inventory have to increase? The actual inventory situation might look like this:

	Inventory	Lead time demand	Reserve stock
A.	Red widgets only	1000 units	300 units
B.	Red widgets	160 units	100 units
	White widgets	420 units	200 units
	Blue widgets	420 units	200 units
	Totals	1000 units	500 units

In this hypothetical example, replacing one product by three products requires an increase in reserve stock to provide the same service level because the lower volume for each of the three products results in greater demand variability.

One group of authors (9) notes that if a company adds branch warehouses—an excellent example of inventory splitting—the inventory reserve will vary with the square root of the number of distribution points involved. If a company is using a reserve stock of 300 units, for example, and adds two warehouses (each assumed to supply an equivalent part of the demand), the reserve required to give the same service level as before is

$$\text{Reserve (each distribution point)} = \frac{\text{reserve for 1 distribution point}}{\sqrt{\text{number of distribution points}}}$$

$$= \frac{300}{\sqrt{3}} = 173$$

Increases in the number of items in the product line also aggravate the lot-size problem. Doubling the number of items going through a department means either running larger than economical lot-sizes, doubling the number of setup hours or some compromise between these two alternatives. This further emphasizes the need to work on shortening setup times as is discussed fully in the second volume (6).

These are typical examples of the problems that face materials control practitioners every day. With the knowledge of the behavior characteristics of inventory, these practitioners can at least understand what is likely to happen and, if ingenious enough in applying statistical concepts, can show management the available alternatives in each case. They can make their decisions knowing *all* the resulting effects rather than learning about these effects after they happen or assuming that the resulting increases in inventory were due to poor materials control.

The most important point to remember about any type of ordering system is that *it should make sense*. Statistics can provide useful tools for practitioners but the results will depend on their good sense and judgment in applying the tools. This is discussed fully in the second volume (6).

Practical Precautions

When first applying statistical techniques, practitioners are advised to try them on a sample of items before applying them across the entire product line in order to gain familiarity with the concepts and the limitations of the techniques. From there, the practitioners may want to extend the statistical calculations of order points to all A items before applying them to the B items. Use with C items should be approached with caution—in fact, it might never be worthwhile to go to the amount of effort needed for most of the low-value inventory items.

Periodic recalculation of order points using exponential smoothing to forecast the demand during lead time and using updated MAD's to determine the reserve stock is feasible. Computers are being used extensively in industry to keep order points updated for thousands of items frequently on a weekly basis. Computer manufacturers and software houses offer programs that can be used readily by practitioners to experiment with these techniques and to determine how well they apply in their own companies. These same programs can then be used to form the nuclei of computer programs for operation. This procedure reduces the work of programming the computer, the time required to get useful results and the costs involved to a minimum. Because these techniques *can be* applied weekly, however, does not mean that they *should be;* professional practitioners are wary of mechanical techniques applied with no manual reviews or controls.

No technique can be applied successfully unless its underlying assumptions are understood. All variations of the order point technique assume that

1. Usage will continue and immediate replenishment is desirable before a stockout occurs.
2. Actual usage occurs at a fairly uniform rate.
3. Early delivery is tolerable but late delivery is intolerable and should be avoided as much as possible.

4. Safety stock will provide adequate protection against stockouts.

5. Capacity and materials will be available to handle the released orders.

Periodic-Review Technique

Another major inventory control tool is the **periodic review technique**, frequently called the *fixed-cycle technique*. In this, the inventory records are reviewed periodically and replenishment orders are placed for each item at each review. The review period may be 1 week, 2 weeks or 1 month, whichever is best for the situation. When ordering, enough stock is ordered to bring the total on hand or on order up to a predetermined target level. Figure 5-15 shows how this system would work over a period of time for one item.

This technique should be contrasted with the conventional order point where the inventory records are reviewed each time an entry is made and a replenishment order is placed when the balance on hand and on order reaches a predetermined order point. In the order point technique, the order quantity is fixed and is usually the EOQ.

The periodic review technique finds application where:

1. There are many small issues of items from inventory, so that posting records for each issue is impractical. Food supermarkets, automobile-parts supply houses and similar retail businesses fit into this category, as do service-parts businesses in electronic and mechanical machinery manufacturers.

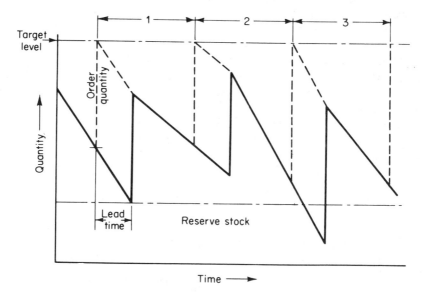

Figure 5-15 PERIODIC-REVIEW SYSTEM.

2. Ordering costs are relatively small. This occurs where orders for many different items from one source are received or orders transferring many items of stock from a central to a branch warehouse are written.

3. It is desirable to order many items at one time to make up a production schedule, for example, so that equipment setups for the family of items can be combined or to obtain a discount from a vendor by means of a combined order or to reduce freight costs by shipping full carload quantities at regular intervals.

The target is the sum of the following:

1. Anticipated demand during the lead time (DLT)

2. Anticipated demand during the review period (DRP)

3. Reserve stock (R)

The first and third are identical to the order point elements. Obviously, if the inventory record is not to be reviewed again for 2 weeks, anticipated usage during this period must be added to the lead time demand, since this lead time cannot begin until 2 weeks have passed. Reserve stocks are calculated by the means discussed earlier in this chapter for order points.

A simple example of a target inventory calculation is as follows:

Lead time	= 1 week
Forecast demand during lead time	= 20 units
Review period	= 2 weeks (average order quantity = 2 weeks' supply)
Forecast demand during review period	= 40 units
Reserve stock	= 30 units

$$\text{Target inventory level units} = DLT + DRP + R \qquad (5\text{-}5)$$
$$= 20 + 40 + 30$$
$$= 90$$

Using this inventory target, the stock would be reviewed every 2 weeks and ordered up to a total of 90 units. The total inventory on hand and on order, for example, might equal 70 units at the first review; 20 more units would then be ordered. During the next 2 weeks, demand might total 45 units, and this would be the quantity ordered at the second review, since 45 units would be needed to restore the total to the target level of 90 units. A few important points about periodic review should be noted:

1. The total lead time is actually equal to the delivery lead time plus the review period.

2. Lengthening the review period is equivalent to lengthening the lead time and will require carrying greater amounts of reserve stock.

3. The ordering quantity is equal to actual demand during the review period just passed.

4. The average inventory level is equal to one-half the demand during the review period plus reserve stock.

Two Simple Ordering Methods

For the many items of low annual value that are usually found in industrial inventories, it is often not worthwhile to use the formal approaches described above. There are two general methods already mentioned that are used for controlling these low-value items without records: the two-bin method and the visual review method. These are worth reviewing.

The Two-bin Method: An amount of stock equivalent to the order point is physically segregated either into a second bin or into a container and this is then sealed. When all the open stock has been used up, the second bin or reserve container is opened and material control is notified to order more stock. This is a practical method for keeping control of low-value items. The most common problems that arise in its application are

1. Without adequate training and proper discipline, this type of system will deteriorate very quickly. Personnel who do not understand the method will use up the reserve stock without notifying anyone, or replenishment material will be received and not properly segregated into open stock and reserve stock.

2. After being once determined, the quantity to be carried in the second bin is never reviewed. As demand changes for the item, this quantity is no longer adequate or may be far too large.

A two-bin method works best in a controlled stockroom where the responsibility for replenishing stock and maintaining the inventory can be assigned to one person. When set up this way, the procedure is called the *bank stock* method. It is very difficult to make it work when materials are stocked on plant floors in the open.

Visual Review Method: Stock is periodically checked (perhaps once a week or once every 2 weeks) and each item is ordered to a preestablished stock level. These levels are stated in easily visible terms like "$\frac{1}{4}$ bin" and "6 deep" for reordering and large order quantities are usually specified. This technique is far more satisfactory than the two-bin method when the responsibility for storekeeping cannot be assigned to an individual. It works well on floor stocks located near the point of use. It works particularly well where lead times are short and vendors ship or cancel (the back orders), thus eliminating the need for any record of material previously ordered except for the last order. It is, of course, the principal technique employed by many retail stores—especially large food supermarkets. There are three principal problems involved in using this method:

1. The necessary periodic reviews of the stock levels are not made.

2. Because of poor housekeeping, stock is not put in its proper location and the reviewer does not find all the inventory actually on hand.

3. Ordering targets are not checked frequently and become outdated and useless as demand changes.

Low-value item control methods involving a minimum of record-keeping can be used very successfully if the following points are kept in mind:

1. The ABC concept of inventory classification is based on carrying relatively high levels of inventory of low-value items and on exerting a minimum of effort in controlling them. Nevertheless, it must be remembered that an assembly or packaging line can be shut down for lack of a C item as surely as for lack of an A item. It must never be forgotten that the basic rule for controlling low-value stocks is to *have plenty.*

2. No good has been accomplished if tighter controls of high-value stocks do not more than offset the inventory increase resulting from looser controls of the low-value stocks. Time saved by the latter should be devoted to reducing high-value inventories.

3. Visual controls are frequently associated with loose controls and perpetual records are associated with tight controls: neither is necessarily so. A common industry case is the example of rivets in the aircraft industry. These are items of low unit value but their tremendously large annual usage makes them A items. Control of such items using visual techniques will save a great deal of record-posting time, but the inventory levels can and should be controlled very closely.

4. The general rule that all items having low annual dollar usage should be controlled using visual review techniques is not a good one. This can result in having a component that is used in a product once a year checked visually every week rather than having the item planned and procured once during the year. Material-requirements planning should be used for such items.

Principle 19. Simple physical techniques may provide more economical control of inventories.

Time-Phasing the Order Point

Several major problems exist with the conventional order-point technique:

1. It lacks ability to develop revised order "need" dates.

2. It provides no information on future orders to be released after the current one.

3. It cannot easily handle known future demand at specific times.

4. It cannot easily handle seasonal or cyclical demand.

5. It acts to trigger ordering with no advance warning.

These difficulties can be overcome and additional benefits provided by *time-phasing* the order point data. Item Z has the following:

Forecast = 20 per week   Order quantity = 100

Lead time = 2 weeks   Reserve stock = 55

On hand = 80 units   On order = 100 units due in week 2

O.P. = (2 × 20) + 55 = 95 units

To provide a more useful picture, the data could be time-phased as shown in Figure 5-16. The logic of this display is the basic logic of procurement and manufacturing:

1. How many are required? (Forecast)

2. How many are now in stock? (On hand)

3. How many are already ordered? When? (On order)

4. When must more be obtained? (Planned orders due)

5. When must they be ordered? (Planned orders start)

Note that the new order is planned for release during the week the available inventory is projected to drop to the order point (95 units), although this is not the method used to determine it. The calculated order point is not used. The technique uses the reserve stock (55) as a target to establish the order due date and offsets the lead time to set the start date. It schedules a receipt to protect the reserve stock from planned demands. The results would be identical if the reserve stock were prededucted from the on hand figure to calculate the starting available total, as is done by many users.

As actual demands are recorded against forecasts in each period, the figures for projected available stock could be recalculated. The technique could thus indicate that released orders are now needed earlier or later than scheduled as well as shifting planned orders as necessary. Faster response to such signals by the supply-

Week	1	2	3	4	5	6	7	8	Etc.
Forecast	20	20	20	20	20	20	20	20	
Released orders		100							
Projected available	60	140	120	100	80*	60	40**	100	
Planned orders: due							100		
Planned orders: start					100				

* Order point reached
** Reserve stock broken into

Figure 5-16 TIME-PHASED ORDER POINT—STOCKED PRODUCT.

ing facility (vendor or plant) could permit maintaining customers' deliveries with lower safety stocks.

Utilizing this time-phased format overcomes the five difficulties cited above with conventional order points:

1. Order need dates can be developed that are different from the due dates placed on the orders when released.
2. Future orders can be projected as far out as forecasts are believed to be reliable.
3. Known future demand "lumps" can be inserted with (or in place of) forecasts in any period.
4. Seasonal or cyclical forecasts can be used directly.
5. Future activity, released-order status and planned orders are all shown in the time-phased display.

Principle 20. Time-phasing order point data greatly increases the power of this technique.

The costs of achieving these benefits are incurred in the far greater data-handling requirements and in the "nervousness" that may be introduced as actual demand varies around the forecast average. The technique reacts to protect the planned reserve stock; it will not use any of this to dampen the effects of variances of actual demand.

Figure 5-16 illustrates the time-phased order point for a stocked product. The technique can also be applied to make-to-order products, as shown in Figure 5-17. Here the forecast is replaced by actual orders as they are received, and manufacturing is scheduled to suit.

Handling Service Parts Demand

The time-phased order point is very useful in replenishing an inventory of service parts where demand originates from customers and must be forecast. It can handle intermittent demand with no demand shown in many periods as well as demand forecasts in all periods. It is applicable where service parts are held in storerooms separate from production stocks and where service parts are no longer used in current production, even if stored together with current items.

Forecast = 20 per period　　Lead time = 2 weeks　　Order quantity = lot-for-lot

Week	1	2	3	4	5	6	7	8	Etc.
Actual-forecast	18	15	21	19	20	20	20	20	
Released orders	18	15							
Projected availiable			−21	−19	−20	−20	−20	−20	
Planned orders : due			21	19	20	20	20	20	
Planned orders : start	21	19	20	20	20	20			

Figure 5-17 TIME-PHASED ORDER POINT—MAKE-TO-ORDER PRODUCT.

Service parts identical to current usage and stored together are controlled by combining the forecast demand for the former with calculated demand for the latter. This is done in MRP techniques described in Chapter 6.

Handling Branch Warehouse Demand

Many companies have widespread distribution networks in which inventory of finished products is stored close to customers in branch warehouses. These are supplied from regional warehouses which may be separate facilities or may be located at a manufacturing plant. The regional warehouses are supplied by one or more manufacturing plants and fill customers' orders themselves as well as shipping to branch warehouses. The time-phased order point provides a good tool to plan for the replenishment of the inventories of branch warehouses. An even better technique is the fixed-cycle–variable-order-quantity (target) method described in detail earlier in this chapter. It works well with the periodic review of stock levels of and regularly scheduled deliveries to branch warehouses. The techniques for this are covered in Appendix VII. The successful application of these techniques is discussed in the second volume (6).

Independent/Dependent Demand

In 1965 a very useful distinction between two types of demand for items in a manufacturing environment was proposed by J. A. Orlicky. He used **independent** to describe any demand for finished products or components unrelated to demand for other items in a company's inventory. Characteristic of this are customers' orders for finished goods, intermediates or service parts. He used **dependent** to describe any demand for items directly determined by schedules to produce a parent (in a bill of materials) or other associated item. Typical of this are raw materials, purchased or manufactured parts or ingredients and manufactured subassemblies, attachments and accessories.

Orlicky proposed this as a rule to determine the selection of the ordering technique to be applied. Independent demand must be forecast, and conventional or time-phased order-point techniques are the proper (and only) techniques applicable. Dependent demand can be calculated, and material-requirements planning is the correct technique. This general rule, or principle, is a useful guide but not a hard and fast law to be followed at all costs. The simpler, less expensive conventional order point, two-bin or periodic review methods can be used very effectively on dependent demand items *where their basic assumptions are valid and where the necessary disciplines are maintained.* This is discussed more thoroughly in the second volume (6).

Principle 21. Orlicky's independent/dependent demand rule provides a good guide to select ordering techniques.

CHAPTER
SIX

MATERIALS CONTROL:
DEPENDENT DEMAND

Material Requirements Planning
Logic

The demands of the great bulk of materials used in manufacturing operations are generated by decisions to produce some item containing them. The components of hard goods, textiles and ceramics and the ingredients in food stuffs, chemicals and pharmaceuticals are not utilized at steady, uniform rates and are not needed until the item into which they enter is to be produced. They have *dependent demand*, defined in Chapter 5.

The initial procurement of such materials, as well as their continuing replenishment, is usually best handled by applying the following logical analysis:

1. When do we want to make how many of this specific product?

2. What components (or ingredients) are required?

3. How many (or much) of each of these are already on hand?

4. How many (or much) are already ordered in addition and when will they arrive?

5. When are more needed and how many more?

6. When should these be ordered?

This is the fundamental logic of MRP. It is equally applicable to purely make-to-order, custom-built products like ships, buildings or special machinery, to periodic batch manufacture of low and high volume products, to process industries and to repetitive mass production.

Principle 22. MRP logic applies to all types of products and processes involving multiple components.

Significant differences in the ways the logic is applied to these different processing methods and in the data formats used with them are required. The requirements for sound materials planning and tight control are identical for all of these, however:

1. A *valid master plan* stating what is to be made, how many are needed, and when items are needed for each product, must be developed. Called the master production schedule (MPS), these numbers drive the MRP and other related programs. All the resultant plans are invalid and unrealistic if the MPS requires output beyond the capabilities of the facilities (plant and vendors) producing it. These important data and the activities and considerations involved in producing them are covered in Chapter 7.

2. *Accurate bills of material* detailing the makeup composition of the products form the structure or framework of modern planning, showing parent-component item relationships of products *as they will be made or procured.*

3. *Accurate information on current inventories,* including a unique part number, quantity in stock and data necessary to describe the item completely for planning purposes is essential.

4. *Accurate information on orders already released* to obtain additional quantities of each item, whether purchased or manufactured, must include quantity ordered and date due. Processing data on successive operations to manufacture items and the times required are *not* needed by MRP.

5. *Reliable lead times* to procure or manufacture batches or specific lots of materials are needed.

6. *An adequate flow of materials* to satisfy all requirements through each facility involved in the total process, including suppliers, must occur.

Precomputer MRP

Prior to the availability of the business computer in the early 1960s, there were few useful applications of MRP logic. Limitations of manual data handling precluded applying true net, time-phased MRP but the *explosion chart* (discussed shortly) provided many companies with a useful planning tool. Figure 6-1 shows a bill of materials for a simple wall lamp listing the component number, its description and the quantity required per assembly and indicating whether these parts are manufactured or purchased. With this bill of materials, a planner can order components in the quantity required for the next assembly lot. For example, if 2000 no. 9 wall lamps were to be assembled, the planner would write purchase requisitions for 2000

Mfg. code 218			Date 8/10/66 Approved AES	
Component		Quantity required	Source	Remarks
Number	Description			
X18	Switch	1	Purch.	
Y2L	Socket	1	Purch.	
9W	Shade	1	Mfg.	
414	Hanger	2	Mfg.	
4107	Cord set	1	Purch.	

Figure 6-1 BILL OF MATERIALS—#9 WALL LAMP.

each of the X18 switch, the Y2L socket, and the 4107 cord set and prepare manufacturing orders for 2000 9W shades and 4000 no. 414 hangers to be issued at the proper time.

This extremely simple example illustrates none of the usual complications that make the job of controlling component inventories extremely complex in many companies. One of the most common complications is that components are used on more than one assembly. Figure 6-2 shows a second lamp, in this case a no. 9 pinup lamp, which differs from the no. 9 wall lamp only in having a different

Mfg. code 314			Date 8/10/66 Approved AES	
Component		Quantity required	Source	Remarks
Number	Description			
X18	Switch	1	Purch.	
Y2L	Socket	1	Purch.	
9P	Shade	1	Mfg.	
414	Hanger	2	Mfg.	
4107	Cord set	1	Purch.	

Figure 6-2 BILL OF MATERIALS—#9 PINUP LAMP.

shade. Obviously, it would be a great deal more economical and efficient to combine requirements for common components. Therefore, before placing an order, the planner should know all requirements for each component in each time period.

Of the many ways of combining requirements, the simplest is the **explosion chart**, as in Figure 6-3. It is really just a series of bills of material listed together with assemblies down the left side and components across the top. The X in the box in the matrix indicates that the component is not used in the assembly shown in the corresponding row. The bills of material for the no. 9 wall lamp and no. 9 pinup lamp were used with the bills of material for all other lamps in this product line to make up this explosion chart.

A planner determining the requirements for any given period of assembly would insert the expected required quantity of each finished lamp in the explosion chart in the second column and then extend that quantity across all components indicated by the open boxes in the matrix, multiplying it by the figure in the upper left-hand corner of the box (which indicates if more than one piece is required per assembly). For example, the no. 414 hanger is used in pairs on the no. 9 wall lamp, so a small 2 appears in the matrix.

Once the requirements have been totaled for each component by adding the figures in the columns, they can then be compared with the total quantity of each item available in inventory. Figure 6-4 shows the inventory record for the no. 9P lamp shade. This figure also indicates the classic perpetual inventory data relationship: Starting balance + received − issued = on hand + on order − allocated = available to plan. As the explosion chart indicates, at the present time there is a need for additional shades to take care of the manufacturing requirements in late March, so an order for 1300 could be written and released to the factory when required, allowing the proper lead time.

During the interim, the explosion chart could be used weekly to determine whether or not components for the next few weeks were coming through on schedule to meet assembly requirements. In this case, the quantity posted in the "total available" row at the bottom of the explosion chart was taken from the "on-hand" column on the inventory record card rather than the "available-to-plan" column.

This type of simple, manual, requirements planning technique has been used for many years. While its users usually found it superior to an order-point system for ordering components, its use often resulted in excess inventory unless it was refined substantially. The explosion sheet can be applied only to a single-level bill of materials; it cannot handle stocked subassemblies or intermediates. It can show only the total quantity required over a period of time and this period must be far enough out to cover the longest manufacturing or purchase lead time of any component. Because of long lead times, many companies did their planning on a quarterly basis and had to plan more than one quarter ahead, showing firm requirements for the current quarter and anticipated requirements for the following quarter. This was necessary because any component requiring more than a week or two to manufacture could well be in short supply at the beginning of the next quarter if not planned in the preceding quarter.

Further problems occur because the planning period is so long. Planning firm

Assembly	Required Qty	X18 Switch	X27 Switch	Y2L Socket	Shade #7W	Shade #7D	Shade #9W	Shade #9D	Shade #9P	Shade #11D	Shade #11P	414 Hanger	418 Hanger	381 Base	411 Base	#4107 Cord Set
#7 Wall			X			X	X	X	X	X	X	2 /	X	X	X	
#7 Desk			X		X		X	X	X	X	X	X	X		X	
#9 Wall	2000	2000	X	2000	X	X	2000	X	X	X	X	2 / 4000	X	X	X	2000
#9 Desk			X		X	X	X		X	X	X	X	X	X		
#9 Pin-up	2500	2500	X	2500	X	X	X	X	2500	X	X	2 / 5000	X	X	X	2500
#11 Desk		X			X	X	X	X	X		X	X	X	X		
#11 Pin-up	2000	X	2000	2000	X	X	X	X	X	X	2000	X	2 / 4000	X	X	2000
Total required	6500	4500	2000	6500			2000		2500		2000	9000	4000			6500
Total available		7105	15,423	7002			4595		1244		4715	29,531	11,648			6400
To obtain		✓	✓	✓			✓		(1300)		✓	✓	✓			(100)

Figure 6-3 EXPLOSION CHART—LAMPS.

Starting balance = 1444

| | (+) | (−) | (=) | (+) | (−) | (=) Availiable |
Date	Received	Withdrawn	On hand	On order	Allocated	to plan
3/12	400	——	1844	——	600	1244
3/14	——	600	1244	——	——	1244
3/23	——	——	1244	——	2500	−1256
3/23	——	——	1244	1300	2500	44

Figure 6-4 INVENTORY RECORD—#9P SHADE.

requirements for a 13-week period requires a forecast of anticipated requirements for each end item; the farther out into the future this forecast is extended, the less accurate it will become. In such a **quarterly planning approach**, the planner typically finds that, as each quarter begins, many components are in short or in excess supply simply because of the forecast errors.

Right after World War II, many industries had large backlogs of customer orders for their products stretching for 12 and sometimes 18 months. These provided a firm base upon which production plans could be made. It was logical and fairly easy to review these orders and make a periodic materials plan, starting with a required date for assembling one type of machine and then working backward to schedule subassemblies, component manufacturing and purchasing of needed materials. Ordering to meet this assembly requirement would take into account the intermediate levels of inventories and normal lead times. The requirements for parts, subassemblies and finished machines were then analyzed by the machine centers to arrive at the levels of production required for the center. Component and subassembly orders were then written with release dates obtained by working back from the planned assembly date, using normal materials-planning logic. In this way (since they far exceeded the lead times) the backlogs served as a known forecast of requirements and planning could be done once each quarter, for example. Even when done manually, this *Quarterly ordering system* was very useful.

During the late 1950s and the early 1960s, these order backlogs dwindled to a point at which they no longer supplied the necessary planning information. Consequently, a great interest developed in forecasting to supply the missing information. Because customers demanded shorter delivery times, many industries changed from building to order to making to stock. The typical approach was to make a detailed forecast by item of finished-goods requirements for each month of the coming year, with a firm production schedule developed for the next quarter. This forecast and schedule was then broken down into subassembly and component schedules, using it exactly as the order backlog had been employed. Once again, start dates were assigned to orders and the orders put in the release file while awaiting their release dates. The work on these orders was then accumulated by machine center to determine the machine load for the quarter to insure that the actual capacity was adequate.

Unfortunately, as the period progressed, actual sales would vary from the forecast and the product scheduled to be produced would differ considerably from that required to meet the latest customer orders. The solution to this problem was to advance the schedule for the desired products and try to expedite them through the plant *in addition to the products for which orders had already been scheduled.* As a result, demands on productive capacity usually became excessive (because the orders being expedited through the plant were really generating an additional workload), although the actual capacity was adequate to meet average requirements. Very few production control systems were sophisticated enough to identify those orders that could be delayed to make room for expedited orders, so the total work load was typically above the planned level.

Another characteristic of this periodic scheduling approach was a large overload at the beginning of each new quarter. As the inventory controller reviewed the requirements for the new period it would be found that many items had been sold in excess of what had been forecast at the beginning of the last quarter and so schedules for the coming quarter required a high concentration of production in the first month in order to take care of the urgent requirements. In theory, the quarterly ordering system attempted to level out production. In practice, when based upon a detailed item forecast instead of a firm backlog of customers' orders, it very seldom succeeded in attaining this goal.

Shortening the time period for planning requires considerable refinement of the simple techniques described so far. Merely showing (as in Figure 6-3) that 2500 units will be required during the second quarter does not pinpoint *when* in the quarter these components will be required and in what quantities. Some manual approaches take the planned assembly requirements and, using the bill of materials, post the required dates on the component record and calculate the start dates based on standard lead times. This approach does not lend itself readily to combining requirements or recalculating component schedule dates as requirements change. This is why, in practice, the manual requirements planning approach is frequently no more effective than the order point technique.

Figure 6-5 is a time-phased plan showing the projected assembly schedule for the no. 9 pin-up lamp by week for the second quarter. This type of assembly plan is one form of a **master schedule**. Such a master schedule might very well be based upon an estimate of when the assembled end product would be reaching its reorder point. The intermittent demands shown in weeks 16, 19, 22, and 25 of Figure 6-5 are actually EOQ's for the end item.

The projected requirements for the no. 9P shade, based upon the assembly schedule for the no. 9 pinup lamp, are shown below the master schedule. This ordering technique specifies in which week components will be required and, based upon the lead time for the components, shows when manufacturing or purchase orders must be released. It can be seen, for example, that the no. 9P shade inventory will be reduced by 500 units in week 16 and 19, when 500 pinup lamps are assembled, and that it will be necessary to order another 256 shades in week 18 in order to have them arrive in week 22, so that another 500 pinup lamps can be assembled as scheduled. Note that the order quantity rule for the shade is lot-for-lot (See Chapter 3).

#9 Pin-up lamp
(master schedule)

				Week							
14	15	16	17	18	19	20	21	22	23	24	25
–	–	500	–	–	500	–	–	500	–	–	500

#9P shade
(materials plan)

On hand = 1244
U/M = pieces
Lead time: 4 weeks

ABC = A
Safety stock = 0
Order quantity = lot-for-lot

	Past due					Week							
		14	15	16	17	18	19	20	21	22	23	24	25
Projected usage	–	–	–	500	–	–	500	–	–	500	–	–	500
Open orders	–	–	–	–	–	–	–	–	–	–	–	–	–
Projected available	–	1244	1244	744	744	744	244	244	244	–	–	–	–
Planned order receipts	–	–	–	–	–	–	–	–	–	256	–	–	500
Planned order releases	–	–	–	–	–	256	–	–	500	–	–	–	–

Figure 6-5 TIME-PHASED ORDERING—LAMP COMPONENTS.

Figure 6-5 shows only the projected assembly requirements for the no. 9 pinup lamp; this is satisfactory for determining requirements for the no. 9P shade which is used only on that lamp. A materials plan for a component common to two or more assemblies has to be based on the sum of the requirements for all assemblies broken into their proper time periods. Similar time-phased calculations could be made for components of the shade if it were decided to make it rather than buying it. This type of ordering is extremely difficult to do manually for anything except a few important items in relatively simple products. For these, however, it can be quite useful.

There are some general principles to remember about time-phased planning:

1. The materials plan must extend over a long-enough period to cover the longest lead time of any component in a single-level bill of materials and the sum of the lead times in a multi-level bill.

2. The materials plan should be revised frequently in order to react to changes in requirements.

3. The shorter the time period used, the more effective the materials plan will be.

For example, a plan in weekly periods revised every week would be more effective than one in monthly periods revised only once a month. Remember, however, the plan is just that—making it more precise and revising it more often can quickly reach a point of diminishing returns. This is discussed fully in the second volume (6).

Prerequisites for MRP

Net time-phased material requirements planning requires very specific data. These are

1. A time-phased master production schedule in which every item is described by a bill of materials (see page 142 and Chapter 7)

2. A unique number identifying each component and the parent in every bill of materials (see pages 142–143 in this chapter)

3. Properly structured, accurate bills of material and tight control of engineering changes (see pages 143–152 in this chapter)

4. Accurate current inventory balances on stocked items

5. Accurate quantities and reliable delivery dates on open purchasing and manufacturing orders

6. Reliable lead times on purchased and manufactured items

These are essential to any MRP program. In addition, there are requirements for practical application of the technique:

1. Computer software and hardware to handle the immense volumes of data required in practically every company.

2. Timely reporting of material issues and receipts, inventory adjustments and order releases and closings.

3. Discipline in handling the discrete batches identified in the plan.

4. People capable of making valid plans and then executing them.

MPS Subsystem

The minimum MPS subsystem must contain quantity and date data for each product to which MRP will be applied. For MRP logic to be used on all components, the horizon of the MPS must extend at least far enough to equal the *sum of all the lead times* making up the longest sequence of procuring some raw material and processing it through the required operations to produce the item described in the MPS; this is called the **cumulative lead time, critical path lead time** or **stacked lead time**. The MPS horizon is extended and *horizon fillers* used at lower levels to provide a reasonable (3 to 6 months) amount of data on future requirements for raw materials. More complete MPS subsystems are described in Chapter 7.

Part Numbering

For use in modern systems, every item must have one and only one part number. The part numbering system used in the lamp examples in this chapter is a very simple one, typical of the type of part numbering system used in small companies, combining numbers and letters without significance or reason. As a company grows and its product line expands, the numbering system begins to get incredibly complicated so that even simple systems start to bog down. Typically, a program is then begun to develop a more reasonable part numbering system—usually with a great many digits, each having some significance (describing the material from which the product is made, the basic method by which it is made, whether it is manufactured or purchased, etc.)—and this part numbering system is introduced. For some components, it soon becomes extremely cumbersome to keep each digit significant and nonsignificant part numbering finally results. It is not uncommon in a poor production and inventory control environment to find three different part numbering systems in simultaneous use. Few managers seem to recognize the connection between the lack of a good part numbering system and lack of results from production and inventory control activities.

The ideal part-numbering system has the fewest digits possible and uses only numerical data. Up to 10,000 different items can be identified uniquely with only four digits. While very few companies have as many as 100,000 items to handle, most have more than 6 digits and many have alphabetic characters, dashes and spaces scattered through the part numbers. The penalties they pay include

1. More errors by people handling data

2. Need for increased file space

3. Slower processing time for programs

There will never be a better time than the present to start phasing in a simple, workable part numbering system. Short, purely numerical numbers should be used for all new products, materials and other items being planned and controlled. A massive program to substitute short numbers for existing long, complex ones is rarely justified; time, design and other changes will eventually remove them. The subject of part numbering is covered in more detail in the second volume (6).

Principle 23. The ideal part number is short, numerical and unique.

Structuring Bills of Material

The lamps used as examples in the earlier sections of this chapter had very simple bills of materials with very few parts required and no subassemblies. In more complex assemblies, it is necessary to plan the manufacture of subassemblies as well as components and final assemblies. If, for example, the lamp manufacturer decided to make the Y2L socket instead of buying it, bills of material would then have to show the components required to put this subassembly together and the other components going into the final assembly.

Figure 6-6 shows this more complex bill of materials but it does not indicate that the #1314 switch, for example, is part of the Y2L socket subassembly. Some notation could be made on the bill of materials to indicate this relationship, such as using an asterisk to show all items used in subassemblies; however, if these subassemblies in turn have subassemblies, the asterisk technique gets very awkward.

Mfg. Code

314

Component		Quantity required	Source
Number	Description		
X18	Switch	1	Purch.
Y2L	Socket assembly	1	Mfg.
1314	Switch	1	Purch.
219	Shell	1	Mfg.
326	Base	1	Mfg.
220	Shell insulator	1	Purch.
222	Base insulator	1	Purch.
405	Screw stem	1	Mfg.
9P	Shade	1	Mfg.
414	Hanger	2	Mfg.
4107	Cord set	1	Purch.

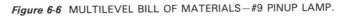

Figure 6-6 MULTILEVEL BILL OF MATERIALS—#9 PINUP LAMP.

Manfacturing code
314

1st level component number	2nd level component number	Description	Quantity required	Source
X18		Switch	1	Purchased
Y2L		Socket assembly	1	Manufactured
	1314	Switch	1	Purchased
	219	Shell	1	Manufactured
	326	Base	1	Manufactured
	220	Shell insulator	1	Purchased
	222	Base insulator	1	Purchased
	405	Screw stem	1	Manufactured
9P		Shade	1	Manufactured
414		Hanger	2	Manufactured
4107		Cord set	1	Purchased

Figure 6-7 PARTIAL INDENTED BILL OF MATERIALS—#9 PINUP LAMP.

A more common approach is to show the bill of materials in idented form, as illustrated in Figure 6-7. Here all the components going into the Y2L socket, the **seccond-level** parts, are indented to the right to indicate that they are components used in the subassembly immediately preceding them. In both Figures 6-6 and 6-7 a manufacturing code number is used in place of the no. 9 pin-up lamp catalogue description.

Because the Y2L socket is used in every lamp, Figure 6-7 shows that any change in this socket or any of its components will affect *every* bill of materials. A slightly different form of bill of materials, which lends itself better to maintenance and updating, can simplify this work. For example, if the bill of materials shown in Figure 6-2 were used but the Y2L socket were coded as a manufactured subassembly, a separate bill of materials (such as in Figure 6-8) could be maintained for that subassembly only. This is called a **single-level** bill. Any change in the subassembly components not affecting its use in the end product would then require changing only one bill of materials—each of the higher-level bills would be unaffected as long as the Y2L socket continued to be used in the final assembly. The use of single-level bills of material also greatly reduces the total file space required, since bills of common items are stored only once in the product structure files. The ability of computers to access and retrieve records at high speed makes such fragmented files practicable; manually searching for such related bills of material would be impractical.

Computers also have the ability to retain information in product structure files permitting the computers to retrieve and present **where-used** bills of material. Like the information in the top of Figure 6-8 (showing all models of lamps in which

Mfg. code   (used on lamps # 7W, # 7D, # 9W,
418   # 9D, # 9P, # IID,
                       # IIP)

| Component | | | |
Number	Description	Quantity required	Source
1314	Switch	1	Purchased
219	Shell	1	Manufactured
326	Base	1	Manufactured
220	Shell insulator	1	Purchased
222	Base insulator	1	Purchased
405	Screw stem	1	Manufactured

Figure 6-8 BILL OF MATERIALS—Y2L SOCKET ASSEMBLY.

the Y2L socket is used), such bills indicate all applications of an item on higher level bills; these are very useful to design engineers in finding out which parent items might be affected by a design change to a component. Both single- and multi-level where-used bills are common.

A useful pictorial representation of a bill of materials is the **family tree**, or **Christmas tree**, shown in Figure 6-9 for the no. 9 pinup lamp. This shows all levels from finished product to raw materials and includes all purchased and manufactured components. While very clear and useful to people studying this product's structure, it is possible to utilize this format in only a very few companies in the formal planning system. It has wider use in studying structuring problems, manufacturing operations and simplification and standardization of products; in these studies it is common to use manual diagrams for typical products. The matrix explosion chart (Figure 6-3) is even more useful in such studies although it can get ponderous. Conventional practice is to number the levels from 0 at the top to the bottom; Figure 6-9 thus has level 0 for the no. 314 lamp and level 3 for most of the raw materials.

The **full, indented** bill of materials for the no. 9 pinup lamp is shown in Figure 6-10. The figure shows one way the bill is commonly set up, indenting the part numbers to show parent-component relationships. Notice that this is a four-level bill (from the no. 314 lamp to four raw materials) with one subassembly (no. 418 socket) and final assembly bills of material plus five bills for single manufactured components made from purchased raw materials. Note also that no. 126 strip appears on two different levels. To be really complete, this bill of materials should include packaging.

In a full, indented bill of materials like Figure 6-10, components and raw materials common to several items (like the no. 126 strip) appear several times. To simplify many activities using such complete bills of material, computer programs are available to develop **summarized** bills. In these, each item appears only once and the quantity per unit of product is the total needed in all applications of each item.

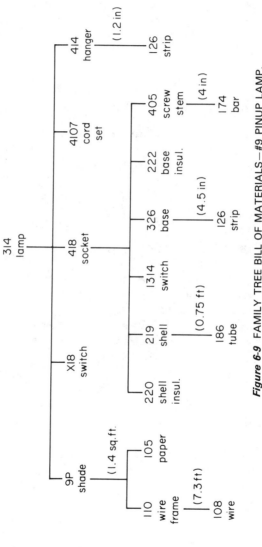

Figure 6-9 FAMILY TREE BILL OF MATERIALS—#9 PINUP LAMP.

Mfg. code 314

Part number	Description	Quantity required	Source
X18	Switch	1	Purchased
Y2L	Socket	1	Manufactured
1314	Switch	1	Purchased
219	Shell	1	Manufactured
186	Tube	0.75 ft	Purchased
326	Base	1	Manufactured
126	Strip	4.5 in	Purchased
220	Shell insul.	1	Purchased
222	Base insul.	1	Purchased
405	Screw stem	1	Manufactured
174	Bar	4 in	Purchased
9P	Shade	1	Manufactured
105	Paper	1.4 sq.ft.	Purchased
110	Frame	1	Manufactured
108	Wire	7.3 ft.	Purchased
414	Hanger	2	Manufactured
126	Strip	1.2 in	Purchased
4107	Cord set	1	Purchased

Figure 6-10 FULL INDENTED BILL OF MATERIALS—#9 PINUP LAMP.

All good computer programs for processing bills of material are capable of automatically assigning **low-level codes**; these indicate the lowest level at which an item appears in any bill of materials in which it is used. The principal use of these codes is in determining when an MRP program has accumulated all requirements for a component and can then proceed to apply on hand inventory and on order amounts against these to calculate net requirements. For example, in Figure 6-9, the no. 126 strip appears on levels 2 and 3; total requirements for the strip would not be developed until amounts needed to make the no. 326 base were determined. The low-level code literally tells the computer when to calculate net requirements for each item. Care should be taken if level codes are used in other applications. Computer programs will always determine the proper lowest-level code as new items are added to bill of materials files but *they may not* reduce the level code as items are eliminated. This poses no problem in MRP netting calculations but may have a significant effect on other uses of the level codes.

When bills of material were handled manually, a common form was the **add-and-delete** bill (also known as **same-as-except** and **comparative** bills). Such a bill could be developed for a new item simply by deleting and adding items to an existing bill. This had the real advantage of highlighting specific differences between similar products, in addition to making the paper work simpler. This form of the bill of materials, however, does not lend itself to use in MRP programs and other modern planning applications and is unnecessary with computer bill processing programs.

Companies manufacturing one-of-a-kind products similar in general configuration (such as ships, heavy machinery, or construction equipment), find a **generic** bill of materials useful. This has arbitrarily assigned part numbers and general descriptions of components and serves two purposes:

1. As a checklist to insure that no components are overlooked in design and procurement.

2. To develop schedules for preproduction activities, including cost estimating, design, tooling, capacity planning, processing and the like.

To permit advance release of some details before design work is completed, **partial** bills of material are issued, so that preproduction, materials procurement and other necessary activities can begin. This is best handled together with generic bills showing both released and unreleased items. Partial bills are also useful in developing and tracking actual cost and production information via the formal system instead of depending on subsystems.

Items other than materials included directly in the products are being included in bills of material to improve the ability to plan and control such materials better. These include cleaning solvents in pharmaceutical, chemical and food processing, testing reagents, tooling, grinding wheels and similar items consumed in the processing. Other special applications of bills of materials are covered in detail in the second volume (6). The use of specially structured bills of material in the technique of *overplanning* is presented in Chapter 7, where master planning is discussed. Chapter 4 in the second volume (6) covers applications of bills of material in many situations.

Principle 24. Bills of material form the framework of modern systems; they must be highly accurate and properly structured.

Engineering Change Control

Because of the key role of the bill of materials, a necessary adjunct to processing programs for bills of material is a set of programs to handle engineering design changes. The basic purpose of these programs is to select the correct formats of bills of material in future materials planning. Engineering changes result from a variety of causes—product improvement, manufacturing problems, cost reduction, quality improvement, product life and government regulations are the principal causes.

Timing of the introduction of the change can be based on any of the following:

1. Temporary need of overcoming some transient difficulty

2. Immediate need (possibly including recall or retrofitting products in use) for function, safety, health or legal reasons

3. Availability of new item(s) to take advantage of the change at the earliest possible moment

4. Minimum cost, including obsolete inventory, tooling, regulatory body approval, equipment alterations, etc.

5. Specific time or unit of product (serial number) to coincide with several other changes (block changes) or to provide a specific configuration to customers

The second category is often called *mandatory*, while the others are known as *optional*. A more complete discussion of the factors influencing the timing of changes and methods of handling data collection and decision making is given in the second volume (6). Among the important considerations in timing are:

1. Depletion of existing component and product inventories

2. Service (spare) parts needs

3. Availability of new items—raw material, tooling, equipment, etc.

4. Impact on plant or vendor capacity

5. Competitive position

6. Profit contribution

7. Regulatory-body approval

8. Product descriptive manual changes

Several techniques are available to introduce engineering changes properly. The most common utilizes an *effectivity date* determined by careful consideration of relevant factors such as those listed above. This date is then entered into the product structure file for both the new and superseded components, as shown in Figure 6-11(a). The computer is thus instructed to use the no. 1314 switch through 09/15 and to start using the no. 1369 switch on 09/16. The date is set to coincide with the availability of the new switches from the supplier.

Under certain circumstances, a very simple (if artificial) bill of materials can be used, as in Figure 6-11(b), to link existing and new components. This requires that the new item replace the old *in every application* in bills of materials (except in spares usage, of course). This is useful when the change is to be effected when all (or down to a specific amount) of the old item are to be used; MRP uses up the existing item and calls for quantities of the new when needed. As indicated in Figure 6-11(b), several changes are necessary in item master data on the existing items:

1. The lot-sizing rule should be set to order discrete quantities needed in each time period (lot-for-lot).

2. Lead time should be set to zero so that the new item is needed *at the same time* as the old one.

3. Safety stock should also be zero if it is desired to use up all the existing item. If some quantity is to be retained for service or other usage, this quantity should be put in the safety stock record.

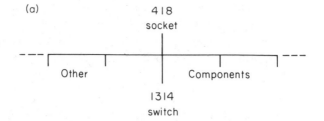

(a)   4 1 8
                                socket

        Other   Components

                                1 3 1 4
                                switch

Engineering Change Notice # 927 directs replacement of
all # 1314 Switches with # 1369 Switch as soon as it can
be obtained

			Effectivity	
Part no.	Description	ECN	Status	Date
1314	Switch	927	Delete	09/15
1369	Switch	927	Add	09/16

(b)   1314   (Set OQ = discrete)
                           switch   (Set L.T. = 0)
                                        (Set SS = 0 or
                                            balance desired)

                            1369
                           switch

Figure 6-11 EFFECTIVITY DATE BILL OF MATERIALS CHANGE.

When such bills of material are used for costing, one item must have zero
cost in its file. If product costs using existing items are desired, set the cost of the
new item equal to zero and vice versa. Pick lists can be produced calling for the
new item as an alternate to the existing one. Use of this technique may also trigger
signals on purchased items which are not supposed to have bills of materials. Obviously, considerable work is involved in adjusting files, and full understanding
by users is essential if this simple technique is to be used effectively. It can be helpful
when it is difficult to set a valid effectivity date because of changing demand, yield
problems and the like. It substitutes the work of altering files for constant monitoring of effectivity dates. Note that product structure files should periodically be
purged of obsolete bills in all cases.

Serial number effectivity is a more complex problem. The serial number used
for control of the timing of the change is usually assigned to the top level product.
It is a mistake to attempt to carry this down through all levels when *planning*
materials. To do so requires a very large amount of data storage and considerably
longer run times; this is justified only when a few, expensive products are involved.
The best solution is to use one of the techniques shown in Figure 6-11 to attempt
to use up most of the existing item and to get the new item about the right time.
Unless very expensive materials are involved, a cushion of existing items can be

planned. When it is time to *execute* the plan, the proper bill of materials can be selected for each serially numbered product.

When expensive materials are involved or when very tight control of changes with serial numbers is required, the master schedule must contain *both* product identifying (model and serial) numbers and net change updating of the MRP program is necessary. Batches of the product below the cutoff serial number in the MPS will then be run with the existing bills and others at and above this serial number will use the changed bill. When the change occurs at middle and lower levels of the bills of material, tight discipline in manufacturing operations is needed to insure using the proper combination of components in the finished products. Because such discipline is difficult to obtain and can be expensive, it is best to avoid assigning serial numbers until final assembly begins or, better still, *after* production has been completed.

Engineering changes greatly complicate the problem of furnishing the correct service parts to customers using the products. For large, complex machinery such as machine tools, power generation equipment and ships, a dossier containing drawings, specifications and a complete bill of materials for the unit as actually built should be prepared for each unit. Copies are given to the customer and one or more retained by the manufacturer to be used when service work or spare parts are required.

For higher volume products like automobiles, home appliances and power tools, even a reasonable number of engineering changes can make the problem of spares unmanageable. The best solution is the *block change*, where many optional changes are implemented simultaneously. This has several advantages in addition to better control of spares:

1. More accurate bills of material
2. More stable, simpler materials planning
3. More accurate cost information
4. Less disturbance of operations
5. Clearer, more accurate documentation

Engineering Change Historical Records

Good configuration control is mandatory for companies in defense, aerospace, drug, atomic energy and food-processing industries; it is a requirement for sound manufacturing planning and control in all others. In addition to part numbering, bill structuring and change control covered already, a comprehensive historical file is needed. This has many uses including determining proper spares, identifying problem sources and causes, locating potential or real defective products and providing data in legal actions.

A typical historical record of engineering design changes includes the following:

1. Part number of component or product
2. New part number superseding it, effectivity date and engineering change number (ECN)
3. Old part number is superseded, effectivity date and ECN
4. Engineering change codes indicating primary reasons for each change
5. Other products or components included in the same change

Responsibility for maintaining these historical data usually is placed on design engineering. Large defense, aerospace and electronics manufacturers, however, set up separate organization groups called *manufacturing specifications* or something similar; their responsibilities include the historical file, together with all other basic files and records.

Historical data for engineering changes can be stored in a variety of ways:

1. *Paper files* are now obsolete.
2. *Computer files* are still expensive because of high volumes of data, although costs are dropping. Bill processor programs provide easy chaining of ECN's to trace history. Storage of complete bills is not necessary, too expensive and too slow in retrieving. Tape files are preferred over disk.
3. *Microfilm and microfiche* are inexpensive and flexible and allow easy retrieval.

Such files find many applications in addition to the primary one of recording engineering changes. They are useful to customers, marketing, sales, patent, legal, quality, planning accounting and production people as well as engineers. Like all files necessary for planning and control of manufacturing, they are worth keeping only when accurate.

Principle 25. Control of engineering design changes to bills of material are as vital to a company's success as the new designs.

Mechanics of MRP

Full, detailed, net, time-phased MRP attempts to set up a very rigorous model representing the way materials will move through a manufacturing plant (or plants) or through a distribution system. Bills of material determine the items that must be scheduled or stocked as well as the sequence and timing in which they are procured from outside sources or manufactured within a plant. The size of the time period (called the **bucket**), usually days (misnamed "bucketless") or weeks (rarely months,) establishes the precision of the plan.

More precise plans are not necessarily more accurate. Inaccurate data, poor discipline and overambitious plans make the model developed in MRP a very poor representation of the environment. More frequent use of the replanning capability of MRP does not help. These two common misconceptions, precision versus accuracy and replanning versus execution, are discussed fully in the second volume (6).

Data included in MRP displays include some or all of the following:

1. **A header** contains a variety of information on each item being planned, including part number, description, quantity now on hand, unit of measure, whether purchased or manufactured (sometimes both), ABC classification, lot-sizing quantity or code for calculating, standard lead time, planned safety stock, responsible planner code, standard cost and quantity allocated. Occasionally other data, like the date of the last transaction, starting work center, the last cycle count date and similar special use information are also included. The more data included, the longer the time to print it, the more cluttered the displays and the greater the amount of paper output. Data needed only occasionally can be accessed when needed by inquiring via the computer data base.

2. **Time period designations** are most often arranged horizontally (like Figure 6-5), but are sometimes done vertically (like Figure 6-12). A *past due* period, which is sometimes subdivided into a number of past periods is always included. Some companies show only a limited number of near future periods in printouts plus a "total beyond," to conserve paper and the user's time.

3. **Requirements** in each time period are generated by plans to manufacture parent items or fill branch warehouse needs.

4. **Open orders** in proper time periods (best described as *will get* and most frequently called *scheduled receipts*) show quantities scheduled to be received in the period indicated when firm, released orders are filled.

5. **Projected available quantities** (best called *will have*) are shown in each time period. Most MRP programs deduct planned safety stocks and allo-

On hand = 1244   ABC = A
U/M = pieces   Safety stock = 0
Lead time = 4 weeks   Order quantity = lot for lot

Week	Requests	Open orders	Projected available	Planned Release	Planned Receipt	Action
17			744			
18			744	256		Order
19	500		244			
20			244			
21			244	500		Order
22	500		-256		256	Receive
23						
24						
25	500		-500		500	Receive
:						
:						

Figure 6-12 #9P SHADE MATERIALS PLAN.

cated quantities from current inventories to get available-to-plan figures to start the MRP netting. Fewer do not, but net to the planned safety stock, scheduling planned orders to come in when the projected available balance drops below safety stock. A few companies time-phase allocations and deduct them from available balances in the proper period. Most users add released open orders to available data but do not add planned orders, letting projected available data become negative and progressively larger. This indicates the period in which the item will drop below planned safety stock level, if any, or will go out of stock unless action is taken earlier to release a replenishment order.

6. **Planned order due** in the proper time periods (best called *need,* or sometimes *plan due*) shows the quantity and time periods in which orders are planned to be completed to meet net requirements. This is often omitted from printouts.

7. **Planned order release** in the proper time periods (best called *start* or sometimes *plan release*) shows the quantity and time periods in which orders are planned to be released to match planned orders to be completed.

The variety of techniques for calculating economic order quantities are covered in detail in Chapter 3; their strengths, weaknesses and problems in applying them are discussed in the second volume (6). Techniques for determining planned safety-stock levels with order points are covered in Chapter 5; there are no valid, rigorous techniques for use in MRP. None of the statistical distributions fits the lumpy, erratic, limited variety of demands experienced in most dependent demand situations well enough to warrant the necessary calculations. A logical method of planning for extra *sets* of components to provide flexibility in meeting variations in level and mix of customer demand is described in the section ''Overplanning the MPS for Flexibility'' in Chapter 7. MRP programs perform far better when *no safety stock* is planned; there are only a very few exceptions to this, discussed in the second volume (6).

The mechanics of MRP applied to the full hierarchy of components of the no. 9 pinup lamp are shown in Figure 6-13. This traces the complete flow of netting and time-phasing calculations from the MPS for the lamp down through the no. 418 socket assembly, no. 219 shell, and no. 186 tube. Similar calculations would be made, of course, for all components; the conventional MRP display would show each item separately, usually printed out in sequence by part number and sorted by planner, not in parent-component relation of Figure 6-13.

Socket assembly no. 418 is used on all lamps and receives requirements from each MPS, including the no. 9 pinup. For clarity, these are shown alone in weeks 16, 19, 22, and 25. Obviously, requirements for the no. 418 socket in other weeks result from schedules to build several other lamps. Because it is a simple subassembly, lead time for the socket is only one week, but it is an important A item. Therefore, its order quantity is small, being stated as a 3-weeks' supply (period order quantity).

Shell no. 219 is used only on this socket assembly, is a B item and has a lead time of 2 weeks because of heat treating operations needed in its processing. An

Mfg. code # 314	Week											
	14	15	16	17	18	19	20	21	22	23	24	25
Master production schedule			500			500			500			500

On hand = 700
U/M = pieces
Lead time = 1 week

ABC = A
Safety stock = 0
Order quantity = 3 weeks

Manufactured socket assembly #418	Past due	Week											
		14	15	16	17	18	19	20	21	22	23	24	25
Requirements		400	300	500	400	300	500	400	300	500	400	300	500
Will get				1200									
Will have	700	300	– –	700	300	– –	-500	-900	-1200	-1700	-2100	-2400	-2900
Need							1200			1200			1200
Start						1200			1200			1200	

On hand = 2800
U/M = pieces
Lead time = 2 weeks

ABC = B
Safety stock = 0
Order quantity = 4000

Manufactured shell #219	Past due	Week											
		14	15	16	17	18	19	20	21	22	23	24	25
Requirements						1200			1200			1200	
Will get													
Will have	2800	2800	2800	2800	2800	1600	1600	1600	400	400	400	-800	-800
Need												4000	
Start										4000			

On hand = 6
U/M = thousands of feet
Lead time = 8 weeks

ABC = C
Safety stock = 3
Order quantity = 12

Purchased tube #186	Past due	Week											
		14	15	16	17	18	19	20	21	22	23	24	25
Requirements										3			
Will get													
Will have	3	3	3	3	3	3	3	3	3	– –	– –	– –	– –
Need										12			
Start		12											

Figure 6-13 MATERIAL-REQUIREMENTS PLAN—#9 PINUP LAMP AND COMPONENTS.

EOQ of 4000 has been calculated for the shell; since requirements are in lots of 1200, excess inventory results although no safety socket is planned.

Tube no. 186 also has only one parent, the shell, is a C item, and must be ordered in minimum lots of 12,000 feet. Safety stock has been planned to guard against vendor delays or poor quality. The change in unit of measure and the length of tubing needed per piece are reflected by showing 3000 feet of tubing required to make 4000 pieces of shell.

Several things are noteworthy in Figure 6-13:

1. Simple words—will get, will have, and so on—are used. Many problems of user misunderstanding and confusion would be avoided if similar simple terminology were used more often.

2. Tube #186 is shown as needing to be ordered *now* to meet a requirement for building 500 #9 pinup lamps in week 25. This is the sum of all the lead times in this hierarchy of components involved. Any changes in the interim (design, larger-than-normal orders, record errors, etc.) will affect *released*, not only planned, orders.

3. The elegance and utility value of these calculations will be destroyed by errors in bills of material, on hand balances and open order quantities, by lack of capacity or discipline to produce the required items on schedule and by scrap or rework.

4. The planned safety stock on tube #186 causes the planned replenishment order to be scheduled 9 weeks before it is really needed—and its lead time is only 8 weeks! While MRP can handle the calculations and replanning, the price of failure to *solve* manufacturing and procurement problems is very high.

5. Lot-sizes mismatched with requirements result in costly excess inventories, as on shell #219.

6. Requirements for data and order quantities in any time period are *not* associated with any specific day in the period. It simply means "some time during the week."

Some convention must be adopted when a calendar date instead of a week number is used to label the period; this is usually the first or last day. Precision and planning are incompatible. Soft (planning) data cannot be precise; hard (execution) data, must be precise, up-to-date and accurate. This is discussed fully in the second volume (6).

Principle 26. MRP simply mechanizes the fundamental logic of manufacturing.

Figure 6-13 illustrates how the explosion process is carried out, beginning with the MPS. Requirements from the MPS of all products on common components are accumulated in the proper time periods on each. When all requirements have been totaled, available on-hand inventory (minus planned safety stock, if any) is reduced period by period by requirements. Released, open orders (will get) are added in the proper time periods. In the period when the projected available figure (will have) becomes negative, a planned order is scheduled to be completed (need). If safety stock has not been prededucted, these orders will be scheduled in the period when the available quantity becomes less than safety stock. Release periods (start) for planned orders are determined by deducting the planned lead time from the need period.

When these calculations have been completed on all level 1 items for which total requirements have been accumulated (as indicated by its low-level code), start-order quantities are dropped as requirements on level 2 items, and the netting and time-phasing is repeated on those for which total requirements have now been developed. Note that *planned orders,* not requirements, for parent items determine component requirements. These calculations thus continue level by level, period by period until all components and all periods in MPS bills of materials and the planning horizon have been covered. The result is a fully integrated plan of when materials should be brought into and move through a plant to support the MPS.

Principle 27. Materials planning simply initiates the procurement process; execution completes it.

Enhancements to MRP

To assist people in using MRP, various enhancements have been added to the basic, elegant program just described. The power and potential difficulties of each is discussed more fully in the second volume (6); suffice it to say here that they should be employed only when they serve a real need and when users understand them fully. *Unnecessary sophistication adds cost, not value.*

As level-by-level calculations proceed down bills of material and lead times are offset for planned orders, the horizon in which data occur grows progressively shorter. A variety of **horizon-filler calculations** are available to extend data through the full planning horizon at all levels. Typical of these are average requirements per period and repeating the previous 4 (or more or fewer) weeks. Since arbitrary data developed by the calculations may affect the timing and quantity of released orders at low levels, care should be taken in their selection.

To provide exception reporting, a variety of **action notices** can be used to alert users to specific conditions without requiring them to study each component display. Precautions in their selection and the use of such notices as a diagnostic tool for system health are covered in the second volume. Although many more are available in modern MRP software packages, the popular ones are:

Release order	Order Past Due	Data missing in
Expedite order	No Requirements	this field
Delay order	Future order covers	
Cancel order	this requirement	

Pegging is the technique of identifying the parent item that is generating requirements on a component. Requirements from several parents on a component in a single period appear as a total. Displays in MRP programs are not arranged when printed to show parent-component relationships but illustrate data for each item separately. Users need to know frequently which parent caused what requirement, particularly when adequate stocks of components are not available. A where-used bill of materials, of course, will show all parents but only one or two may be involved in the critical period. Pegging provides information on the component display, as shown in Figure 6-14, which leads the user directly to the correct parent.

Such pegging is called **full single-level pegging** and identifies the time period, the parent item and the quantity required for it. When items are common to many parents and parents are ordered frequently, this requires significant storage capacity for the data and long printing time. Note that one parent will appear many times on each component's display. Since the parent display is (or can be) also available for the user's use, file space and printing time can be saved by **partial single-level pegging,** which gives the part numbers only of parent items causing requirements. This can be limited further to show only those parent items involved in a short horizon. The second volume (6) contains other uses and cautions when pegging is used.

In some situations it is desirable to override the way the MRP program normally handles planned orders. For example, the number of full sets of components may be less than needed to complete the next lot of the normal order quantity for a parent item, or the next lot of an item may have to be completed in less than the planned lead time. For several reasons it may be undesirable to release firm orders at the current time, which would solve both problems. The **firm planned order** forces the computer to accept special lead times or order quantities for any order so designated, which is otherwise handled like all other planned orders. Figure 6-15 compares the ways in which planned, released and firm planned orders are handled in MRP programs. Since such special orders obscure the normal logic of the system, they should be used sparingly and only by qualified users. The second volume (6) contains further comments on these and other special orders as well as on other enhancements.

Allocations

When planned orders are released for procurement or production, specific changes are made in MRP data. For purchased materials, these changes are relatively simple and easily illustrated. Using the #186 tube in Figure 6-13 as an example, a decision to release a purchase order to the supplier would result in

1. Removing the order quantity (12) from both START and NEED lines to the WILL GET line in week 22.
2. Changing the WILL HAVE line from 0 to 12 for week 22 and all subsequent weeks (up to the next requirement, of course).

These changes are usually made by a computer subroutine program called **order release.** Nothing further is needed for a purchased item.

For manufactured components, however, the situation is much more complex because these have components also. The action of deleting the planned order and adding the released order is identical to that taken on purchased materials.

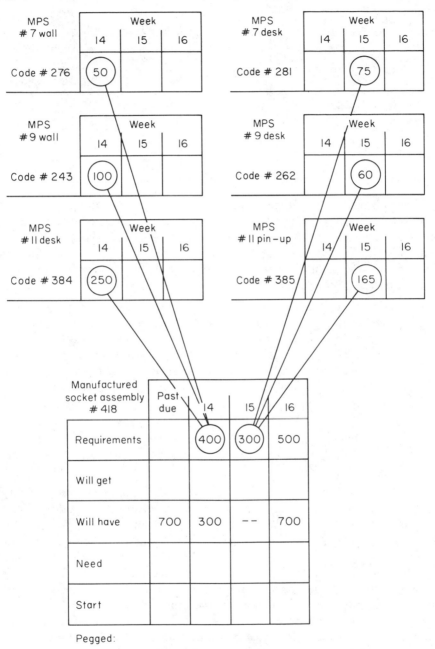

Figure 6-14 PEGGED REQUIREMENTS—SOCKET ASSEMBLY #418.

	Exploded to lower level ?	Rescheduled automatically ?	Exception messages generated ?	User control of quantity, start, and need dates ?
Planned order	Yes	Yes	No	Only via rules in MRP program
Released order	Only when first released	No	Yes	Yes
Firm planned order	Yes	No	No	Yes

Figure 6-15 MRP ORDER HANDLING.

However, planned orders generate requirements on components in the START week and released orders show quantities in the week the order is scheduled to be completed. To keep parent and component records in balance, (Orlicky calls it "maintaining interlevel equilibrium"), the quantity of each component needed to produce the quantity ordered for the parent is **allocated** (also called *reserved, mortgaged,* and *assigned*). This is done in two ways:

1. The most common and the easiest way is in a single separate file with quantities in it appearing in the header of the MRP display. All allocations for any component are grouped and have to be pegged if the user wants to identify specific quantities associated with individual parent orders. Figure 6-16 shows the results from firming up the planned order for #418 socket assembly and the allocation on #219 shell for week 18.

2. A time-phased file similar to requirements data on an MRP display permits releasing future orders if desired without placing an immediate demand on all components as the separate header file does. This would be useful where erratic ordering would make it desirable to release orders early frequently.

Allocated quantities substitute for component requirements when planned orders for parents are converted to released orders. This situation is transient, lasting only until the allocated quantity is delivered from stores inventory to work-in-process. When actual physical issues are reported, the On Hand and Allocated quantities are both reduced *by the amount issued.* If this is equal to the quantity ordered and allocated, the MRP display data remains in balance. If it is less, a back order requisition should be generated to insure delivery of the balance unless the present order quantity is reduced; in that case the remaining allocated balance for this order must be deleted. The MRP rerun will rebalance the planned orders for the parent to recognize the smaller quantity on the parent order. If the issued quantity exceeds that allocated, the excess quantity allocated must be deleted to avoid understating other allocations. The excess issued is viewed by MRP as an inventory "loss" and—when rerun—it will advance future planned orders unless some way is found to account for the excess. Discipline in executing the plan is essential to avoiding a multitude of "tinkering" adjustments.

On hand = 700 ABC = A
U/M = pieces Safety stock = O
Lead time = 1 week Order quantity = 3 weeks

Manufactured socket assembly # 418	Part due	Week									
		17	18	19	20	21	22	23	24	25	
Requirements		400	300	500	400	300	500	400	300	500	
Will get				(1200)							
Will have	700	300	-/-	700	300	--	-500	-900	-1200	-1700	
Need				(1200)			1200		1200		
Start			(1200)			1200			1200		

On hand = 2800 Alloc = 1200 ABC = B
U/M = pieces Safety stock = O
Lead time = 2 weeks Order quantity = 4000

Manufactured shell # 219	Part due	Week									
		17	18	19	20	21	22	23	24	25	
						1200			1200		
	2800	1600	1600	1600	1600	400	400	400	-800		
									4000		
							4000				

Figure 6-16 ORDER RELEASE AND ALLOCATION.

The allocation routine, whether single or time-phased, provides an excellent way to determine whether or not all the needed components are available to permit releasing an order. If there is a shortage of any item, it will be revealed by a negative number in WILL HAVE (or Projected Available) data. Called *staging on paper,* this allows the formal planning system to be used to develop shortage lists as far into the future as desired without physically segregating the materials. The advantages are obvious. An allocation program is both a planning and an execution technique. The latter application is discussed fully in the second volume (6).

Updating MRP

Manual materials plans, in addition to being poorly integrated, literally were almost never up-to-date. Changes in sales forecasts, releases of new designs and many other factors just could not be handled promptly. The development of computer programs provided the capability of getting full integration and of keeping the plan more up-to-date by frequent rerunning of all the data. Called **regeneration,** this approach discards one plan and develops a completely new one. Because of the long computer run time required, it is usually done weekly or at longer intervals.

Experienced users of MRP usually develop a desire for more specific and timely planning data and to spread the computer run more evenly during the week. This can be done by programs running only the changed portions of the data. One approach, called **requirements alteration,** introduces and processes only *changes* in the MPS; it uses the latest information found in the files (bills of material, on hand and on order balances, safety stock, lead times, etc.) which have been updated recently. Products whose MPS have not been altered would not be processed in the MRP explosion. The technique is particularly useful for adding MPS data in time periods at the far end of the planning horizon as these move into it. It is useful in focusing attention on needed actions since the action notices generated are the result of the MPS changes introduced plus those relating to component availability. Requirements alteration is usually run when a new planning period comes onto the horizon and when significant changes are made to the MPS.

Even more planning flexibility can be introduced by having the system replan data after individual transactions reporting scrap, record errors or other significant deviations from previously planned data. When done periodically, this is called **batch net change.** Where MPS changes and deviations are frequent, daily runs are made.

In more stable, disciplined environments, semiweekly, weekly or even biweekly replanning may be adequate. Regeneration runs are usually made periodically to purge accumulated errors; the period usually lengthens as better disciplines are instituted in the requirements alteration and net change transaction handling. The second volume (6) contains more in-depth discussion of the application of these techniques and of replanning versus execution activities. Figure 6-17 compares the three ways in which MRP programs can be updated.

MRP in Make-to-Order Operations

Makers of custom-built products have been slow to implement MRP programs. This resulted primarily because MRP was misunderstood to be only a full-horizon, classical net, time-phased, multilevel technique, as it is presented in most of the literature. Manufacturers of purely make-to-order products (the true *job shops*), including ships, airplanes, special machine tools and electronic units, missiles and heavy construction machinery have difficulty developing a conventional MPS; their products are very low in volume (if more than one) and are produced intermittently (if more than once). Bills of material are developed and released in fragments and

	Regeneration	Requirements alteration	Net change
Inventory, open order files updated	Yes	Yes	Yes
All master production sched. exploded	Yes	No	No
Frequency of MRP run	Weekly Bi-weekly Monthly (rare)	Daily Semi-weekly	Daily
Effects of every transaction analyzed	No	No	Yes

Figure 6-17 UPDATING MRP.

often are not final and complete until after the product has been shipped. Design changes are frequent, many occurring at the last minute during acceptance tests.

At the same time, most such manufacturers were planning to use only gross requirements and very liberal lead times for both purchased and manufactured materials. They had very little ability to net out materials already available, using only manual or crude computer subsystems. Thus they recognized that the logic of MRP applied but they did not clearly see how to apply it. Application of MRP requires:

1. Generic bills of material (see page 148) for products produced repetitively, even if fully custom-made
2. Partial release by engineering of components to schedules that meet as much as possible the needs of planning people who order materials and schedule facilities
3. Common use by engineering, planning, purchasing and production of one bill of materials file
4. Broader time buckets (weeks and months)
5. Lead times with minimum cushions

When the lead time the customer allows is significantly shorter than the total time required to procure and process materials, raw materials, some purchased components and some manufactured items must be carried in inventory. Since their requirements cannot be calculated in the standard MRP program, such materials must be obtained and controlled by

1. Classical or time-phased order point techniques (see Chapter 5)
2. Use of modular planning bills of material in MRP driven by generic master production schedules (see Chapter 7)

Tight discipline is essential in releasing bill of materials information, managing design changes, handling transactions, reporting receipts and issues, maintaining accurate inventory and open order status and, particularly, adjusting capacity to handle loads that will vary. An integrated MRP program with replanning power is not only applicable to make-to-order products, it is required.

MRP in Repetitive Manufacturing

At the other end of the scale of those who have difficulty in applying MRP programs are companies in repetitive production, where large volumes of discrete, often very different, products are made in a flow process. Typical of these products are automobiles, household appliances, television sets, radios, pharmaceuticals, toiletries and fine chemicals. The basic difficulty here is the need in conventional MRP for discrete orders for manufactured items. Such companies think rather in terms of rates of production, per shift or per day, and of cumulative totals to specific dates.

There is no difficulty with purchased materials which are planned the usual way. The planning problem is also greatly simplified by shallow bills of material and little if any stocking of such products as semifinished items, intermediates, subassemblies etc. between raw materials and finished products. Figure 6-18 shows how MRP can be adapted to repetitive manufacturing, using cumulative totals for operating days, requirements, receipts, and planned order rates. Note that WILL GET and CUM RECPTS show released order data; NEED and START data are only planned at this time. In this period, two holidays are planned, Good Friday and Memorial Day, in weeks 16 and 22. Requirements will increase twice, during weeks

Manufactured motor #13245	Past due	Week								*Holiday
		14	15	*16	17	18	19	20	21	*22
Cumulative days		69	74	78	83	88	93	98	103	107
Requirements		12	12	12	12	17	17	17	17	22
Cumulative requirements		140	152	164	176	193	210	227	244	266
Will get		12	12	10	12					
Cumulative receipts		132	144	154	166					
Will have	7	7	7	5	5	8	11	14	17	11
Need						20	20	20	20	16
Cumulative need		132	144	154	166	186	206	226	246	262
Start					20	20	20	20	16	20
Cumulative start		144	154	166	186	206	226	246	262	282

Figure 6-18 CUMULATIVE MRP FOR REPETITIVE MANUFACTURING.

18 and 22, by 5 units per week each time but production will be changed only once in week 18, increasing from 12 to 20 units per week. This will increase inventory from the present 7 to 17 until requirements change again but another production change will not be necessary until this inventory is used up. This is typical of MRP applications when production and requirements can be closely matched. Note the short lead time, also typical of repetitive manufacturing. The item being manufactured is an electric motor used on a home appliance.

When minimum production rates are considerably higher than requirements, the item will be run intermittently, building up inventory while running and drawing it down when not. The daily rate, requirements and tolerable high and low levels of inventory control the timing and number of periods in which production runs. Very little modification of the computer programs is needed to display the cumulative totals and to schedule to a given rate each period.

MRP in Process Industries

Process operations vary all the way from petroleum refining, where dedicated, single-purpose equipment is operated continously to produce a narrow line of products, to food processing, where general-purpose equipment runs intermittently to produce batches of a wide line of products. Many plants producing chemicals, pharmaceuticals and cosmetics combine several types. Conventional time-phased MRP is being applied without modification to the intermittent production of batches of such products. When a broad line of products is produced with infrequent interruptions of flow-line equipment (paper, cigarettes, soft drinks), the modified MRP programs discussed for repetitive manufacturing are used.

Continuous operation of catalytic cracking units, pipe stills and petrochemical plants in refinery operations and clay, cement and steel mills require fairly simple calculations only intermittently to balance sales, production and inventories, set flow rates for feed stocks and develop requirements for packaging materials and shipping containers, together with a very few catalysts, fillers, additives or alloying elements. The low volume of calculations requires very little computing power, although a formal, systematic approach always produces better results than fragmented manual techniques. The real problems in these operations are controlling the process (and thus the quality of products), reacting promptly to changes in feed-stock composition, coping with inflexible capacity and striking a balance between too little and too much excess capacity.

MRP: Technique versus Logic

There is no one best format for MRP; only its logic (see page 133) is universally applicable. Its application must be determined in such a way that it is suitable to the operation. Here is an example of an ingenious, effective adaptation. A well-known manufacturer of stoneware dishes produces over 1000 tons per week of some 1800 catalog items plus frequent promotions of various sets of products.

These are all made from 12 items of clays, frits and glazes, plus decorative decals and packaging materials. The supply of the 12 raw materials was planned as follows:

1. Clay requirements were calculated from ratios showing rates of usage relative to manning levels in the various processing facilities. These were checked regularly against actual consumption and adjusted to reflect the latest performance. This answered, What will we make, how many and when? in terms of clay requirements.

2. Bills of material were available showing finished products made from bisque (first firing) ware, produced from green (unfired) ware molded from clay. A major problem was evaluating relative quantities of components per unit of parent items since breakage, porosity and other causes resulted in losses up to 25% of some batches. Hence, bills were not used in ordering raw materials.

3. Raw materials were received and stored in freight cars, hopper trucks and bags on pallets. These were inventoried every day by the materials planner on the way from home to office. Simple Kardex records maintained by the planner showed on hand, issues, receipts and on order transactions and balances. This answered the question, What do we have now?

4. Details on open purchase orders of such facts as material-specification number, vendor number, purchase-order number, and rail or truck waybill number were kept on a large desk-blotter calendar in due date boxes. Materials en route were checked daily with rail and truck shippers and 3 days in advance of shipping with vendors. No purchase requisitions were needed; the planner was the buyer. This answered the question, When will we get some more?

5. Based on vendors lead times and shipping days required (about 2 weeks for rail and 1 day for trucks), the planner telephoned new order releases against blanket purchase orders on specific vendors. The planner answered, When do we need more? from the Kardex data by inspection and analysis, using requirements calculated from ratios together with manning levels set and modified at weekly production meetings.

Compare the simplicity of this with full, net, time-phased MRP in the classical display. Yet one person (with another trained as backup) used this so effectively that the company operated with *an average of only $1\frac{1}{2}$ days' supply* of raw materials and needed maximum storage capacity for only 3 days' supply. These people did not know that what they were doing was called MRP and Just-in-Time!

Principle 28. The logic of MRP is universally applicable; the way it is applied depends on the environment.

MRP techniques can do three very valuable jobs:

1. Suggest (not dictate) the proper time to release orders
2. Indicate the proper date by which orders are needed and keep these dates valid during order processing times.

3. Provide information to assist capacity requirements planning and machine and work center loading.

MRP is *not a system*. It is simply one technique (albeit an important one) in a system. Success in its use depends on the many factors discussed in this book and amplified in the second volume (6). The following contribute to the reasons for lack of success in the use of MRP:

1. It is part of an incomplete system (see Chapter 1).

2. It is driven by an invalid or mismanaged MPS (see Chapter 7).

3. Data are inaccurate.

4. Bills of material are structured improperly (see pages 143–148 in this chapter and Chapter 7).

5. Users are underqualified.

## CHAPTER SEVEN

MASTER PLANNING

The Planning Hierarchy

The planning process in a manufacturing business is a series of revisions to a hierarchy of more or less tightly integrated plans. For their own reasons, companies adopt a different number of levels in their hierarchies and call these levels a variety of names. Closer attention to this planning process in the 1970s by managers, consultants and educators has led to development of standardized names and clearer identification of the functions required to be planned. These are summarized in Figure 7-1.

Strategic plans begin with an examination of the basic nature of the business and the direction management wishes it to take in the next 5 to 10 years. Fairly specific actions are defined, obviously subject to further definition and revision as time passes. For example, new technologies and expanded geographic markets may be targeted; actual developments over time may require considerable changes in future plans. Strategic planning points general directions, not specific courses to get there and usually does not set detailed objectives. Such planning is concerned with the total business.

Each major organization group—marketing, manufacturing, engineering and finance—must have its own strategic plan. In the past, these plans frequently were poorly integrated and often were nonsupportive. While marketing was moving in the direction of attacking specific sections of a broad market requiring flexibility and a wide variety of low-volume products, manufacturing was driving for low costs, requiring stable demand, high volumes and standardized products. Also, in the

Plan horizon	Attempts to answer
Strategic plan 5 — 10 yrs	What business are we now in? What do we want to be in? What must be done now to get ready? What will be required next?
Business plan 2 — 5 yrs	How do products, markets rank now? Which are declining? How fast? Which are mature, stable? Which are growing? How fast? What new products are needed? What actions are needed?
Production plan 2 — 5 yrs	How well is present plant utilized? What demands will be made on it? What new technologies will be involved? What new products will be introduced? What products will be dropped? What new plant, equipment will be needed?
Master production schedule 1/4 — 1 yr	What specific products are to be made? How many? When? What other materials are needed? How many? When? What capacity constraints exist? What material constraints exist?

Figure 7-1 PLANNING HIERARCHY.

past, the attention of top management was on mergers, acquisitions and divestments, buying and selling businesses based on their financial performance as "cash cows," generating high volumes of cash flow, or poor return on capital. While there are real benefits from mergers (better utilization of physical resources, smoothing of demand cycles, increasing share of market, and acquiring new technologies) and while some businesses have outlived their economic lives (making horse-drawn vehicles and wooden barrels), this obsession with financial criteria and manipulation failed to recognize that *operations could be improved* by better planning and control utilizing modern techniques.

Peter Drucker (4) said that strategic planning deals with the future effects of present decisions, not with future decisions. It is not an attempt to forecast what will be done some time in the distant future but rather to decide what must be done now to prepare a company better to handle what the future might bring and, even more important, to *influence the future favorably*. Its focus is on the total business, what it is now, what it should be and what must be done now to get there.

Strategic planning sets the "big picture" framework within which all other planning and execution will be done. It defines the company's business in the broadest possible terms: not making glass bottles but providing packaging, not refining crude oil but meeting energy requirements. It identifies strengths and weaknesses in order to build on the former and compensate for the latter. It is concerned more with the environment, competition, government, availability of resources and similar factors than with internal operations. Contingency plans, exploring various reactions to unpleasant surprises, are a vital part of strategic planning. Additional comments on strategic planning are made in the second volume (10) but thorough coverage of this topic is beyond the scope of these two books.

Business plans focus on products and markets. Top management's role is to coordinate the plans of individual departments. Marketing should define the company's role in the marketplace (broad line versus special niche), set targets for the desired share of market for major product families, identify those worthy of allocating more resources, define needed new product characteristics, establish channels of distribution and set targets for customer service levels. Manufacturing should translate marketing's plans into the necessary supports in people, facilities, equipment and materials in broad, general terms. Details are unlikely to be accurate enough to warrant the effort of developing them. Engineering should develop the directions in which technology is moving and the potential effects this may have on products and processes. They should also identify research, development and application opportunities requiring actions now for future benefits. Financial plans convert the others into needed capital projections, cash flow, major budgets and profit estimates.

Business planning makes the transition from the broad, general terms of strategic planning into the more detailed production planning. Too much emphasis on (apparently) precise financial data and overreliance on tangible factors (such as equipment costs) has stifled initiative and risk-taking in several industries now in decline. Perhaps more important than the risk of doing something is the risk of *not* doing it. Risk is inherent in making future projections; business planning should not emphasize reducing risks, it should identify actions needed to maximize the benefits of taking risks.

Production plans develop the next level of detail supporting the business plans. They usually have the same horizon but focus on facilities and production required to support the business plans. The front end (1 to 2 years) is particularly important since it will interface with detailed operating plans. A typical production plan will be developed as follows:

First year, 12 monthly periods, subfamilies

Second year, four quarterly periods, families

Third year, two semiannual periods, family groups

Fourth and fifth years, annual totals, family groups

Production plans have three functions:

1. To define in more detail the manufacturing portion of the business plan

2. To set rates for manufacturing families of products

3. To provide the basis for management control of operations

To answer the questions posed in Figure 7-1 for the production plan, somewhat more detail is needed than is usually provided in business plans. These are usually stated in financial terms, but manufacturing needs units of products for plant utilization, future loads and physical capital budgeting, all part of production planning. Equivalent units expressing product relationships meaningful to manufacturing (a two-door refrigerator/freezer unit might be equivalent to two standard refrigerators) can be used for capacity and cost determinations.

Very adequate management controls can be developed using the rates of production of families of items stated in production plans. Figure 7-2 shows a common application of a production plan for management review. Often called a sales-production-inventory (S-P-I) or production-sales-inventory (P-S-I) report, this plans and monitors the total inputs to and outputs from finished product inventories. Such reports form the basis for effective control of inventories and production through the *totals*. This is discussed in detail in Chapters 8 and 9. These reports also provide data for developing the master production schedule which is discussed later in this chapter.

Ideally, every plan would include provision for data comparing actual performance and every performance report would show planned data. This is difficult to do with strategic and business plans and is really necessary only at fairly long intervals. It should be done regularly and often for production plans and master production schedules. These plans provide sufficient information in detail to make such comparisons useful as early warning signals of the need for corrective action. In Figure 7-2, for example, tolerances defining significant deviations have been

Period		1	2	3	4	5	6	7	8	9
Production (P)		(tolerance = ± $100)								
Planned	Period	450	450	450	450	450	450	475	500	500
	Cumulative		900	1350	1800	2250	2700	3175	3675	4175
Actual	Period	435	440	450	430	445	430	460	480	475
	Cumulative		875	1325	1755	2200	2630	3090	3570	4045
Deviation	Period	(15)	(10)	—	(20)	(5)	(20)	(15)	(20)	(25)
	Cumulative		(25)	(25)	(45)	(50)	(70)	(85)	(105)	(130)
Sales (S)		(tolerance = ± $100)								
Planned	Period	450	450	450	475	475	475	500	500	500
	Cumulative		900	1350	1825	2300	2775	3275	3775	4275
Actual	Period	430	470	480	415	425	460	510	490	480
	Cumulative		900	1380	1795	2220	2680	3190	3680	4160
Deviation	Period	(20)	20	30	(60)	(50)	(15)	10	(10)	(20)
	Cumulative		0	30	(30)	(80)	(95)	(85)	(95)	(115)
Inventory (I)		(starting = $3000)		(tolerance = ± $200)						
Planned		3000	3000	3000	2975	2950	2925	2900	2900	2900
Actual		3005	2975	2945	2960	2980	2950	2900	2890	2885
Deviation		5	(25)	(55)	(15)	30	25	—	(10)	(15)

All data in $000

Figure 7-2 P-S-I REPORT.

set and sales and production are both low, although inventories are in line. Monitoring these three factors independently would not reveal the true situation as effectively. Many managers prefer a cumulative graphical presentation like Figure 7-3 (the time scales have been shifted for clarity) instead of the tabular format of Figure 7-2. For additional examples and discussion, see the second volume (10).

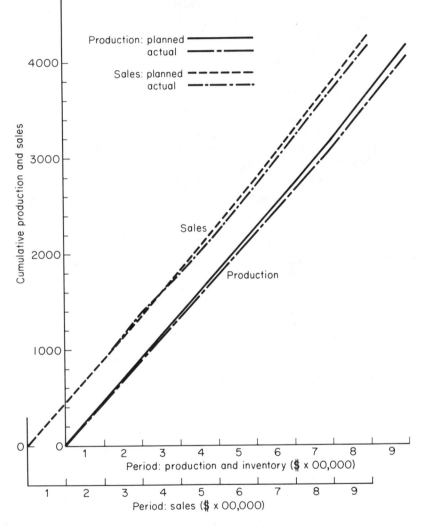

Figure 7-3 GRAPHICAL P-S-I REPORT.

Broad experience with production plans indicates the following characteristics:

1. Formats are essentially the same for job shop, intermittent, process and repetitive manufacturing; time periods and horizons may be different.
2. The basic logic questions (see page 133) also apply to them.

3. The temptation to plan more than can be produced is irresistible—and too often fatal to good results.

4. Careful thought in defining families and aggregations will contribute more to good results then providing systems capable of handling more details.

5. Teamwork among *all* managers is crucial to sound planning and good results.

Different portions of the production-plan horizon are used for different purposes. Data at the front end are converted and compared to the MPS driving the formal materials plan and are also used via rough-cut capacity-requirements planning for input/output control of work-in-process and lead times. Farther out, production plans provide information for work force totals for hiring, training, transfer or layoff. The same data are used for adding, replacing or removing capital equipment and expanding or contracting plant space. Skills and equipment to handle new technologies usually relate to the middle range of the plan. Capital requirements need to be evaluated over the full horizon.

Principle 29. Data farther out in the planning horizon can and should be in less detail, more aggregated.

The Master Production Schedule (MPS)

Even more detail is needed in the master production schedule than in production plans since it drives the formal system integrating priority (material), capacity and cost planning and control. Products specified in the MPS must be described by specific, individual bills of material. The MPS has three functions:

1. To interlock the business plans and day-by-day operating plans

2. To provide a "control handle" for management on daily operations

3. To drive the formal, integrated planning and control system.

In the absence of a well-integrated formal planning capability provided by modern systems, managers have no way to determine whether or not the dozens of people making hundreds of decisions on thousands of items are working in support of strategic business and production plans. Present day knowledge and modern information management systems make possible a fully integrated planning hierarchy characterized by

1. Shorter horizons and time periods from top to bottom

2. Increasing detail from top to bottom

3. Periodic replanning capable of maintaining the integrity of all plans

4. A variety of plans developed to meet specific needs

Principle 30. Stand-alone, independent and multipurpose plans are worse than useless; they are dangerous.

The MPS focuses on products to be made and, through the detailed planning system, identifies the resources (materials, work force, plant equipment and capital) needed and the timing of the need. Although now widely accepted and used, the name is poor. *Master* and *production* are good terms properly applied here; however, while *schedule* properly connotes timing and specifics, it conveys to middle and top managers a picture of minutia, order dates and other (to them) trivia. A change in name is now too late. Their misconceptions must be overcome, however; the MPS provides one of their **handles** on the business (13).

The fundamental purpose of the MPS is *to initiate procurement of the resources necessary to implement the plan.* Note the emphasis on *starting,* not completing, the processes of getting the needed materials, people, equipment, capital, and the like. The planning phase projects estimates of how many of what will be needed when; the execution determines finally—usually much later—specifically what will be obtained and produced. This is a vital distinction, not just semantics.

What the MPS Is

By definition, the MPS is a detailed statement of how many items are planned to be produced and when. Thus any company's MPS is a matrix of items scheduled and time periods covered *for each item* scheduled. The time periods used most often are weekly, although occasionally biweekly or monthly periods are used for large, complex products like power generation equipment and ships. Some theorists, carried away by the supposed power of replanning, advocate daily time buckets but these are impractical; they may be more precise but they cannot be more accurate. This is discussed in Chapter 2 of the second volume (10). The MPS states what can and should be produced; it is not a **wish-list** of what management would like to produce.. The problems resulting from overstating the MPS are very immediate and serious. They are discussed also in detail in the second volume (10).

As stated earlier, the MPS provides management with one of its handles on the business. It does this by providing

1. A means to authorize and control work force levels, inventory investment and cash flow supporting customer service, profitability and capital investment goals.

2. A mechanism to coordinate marketing, sales, engineering, manufacturing, and finance activities to develop a common plan and improve teamwork.

3. A device to reconcile marketing and sales need with manufacturing capabilities.

4. A means to measure the performance of each group in executing the common plan.

What the MPS Is Not

A sales forecast is not an MPS; it projects customer demand, while the MPS states production to meet this demand. Major differences arise when batches are produced intermittently to meet steady demand, when production is level but demand is seasonal or erratic and when finished goods inventories are being raised or lowered significantly. Only rarely, when these situations do not exist, will the MPS and the sales forecast be identical.

The MPS also is not an assembly or packaging schedule, the latter are execution activities. For consumer products, pharmaceuticals, cosmetics, foods, fine chemicals and simple hard goods (those with few levels and components in bills of material), the MPS and finishing schedules may be identical in the numbers used, but their conceptual differences must be kept clearly in mind if they are to be applied properly for maximum benefits.

Principle 31. The MPS drives the planning, not the execution, process.

Inputs to the MPS

Many factors must be given consideration in developing the MPS; these are both technical and nontechnical and include:

1. Whether products are stocked, built-to-order or a combination of both.
2. Number and location of warehousing and producing facilities
3. Service part policies
4. Customer service goals
5. Interplant transfers of components
6. Make versus buy policies
7. Customer orders and demand forecasts
8. Safety stock levels
9. Policies on stability of employment and plant utilization
10. Product structure, as defined by bills of material

Obviously, preparing the MPS is not a clerical task. It is a high-level planning operation which should be thoroughly understood and directed by top managers.

For both stocked and made-to-order products, the logic of the time-phased order point provides an effective way to consider simultaneously a number of stocking locations, demand forecasts, safety stock levels, customer orders already received and production lots already in process in developing input data for the MPS. The mechanics of the technique are described in Chapter 5 and its application to finished-product planning is discussed more fully in the second volume (10). The planned order data output of the time-phased order point provide a starting point for master scheduling each product. The S-P-I report also is used frequently to develop inputs to the MPS; note that is logic is very similar to that of the time-phased order point.

The MPS can be set up in two different ways:

1. Showing *quantities of end items* (the highest level of the bills of material used with the MPS to develop MRP output) *finished* and ready for delivery to customers, warehouses or affiliated plants

2. Stating *numbers of sets of components* ready to build the end items in the quantities stated in the MRP *starting* in the time period used

The selection of one of these ways will be based on the type of product. When a product offers several options to customers on functional features (not just color or packaging) or if a variety of attachments and accessories can be included if selected by customers, the MPS is stated as method 2. This type of product includes computers, machine tools, automobiles, trucks, airplanes and heavy off-highway vehicles. This way is also used for simpler products with many common parts or ingredients if finishing is quick. Typical of these are pens, automatic pencils, telephones and electronic calculators. When the first way is selected, the planned order receipt quantity and timing provide input from the time-phased order point to the MPS; when the MPS states sets of parts to begin finishing, the planned order release data are used. The mechanics of this are illustrated in Chapter 3.

The MPS must contain all significant demands on plant facilities. These come from customers for products and service parts, from distributors, dealers, and company distribution centers warehousing them, from affiliated facilities using components or products, and from plans to build up inventories of such items (note that such demand is negative when inventories are being reduced). Loads on the plant will be understated significantly if any of these is omitted.

In a hierarchy of feeder-user plants, the MPS for the feeder plant must be derived from the planned orders developed by the MRP program in the user plant. In textile manufacturing, for example, yarn production must be planned to meet the needs of greige goods facilities which, in turn, must support the output of materials, garments and the like in the finishing plants. Making independent plans for such integrated facilities is wasteful, particularly if all belong to the same corporate family. Likewise, there are real benefits for companies working closely with their suppliers even when they are in different corporations and even when the user plant takes only part of the suppliers' output. Just-in-time deliveries of purchased materials require this type of cooperative planning and execution.

MPS in Different Businesses

The key to effective master scheduling in any business is the proper structuring of bills of material and selection of the correct level in the bills at which to set the MPS. Businesses can be classified in four ways relating to their bills:

1. A few significant items are produced from many components.

2. Many products are made from many components, with a significant degree of commonality.

3. Very many possible combinations of modules are assembled from relatively few subgroups of components.

4. Very many finished products are made from very few components or raw materials, with many package variations.

These are illustrated in Figure 7-4, which also shows the proper level for the MPS. Type 1 requires that the MPS be set at the top of the bill of materials, as does type 2. The major difference is the practicality of handling management review of the many products in type 2. This review requires grouping together families of similar products. Products in type 1 are ships, buses, large machine tools, heavy machinery, cranes and hoists for construction and elevators. Type 2 products include small home appliances, kitchen and workshop tools, electric motors, food products, pharmaceuticals and cosmetics.

Type 3 covers such products as automobiles, computers, machine tools, electric motors and controls, home heating and air conditioning units and farm equipment. In this type of product, the customer can choose among many options for individual features, resulting in an extremely large number of different combina-

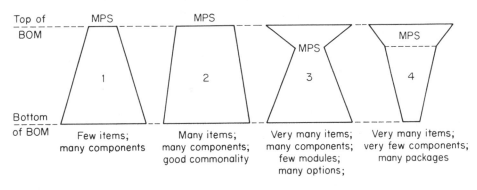

Figure 7-4 PROPER MPS LEVEL IN TYPES OF PRODUCTS.

tions of these options. If the manufacturer of lamps used as examples in Chapter 6 decided to offer a new line of Rite-Lite lamps to their customers like that shown in Figure 7-5, relatively few selections lead quickly to a potentially large number of lamps. The number is easily calculated, assuming any combination can be built:

3 bulbs × 4 bases × 5 shades × 4 columns × 1 cord = 240 lamps

If the maker decided to export lamps to two other countries using 220-volt power instead of the U.S. standard 110-volt power and needing different plugs on the cord set for each, the number of lamps is

6 bulbs × 4 bases × 5 shades × 4 columns × 3 cords = 1440 lamps

The many end products are obviously impossible to forecast accurately and master schedule with any hope of validity. The MPS cannot be made at that level of the bills of material. The proper level to master schedule such products is one level down—the major subassemblies. A reasonable forecast for *total lamp* sales in the United States could be made for example, 2000 per week. The MPS for the U. S. cord set would be 2000 per week, of course, since these cord sets are used

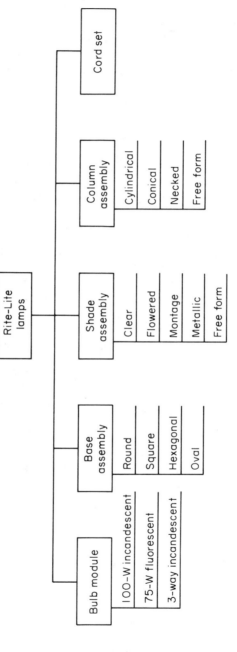

Figure 7-5 LAMP OPTIONS.

in every lamp. Each of the options could then be forecast *as a fraction* of the total lamp demand, based on historical sales data modified by expected future trends. For example, for the bulb module:

>0.5:　　100-watt incandescent　　= 1000 per week
>
>0.2:　　75-watt flourescent　　= 400 per week
>
>0.3:　　3-way incandescent　　= 600 per week

Individual options in the major assemblies could be handled the same way. This technique, called **modular planning**, requires far fewer MPS's to be developed; the total number for the U. S. products is

3 bulbs + 4 bases + 5 shades + 4 columns + 1 cord = 17 MPS's

When the export varieties are added, the number increases only to 22 MPS's, a very manageable number.

Note that the components in the bulb module bill of materials would actually be assembled in different parts of the lamp. The sockets would be installed in the column and the switches in the base with the fluorescent ballast where used; wires would connect the two. For planning purposes, however, these components are grouped into a module associated with *one specific option* available to the customer. In just this way automobile manufacturers group components for air-conditioning options in one planning module although the physical parts are scattered through the vehicle.

As stated earlier in this chapter, the MPS initiates procurement actions; these actions are completed in the execution phase. The specific configuration of lamps and automobiles actually built would be determined by the choices customers exercise. Final-assembly bills of materials would be issued after customers' orders (frequently dealers, distributors or agents) are received. If the planning has been effective, the needed modules and major assemblies will be available. Planning is never perfect, nor are sound plans executed perfectly, so some shortages can be expected. Ways to minimize such shortages and to react more quickly to them are covered in detail in Chapter 2 of the second volume (10). The technique of over-planning the MPS to aid in minimizing shortages is covered in the next section of this chapter.

Type 4 in Figure 7-4 covers such products as toilet articles, cosmetics, medicines, fine chemicals, photographic film, candy, minerals, petroleum derivatives like wax and motor oil and countless others. For this group, very few raw materials and purchased components are converted into a very wide variety of finished bulk products, which are then offered to markets in a number of different packages. This group includes the process industries. Varying raw material characteristics and properties, uncertain yields and inflexible capacity in expensive capital equipment change the planning process in this group from that of the other three. Planning cannot be so precise and is usually directed toward proper utilization of equipment rather than minimizing inventory.

Selection of the proper level to master schedule any product family is governed by three criteria:

1. Have the fewest possible number of items in the MPS to improve management review and control.

2. Cover the maximum possible number of components in the MRP program driven by the MPS.

3. Generate the maximum possible information on loads on manufacturing facilities, particularly bottleneck vendors and machine or equipment centers.

The criteria are obviously in conflict, with item 1 opposing items 2 and 3. The choice of level is fairly easy for type 1 and type 3 products in Figure 7-4. For type 2 products, the compromise needed is between the large number of MPS's and adequate capacity and materials plans. The selection of families of products as a single MPS item provides a good compromise, since these establish both the bulk of the loads on facilities and the demand for common components. The planning process can be improved greatly if product design engineers and process selection engineers clearly see the requirements for good planning and control. The benefits of teamwork here are enormous, but this subject is beyond the scope of these two volumes.

Type 3 products likewise face the problem of too many items in the MPS. Here, too, families of products can partially solve the problem, particularly in the capacity data. Figure 7-4 shows the MPS somewhere below the top end product level of bills of material. This is the *bulk-product* level for packaged items, which has the ability to reduce the number of MPS's to a small fraction of the total number of products. To meet the second criterion above, an *inverted bill of materials*, described in Chapter 4 of the second volume (10), can develop requirements for troublesome packaging materials and also permit utilization of the technique of overplanning the MPS discussed in the next section of this chapter. The third criterion can also be approached with this technique and is frequently met through the use of families of products.

Principle 32. The best MPS has the least number of items and serves the needs of adequate material and capacity plans.

Overplanning the MPS for Flexibility

In the case of the Rite-Lite Lamps in the preceding section, it was practical to develop an MPS for each option; data were shown for each bulb selection, with a total rate of lamp production of 2000 per week. Such estimates of lamp selections are *averages*; the actual mix of orders any week could vary significantly, for example:

100-watt incandescent: 0.3–0.7

75-watt fluorescent: 0.1–0.3

3-way incandescent: 0.2–0.4

Flexibility to meet the maximum demand in any week could be planned by the technique called **overplanning the MPS**. It cannot be emphasized too strongly that *this does not mean overloading or overstating the MPS*; materials and capacity must be available to produce and maintain the additional sets of components.

The MPS for the first option, using this technique, would be increased *in one week* from the 1000 per week average to 1400. The extra 400 sets of components would provide inventory to fill extra customer orders for this option when needed. If the average demand of 1000 is correct, the extra sets used would be replenished when actual demand by customers for this type of bulb dropped below average. Such excess is analogous to safety stock but it is carried in *matched sets* of components associated with each option on which the technique is used.

The choice of the particular week in which to place the overplanned quantity (400 in our example) depends on the condition in which the components are desired. If the quantity were placed in the first week, the plan would make available finished components ready for assembly into finished products. If, on the other hand, it were placed farther out, at the end of the product's cumulative manufacturing lead time, the plan would be aiming only for excess quantities of purchased raw materials and lowest-level components. For custom-built products, not just those assembled to order, this would be the proper application of the technique. The overplanned quantity can be located in intermediate weeks to take full advantage of the flexibility of holding common components or ingredients in their semifinished or uncommitted form before locking them up in specific higher-level configurations. This adheres to the basic strategy for manufacturing stated in Chapter 1 of the second volume (10).

To make most effective use of overplanning for flexibility in meeting customer-demand mix changes, bills of materials for option modules can be restructured to separate the components common to all options from those unique to each option. The various shade assemblies in Figure 7-5, for example, could be built with common wire (including the length if design were cleverly done), common ferrules to secure the shade to the column and clips for the shade material. Overplanning each option using its full bill of materials would plan for excess sets of such common components when actually none are required to respond to mix changes. Sorting out the unique components in a separate bill and overplanning only this enables the investment in excess inventory to be limited to only those items really needed for flexibility. Note that this requires one more MPS to be generated, since two bills of material are now exploded (for common and unique items) instead of one for each option. This also drops the MPS one level lower in the product structure. Bills of material for the higher level option assemblies (shades, bases and columns), which are true subassemblies, and bills for finished lamps would *not* be used in the planning process and would not have to be developed and loaded into product structure records until customers actually ordered specific configurations. These bills would be execution bills, used for assembly scheduling, requisitions or pick lists for storerooms and recording, costing and payment of actual production.

For the flexibility to produce a larger total of lamps than 2000 in any period, the MPS for every common component module (including the cord set) could be overplanned by the same quantity. Again, capacity would have to be adequate to produce and maintain this extra material. If unique sets of components were already adequately overplanned for mix flexibility, they would not have to be increased to provide for building additional total lamps. Use of the overplanning technique with an MRP program permits evaluting the total extra investment needed to provide flexibility to meet market changes. The calculations necessary to do this, also used to prepare inventory budgets based on the operating plan, are covered in Chapter 3 of the second volume (10).

Principle 33. Structuring bills of material properly is a vital part of master production scheduling.

The MPS Horizon

For every product, some raw material or component must be purchased and then converted through some sequence of manufacturing processes into the finished item. This is shown graphically in Figure 7-6. The longest planned time span required to do this, equal to the sum of the planned lead times on the **critical path** (called variously the *cumulative lead time,* the *stacked lead time* and the *critical path lead time*), determines the minimum horizon over which the MPS must extend if MRP is to be able to plan replenishment orders for all components. This ranges in various industries from a few weeks to 2 or more years. If the MPS does not extend at least that far, order point techniques will have to be used on low-level components and raw materials.

The critical path is sometimes called the *firm* portion of the MPS but this term is misleading; it connotes that the MPS should not be changed in this period—

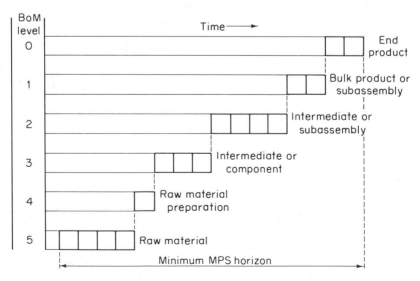

Figure 7-6 PLANNED CUMULATIVE LEAD TIME.

but this is not so. "Freezing" the MPS in the period, allowing no changes, says

1. We are planning to make it whether we need it or not.
2. If we didn't plan it, we can't make it.

Both statements are not only fallacious, they are dangerous and unnecessary. The MPS drives the planning system to initiate procurement of resources, as stated earlier in this chapter. It is hoped that the needed materials, work force and other resources required will then be available when it is time to execute the plan. Perfection in planning or execution is impossible, of course, and corrective actions will always be needed during the execution phase to overcome deficiencies. This is covered thoroughly in Chapter 2 of the second volume (10).

The description *firm* should be interpreted to mean that changes cannot be made capriciously and without study of their specific effects. Within this horizon, any changes in the MPS will have an immediate effect on some real orders, released to suppliers or to the plant, not just on planned orders in the system. It could properly be called the *active* portion of the planning horizon. Costs incurred by changing timing and quantities on such orders include those associated with excess inventory, expediting, obsolescence, lost orders, delayed deliveries, scrap, rework and overtime. Some or all of these could also be incurred by not changing orders; this requires detailed analysis of desired changes when executing the plan. The benefits of reducing this horizon are obvious:

1. A more valid plan
2. Fewer real orders impacted by changes
3. Greater flexibility to meet changes during execution
4. Real competitive advantages

The need for more information on future requirements of low-level components, raw materials, work force and equipment capacity extends the MPS horizon well beyond the minimum. Few MPS's have horizons of only 3 months but some are as short as 6 months; most have a horizon of 12 months and some are 2 or 3 years in total horizon. Data in various portions of the horizon are used for basically different purposes:

Near-term: materials planning, plant scheduling

Midterm: work force levels, shifts, equipment loading

Far-term: plant, equipment, capital requirements

Three, four or more such zones can be identified in each company. The amount of detail needed decreases as the horizon lengthens, as indicated in Figure 7-7, and the time period may also increase. The MPS, therefore, *need not be stated in identical terms* throughout its full horizon. The transition between zones, of course, will pose problems in converting data to more detailed figures. Identifying the proper zones for any company will simplify planning and greatly improve its validity.

	Zone 1	Zone 2	Zone 3
Controlling constraints:	Material	Long leadtime material	Critical raw material supply
	Workforce	Equipment	Capital
	Equipment	Plant	
Detail needed: Bill of materials	Finished product	Typical product	Partial
Processing	Full routings	Bills of labor	$ averages
Time period	Week	Month	Quarter or half-year

Figure 7-7 MASTER SCHEDULE TIME ZONES.

The MPS Format

As presented earlier, time-phased order points, P-S-I and other high-level calculations are used to develop data for the preparation of the MPS for each end product. The specific formats used are as different as the individual companies using them; illustrations used in these two volumes are typical and are designed to show the mechanics of the techniques and relationships among the data. These simply identify what is *desired*.

Any MPS is simply a file of data for each end product in it (this can be a finished product, major subassembly, planning module or spare part) showing how much is planned and when, in specific time periods. Dr. J. A. Orlicky suggested that the MPS be viewed as a continuous "scroll" being steadily (if intermittently) moved to drop past periods off one end and reveal future periods on the other, maintaining a constant horizon (9).

Before any MPS can be deemed usable in planning, what is *desired* to be produced must be reconciled with what is *possible* to produce; this requires knowledge of constraints on material availability and capacity and the capability of determining the *aggregate* effect of all MPS end items on these constraints. Details on individual end items make up the schedule but the crucial question is, Can all items be produced when desired? Figure 7-8 shows a typical format of MPS for several end items making up one product family. Here the family comprises items processed in the same facilities; it is a manufacturing family rather than a marketing family containing different products sold in the same market. It is significant that some items are to be produced steadily, some intermittently, some seasonally and some at higher or lower trending rates. The facility must handle all of them. It is a mistake to call the quantity in any time period for any item an order, although many do; it is not a commitment to produce something as implied by the work order but rather a plan to provide adequate resources to produce something.

Weeks	1	2	3	4		23	24	25	26
Family #1:									
End item A	50	–	50	–		60	–	60	–
End item B	610	610	610	610		610	610	610	610
End item C	340	360	380	400		300	310	320	330
End item D	180	180	180	180		150	150	150	150
End item E	15	–	–	–		–	–	20	–
End item F	205	205	205	205		225	225	225	225
Family #1 total/mo	5575					5340			

Figure 7-8 MPS FORMAT.

The family totals for individual months provide data to link the MPS details to the production-plan totals as discussed earlier in this chapter. Weekly data for individual items or monthly figures for families are used in rough-cut capacity requirements planning (covered in Chapter 9 and in Chapter 5 in the second volume (10). Weekly data for each end item are fed into the MRP program to explode through its bill of materials. The important considerations in this stage of master scheduling are

1. Holding as closely as possible to desired output

2. Leveling the loads on facilities, particularly bottleneck operations or suppliers

3. Including all important demands on facilities

4. Allowing for flexibility in handling unexpected mix changes or additional demands

The first three considerations are self-evident or have already been discussed. The fourth is highly controversial and widely misunderstood. It is a mistake with very serious consequences to overload the MPS beyond the abilities of the manufacturing facilities to handle the load. This is discussed in detail in a later section of this chapter in the section, ''Problems with the MPS.'' Customer service will be poorer, costs higher and inventories excessive; this is exactly the opposite of the desired effects of good planning and control.

Except in a limited number of process and repetitive manufacturing plants, it is extremely difficult to determine accurately how well facilities will be able to handle the mix of materials, processes and products planned in the MPS. The ''right'' capacity for any set of MPS's cannot be calculated precisely; this is discussed more fully in Chapter 9. The inevitable result is that the total MPS will not be matched with capacity; it will be either overstated or understated. Normal tendencies of managers and planners, including optimism about sales, generating pressures for higher output, avoiding idle time for workers, and developing high equipment utilization, result almost invariably in overstatement of the total MPS.

Careful thought of those familiar with how plants really operate will lead to the following conclusions:

1. Some excess capacity to handle "unplanned demands" (new and additional products, scrap replenishment, record errors, use of alternative operations, etc.) is a much better solution than safety stocks.

2. Feeding orders smoothly to vendors and plant facilities to match their abilities to handle them will be far more effective than releasing only what the MRP or order points direct.

3. Excess capacity will never be wasted by professionally qualified planning people and makes it far easier to adjust quickly than having too little capacity.

The truth is that actual output of plants will be *increased* by understating somewhat the MPS total compared to output with overstated total MPS loads. This is counterintuitive and violates commonly held beliefs about the value of high utilization of facilities and the costs of idle time. Professionals recognize its truth and value. Further discussions of relevant details are given in Chapter 9.

The MPS *must not include past-due data* indicating that end items planned in some previous time period have not been produced. This is the worst way to overload the schedules. Actual production should be compared with planned production, of course, but the score should be kept on some other report, not the MPS. It is permissable to plan larger-than-normal quantities in earlier time periods if essentially all or at least the bulk of the work has been completed and the balance required is within available capacity. Otherwise, overdue and overload items must be rescheduled into future time periods.

MPS end items must be identified with numbers recognizable by product structure records containing the proper bills of material. Catalog numbers or other finished goods identifiers can be included also for ready reference by other users. All data must be in units of product, not financial, value. Periodic review and revision by management requires printed copies easily legible without mysterious abbreviations, usually on preprinted forms, which computers can produce easily and economically.

Misconceptions About MPS

There are several misconceptions commonly held about the MPS:

1. The sales forecast is the MPS. See the section, "What the MPS is not."

2. The final assembly schedule is the MPS. See the same section as in (1).

3. When materials are late in arriving, the MPS must be changed. Planned lead times include allowances for queue times, which provide opportunities to *get back on schedule,* even when materials are delayed. Except for customer-dictated changes, revising the MPS should be viewed as an admission of failure.

4. Quantities in the MPS are "orders." The end items in the MPS are planned in the quantities indicated but the items may never actually be built. This is obvious when planning (modular) bills of material are in-

volved (such as the bulb module in Figure 7-5). Orders are released to set assembly, finishing and packaging schedules in the execution phase but these will often be different from the MPS data. The use of the term *"orders"* confuses the distinction between planning and execution and is not recommended.

5. Some part of the MPS must be frozen. See the section, "The MPS Horizon."

6. There are too many items to develop MPS. This implies that there is some valid alternative; there is none. Frequently, it is said by people who do not understand how to structure bills of material and use families to end items to reduce the number to a manageable total.

Problems With MPS

Five major problems destroy the effectivity of the MPS and the planning system it drives:

1. Overstating or overloading
   a. Including a past due time period
   b. Overloading the first few periods (called *front-ending*)
   c. Overloading generally over the whole horizon.
2. Excessive nervousness
3. Invalid data
4. Uneven loading
5. Overautomation

The specific effects of overloading are easily discernable—bottleneck work centers and vendors will have a significant and increasing number of past due orders. These cause shortages, interfering with production and shipment of customers' products, and also expediting and use of substitute materials and alternate operations. Output from nonbottleneck operations will be according to plan and will generate excesses of mismatched components. The net effect is poor customer service, excessive costs and high inventories. This is true whether the overloading is from past due orders, front-ending, or general excesses, over the horizon. When the business economy is healthy, demand is high and there is a compelling need to increase output. While actual capacity increases only slowly, there is an irresistable urge to increase the plan quickly, usually overstating it. This causes more harm than good. In the earlier section, "The MPS Format," the difficulties in getting realistic MPS data and the real advantages were covered.

Nervousness generated by frequent changes to the MPS can easily be handled by computers (in fact, they thrive on it) but can interfere drastically with efforts to execute the plan. An excessive number of action notices to change priorities or capacities and conflicting signals canceling previous actions destroy the morale and the abilities of good people to get things done. Only rarely can production rates fluctuate significantly; plants produce much more economically at stable rates.

Some switches can be made among materials—but only at the cost of excess inventories of components started but not needed now and of expediting. The only real cure for tinkering with the MPS is much shorter lead times for planning, as discussed in Chapter 9, and cushions of inventory strategically planned, as discussed in Chapter 2 in the second volume (10). In time-phased order point planning for finished product inventory replenishment, the use of the firm planned order (Chapter 6) can dampen changes to the MPS from erratic customer ordering, utilizing safety stocks at the finished product level. Effective master scheduling requires managers to walk a fine line between incessant replanning and inflexible planning.

Invalid data used in developing inputs to the MPS include poor forecasts, wrong finished goods inventories, incorrect customer orders and mistakes in shipments. Tracking signals to alert people to forecasts performing poorly, cycle counting to detect and eliminate the causes of record errors and tight discipline in handling MPS data are essential.

Strenuous effort can be made to develop level MPS data but this will not insure level loads on facilities, even starting (gateway) work centers or vendors. Lot-sizing and the occurance of two or more lots in a given time period result in erratic release of work by even well-designed MRP programs. Some relief can be gained by carefully separating the time periods in the MPS end items that generate significant loads on specific work centers. The real solution to this problem is cutting setup times, reducing lot-sizes and smoothing input through well-managed input-output control techniques as described in Chapter 10.

Computer-updated forecasts and distribution requirements planning systems using time-phased order points cannot be allowed to drive directly into MPS data. It is very tempting to allow this to happen when a multitude of products and a large number of service parts are involved. Many software packages are designed this way. Manual intervention is essential to dampen nervousness, smooth loads and insure realism in all MPS's. Even though this intervention is difficult, it must be done.

Principle 34. MPS must be well managed, complete and capable of being executed.

Uses of MPS

The MPS is probably the most important set of data under management control. It has many uses, together with the integrated, formal planning and control system it drives; the most important of these are

1. It interlocks the higher level production plan and the day-to-day schedules. This insures that the latter support the former and also that early warning signals are generated before it is no longer possible to keep both in step.
2. It drives the several detailed plans, including
    a. Materials requirements
    b. Capacity requirements (work force and equipment)

These establish the proper timing and quantities of materials, people, machinery, tooling, supplies, testing and other equipment needed to produce the end items in the MPS. The result is a fully integrated set of plans linking a manufacturing plant and its suppliers.

3. It drives the financial plans leading to flexible budgets for stocked components and work-in-process inventories, purchase commitments, direct labor and cost of goods sold. These are major factors in financial analyses which can be calculated directly from the operating plans. Secondary calculations can be made of indirect labor, factory overhead and net sales income, necessary for formal profit planning.

4. It makes customer delivery promises on make-to-order products. As customer orders are booked, these can be viewed as *consuming the MPS* if they are converted into modules and end items in the MPS and subtracted from it in the appropriate time period. The remaining balances, often referred to as *available to sell,* provide a sound basis for making delivery promises to customers on new orders. In an environment of sound planning and effective execution, developing promises is easier, and much higher levels of on-time delivery can be attained . These are far better than with formulas for lead times or rules of thumb which cannot give adequate consideration to existing loads.

5. It monitors actual performance of: marketing, in evaluating market needs and desires; sales, in getting customers orders; engineering, in adhering to schedules for design and development work; planning, in developing sound plans; and manufacturing, in executing the plans. By this means, the sources and causes of falldowns are made clear, finger-pointing is eliminated and performance is improved.

6. It coordinates managers' activities. The work of developing and maintaining the MPS forces a consensus on an operating plan that best meets their individual needs and desires. This provides a basis for teamwork in executing the plan. No other process is as effective in overcoming the "all-star syndrome," in which one manager tries to excel at the expense of the, others on the team.

Management's Role with MPS

The set of MPS's provides a real handle on the business for top management. To make the best possible use of this fine tool, they must

1. Understand its functions and uses fully. These are covered in the preceding section.

2. Set policies and guidelines for those making detailed decisions in planning and execution. Specific discussion of these is far beyond the scope of these two volumes but their basic purpose must be to define as clearly as possible what management desires in stable employment, customer ser-

vice, product quality, safety and reliability, utilization of resources and similar matters affecting decisions on operations.

3. Resolve conflicts among those with divergent views. Each manager has strong ideas on what is best for the company, usually based on the views of individual departments and specialties. It is rarely possible to reconcile differences on the basis of tangible factors; arbitration may be necessary to insure workable compromises.

4. Insist planning be realistic. There is an irresistable urge to plan optimistically, particularly in periods of growth or recovery from recessions, to keep the work force lean and to utilize plant and equipment at highest possible levels. The result is overloading of the MPS, the most frequent cause of problems in managing manufacturing facilities. Top managers must understand the effects of this on operations and strive to give adequate consideration to flexibility and speed of response to changes. While not so easy to define and measure quantitatively, these may be more important to sharp competitive situations than low headcount and high machine utilization.

5. Review the MPS regularly and rigorously, comparing it to actual performance in operations. This valuable control tool deserves a prominent place on the agenda of operating and executive committee meetings among top-level managers. High-level decisions can be converted into low-level details via the formal planning systems. Coordinating the whole organization is feasible.

With a valid, well-managed MPS, success is not guaranteed—but without it, failure is.

CHAPTER EIGHT

AGGREGATE INVENTORY MANAGEMENT

The Need for Aggregates

Practically every technique used in manufacturing planning and control deals with one item—a product, component, raw material, work or purchase order, work center or vendor. For many years practitioners in this field believed that doing the right things on each item (ordering *the economic* lot-size, planning *the correct* safety stock, getting *adequate* capacity) would result in the correct totals. This has not worked well. In fact, exactly the opposite approach is necessary to get control of inventories and to manage production—start with the totals.

Four questions must be answered to control inventories effectively:

1. How much do we have now?
2. How much do we want?
3. What will be the output?
4. What input must we get?

Information should be available *any time it is desired* on the total inventory by classification, by location, by product family or by facility. If records are coded properly, computers can total the items and their values in minutes for any desired groupings at any time such totals are requested.

Few companies have developed rigorous ways to budget inventories; most use turnover ratios (shipments at cost value divided by total inventory at cost value), inventory as a percentage of sales (the inverse of turnover) or some other rule of thumb indicating some desired improvement over current operations. Usually the improvement projected is modest (10 to 20%) although the real potential is enormous (50 to 90%). Data available in modern MRP-based systems make it possible to *calculate* the inventory levels associated with the operating plan over its full horizon.

Calculation of inventory amounts based on the operating plan is a much better technique than turnover ratios or inventory to sales percentages. These give no clue as to the right level of inventory, nor can they be related to detailed operating plans. Using published turnover data for other companies is misleading, since products, markets and processes may be significantly different; policies on customer service, distribution, stability of employment, product service support, and similar factors may vary widely; and they may not be managing inventory well.

Theoretical calculations of target inventories using the formula

$$\text{Average inventory} = \tfrac{1}{2}(\text{order quantity}) + \text{safety stock} \qquad (8\text{-}1)$$

are also poor for setting inventory budgets. These formulas invariably understate the right level because of one or more of the following:

1. Actual usage is not uniform as the theory assumes.

2. Parts, ingredients and components are used in matched sets, not individually and independently.

3. Significant amounts of inventory in work-in-process, anticipation inventory built for seasonal products, material in transit, etc. are not included.

4. Cushions of inventory added to insure keeping people and machinery busy, take advantage of purchase discounts, hedge against price rises or interruptions in supply, etc. are omitted.

Somewhat better than turnover ratios, inventory-to-sales percentages and theoretical calculations for setting inventory budgets are **time cycles**. The flow of material, usually stated in dollars per day relief rates, is set to support shipping rates. The technique is best when product family data are used. Relief rates and time cycles are specified for each storage and processing stage from raw materials to finished goods as shown in Figure 8-1. Two serious problems with this approach are the average estimates of relief rates and standard days. Actual data can and will vary widely around these averages and the day's estimated are arbitrary without regard to what is really needed.

A strong point, however, is that it focuses attention on the long cycles, indicating fertile fields with significant inventory reduction potential. Such projections can then be adjusted to develop inventory budgets that are flexible, realistic and achievable. This is covered fully in Chapter 3 of the second volume (6).

Aggregate Input/Output Control

The outputs from inventories are ultimately **shipments** to customers, warehouses or affiliated plants. Every company has carefully budgeted and monitored figures for these. Very few use them, however, in controlling inventories.

Manufacturing stage	Planned relief $/day	Standard days	Standard $
Raw material stores	2,550	15	38,250
W. I. P. – fabrication	5,250	30	157,500
Component stores	9,720	10	97,200
W.I.P. – subassembly	12,360	2	24,720
Component stores	12,360	10	123,600
W.I. P. – assembly	12,700	2	25,400
Finished goods	12,700	10	127,000
Materials in transit	12,700	5	63,500

Total standard $657,170

Finished good relief = $12,700
Inventory goal = $657,170/$12,700 = 51.7 days

Figure 8-1 INVENTORY GOALS VIA TIME CYCLES.

The inputs to inventories are called **production** and consist of three parts: purchased materials and services, direct labor and factory overhead. Where overhead costs are allocated on the basis of direct labor, they can be considered one factor.

The fundamental inventory control equation is

$$\text{Inventory now + production} - \text{shipments} = \text{inventory goal} \qquad (8\text{-}2)$$

This relationship of inputs and outputs also applies to make-to-order companies:

$$\text{Bookings now + new orders} - \text{production} = \text{bookings goal} \qquad (8\text{-}3)$$

Here bookings are unshipped orders. In this type of operation, production is made to order and shipped immediately, so total production can be substituted for shipments, the true output factor in equation (8-2).

Figure 8-2 shows a management control report typical of many now used successfully in industry. The plan is set up to reduce inventory in one product family by 20% over a full year. To accomplish the reduction, inputs of purchased material and productive labor must be reduced below the level needed to maintain a constant inventory. The amount of this reduction (overcorrection) depends on the time period allowed; a shorter time to do the job will require more stringent cuts.

Even in the absence of formal, detailed planning systems, this control report can be developed easily. Practically every company knows the purchased material and direct labor content of individual products or, at least, total production, usually expressed as percentages of the cost of goods sold. Some companies' cost data are set up this way. These percentages can be used to develop the plan data for these two factors, multiplying the planned shipments by them and adjusting the results downward to reduce inputs as necessary to achieve the inventory cuts. A sound formal system, of course, permits planning the actions necessary to achieve these cuts in detail. Actual data are posted periodically and deviations from the plan are calculated. A tolerance range set for each of the four variables will bring

Inventory Jan. 1 = $3,000,000
Goal Dec. 31 = $2,400,000

Month	Purchased material			Productive Labor			Shipments			Inventory		
	Plan	Actual	Deviation	Plan	Actual	Deviation	Plan	Actual	Deviation	Plan	Actual	Deviation
Jan.	240	260	20	160	150	(10)	450	430	(20)	2,950	2,980	30
Feb.	240	230	(10)	160	165	5	450	470	20	2,900	2,905	5
Mar.	270	260	(10)	180	175	(5)	500	480	(20)	2,850	2,860	10
Apr.	270			180			500			2,800		
Etc.												

All data in table in $000

Figure 8-2 INVENTORY INPUT/OUTPUT REPORT.

to management's attention significant variance from plan. For example, the acceptable tolerance on receipts of purchased material might be set at ± $10,000; actual receipts in January of $20,000 higher than the plan would alert management that some action was needed immediately to get back on plan. The provision of such early warning signals is invaluable in getting a sound plan executed well with a minimum of data to review and far less drastic corrective actions needed.

Detailed plans must be consistent with these overall aggregate controls. Inventory budgets must be feasible, not "blue-sky" guesses. Basing them on the operating plan as discussed in the preceding section of this chapter is the best way to insure this. Modifying the operating plan to achieve management's objectives with inventories is easy; the mechanics are discussed in Chapter 3 of the second volume (6) and additional coverage is included in later sections of this chapter and in Appendix II. Shipping targets must be consistent with the MPS driving the formal plan. Significant deviations from purchased materials targets must trigger prompt action to review receipts due in the immediate future to cut them without crippling operations. Reasons for the excesses must be determined to prevent repetition in the future. Direct labor deviations must be handled similarly, together with any overhead costs out of line. This latter factor requires detailed expense budgets but these are common in industry.

> **Principle 35. Inventories must first be managed in aggregate before they can be controlled in detail.**

The inventory input/output control report presents all the major factors on one page for management review. They alert managers by exception to factors going out of control and provide early warning signals. Timely, accurate data based on well-integrated plans provide another powerful handle for management on manufacturing operations. To assist managers in making difficult decisions on inventory levels, aggregate techniques are available for each of the major types of inventory: lot-size, safety stock, anticipation and transportation.

Aggregate Lot-Size Inventory

In Chapter 3 and Appendix II some of the problems arising in the application of EOQ's are discussed. These center around the accuracy of demand forecasts and costs used in the formulas and the basic assumptions in the derivation of these formulas that these costs are proportional to the lot-size selected. Even more important reasons for the surprising lack of application of this potentially powerful concept, however, are the problems arising because practitioners must deal with *total* inventories and with *changes* in operations. EOQ formulas apply to individual items and indicate a desired optimum condition for each item based on some definite assumptions regarding costs. They do not indicate the total results in either inventory or operating conditions (setups needed, number of orders to be handled, etc.), which can be expected, nor do they give any consideration to changes in these from the present situation. More detailed coverage of such problems is also included in Appendix II of the second volume (6).

Intuitive order quantities are seldom economical. If set by manufacturing people concerned with the costs involved in setting up machines, they will be too large and, conversely, they will be too small if established by individuals more concerned with the costs associated with carrying inventory. Introduction of EOQ's in such cases may not really improve the actual situation and can even have an upsetting effect. The larger number of orders generated in a period of time by EOQ's that turn out to be smaller than the present lots may be beyond the capacity of those employed in setting up. They may even be beyond the capacity of the equipment, if time cannot be spared from production for setup and changeover. If present order quantities are too small, EOQ's will cause substantial increases in the lot-size inventory and may strain financial resources or overcrowd available space. To prevent such unpleasant surprises, EOQ's should not be introduced (or changed substantially) without studying the total inventory and the changes in operating conditions that will result from the action.

When inventories are reduced by the introduction of EOQ's, whether or not the savings resulting from such areas as reduction in invested capital, lower obsolescence and deterioration, or lower taxes can actually be pinpointed, the inventory reduction should be of real value wherever capital so released can be put to work promptly in other areas. When EOQ's produce fewer orders, however, savings may never be realized. Unless *fewer* buyers or setup people are actually employed, larger order quantities (and correspondingly fewer orders to handle) will only increase carrying costs of inventory without achieving the offsetting savings in operating costs.

Obviously, to prevent increasing total costs by applying EOQ's, all effects on total inventory and total operating conditions must be investigated. A basically different approach to EOQ determination is needed. The standard EOQ equation, formula (3-1), in Chapter 3 shows that the EOQ *and the total lot-size inventory* can be increased if a lower value of the carrying cost is used and can be reduced if a larger value is employed. R. L. VanDeMark (11) suggested this as long ago as 1960. In 1961, R. G. Brown (2) suggested that the carrying cost should be considered a management "policy variable" to control the cycle stock or lot-size inventory. This interpretation holds the key to the true function and application of EOQ's in the management of lot-size inventories.

This concept now has many adherents among professionals who consider that the inventory carrying cost, while it is a very real business expense, cannot be identified as a single magic number any more than the cost of a stockout—an equally real business expense—can be expressed as a specific dollar value. These two costs are concepts needed for the derivation of useful mathematical formulas; the search for fixed, true numbers to be used can be a frustrating experience and should not obscure the real-life factors that determine the economies.

How can the advantages of using the EOQ concept be realized without having a precise value of carrying cost to use in the formula? Some simple examples of the use of inspection to redistribute the number of orders among a family of items to get a lower inventory investment are discussed in Chapter 3. A simple technique to calculate individual order quantities to obtain the lowest total lot-size inventory for a family of items without changing the number of orders written is also described in Chapter 3. It was shown that total inventory could be held constant and that a reduction could be obtained in number of orders written by a variation of the same technique.

While this oversimplified technique was developed principally as a teaching tool, it does give some insight into the type of approach that can be used when applying EOQ in the real business world, where constraints are almost always present. The following are some of the limitations in real life that must be considered when applying the EOQ concept:

1. A limit on the space available for storage
2. A limit on the number of orders the clerical force can process
3. A limit on the number of setups the labor force can make
4. A limit on the time production equipment can remain idle while it is being set up and still produce the total requirements
5. A limit on the amount of money that can be invested in inventory

A technique for handling EOQ's in aggregate and dealing with problems of constraints on the EOQ calculation was developed as a part of a special project (3) for APICS. Appendix III describes this technique, called LIMIT, in detail. LIMIT provides a means to calculate directly the proper lot-sizes for a family of items to meet some constraint such as a maximum on setup hours or on the total inventory resulting. Families of items processed in the same facility (blending, mixing, screw machines, sheet metal presses, packaging lines and complex testing equipment are typical) are handled together.

Trade-off curves like Figure 8-3 are easily developed for such families using the square root EOQ formula or any of the others. Lot-size calculations are made for each item in the family using a range of values of the cost of carrying inventory (in effect saying, What if the carrying cost were 20%, 25%, 30%, 35%, ...)? For each value of carrying cost, the average inventory investment is determined for all items in the family, together with the total cost of ordering all the items

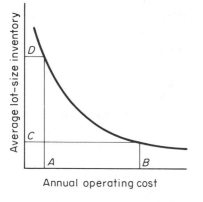

Typical calculation

Item	Annual usage $	Setup cost $	EOQ $	No. setups/yr.	Annual S.U. cost $
A	2000	10	447	5	50
B	5000	5	500	10	50
C	1500	12	424	4	48
D	4000	6	490	8	48
E	1000	15	387	3	45
		Totals	2248		241

For carrying cost = 20%

Figure 8-3 LOT-SIZE INVENTORY VERSUS OPERATING COST.

in some period, usually a year. Each value of carrying cost corresponds to one point on the curve in Figure 8-3. A typical calculation is shown in the table at the bottom of this figure. Five items make up this family, a carrying cost of 20% of the inventory value is used and EOQ's are not rounded as they would be when orders are written. The average inventory is one half the total of EOQ's. The setup cost is assumed to include first-piece scrap and inspection, writing orders and other related charges, in addition to the labor cost of actually setting up the facilities. This is better called **ordering cost**.

The curve represents the ideal or theoretical situation; actual operations will always be above it—higher operating costs for a given inventory, larger inventory for a particular operating cost, or both. This is caused by fallacies in the theory, covered in Chapter 3, and failure to run the EOQ in order to expedite a split lot. Each point on the curve corresponds to some specific value of carrying cost; this is the amount to be used in specific EOQ calculations after a decision has been made concerning where management would like to operate. Such decisions can be based on return on investment; the distance *AB* represents the reduction in operating cost possible by increasing the inventory from *CD*. Constraints on setup would erect a fence at the corresponding operating cost ceiling. Inventory could not be decreased below this value regardless of the economic benefits until the constraint is removed by cutting setup times or adding more people or equipment.

Principle 36. EOQ theory should be used to draw trade-off curves for management decision making.

The techniques discussed in this chapter can be very helpful in calculating lot-sizes. They certainly will not solve all related production and inventory control problems but they do represent a more realistic approach than the standard EOQ and discount calculations. The techniques must be used with judgment because they do not take into consideration all of the possible variables that enter into such decisions. One point to remember is that reductions in order quantities generate more reorder periods and thus more frequent exposure to stockout. Consequently, the total inventory will not be reduced in direct proportion since reserve stock will increase. Appendix IV shows an example of this phenomenon.

Before using lot-sizes calculated by any method, the lot-sizes should be reviewed by manufacturing *and* materials control personnel most closely associated with the manufacturing area that will produce the pieces to be sure that they are *reasonable*. In computer programs, lot-sizes should not be rounded but should be printed exactly as calculated. This should be done deliberately so that the lot-sizes will be reviewed for reasonableness and then rounded as part of this review.

The individual reviewing the lot-sizes should adjust them to take into consideration spoilage, deterioration, exceptional bulk or other factors not included in the calculations. Reference to Figure 3-5 in Chapter 3 will show that total cost increases only slightly as the lot-size varies from the EOQ—particularly for *larger* lot-sizes. The minor loss of economy due to slight variations in the lot-size is more theoretical than real. The value of having lot-sizes that make sense is very tangible.

The standard LIMIT program works best where there is one major machine group (such as a screw machine or punch press department) under consideration. When an item goes through a sequence of operations, the decision information presented by LIMIT is not as clear-cut as it is when there is only one major machine group that is being set up. If, for example, an item goes through six different operations in sequence, LIMIT would handle all these as one operation. The program can still be useful under these circumstances if the following suggestions are considered:

1. Run the LIMIT program, first treating each major machine group as a separate operation. This will show what the desired lot-sizes would be if each operation were run separately.

2. Run the LIMIT program again, adding all the setup times together for all operations and treating the group of operations as if it were one machine group.

3. Compare the lot-sizes that result from these calculations to determine the most practical lot-sizes. It may be desirable to break up the operation sequence with an inventory of parts held in semifinished condition. A detailed treatment of all the possible alternatives is beyond the scope of this book.

Even in circumstances where EOQ calculations are made as a simulation program in order to study different lot-sizes, the aggregate approaches definitely help the practitioner to avoid the pitfalls of the standard EOQ approach by showing where setup hours will have to be increased or when the total inventory will increase as a result of economic lot-size decisions. An aggregate calculation can be of great value even if the calculated lot-sizes are not used because the program focuses attention on inventory and setup totals. To use the LIMIT program this way, the lot-sizes that have been determined by some desired means are entered into the LIMIT program as *present lot-sizes,* and the program then makes the balance of the calculations.

There are other effects of the lot-size decision that often must be considered. If, for example, there is only one machine to perform a particular type of work, the portion of its capacity occupied in producing the total parts required in a year may leave very little time for setup and lot-sizes will consequently be very large. These lot-sizes will not be chosen from the point of view of the economics of balancing setups versus inventory but to meet the setup restrictions on the equipment.

The effect lot-sizes will have upon inventories due to the cycling problem must also be considered. Large lot-sizes require long running times and larger inventories have to be carried on each item to cover the additional time each item waits to be processed. It is almost certain that some jobs will be in the machine or waiting for it when the order for another item is generated. This item will then have to wait for the current backlog of orders to be completed before it can be run. This waiting time can be many times the normal processing time and will increase inventories significantly. The value of reducing the required setup time is very high.

Other real-life effects are not considered in the theory of EOQ but are easily evaluated by aggregate calculations. The ability to handle the total number of set-ups required by the lot-sizes used is one such factor. Often special skills are required and individuals are assigned solely to setup work. Their capacity limits the number of setups that can be handled and thereby restricts the lot-sizes that can be selected. The ideal number of setups is that which keeps the setup people fully occupied but not overloaded.

Another constraint is the amount of capital available for this type of inventory. Lot-sizes are not economical if they tie up capital that could be employed better elsewhere. Trade-off curves like Figure 8-3 help make the decision on whether the return on investment of lot-size inventories is adequate or not.

Purchase decisions involving discounts have suffered from the same "one-item-at-a-time" approach. The decision to take the discount or not is usually based on whether the savings from lower unit prices and fewer orders exceed the cost of carrying the additional inventory. The decision hinges on knowing the carrying cost and the approach gives no indication of the total impact on capital investment of *all* discount decisions that might be taken. Viewing the net savings as return on investment and ranking a number of potential discounts in order of return on the added investment would permit taking only those discounts which meet management's desired return similar to goals set for capital equipment. The objection is frequently raised that all items on which a company may be able to get discounts cannot be identified early. This is true, of course, but it is no excuse for not using the technique for all known discount situations and making a real effort to be sure all A items (those with high usage value) are covered. These will obviously generate the bulk of the return and are most likely to have discount possibilities.

This is typical of actual situations, where production and inventory control decisions are highly complex. No single calculation can take into account all of the variables encountered in manufacturing situations. Formulas, techniques and programs discussed in this chapter can be a great aid to good judgment but should be used with discretion and with the realization that they alone do not solve all of the problems.

These techniques attempt to deal with the total lot-size inventory and to show the real-life implications of the mathematical calculations. Other techniques are needed to deal wth other segments of the inventory in aggregate.

Aggregate Safety Stock Inventory

The balance between customer service and inventory investment is seldom the result of a well-thought-out policy in most businesses. It is not always recognized by management that there is a basic relationship between inventory levels and customer service and that these are not independent variables. The better the desired service to customers, the higher the finished-goods inventory must be in a business already using manufacturing-control systems effectively.

Chapter 5 showed the method for computing statistical reserve stocks using a mean absolute deviation computed from the demand data for a particular item.

An item designated "item M" is used next to illustrate the calculation of the relationship between service and inventory investment over a range of service levels. The pertinent data needed to make the calculations are

$$\text{Annual forecast} = 26,000 \text{ units}$$

$$\text{Order quantity} = 2000 \text{ units}$$

$$\text{Mean Absolute Deviation} = 209 \text{ units}$$

$$\text{Unit cost} = \$1.35$$

The reserve stock required for each service level can be calculated using the method shown in Chapter 5. A typical calculation for one such level is as follows:

$$\text{Tolerable number of stockouts per year} = 4$$

$$\text{Number of exposures per year} = \text{annual forecast divided by}$$

$$\text{order quantity} = \frac{26,000}{2000} = 13$$

$$\text{Service fraction} = \frac{(13 - 4)}{13} = \frac{9}{13}$$

$$\text{Service ratio} = \frac{9}{13} = 69.2\%$$

$$\text{Required number of MAD's (from Figure 5-7)} = 0.75 \text{ (estimated)}$$

$$\text{Reserve stock required} = 0.75 \times \text{MAD} = 0.75 \times 209$$
$$= 157$$

Similarly, the required level of reserve stock inventory can be calculated for different service levels. Figure 8-4 shows this calculation for item M at nine differ-

---

Data:
 Mean absolute deviation = 209
 Order quantity = 2000
 Annual forecast = 26,000
 Unit cost = $1.35

SO/Year	Exposures	Service fraction	Service ratio	Required #MAD	Reserve
4	13/Year	9/13	69.2%	0.75	157
2	13/Year	11/13	84.5%	1.29	268
1	13/Year	12/13	92.4%	1.80	376
One in 2	26	25/26	96.1%	2.20	460
One in 3	39	38/39	97.4%	2.40	501
One in 4	52	51/52	98.1%	2.60	544
One in 5	65	64/65	98.5%	2.70	565
One in 10	130	129/130	99.2%	3.00	626
Never	---	---	100%	5.00	1044

Figure 8-4 SERVICE VERSUS RESERVE-STOCK TABULATION.

ent service levels. The amount of reserve stock inventory required for theoretically perfect service (never out of stock) is almost seven times the amount that would be required if four stockouts per year could be tolerated. It must be remembered that these calculations assume that *operations are well planned and tightly controlled.*

This relationship is plotted on a curve in Figure 8-5, which shows the reserve stock inventory (in pieces) required for various levels of service. Here, the number of stockouts per year has been expressed as *stockouts in* 10 *years,* in order to have a uniform scale for all conditions included on the curve. This curve clearly illustrates the rapid increase in reserve stock as the required level of customer service is increased. Using such a curve, a reasonable level of customer service can be selected

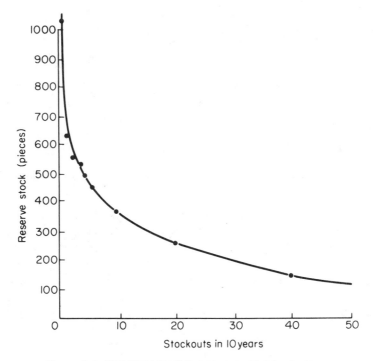

Figure 8-5 SERVICE VERSUS RESERVE STOCK CURVE.

and the required reserve stock can be determined to attain that service level. The service ratio corresponding to the point selected is then used to calculate reserve stocks for each item in the family (5).

In most situations where reserve stock inventory has previously been determined intuitively, this statistical solution provides an immediate improvement in the relationship between inventory and customer service. The most important aspect of this curve, however, is that it puts the conflict between customer service and inventory investment into perspective, showing materials control and other management personnel the levels of finished goods inventory required to give corresponding levels of service to customers. This type of curve is a very useful management tool.

The number of items held in inventory is in the thousands in most businesses and it would not be practical or significant to develop and analyze data and curves like this for each item. Materials-control people must determine the required reserve stock for each item in order to plan its replenishment properly but these should be set after management has decided on the specific level of service to be provided. Furthermore, to make its decision on service level, management needs service versus investment data not on individual items but on the total inventory of all items. The individual inventory items are significant to the inventory planner but at higher levels of management, the concern is with the aggregate inventory investment.

The same general method used to plot a service versus investment curve for one item can be extended to a group of items and the inventory investment required for an entire product line can be shown in relation to the customer service that will be provided.

In the following example, a service versus investment curve will be calculated for a family of four items, item M (used in the previous example), item N, item O and Item P. Assume the following data:

Items	Annual usage	Order quantity	Unit cost	MAD
M	26,000	2000	1.35	209
N	96,000	8000	0.70	1600
O	12,000	2000	0.90	271
P	6,000	1500	0.85	240

Choosing a lowest service level of eight stockouts per year for the entire group of items (equivalent to two stockouts per item per year), the reserve stock calculations are made for the other items in the group in the same way as for item M.

This calculation is shown for each of the four items in the top section of Figure 8-6, where the required reserve stock for each item is shown in the column headed *Reserve*. The next column shows the average cycle stock equal to one half the order quantity for each item. The following column shows the total of the reserve stock plus one half the order quantity (this is the average inventory in units). In order to express these inventories for the whole group in common terms, the average inventory is then extended by the unit cost for each item and the total average inventory is expressed in dollars in the last column.

Figure 8-6 shows that a total average inventory of $7518 would be required in order to provide a service level of eight stockouts per year for this group of items or two stockouts per year per item. The figure also shows similar calculations for a total of four stockouts per year for the group of items and for subsequent increasingly higher service levels.

Figure 8-7 shows the total relationship of service versus investment for this

Item	No. Exp.	Serv. Fract.	Serv. Ratio	#MAD	Reserve	1/2 O.Q.	Avg. Inv. Units	Unit Cost	Avg. Inv. $
For 8 Stockouts per year (2 per item):									
M	13	11/13	84.5%	1.29	268	1000	1268	1.35	$1710
N	12	10/12	83.4	1.20	1920	4000	5920	0.70	4140
O	6	4/6	66.7	0.54	146	1000	1146	0.90	1030
P	4	2/4	50.0	0	0	750	750	0.85	638
									$7518
For 4 Stockouts per year (1 per item):									
M	13	12/13	92.4	1.80	376	1000	1376	1.35	$1860
N	12	11/12	91.6	1.75	2800	4000	6800	0.70	4760
O	6	5/6	83.3	1.20	325	1000	1325	0.90	1192
P	4	3/4	75.0	0.84	202	750	952	0.85	810
									$8622
For 2 Stockouts per year (1 every other year per item)									
M	26	25/26	96.1	2.20	460	1000	1460	1.35	$1970
N	24	23/24	95.8	2.16	3460	4000	7460	0.70	5220
O	12	11/12	91.6	1.75	474	1000	1474	0.90	1325
P	8	7/8	87.5	1.45	348	750	1098	0.85	932
									$9447
For 1 Stockout per year (1 every 4 years per item)									
M	52	51/52	98.1	2.60	544	1000	1544	1.35	$ 2085
N	48	47/48	98.0	2.56	4100	4000	8100	0.70	5660
O	24	23/24	95.8	2.16	585	1000	1585	0.90	1428
P	16	15/16	93.7	1.92	461	750	1211	0.85	1030
									$10,203
For 1 Stockout every two years (1 every 8 years per item)									
M	104	103/104	99.1	2.95	616	1000	1616	1.35	$ 2181
N	96	95/96	99.0	2.91	4660	4000	8660	0.70	6060
O	48	47/48	98.0	2.56	694	1000	1694	0.90	1525
P	32	31/32	96.9	2.33	560	750	1310	0.85	1113
									$10,879
For 1 Stockout every three years (1 every 12 years per item)									
M	156	155/156	99.4	3.14	656	1000	1656	1.35	$ 2219
N	144	143/144	99.3	3.10	4960	4000	8960	0.70	6260
O	72	71/72	98.6	2.75	745	1000	1745	0.90	1571
P	48	47/48	98.0	2.56	615	750	1365	0.85	1160
									$11,210
For "Never"(99.9%)									
M	---	---	99.9	4	835	1000	1835	1.35	$ 2480
N	---	---	99.9	4	6400	4000	10,400	0.70	7270
O	---	---	99.9	4	1083	1000	2083	0.90	1878
P	---	---	99.9	4	960	750	1710	0.85	1452
									$13,080

Figure 8-6 SERVICE VERSUS INVESTMENT CALCULATONS.

No. of Stockouts Group service level		1/2 O.Q. $	$ R	Total average inventory
1-Yr. base	10-Yr. base			
8	80	$ 5687	$ 1831	$ 7518
4	40	5687	2935	8622
2	20	5687	3760	9447
1	10	5687	4516	10,203
1/2	5	5687	5192	10,879
1/3	3.3	5687	5523	11,210
"Never"	0	5687	7393	13,080

Figure 8-7 TOTAL SERVICE VERSUS INVESTMENT DATA.

group of four items. It is a summary of the preceding table, with all the data expressed in dollars. In Figure 8-8, these data are plotted as two curves, the lower curve showing the reserve stock and the upper curve showing the total inventory investment required for various service levels. The cycle stock (lot-size inventory) lies between the two.

Most important from a practical point of view is the fact that in almost every real situation where the statistical computation replaces intuitive approaches to order points, a substantial improvement in the service versus investment relationship can be attained immediately. It might be found, for example, that the current inventory investment equals $11,000 for the items shown in Figure 8-8 and that approximately ten stockouts were occuring in 10 years for the group. Using statistical methods to redistribute the reserve stocks, the curve shows that $11,000 worth of inventory investment should result in only four stockouts in 10 years for this group. This is the same kind of improvement that was attained in Chapter 3 when lot-sizes were calculated using the square-root relationship of the EOQ concept instead of intuitive methods. An immediate improvement was available to the practitioner and other alternatives leading to even greater economies were shown.

In making this particular group of calculations, it was assumed that the number of stockouts should be kept equal for all items in the group. That is, if the total number of stockouts desired for the group equaled eight, then it should be spread evenly across the items in the group so that each item would have two stockouts per year. This is not always the case; it might sometimes be desirable to have less frequent stockouts on some items than on others. This could be done by allocating the number of stockouts as desired among the items in the group and then calculating the appropriate reserve stocks.

Looking at the curve in Figure 8-8, it can be seen that the total investment in reserve stock needs to be increased almost fourfold as the service requirement is increased from two stockouts per item per year to *never* out of stock. Using such a curve, management can see the service versus investment alternatives that are available, and they can—with the help of materials control professionals—determine

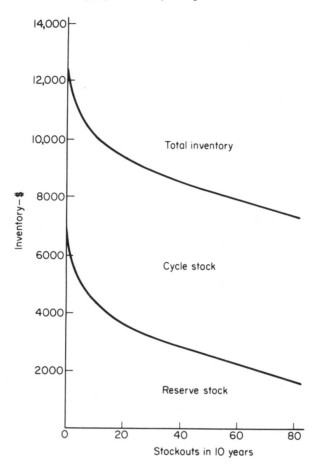

Figure 8-8 TOTAL SERVICE VERSUS INVESTMENT CURVE.

a reasonable level of inventory for any group of items. The basic conflict between those who feel that inventory turnover rates are by themselves a good indicator of business efficiency and those who feel that customer service is the only measure of the effectiveness of inventory control can thus be quantified using statistical approaches to determining reserve stock.

This is the type of information with which managers are used to dealing. The calculations certainly do not give them the final answer directly. If, for example, the cost of a stockout were known, a formula could be developed to balance this cost against that of carrying the necessary inventory and there would be very little need for management judgment. Unfortunately, neither of these costs can be determined accurately; in most business situations both vary widely over time. In most businesses, they are recognized as real, yet highly intangible, costs that are not susceptible to being captured and expressed in specific numbers.

Experienced management personnel are accustomed to making decisions where all the desired information is not available. They are constantly called on to use their experience and judgment in such situations. Nevertheless, materials control personnel cannot merely collect information, express it in a form usable to management and then depend upon management to make a decision. Considerable help and guidance should be provided by these professionals who are qualified to recognize the implications of decisions regarding inventory level or desired customer service level.

With this approach, a far more rational decision on inventory investment can be made. Significant improvements can usually be made in the relationship between inventory investment and customer service. Once materials control people have presented this decision information and a particular inventory and customer service goal has been set, it becomes the job of these people to operate the inventory control system so that these goals are met. This is done by setting up the reserve stock levels that correspond to the service versus investment level chosen and operating the inventory system to achieve these stocks.

Principle 37. Studying alternatives using trade-off curves results in better decisions than calculating reserve stocks for a given level of customer service.

The first known application of a total service versus investment curve for an entire product line was made in 1959. This application covered a group of 80 different items that constituted one family of purchased parts. EOQ's were calculated for each item and reserve stocks were computed as described here. Both cycle and reserve stocks are included in the inventory figures shown in this curve, Figure 8-9, expressed in dollars of total inventory.

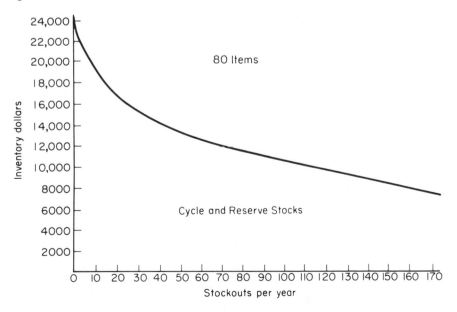

Figure 8-9 FIRST TOTAL SERVICE VERSUS INVESTMENT CURVE.

It can be seen that zero stockouts per year would require approximately $24,000 worth of inventory for the group. If it were decided to operate with $18,000 worth of inventory, there would be approximately 15 stockouts per year distributed among all the items in the group (equivalent to approximately 1 stockout in 5 years for each item). The curve also shows that a further reduction from $18,000 to $12,000, for example, would result in a drastic increase in the number of stockouts per year to approximately 70, or very close to 1 stockout per item per year, thus illustrating the critical zone in the relationship between customer service and inventory investment.

When this analysis was first made, the total inventory for this group of items was approximately equal to $30,000, and the number of stockouts was between 80 and 100 per year. The statistical calculations indicated that a substantial improvement in this relationship was possible and it was determined to try to keep the inventory level at approximately $18,000 and the stockouts at approximately 15 per year. In practice, the system worked very well; the inventory level seldom went above $21,000 or below $16,000, and there were 22 stockouts during the first year of operation.

One reason that actual stockouts exceeded the level indicated by the statistical calculations was the method for counting stockouts. Statistically, a stockout is defined as an instance when stock is not available to meet the total demand at that time. Usually no attempt is made to measure the duration of any stockout. In practice, it was more practical to count the number of items out of stock each week and consider each occurrence as a stockout. Thus it was possible for one item to go out of stock and remain out for 3 weeks, in which case the number of stockouts would be counted as three rather than one.

After running the system for a short period of time, it was possible to correlate the statistical measure of service with the method of measuring actual customer service and to set the statistical measure of service somewhat higher than the level desired in order to attain the latter in practice. Interestingly enough, although the number of stockouts was actually half again as much as the number predicted by the statistics, the improvement in service was so dramatic that this minor discrepancy caused no great concern. Management appreciated the "near miss" as far better performance than the blind shooting which had preceded it.

One problem brought into focus by this approach to inventory control was that of unmanaged lead time. Vendors for this group of purchased items, like so many other manufacturers, usually experienced an increase in lead time when business was good and a decrease in lead time when business was dropping. When they shipped in shorter-than-planned lead time, the result was a higher inventory. When their lead time was extended, the inventory level dropped and customer service suffered as a result of late deliveries. It became necessary to watch delivery lead times and performance very closely in order to keep the total inventory investment under control without excessive shortages. The real solution to this problem is *not* to increase reserve stock or to advance delivery dates. The proper way to handle this **lead-time syndrome** is covered in Chapter 5 of the second volume (6).

In operation, this was highly successful inventory management. It represented a substantial improvement in the service versus investment relationship. Managers were pleased that they were at last able to determine the total inventory investment for this product line and choose the levels of inventory and customer service that they desired. Materials control and line personnel had a challenging job in attaining the service and investment levels that they had predicted, yet these levels were not as difficult to attain in practice as had been anticipated. Overall, everyone concerned was highly satisfied that they were at last able to manage the total inventory investment directly rather than attempting this through a lot of individual decisions whose total effect could not be foreseen.

This particular application used manual calculations. These required constant revision, updating them for changes in the forecast and demand variations. Because of the experimental nature of this first service versus investment calculation, it was applied to a low-dollar-value product group. Eventually, after being in use for approximately 2 years, it had to be abandoned because of the excessive amount of manual effort involved in its upkeep. Since that time, computers have become available and are being used to obtain periodic stock status reports, applying exponential smoothing to forecast the demand for individual items and calculating the MAD of forecast error on a regular basis. The reserve stock is then determined and incorporated with the updated item forecast into a floating order point for each item.

With this type of information regularly available, the maintenance required for aggregate inventory management of the type presented in this section is reduced to manageable proportions. Figure 8-10 shows a total service versus invest-

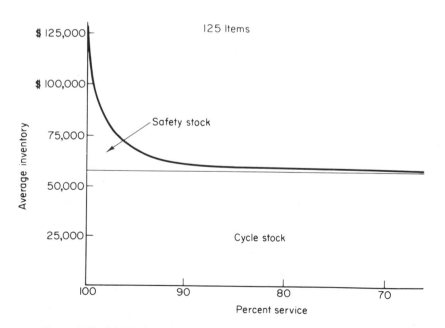

Figure 8-10 COMPUTER TOTAL SERVICE VERSUS INVESTMENT CURVE.

ment curve for a group of 125 finished products calculated using the technique described in this chapter. Various levels of service for the entire product group were simulated and the group curve was developed from these simulations. Using the computer, these simulations take a very small amount of time and the use of statistical concepts to develop a service versus investment chart periodically becomes very practical.

The horizontal scale in Figure 8-10 is labeled "percent service" rather than "number of stockouts per year", as in Figure 8-9. The number of stockouts per year can be converted to a percentage of service quite easily, as follows:

1. Total number of items in the group = 125.
2. Total number of selling weeks in the year = 52.
3. Total number of stockouts possible = 125 × 52 = 6500.
4. If there are 650 stockouts (number of items out of stock each week totaled for the year) during the year, this is equivalent to 90% service $[(100 - 650/6500)\%]$.

This expression of customer service is frequently a desirable one to use. It is important to remember that the statistical measure of service used here does not measure the duration of stockouts. Chapter 5 contains other statistical measures of customer service that can be used; there may be some situations where these are more appropriate to the particular application. In general, however, any statistical measure of customer service must be correlated with the actual customer service and the statistical measure will usually need to be set higher than the actual level of service desired.

The following steps are employed in using the statistical order point method for determining a service versus investment chart:

1. Calculate a MAD for each item in the product group and develop a method for updating it regularly. This will probably involve the use of some statistical technique to forecast demand during lead time and may involve an adjustment (as in Figure 5-9) if the forecast interval and the lead time interval are not identical.

2. Run a sample calculation to develop the total service versus investment curve, including the cycle stock inventory (sum of one half the order quantities) and the reserve stock in the total. In setting targets to which the inventory will be reduced at stated times in the future, do not forget to include any slow-moving stock. The best-regulated inventory control systems cannot avoid having some slow-moving stock. It is not reasonable to compare the present inventory level with a theoretical inventory level and assume that the reduction can be made immediately, since some "dead stock" items in it may not move for a long time.

3. Compare the levels of inventory required for present customer service and show the improvement possible using statistical inventory control tech-

niques. If the calculations do not indicate an improvement, the implication is that reserve stock is now distributed very equitably across the items in inventory. This is highly improbable if intuitive methods are now being used and it would indicate that the calculations and current service data should be checked.

4. Show management the present service versus investment relationship and the improvement possible using statistical techniques and then help them to choose the ''best'' inventory level.

5. Set the reserve stocks at the agreed level and run the inventory control system.

There are some practical hints of value when starting this aggregate control approach:

1. The inventory of items included almost invariably increases very quickly when the changes are first introduced. This occurs because items that are *below* the right levels are ordered all at once. There are usually many other items for which the inventory is too high and it is necessary to wait for them to be worked off. Consequently, an upward bulge in the inventory level can normally be expected. A sample check will indicate the amount to be expected and management *should be warned* that it will occur. Even better, parallel actions should be taken to *reduce some other type of inventory* to offset this increase.

2. These techniques alone should be used only for finished products. Statistical safety stock theory does not apply to components of other manufactured items (dependent).

3. Use weekly sales histories in developing demand data whenever possible. Monthly sales figures are usually more difficult to use since they must be adjusted to compensate for the different number of selling days in each month.

4. It is well to try the system manually for a small number of items in order to understand it thoroughly. This can be done using a desk or pocket calculator.

5. *A computer is not necessary;* this type of calculation can easily be done manually for a small number of items. Once it has been proven for a low-value inventory (where mistakes are not as serious), a manual system can then be used for the highest dollar value items (the A items).

6. With computers, however, the aggregate approach is more practical. All major computer manufacturers and many software suppliers have packaged programs containing the statistical techniques needed. While these computer programs are rarely identical in the calculations for the techniques described in these two volumes, they are basically designed around the same principles. A thorough understanding of the principles in these chapters is necessary if the practitioner is to use these programs effectively.

7. Service versus investment charts need be made only periodically. They are only approximations at best, and small changes in forecasts, errors, costs and other data need not trigger recalculations.

8. When starting any new technique, it is important to remember to insure that it does *at least* as good a job as the old way, even in the beginning. A company's reputation for service can be damaged for a long time by one brief lapse in the service level. The practitioner who risks this reputation while trying out new techniques, no matter what their potentials, is not acting in the best interests of the company.

The concept of aggregate inventory management is so significant that two types of aggregate inventory calculations have been presented in great detail. This type of calculation can be made for any type of inventory by the practitioner who understands basic inventory concepts.

Aggregate Work-In-Process Inventory

With the possible exception of small amounts of rework, work-in-process is lot-size inventory. Figure 8–11 shows the typical lot situation, where the order quantity is eight pieces and the lead time (LT) is weeks required to make the batch. The average work-in-process (WIP) for this batch is $(q \times LT)/52$ and n batches are processed during a year, determined by the annual usage, A, divided by the lot size, q. Average annual work-in-process is:

$$\text{Average WIP} = \frac{nq\,(LT)}{52} = A \times \left(\frac{LT}{52}\right) \qquad (8\text{-}4)$$

The significance of this equation, in addition to providing a way to calculate aggregate work-in-process, is that the *average work-in-process is independent of the lot-size* and varies directly with lead time and annual usage. This highlights clearly the advantage of cutting lead times in reduced investment in work-in-process.

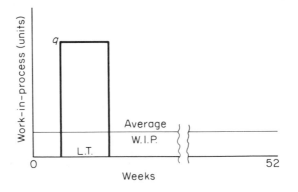

Figure 8-11 AVERAGE WIP VERSUS LOT SIZE.

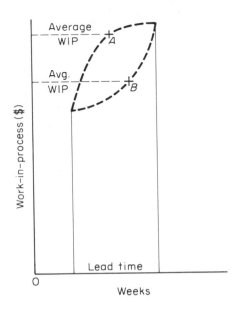

Figure 8-12 VALUE ADDED IN WIP.

It also shows that both increasing lot-sizes to compensate for scrap losses and adding rework operations add to operating costs and capital investment requirements.

The average *value* of a lot depends on how material, labor and overhead are added during processing. For most manufacturing operations, all the material is introduced into work-in-process at the release of the order. When the bulk of the labor (and overhead) is expended in the early stages of processing, the average value will be closer to that of the finished batch as shown by point *A* on Figure 8-12. When finishing or packaging represent the bulk of labor (and overhead), the average value of work-in-process is much lower, closer to the material cost shown by point *B* on Figure 8-12. However, large, complex products and those made on assembly lines have materials of significant value introduced at various stages of the process, while labor and overhead are applied at fairly steady rates. This is illustrated in Figure 8-13. The average work-in-process value for the total process is the weighted average of the averages for the individual phases. Using Figure 8-13, the average total work-in-process is:

$$[(\text{Average WIP} \times \text{LT})_1 + (\text{Average WIP} \times \text{LT})_2 +$$
$$(\text{Average WIP} \times \text{LT})_3 + (\text{Average WIP} \times \text{LT})_4] \qquad (8\text{-}5)$$
$$\div \text{ Total LT of all phases}$$

In this discussion work-in-process is defined as material *released to the plant to be worked on* and does not include material actually or technically in stockrooms awaiting such release for further processing. Stockroom inventories were covered in the two preceding sections of this chapter. Many companies use wall-to-wall inventory evaluation approaches, wherein *all* inventory in the plant is considered work-in-process, even finished products, until shipped to customers or warehouses. Prac-

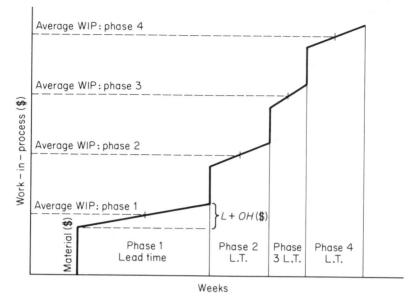

Figure 8-13 LARGE AND ASSEMBLY-LINE PRODUCTS WIP.

titioners must understand their companies' accounting practices if their studies are to be compatible with other data used by management.

Aggregate Anticipation Inventory

Anticipation inventory is carried for two basic reasons:

1. To level out production rates of products having seasonal demand, sales promotions or demand inflated temporarily by price changes
2. To carry over periods when production is low or interrupted temporarily by vacation shutdowns, plant moves or machinery overhaul and replacement

The benefits from carrying it come in two classes:

1. Lower investment in plant and equipment than that required to meet peak demands
2. Reduced costs of hiring, layoff, training, overtime and downtime

Anticipation inventory is usually planned for families of products that determine the loads on specific manufacturing facilities. The popular technique is the S-P-I report illustrated and discussed in Figures 7-2 and 7-3. The costs involved are rarely found in the standard chart of accounts in companies and, therefore, have to be engineered—that is, estimated for each situation studied.

The major problem in aggregate anticipation inventory studies is the lack of accurate data. Seasonal forecasts, results of sales promotions and price changes, cost data and plant output rates are difficult to evaluate at best. Using consistent data, however, aggregate analyses can indicate clear choices among various alternative ways of preparing for wide fluctuations in demand or supply. Comparison of actual performance with even unusual plans can provide early warning signals that restudy and changes in operations are needed.

Aggregate Transportation Inventory

This includes all products and other materials belonging to the company that are in transit to or from the company. This investment is necessary to keep such materials flowing. The amount needed is a straightforward calculation:

$$\text{Transportation inventory (\$)} = \text{shipments per week (\$)} \times \text{weeks in transit} \tag{8-6}$$

Thus the value of this inventory is directly proportional to the amount shipped and the in-transit time. The amount shipped is determined by operations—production rates and shipping (sales) rates. The in-transit time is variable, depending on the method of shipment chosen.

The faster the shipment, the higher its cost and the lower the inventory required. Cargo ships are the least expensive; rail, trucks and airfreight are increasingly more costly. The total freight savings from using slower methods is the return on the additional capital investment in inventory. Obviously, if more return can be generated by alternative uses of the capital, the faster method should be selected.

Other significant factors are involved:

1. Safety stocks in field warehouses can be reduced if the replenishment lead time (mostly in transit) is cut.

2. Water and shock damage tend to be higher for ships and trains.

3. Theft and pilferage are lower in trucks and air freight.

4. Earlier collections of customer invoices, reducing accounts receivable, has real financial value.

5. Field warehouses can be eliminated for high value, low bulk and mass products (that is, electronic components) and customer service maintained or even improved by fast airfreight shipments.

Data on each of these factors must be developed from experience in individual companies. Analyses for replenishment of field warehouse inventories are detailed in Appendix VII.

Aggregate Hedge Inventory

These result from "spot" decisions to buy more of commodities like precious metals, grain, animal fibers and hides, minerals and wood that have significant fluctuations in market prices. Another type is generated by decisions to purchase additional quantities of materials before a scheduled price rise occurs or the supply is interrupted by strikes. Each decision can be made on the basis of whether or not the saving from buying now is an adequate return on the additional investment in the extra inventory.

The only significance in aggregating such quantities is in showing the total demand on capital. This is simple addition. The only contribution materials planners can make is to provide information on future requirements for such commodities and materials and current inventory amounts. A discussion of the potential risks and pertinent market situations is beyond the scope of this book.

Managing the Total Inventory Investment

Most managers charged with inventory responsibility are today in the unpleasant position of trying to execute inventory policies that have never been clearly formulated. Setting rational inventory policy requires a knowledge of existing alternatives and this requires looking at cost and other data in aggregate. The calculations required are rather tedious but are completely feasible in any company using modern computers. The inventory manager who can present aggregate inventory information to higher levels of management and assist them in making reasonable policy decisions will be able to work with clearly established policies that recognize the basic trade-offs in inventory management. The inventory manager who cannot present aggregate information will almost certainly have to work under a constant stream of criticism arising inevitably when policy has not been clearly established. In fact, it is questionable whether the managers who do not prepare aggregate inventory information can truly be said to be *managing* inventories. They are certainly not professional in carrying out their duties.

As managers become more professional, properly using the principles and techniques of inventory management, the true trade-offs in manufacturing become obvious. Those who do not understand the principles and techniques struggle to get enough inventory of the right items to minimize a few vaguely defined ''costs'' and to prevent shortages from unexpected upsets. This is planning to handle unplannable occurrences—inherently a contradiction and futile in practice.

Aggregate planning reveals the real alternatives:

1. Improve quality and eliminate rejects
2. Reduce late vendor deliveries and behind-schedule operation
3. Increase reliability of machinery and equipment
4. Shorten setups to permit running only what is needed now
5. Smooth out and speed up flow, shortening lead times
6. Provide flexibility and fast response to handle upsets

Essentially this approach views inventory *as a liability,* not an asset. It shows the real trade-off—*solve the problems or suffer;* carry inventory, support the investment and expect trouble anyhow. The answer to the perennial question, How much inventory is enough? is less, always less.

Principle 38. Inventory is a liability; less is better.

CHAPTER
NINE

CAPACITY REQUIREMENTS PLANNING

Lead Time: Kinds and Elements

In distribution, where inventories are purchased, stored and resold, inventory control can be a fairly independent function balancing the purchasing economies with the objectives of customer service and minimum inventory. In a manufacturing organization, inventories exist either as a result of production or to support production. A manufacturing concern can change the timing and lot-sizes of orders, as dictated by priority considerations, but any resultant *change in* total *inventory levels will not be achieved until production rates are changed to increase or decrease* total *factory output.* Moreover, an inventory control function that ignores a plant's operating efficiency (specifically, the need to maintain smooth, fast flow and a fairly stable rate of production for quality, morale, and cost considerations) is usually characterized by long lead times, poor service and high inventories. The reasons for this involve the basic relationship of lead time to inventories.

Two different types of lead time must be managed:

1. Work center lead time
2. Order lead time

Work center lead time is the *average time an order spends in the queue at a work center before being processed.* Figure 9-1 illustrates a typical work center in which several orders are awaiting processing. The length of the queue, which is the work center lead time, is the sum of the setup and running times for the

$$\text{Average } Q = (SU + RT)_1 + (SU + RT)_2 + (SU + RT)_3 + \ldots + (SU + RT)_n$$

Figure 9-1 WORK CENTER LEAD TIME.

individual orders at the center. On the average, this is how long the next order must wait to get started being processed at the center.

How long each specific order really will take is, of course, a function of the priority it is assigned. Higher priority orders will bypass those of lower priority and move into the center more quickly. The average time, however, is a direct function of how many orders are there. This is unaffected by the priorities of orders; it depends on the relative rates at which orders arrive and leave the center—its capacity.

Principle 39. Managing work center lead times requires managing capacity.

Planned levels must be set for each significant work center. These should consider the variability of arrival rates of work and the importance and cost of idle time in the work center. Critically loaded, high-cost operations with widely varying input rates need high standard queue levels. Specific techniques for setting such planned average queues is covered later in this chapter. Ideally, engineers, tool designers, shop supervisors, setup people and workers will combine their efforts to smooth out and speed up the flow of work so work-in-process inventories can be reduced. This too is discussed in more detail later in this chapter and also in the second volume (9).

Order lead time—the time it takes to replenish an inventory item—is composed of many basic elements:

1. Paper work time
2. Setup time
3. Running time
4. Move time
5. Queue time

Paper work time (also called *preparation* or *administrative* time) is the time required to do all work related to initiation of either purchasing or manufacturing orders. For the first release of such orders, it can involve a significant amount of time to produce the necessary routings, specifications, vendor selections, etc. and must be considered in planning and scheduling activities.

For materials processed repetitively, paper-work time does not have to *and should not be* included in planned order lead times. Ordering techniques like the time-phased order point and MRP provide visibility of orders coming up for future release far enough ahead to provide the time needed for processing paperwork and related activities. This is illustrated in Figure 5-16, Chapter 5, and Figure 6-5, Chapter 6. Omitting the paper work elements results in shorter planned lead times, later release of work, lower levels of work-in-process and, most importantly, a shorter active horizon in the manufacturing plan. The importance of this in the total planning and control process is covered in Chapter 7 and also in Chapter 2 of the second volume (9). This affects all starting or gateway work centers which include all in-house or vendor facilities receiving orders to begin processing raw materials, subassemble or combine components and finish assemble or package end products.

Running and **setup times** require no explanation; **move time** is the actual time spent in transit between operations, including the time a job spends waiting to be moved; **queue time** (work center lead time) is the time that a job spends at a work center without being worked on because there are other jobs ahead of it. In most functionally organized plants and in many process plants, checking a sample of manufacturing orders to see what percentage of the manufacturing lead time was made up of the running, setup and move times typically shows them to be less than 10% of the total manufacturing lead time.

The element that constitutes the great bulk of lead time is queue time—time spent waiting because there are other jobs in process. The bulk of the work-in-process inventory is typically not being worked on, indicating that controls over total levels of work-in-process are poor. In companies where there is very little specific effort to control work-in-process, the result is long queues and long lead times. In practice, a manufacturing planning and control function that lacks sound capacity planning and control makes high levels of work-in-process an operating necessity.

As an example, consider a company attempting to control inventory without regard for whether or not plant capacity is adequate. Replenishment orders are generated at random by the inventory control technique and are then sent to the plant. Inventory control personnel assume no responsibility for level loading or smooth flow of work in the plant.

Plant operating people recognize that increases in the number of orders that they have received in the past represented just a random effect. Having as one of their prime objectives the maintenance of a stable work force, they will build backlogs of work in order to insure a supply of work. This will increase lead times, so that the wanted dates on the orders become less and less meaningful and proper sequencing of manufacturing orders becomes extremely difficult. The only way to insure getting a specific order through the plant is to expedite it. Thus the situation typically degenerates into inventory control and expediting.

The usual reaction of the inventory control system to longer lead times is to increase them in the order points or materials plan. This simply generates more orders which in turn creates a higher level of work-in-process, which generates longer lead times. This is the infamous "vicious cycle" described in detail in Chapter 5 of the second volume (9). The fact that plants tend to operate this way can be confirmed by looking at the work-in-process on their manufacturing floors. In those plants lacking sound capacity planning and control, levels of such inventory are high, materials lurch through the plant rather than flowing smoothly and even starting work centers have significant backlogs. Lead times are long and highly variable. In the absence of adequate capacity planning and control, work-in-process will follow a variation of Parkinson's law—it will expand to fill the available space (or shop containers or computer disk files).

Control over work-in-process—and hence over order lead times—requires that capacity requirements be planned and adequate capacity provided to support the master production schedule. Priority planning and control cannot be effective without this, no matter how sophisticated and dynamic that portion of the system is.

Principle 40. Managing order lead times requires managing both priority and capacity.

A Rational Approach to Capacity Planning

Generating individual orders far enough in advance to give manufacturing personnel or suppliers a means to plan capacity is unrealistic when the basis for generating these orders is a forecast. Also, if orders are released only as required by the priority plan, lead times tend to get extremely long and highly variable. Both approaches usually degenerate, in practice, into expediting systems.

Since no companies have perfect forecasts, any successful system must be capable of coping with imperfect predictions. This can usually be done if basic forecast characteristics discussed in Chapter 4 are understood and applied. The two major characteristics involved are:

1. Forecast accuracy is a function of time; the farther in the future the forecast is made, the less accurate it is likely to be.
2. Forecast accuracy is a function of the number of items in the group being forecast; the larger the product group, the more likely the forecast is to be accurate.

Principle 41. Capacity plans should use the broadest possible product groups that go through similar manufacturing operations.

Utilizing Principle 41, plans can establish the flow rates for such operations, while individual manufacturing orders are scheduled to the planned rate at the last possible moment and are based on the latest requirements—whether these requirements are generated by an order point or materials planning technique.

Choosing meaningful groups to plan requires a thorough knowledge of the plant's manufacturing processes. These groupings are seldom the same ones used by the marketing department or in inventory control. The groups must be meaningful in terms of *demand on the manufacturing facilities*. The important point is that forecasts are inevitably going to be more accurate for groups than for individual items, and even a crude capacity plan is far better than no plan at all. Such a plan provides

1. A means of *planning* production rates
2. A means of *controlling* production rates to meet the plan
3. A means of *regulating* the rate of release of work to the plant in order to control the level of work-in-process

The balance of this chapter is devoted to the development of capacity plans, emphasizing their use in the presentation of alternatives to higher levels of management as well as in planning production rates for specific facilities. The use of such plans to control order releases to meet the planned production rates is covered in Chapter 10. Chapter 11 presents the techniques and principles involved in the use of capacity plans to control work output.

A good capacity plan is a projection of the level of production required for a specific facility but it is *not* a firm commitment to the individual items to be made. The production plan establishes the framework within which inventory control techniques will operate. It sets the rate at which orders must be generated to feed the plant as well as the rate of plant output required to support the master production schedule.

Experience has shown that of all the improvements that can be made in manufacturing control, the capacity plan is usually the most significant and rewarding portion of the system. Benefits are higher and more immediate. Companies with seasonal production are especially vulnerable to high costs and inefficient operation when they lack effective capacity planning. The plan lays out in advance the program for building inventory ahead of the peak selling season and charts a course against which actual performance can be measured. Without a capacity plan, it is typical in this type of operation for management to become alarmed by the inventory buildup ahead of the peak season but to lack specific information about the level of inventory needed. Too frequently, the reaction is to get nervous over uncharted inventory increases, cut back production rates just before the peak season and then react at considerable expense to increase the production rate again when sales rates pick up and the inventory disappears. With a capacity plan, the inventory buildup can be compared regularly to the planned levels and the question of too-high or too-low inventory can be decided in time for corrective action to be effective without the problems of baseless discussions and panic decisions.

Making the Production Plan

The **production plan** is the common name given to capacity plans for plants or major groups of manufacturing facilities. It applies equally well to commodity groupings of purchased materials. Two requirements must be observed in making a production plan:

1. The production plan should cover product families or groups that are processed by some common manufacturing facilities. This, of course, means that the forecast used for production planning must be for these product groups and not for product groups that have meaning only to the sales department. Ideally these will be groups of products for which individual master production schedules will be developed.

2. The production plan should be expressed in the simplest terms meaningful to plant operating personnel; that is, the measures of production should be in units such as pieces, hours, etc.

The steps involved in making a production plan are:

1. Determine the period to be covered by the production plan. Many companies make a general, overall monthly production plan 1 year in advance that is used to establish overall inventory/production policy and as a basis for checking requirements for equipment capacity. They then make a detailed weekly production plan to plan and stabilize requirements for workers.

2. Establish the base inventory level. This is the minimum inventory that should be on hand to meet the customer-service level set by management policy. The logic for determining aggregate inventory levels using materials planning was discussed in Chapter 8.

3. Spread the sales forecast over the planning period. This should take into account regular cycles or peaks produced by sales promotions that have a significant effect on sales rates.

4. Determine the total inventory for the product group at the beginning of the planning period. This is usually net inventory available for new business but may also include items manufactured but not yet packed or delivered to warehouses.

5. Set the desired inventory level at the end of the period. This is the base inventory level mentioned in (1) plus any inventory that has to be added to cover plant shutdowns, seasonal peaks or other requirements at the end of the period.

6. Calculate the change in inventory level desired during the planning period. This is simply the difference between beginning and ending inventories.

7. Calculate the total production required for the planning period. This is equal to the total sales forecast plus or minus any desired change in the inventory level from the beginning to the end of the period.

8. Spread the total production over the period as desired. This should be done considering holidays or other periods of lost production and the time required to increase or decrease production rates from present levels.

Starting with the actual inventory, if the desired inventory at the end of the planning period and the forecast of sales during the planning period are known, the weekly production rate can be calculated by using this simple formula:

$$R = \frac{(D - S + F)}{N} \tag{9-1}$$

where:

R = weekly production rate to achieve level production over the planning period

D = desired total inventory at the end of the planning period

S = actual total starting inventory

F = total sales forecast for the planning period

N = number of weeks in the planning period

As an example, assume the following for a product line of stamped ashtrays:

1. Actual starting inventory is 130,000 units.
2. Desired inventory at the end of the planning period is 110,000 units.
3. Total sales forecast equals 140,000 units.
4. There are 5 weeks in the planning period.

Then

$$R = \frac{D - S + F}{N}$$

$$= \frac{110,000 - 130,000 + 140,000}{5} = 24,000$$

Figure 9-2 shows the weekly production plan that results. The starting inventory is 20,000 units higher than the desired inventory at the end of the planning period. Therefore, the total production must be less than the sales forecast. Note that the production plan has two lines for each week, planned and actual. During October, the actual sales, production and inventory will be posted against the plan in order to track and control the production rate. A production plan should be used as a budget to compare actual performance against planned performance

All stamped ashtrays (Figures in "pieces")			
Week date	Sales	Production	Inventory
Start			130,000
10 – 3 Planned Actual	20,000	24,000	134,000
10 – 10 Planned Actual	25,000	24,000	133,000
10 – 17 Planned Actual	30,000	24,000	127,000
10 – 24 Planned Actual	30,000	24,000	121,000
10 – 31 Planned Actual	35,000	24,000	110,000

Figure 9-2 WEEKLY PRODUCTION PLAN.

and to indicate when corrective action must be taken. This is identical in format to the S-P-I report presented in Chapter 7.

The production plan, in addition to planning and controlling the level of production, also regulates the flow of orders into the plant. The techniques for doing this are covered in Chapter 10.

A production plan is a simple—yet essential—tool, and the information required is usually readily available in most companies. In fact, many companies that do not use production plans as such have all this information and are comparing performance against plans—but are doing this separately for sales, production and inventory. Most marketing and sales departments compare actual sales against forecasts. Financial people keep track of the actual inventory level against the data on which financial budgets have been based. Like much financial data, however, these figures are usually at least 1 week old and are of little use in controlling inventories. The materials control manager or plant manager keeps records comparing actual production with the planned production rates updated daily.

Although this information is not often integrated, it has little meaning when considered individually. Manufacturing control decisions can best be made when all three factors—sales, production and inventory—are viewed together. It would be wrong to insist that a plant meet a planned increase in production rate if sales were not up to forecast and inventory was higher than planned. On the other hand, if production were up to the planned rate but sales were exceeding the forecast (causing inventory to drop below the planned level), the manufacturing rates would obviously have to be increased. Looking at the three factors together in a production plan is the first and basic step in establishing sound control of manufacturing operations.

Production plans in periods immediately preceding vacation shutdowns or other interruptions in production require that a difficult choice be made. Because of lost production, inventories may drop below desirable levels and, consequently, customer service will probably be poorer than desired. Two alternatives are available: either run at a higher level during the earlier part of the year and then reduce production to hit the year-end inventory goal or set a higher year-end target inventory and maintain production at a level rate throughout the year. These are typical of the "least-worst" choices in manufacturing.

In any case, production plans are only approximations. The chance that sales will be exactly as forecast is almost nil, as is the chance that the plant will manufacture exactly to the planned level of production. There is a point of diminishing returns where added refinement of the production plan becomes meaningless. Capacity planning does not require being carried away by the illusion of precision in the numbers. Production planning is frequently referred to as "rough-cut capacity requirements planning," but this should not be interpreted as crude or poor. Perhaps "first-cut" is better.

Principle 42. Production plans, even though rough-cut, provide effective means for capacity management.

The Seasonal Production Plan

When making a seasonal production plan, three alternatives are available to the planner:

1. Hold a level production rate at the expense of carrying high inventories
2. Hold inventories down by varying the production rate to meet the seasonal sales requirements
3. Some combination of these two extremes, with changes in the production rate made at strategic times to minimize excess inventory and meet the seasonal requirements

These three alternatives are illustrated by the following example. Figure 9-3 shows a yearly production plan for making all-steel, cartridge, automotive-type

All–steel, cartridge, automotive–type filters (all figures in thousands of hours of labor)								
			Sales		Production		Inventory* (Sept. 30 1 200)	Remarks
Month		Wk	Month	Cumul.	Month	Cumul.	1 200)	
Oct.	Planned	5	800	800	1120	1120	1520	Prod. = 224/wk
	Actual							
Nov.	Planned	4	600	1400	896	2016	1816	
	Actual							
Dec.	Planned	4	500	1900	896	2912	2212	
	Actual							
Jan.	Planned	5	1000	2900	1120	4032	2332	
	Actual							
Feb.	Planned	4	800	3700	896	4928	2428	
	Actual							
Mar.	Planned	4	800	4500	896	5824	2524	
	Actual							
Apr.	Planned	4	900	5400	896	6720	2520	
	Actual							
May	Planned	5	1200	6600	1120	7840	2440	
	Actual							
June	Planned	4	1000	7600	896	8736	2336	
	Actual							
July	Planned	2**	1000	8600	448	9184	1784	
	Actual							
Aug.	Planned	5	1500	10,100	1120	10,304	1404	
	Actual							
Sept.	Planned	4	900	11,000	896	11,200	1400	
	Actual							

*Base Inventory Level = 1400 M hours
**Vacation shutdown = 2 weeks

Figure 9-3 SEASONAL PRODUCTION PLAN 1.

filters. Two points in particular are worth noticing about this plan. The first is that it does not cover a calendar year but covers instead a *selling year.* Production and inventory are planned to meet the seasonal demand pattern which starts from a low in December, increases to a peak in August and then drops back down. The plan should start near the end of the selling season, since inventory will be lowest just as sales drop below the production rate. The second point worth noticing is that this plan measures inventory, sales and production in terms of *labor-hours,* which is the only meaningful measure for this large and mixed product group where some of the individual products in a group take far longer to manufacture than others. Nevertheless, all these products go through the same basic manufacturing equipment.

Seasonal production plan 1 (Figure 9-3) attempts to level out production and maintain it throughout the year. Inventory from January through June is quite high but production is maintained at a steady rate. Seasonal production plan 2 (Figure 9-4) changes the production rate four times during the year but succeeds in main-

All–steel, cartridge, automotive – type filters (all figures in thousands of hours of labor)			Sales		Production		Inventory* (Sept. 30 1200)	Remarks
Month		Wk.	Month	Cumul.	Month	Cumul.		
Oct.	Planned Actual	5	800	800	805	805	1205	Prod.= 161/wk
Nov.	Planned Actual	4	600	1400	645	1450	1250	
Dec.	Planned Actual	4	500	1900	645	2095	1395	
Jan.	Planned Actual	5	1000	2900	1000	3095	1395	Prod.= 200/wk
Feb.	Planned Actual	4	800	3700	800	3895	1395	
Mar.	Planned Actual	4	800	4500	800	4695	1395	
Apr.	Planned Actual	4	900	5400	950	5645	1445	Prod.= 238/wk
May	Planned Actual	5	1200	6600	1190	6835	1435	
June	Planned Actual	4	1000	7600	950	7785	1385	
July	Planned Actual	2**	1000	8600	620	8405	1005	Prod.= 309/wk
Aug.	Planned Actual	5	1500	10,100	1550	9955	1055	
Sept.	Planned Actual	4	900	11,000	1240	11,195	1395	

*Base inventory level = 1400 M hours
**Vacation shutdown = 2 weeks

Figure 9-4 SEASONAL PRODUCTION PLAN 2.

taining a much lower level of inventory. Seasonal production plan 3 (Figure 9-5) varies the production level twice during the year and arrives at a level of inventory that is a compromise between the first two plans.

Basically, a seasonal production plan attempts to balance inventory investment against the costs of changing the production level. Just as with the economic ordering quantity problem, the costs needed to solve this planning problem are not readily available. Primary factors in these costs are overtime, hiring, and training and layoff (all of which can be *estimated* with some confidence). Other costs are more nebulous, though real just the same. Training new employees and low morale of workers facing layoff reduce quality, with higher scrap and rework losses. Frequent layoffs give a company a poor reputation in the labor market and make it difficult to hire and keep high-caliber workers.

Production-rate changes, particularly increases, are very difficult to accomplish as scheduled. New employees are not able to produce at desired rates for varying

Month		Wk.	Sales		Production		Inventory* (Sept. 30 1200)	Remarks
			Month	Cumul.	Month	Cumul.		
Oct.	Planned Actual	5	800	800	975	975	1375	Prod. = 195/wk.
Nov.	Planned Actual	4	600	1400	780	1755	1555	
Dec.	Planned Actual	4	500	1900	780	2535	1835	
Jan.	Planned Actual	5	1000	2900	975	3510	1810	
Feb.	Planned Actual	4	800	3700	780	4290	1790	
Mar.	Planned Actual	4	800	4500	780	5070	1770	
Apr.	Planned Actual	4	900	5400	780	5850	1650	
May	Planned Actual	5	1200	6600	975	6825	1425	
June	Planned Actual	4	1000	7600	1272	8097	1697	Prod. = 318/wk.
July	Planned Actual	2**	1000	8600	636	8733	1333	
Aug.	Planned Actual	5	1500	10,100	1590	10,323	1423	
Sept.	Planned Actual	4	900	11,000	1272	11,595	1795	

All-steel, cartridge, automotive-type filters
(all figures in thousands of hours of labor)

*Base inventory level = 1400 M hours
**Vacation shutdown = 2 weeks

Figure 9-5 SEASONAL PRODUCTION PLAN 3.

periods and some, never able to attain even minimum rates, must be replaced. Component production increases usually precede finishing rate increases; manufacturing supervisors are usually reluctant to add people until they can see the materials there to work on.

Figure 9-6 compares the three production plans using estimated data for value of inventory, cost of carrying inventory and the cost of changing the production level as shown. With these assumed costs, plan 2 gives the lowest total cost.

It should be noted that plans 2 and 3 require far more capacity to handle the peak production than plan 1. This may be close to or even beyond the maximum capacity of machinery and equipment available. Management should also recognize that with plan 2, inventory will be well below the base level right after vacation. It should also be noted that production is at a high rate going into the slow selling season in plan 3. Unless sales are considerably higher next year, another change in production level may be required sooner in plan 3 than in plan 2. This even more strongly makes plan 2 the lowest-cost plan.

All–Steel, Cartridge, Automotive – Type Filters

	Average inventory level (M hrs)	Average inventory (M dollars) (1)	Average inventory carrying cost (2)	Changes in production level	Cost of changes (3)	Total cost (M dollars)
Plan #1	2060	$41,200	$8240	1	$150	$8390
Plan #2	1313	26,260	5252	4	600	5852
Plan #3	1622	32,440	6488	2	300	6788

(1) $20.00 per labor hour; (2) 20%; (3) $150M per change.

Figure 9-6 COMPARISON—PRODUCTION PLANS 1, 2 AND 3.

Practical Factors in Production Planning

A few considerations worth keeping in mind when making production plans are:

1. Some definite period of time is required for changing production levels. The change in production rate must be given to the plant soon enough for it to react.

2. The number of holidays during the year may be a substantial factor affecting the level of inventory. Setting a daily production rate and the working days per week in the production plan will handle this.

3. Many workers may have 3-week or even 4-week vacations which result in production losses beyond the 2-week vacation shutdown. June through August is likely to be a period of slack production and it is important to pinpoint just where lost production will occur during this period.

4. Overtime is expensive but in some circumstances is more desirable than adding people (from a pure cost viewpoint). A good rule of thumb used

by many practitioners is never to plan to use overtime. Their reasoning is that overtime provides flexibility in meeting unexpected surges in sales or overcoming losses in production caused by equipment breakdowns or similar failures. Moreover, planned overtime is much easier to start than it is to stop.

5. Seasonal production plans should attempt to store production *hours* in the cheapest form. Given the alternative between fabricating and storing a high-value component that requires very little labor or processing a low-value one with high labor content, the latter is definitely the better choice.

6. When making a production plan, it is important to obtain and use the most accurate data available and to present information to management to show them the real alternatives.

7. Production plans are usually made on a monthly basis for the year. In fast-moving operations, they may be made on a weekly basis for each quarter in order to give enough detail to permit following closely the planned production rate, sales and inventory levels.

8. One of the most frequently asked questions about production plans is, How often should they be changed? This question really misses an important point—the objective is to *change production plans only when necessary*. It is extremely important to determine ahead of time what set of circumstances will require a change in the production level. When these rules are not established ahead of time, there may be weekly discussions, causing friction among managers of different opinions as to whether or not the present circumstances require a change in production level. Chapter 11 discusses decision rules that can be established for determining when to change production plans.

9. A plant should have a production plan for each major manufacturing facility that it wishes to control. In fact, if there is a chance that it may be desirable to run two work areas within an overall manufacturing area at different production rates, two production plans—one for each of these submanufacturing areas—should be established. This might occur when one facility is feeding components into an intermediate inventory ahead of a finishing department. Separate production plans for the fabrication and finishing operations make it possible to control (either raise or lower) the production rates of each independently. This is covered in detail in the next section of this chapter. As was stated previously, too much refinement and precision should be avoided in developing any production plans.

10. Picking the right measures of capacity to use in planning is particularly important—the production plan should use the simplest terms that are meaningful to manufacturing people. One of the best methods for determining meaningful terms is to ask manufacturing supervisors about

changing production levels: What personnel changes would have to be made if the number of *pieces* on the production schedule were increased? If these terms are meaningful to them, go no further. If they require *hours,* which are much harder to get, the added work is usually justified since it is important to generate information that is useful to those responsible for getting action in the plant.

An alternative that has proven to be very useful in many companies is *equivalent units.* For production planning purposes, a dual gasoline pump, capable of putting two different grades of motor fuel into two cars simultaneously, would be equivalent to two single pumps, serving only one vehicle with one product. Other models can be related to the standard single unit also. For example, a dispenser, lacking pumping unit motor and related hardware (they are in the underground storage tank), would be counted as three fourths of an equivalent unit.

11. Cumulative sales and production figures should be shown in the plan. These permit comparison of actual sales and production against planned values and against one another over the period. Marketing may decide not to change the forecast because of a lower sales rate in the preceding period because they do not believe the deficit will be made up. The future plan, therefore, starts with the actual cumulative sales figure. If they anticipate overcoming this deficit *in addition* to selling the future forecasted units, the sales rate in the plan will have to be increased. Note that the cumulative totals of *actual* sales and production for one period become the starting figures for the next. The development of the production rates in making the new plan should be based on the desired inventory level at the end of the quarter and the expected total demand. Using these figures in making the plan takes care of production deficits in the preceding quarter.

12. In making a production plan for finished goods in a make-to-stock plant, the service versus investment chart (see Chapter 8) is an extremely valuable tool. It helps establish the base inventory levels at which the production plans aim. It is important to remember, however, that the service versus investment chart is based upon the average demand during the year. Where demand varies greatly during the year, the safety stocks required for a particular service level also vary. In applications where there is a wide variation in demand during the year, the service versus investment chart should be based upon the demand experienced at the time the inventory reaches its low point when there is no anticipation inventory on hand to assist the normal safety stocks in giving customer service protection. The service versus investment chart can also be used to evaluate the effect on customer service of dips below the base inventory level. Some production-plan alternatives include a period during the year when inventory temporarily dips below an ideal level. This is illustrated by the seasonal plan for ashtrays in Figure 9-4. The desirability of such an

alternative can be evaluated better if a definite measure of the effect on customer service can be obtained. The service versus investment chart gives this measure.

Rough-Cut Capacity Planning for Functional Departments

Capacities of functional departments performing basic starting, fabrication or finishing operations are more difficult to plan and control. When this is attempted using only inventory control techniques and backlog measuring techniques (such as machine loading), the erratic rate of order flow in these departments results in excessive and highly variable lead times and in very slow reaction to changes in the total demand caused by increasing or decreasing business. The same general principles of establishing a planned level of operation for these departments and then scheduling specific orders to meet this plan can reduce the lead time for components drastically, level out manufacturing operations very significantly and shorten reaction time when the business level changes.

A capacity requirements plan for a functional department making components can be set up by converting the master production schedules for *all* products into standard hours of work requirements. A simple technique for converting units of product in the MPS to standard hours of work in individual centers involves the use of the bill of labor. Figure 9-7 shows a typical bill of labor and illustrates its structural resemblance to a bill of materials—hence the name. The product (one listed in the MPS) requires the indicated total standard hours of work in specified work centers to do *all work required*. Not all work centers involved in the processing are included; listed are only those for which production plans are to be prepared. The hours include estimates for both setup and processing times.

Product #13254

Work Center	Total* Standard Hours
92	10
88	8
74	14
53	28
36	9
10	17

*Setup and processing

Figure 9-7 TYPICAL BILL OF LABOR.

Accurate data yield better results, of course, but even rough estimates permit useful plans to be developed. Such data are sometimes found in cost accounting records. A very sound beginning to rough-cut capacity requirements planning for functional centers can be made if only bills of labor for product families are available, providing that these are the same groups of products for which overall production plans have been made or for which totals can be determined from the MPS. The mechanics of developing capacity requirements for individual work centers is identical to that described next for individual products, except that the quantities and time periods used will be the same as for families in the production plan instead of those for products in the MPS.

The next step is to accumulate in each time period in the MPS the total hours of work required to produce all products scheduled in that period. The results of one time period are shown in Figure 9-8. Note that these calculations assume

1. That the hours of work will all be needed in the same time period (no lead time offsetting)

2. That only the quantities of items in the MPS will be produced (no lot-sizing)

3. That all items will have to be produced (no significant changes in inventories of items)

Finally, a summary capacity-requirements plan is developed, as shown in Figure 9-9. The column headed "Present capacity" shows recent actual output (average of 3 or 4 weeks) in standard hours; this is called **demonstrated capacity**. The capacity required is averaged for three or four periods before being compared to the present data. *This removes all limitations resulting from the first two assumptions just given.* The comparison with present capacity reveals bottleneck centers with inadequate capacity (work center no. 53) as well as those with excess capacity (work center no. 10). Changes in data over the horizon show needed capacity adjustments.

The third assumption poses no problem unless it is planned to reduce component inventories significantly. Calculations can be made for such reductions, if desired. Quantities of components now in stock can be converted into standard hours of capacity stored for each work center.

Principle 43. A capacity requirements plan cannot be deferred; rough-cut approaches are very practical.

A typical capacity plan is shown in Figure 9-10. Quantities of components in inventory are converted into standard hours of machining, as are orders withdrawing components for production in downstream operations and production rates replenishing such components. If no significant changes are to be made in com-

Products	13254	13255	13256	13257	13258	Total for period
MPS units	55	—	20	40	30	
Work center 92	550	—	200	400	300	2150
Work center 88	440	—	160	320	240	1410
Work center 74	770	—	280	560	420	2560
Work center 53	1540	—	560	1120	840	4420
Work center 36	495	—	180	300	270	1560
Work center 10	935	—	340	680	510	2980

Figure 9-8 PERIOD CAPACITY REQUIREMENTS PLANS.

(All data in Standard Hours)

Work center	Present capacity	Required capacity						
		Period 1	Period 2	Period 3	Period 4	Period 5	Period 6	Period 7
		Average =						
92	2120	2100						
88	1460	1470						
74	2660	2640						
53	4140	4510						
36	1510	1520						
10	3280	2910						

Figure 9-9 SUMMARY CAPACITY REQUIREMENTS PLAN.

ponent levels, the plan would show only the producton data. Occasionally, it is desirable to increase the levels of component inventories temporarily in preparation for periods of reduced production, such as would occur if factory equipment layouts were being rearranged or if a key piece of equipment were to be shut down for overhaul. Figure 9-10 shows a buildup of components ahead of a plant shut down for vacations. Having a production plan for each major facility enables planning for different production rates for individual facilities when it is necessary to change component inventory levels added to by one and depleted by another.

(In Standard Machining Hours)

Week Ending		Orders		Production		Component Stockroom Inventory
		Weekly	Cumulative	Weekly	Cumulative	
4/7	Planned	2800	64,190	4300	55,390	12,820
	Actual	2750	64,200	5100	55,390	13,670
4/14	Planned	2800	66,990	4300	59,690	14,320
	Actual	3400	67,600	7580	62,970	17,850
4/21	Planned	2800	69,790	4300	63,990	15,820
	Actual	3260	70,860	4490	67,460	19,080
⋮						
6/30	Planned	2800	97,790	4300	106,990	30,820
	Actual					

Figure 9-10 CAPACITY PLAN—FUNCTIONAL DEPARTMENT.

Capacity requirements plans based on bills of labor are usually considered rough-cut. In the early stages of implementation of modern integrated systems, however, they can make possible significant improvements in operations. Work-in-process and lead times can be slashed dramatically using simple, manual capacity planning and input/output control techniques.

As more accurate data become available, these rough-cut approaches should be refined. Such refinements include

1. Smaller families or even individual products
2. More complete, accurate data in hours of work required
3. More work centers
4. Shorter planning intervals

The timing of changes in production levels is very important. It is a difficult task to keep a manufacturing plant's work centers in balance and it becomes even tougher as inventories drop and lead times shorten. When work-in-process is low, assembly and finishing rates cannot be increased and sustained a long time until production rates of components are picked up. Any change in production levels that requires hiring and training skilled people requires a considerable period of time to accomplish. Unless work-in-process is to be reduced, it is meaningless to increase the required production rate from a department before the material input rate has been increased. In a complex factory, production rate increases through a sequence of departments have to be coordinated very carefully depending upon the starting inventory and lead time through the series of operations. Sound capacity planning is necessary to accomplish such changes on an orderly basis with a minimum of lost time and upset.

For service departments within a plant, such as painting, plating or mixing, production rates for significant equipment groups must also be planned— recognizing that it is not always possible to control precisely the flow of material into these departments since work does not originate there but comes from many other work centers. The scheduled input of orders into source departments should be balanced as closely as possible to meet the planned production rates in service departments and to insure smooth flows of materials to them. This is covered in detail in Chapter 10.

Detailed Capacity
Requirements Planning

When the proper data and computer programs are available, very detailed calculations of capacity requirements are possible. The data requirements are

1. Valid due dates on all released and planned orders
2. Up-to-date routings and processing information
3. Accurate standards for setup and processing time
4. A scheduling program to handle all operations
5. A loading program to assign work to time periods
6. Standard queue allowances for all work centers
7. Estimates of load due to unplanned occurrences

Scheduling and loading techniques are covered in detail in Chapter 10, which also provides information on ways to determine standard queue allowances.

Figure 9-11 shows a typical work center load report for gateway (starting, subassembly, final assembly, finishing and packaging) and other types of work centers. It includes both released and planned orders and must extend far enough into the future (well beyond the 8 weeks illustrated in Figure 9-11) to provide useful information. In gateway centers the load, of course, will be a paper load of released orders; in others it will be made up of a combination of real orders (physical materials actually at the center) and planned orders (orders scheduled to be there in the period indicated). Note that released orders may be real or planned in this context, depending on whether or not they have arrived in the center on schedule. Figure 9-11 is typical because it shows

1. A significant amount of late work (see Chapter 10 for a discussion of the meaning of this)

2. A heavy total load in the immediate future, mostly from orders already released

3. Erratic loads in various time periods

4. A sharp falling off of the *released* order load in the future

Such a load will be a good representation of the actual plant situation only if the assumptions and data on which it is based are valid. It is a classic illustration of the illusion of precision, often confused with accuracy. It is easy to misread such data unless the techniques of loading and scheduling are understood thoroughly. This is discussed in Chapter 10.

It is a *mistake to assume that the load in each period must be handled by the work center.* While such fluctuations in capacity are possible in some work

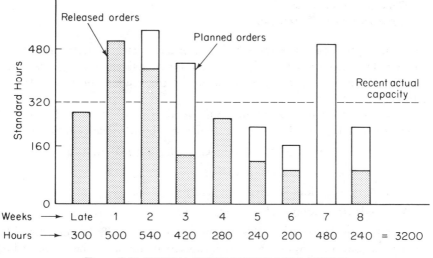

Figure 9-11 TYPICAL WORK CENTER LOAD REPORT.

centers, they are difficult at best and often impossible. It is an even *more serious mistake to assume that the work center capacity must be adequate to handle the average load* shown (100 hours per week in Figure 9-11). There are two reasons:

1. The formal plan does not include all the load it will be necessary to handle.
2. Some of the load must remain in the center to provide the planned standard queue.

In addition to the detailed load calculated by the formal plan, there will be demands on capacity for

1. New products not in the current MPS
2. Use of alternate routings and processing in times of crisis
3. Scrap replenishment and rework operations
4. Additional processing needed for any reason
5. Record errors resulting in additional material requirements

Partially offsetting these will be reductions in load from products dropped from the line, changes and improvements in methods, new equipment and excess inventories uncovered. These can be only estimated to determine the net additions or subtractions from the formal plan.

As long as it is necessary to have work-in-process (queues) to absorb fluctuations in loads on work centers, the hours of the load represented by these planned queues must be deducted from the total load to determine the capacity requirements for the work center. For obvious reasons, successful companies are working constantly to reduce these fluctuations and cut work-in-process.

Principle 44. Capacity must be adequate to support the MPS and handle additional unplanned demands.

Capacity Planning for Purchased Materials

Establishing a production rate and scheduling orders to meet this planned rate are also required for effective control of purchased raw materials and components. These are particularly necessary when a large portion of the vendor's business is from a few principal customers.

Capacity requirements from important vendors should be included on bills of labor, such as Figure 9-7, on which should be shown capacity measures like

1. Thousands of pieces (for fasteners, packaging materials, etc.)
2. Pounds or tons (for raw materials)
3. Gallons (for liquids, chemicals, etc.)
4. Molds (for castings, plastics, etc.)

Rough estimates make possible an effective start but refinements should be developed as quickly as possible to improve capacity planning for the vendor. Close cooperation between customers and suppliers makes it possible to develop, smooth out and reduce loads on the latter's facilities, using the detailed calculations discussed in the preceding section.

Changes in the rate of orders flowing to vendors generate severe ups and downs in their output requirements and result in widely varying service to customers. The fact that this is the vendor's problem does not lessen its effect on the customer's inventories and operations. A vendor's natural reaction to erratic ordering by customers is to generate a substantial backlog of orders in order to operate efficiently. By giving each vendor a capacity plan to work to and scheduling the mix of individual items regularly to meet this plan, suppliers' lead times can be reduced very substantially. As each mix schedule is issued, a review of the status of both new orders and previous orders should be made with the vendor. Such close communication is of great benefit to both vendor and customer. Regardless of the portion of the supplier's output taken by any customer, careful capacity planning and input/output control can result in just-in-time deliveries. This is covered in detail in Chapter 10.

The procedure for developing detailed capacity requirements plans is

1. Update the due dates of all released and planned orders in the MRP program over its full horizon.
2. Schedule all operations on both released and planned manufacturing orders (using the detailed techniques covered in Chapter 10).
3. Load all work centers with all orders scheduled (using the infinite-loading technique described in Chapter 10).
4. Average the loads over monthly or bimonthly periods.
5. Add estimates of known additional work not in the formal plan.
6. Add allowances (usually percentages) for unplanned random occurrences (scrap, rework, alternate operations, etc.).
7. Deduct estimates of known improvements (tooling, methods, new equipment, etc.) reducing work content.
8. Deduct standard queue from first period in capacity requirements plan.
9. Compare capacity requirements with present (demonstrated) capacity of each work center, highlighting significant excesses or inadequacies.
10. Plan and implement corrective actions.

This and other rigorous, highly detailed techniques can be applied successfully only where the data are accurate and complete and the environment is sufficiently disciplined so that the plans represent closely what will or can be made to occur. Simply having the necessary computing power is no reason to use this detailed capacity requirements planning approach.

Principle 45. Detailed capacity requirements plans may look highly precise and still be very inaccurate.

Planning Capacity
in a Make-To-Order Plant

While the techniques of capacity planning are relatively easy to understand, they are more difficult to apply in a make-to-order plant. Many who operate in such plants believe that a customer order must be on hand before valid planning information is available and, therefore, they can plan capacity only from backlogs of customer orders. This ignores the basic forecast characteristic discussed earlier—large groups of items can be forecast with some accuracy, even where individual items cannot. Planning from forecasts rather than backlogs reduces lead time and this can be a real competitive advantage even if it is not necessary to meet customers' delivery requirements.

The first step in capacity planning in a make-to-order plant is to decide upon the definition of manufacturing groups. These are not as readily apparent as they are in a make-to-stock plant. Nevertheless, there are usually groups of like products that go through similar manufacturing facilities which can be identified if the ultimate purpose of planning the rate of production is kept in mind. Even if the groups so identified do not account for the full load on the facilities, preparing a production plan for even a portion of capacity is far better than doing no planning and almost invariably justifies the cost.

The next step is to look at the history of total demand for the product groups selected. Figure 9-12 shows this type of analysis. This example covers a paper-manufacturing company making a variety of grades of paper. Incoming orders for a group of coarse papers have been tallied for a 10-week period. This analysis does not break the incoming orders down into individual items but instead totals them in terms meaningful to production (in this case, production hours). The forecast made previously was approximately 200 hours per week.

Cumulative sales deviated from forecast between plus 1 week (195 hours) and minus $\frac{1}{10}$ of a week (20 hours) of production. One of the great values of this type of approach is that it determines how much unreleased order backlog is necessary if a backlog is needed at all in this plant. Rather than just assuming, for example, that three to four weeks is normal for this particular business, Figure 9-12 indicates that 1 week of backlog would be satisfactory to keep production going at a fairly level rate. This information could be used to set up a decision rule for changing the production rate. Based on these data, whenever the total backlog is greater than 1 week of work at the planned rate, the production level has to be increased.

One of the distinct advantages of this type of analysis is that it focuses attention on the total demand rather than on individual orders, so that significant trends and factors are no longer buried in a maze of detail. Statistical approaches detailed in Chapter 5 can be used to refine this type of capacity planning in a make-to-order plant.

Many factories are comprised of both make-to-order and make-to-stock plants, having the bulk of their business in make-to-stock products but receiving many orders for specials. The capacity plan for these should allow a portion of the total work-hours each week for specials, averaging the ups and downs inevitable in incoming order rate for special products.

Forecast = 200 hrs / week				
Week	Orders	Cumulative Orders	Cumulative Forecast	Deviation
1	210	210	200	+ 10
2	220	430	400	+ 30
3	150	580	600	− 20
4	230	810	800	+ 10
5	300	1110	1000	+110
6	270	1380	1200	+180
7	215	1595	1400	+195
8	180	1775	1600	+175
9	140	1915	1800	+ 115
10	210	2125	2000	+ 125

Figure 9-12 INCOMING ORDERS FOR COARSE PAPERS.

Graphical Capacity Planning Techniques

In the previous sections, production and capacity plans were tabular, using hours and pieces. However, some practitioners prefer graphical techniques. Figure 9-13 is a graphical representation of the monthly production plan for filters shown in Figure 9-3. The production plan shows clearly that production exceeds sales during the early part of the year and, consequently, inventory builds up. Inventory is reduced during the peak selling season (May through September), when sales greatly exceed production. Upon close inspection of this production plan, though, some problems are apparent. Because the plan is based on a shop calendar that has two 4-week months and one 5-week month in every quarter, the graph of this production plan indicates that the production rate is quite erratic when, in fact, it is level at 228,000 hours per week.

To make this graphical production plan representative of the true situation, the time scale could be in weeks, days or 4-week periods to eliminate distortion. Another approach, however, is to plot sales and production cumulatively (as shown in Figure 9-14. In this case, the spacings for the months have been adjusted to be proportional to the number of production weeks available in each month. Consequently, the cumulative production total is a straight line, which is of more value in planning and following production than the monthly production line graphed in Figure 9-13. Figure 9-14 also shows that inventory is built up during the early

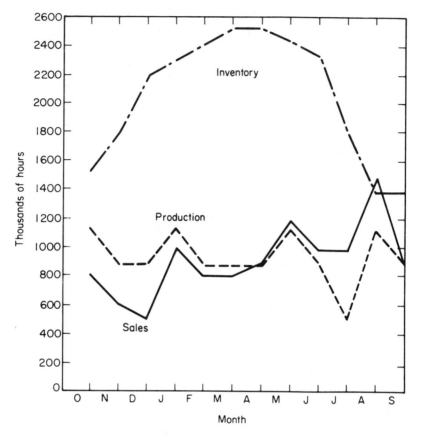

Figure 9-13 GRAPHICAL PRODUCTION PLAN.

part of the year, but that as the sales and production cumulative lines close the gap, inventory is reduced.

Figures 9-13 and 9-14 illustrate standard approaches to graphical production plans. It is evident that they require more work than tabulating data and that some study is required to understand them. Some people prefer graphs, however, and can understand them more readily than columns of numbers. Graphical plans can become extremely complex, particularly when actual figures are plotted against the planned data; this, of course, is one of the most important uses of production and capacity plans.

Many practitioners feel that graphical techniques have been somewhat over-emphasized in business literature. Most graphical production plans fail exactly where they should succeed: conveying the picture rapidly. The people who are to take action to correct deviations from plan want information in terms of hours, workers, pieces, tons, etc. If given a graphical production plan, they must translate the graph into numbers in order to determine the action required.

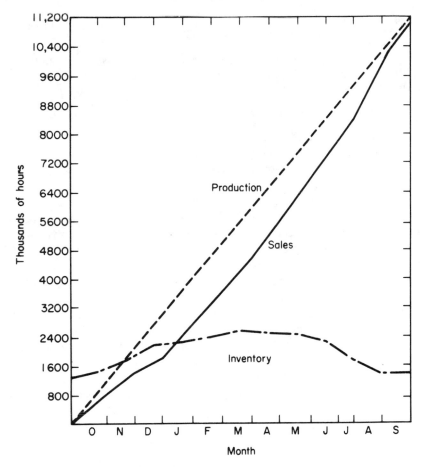

Figure 9-14 GRAPHICAL CUMULATIVE PRODUCTION PLAN.

Integrating Priority
and Capacity Planning

Four kinds of capacity must be recognized:

1. **Theoretical capacity** (also called nominal, rated and standing capacity) is the amount of output that should be produced by existing facilities. (Five people working 40 hours per week should produce 200 hours of output. Automatic machines are designed to turn out a given number of pieces per hour.) *This must exceed the other three kinds* of capacity.

2. **Required capacity** is the amount needed to support the MPS. Capacity requirements planning techniques are intended to yield this. It should include allowance for unplanned demands on capacity.

3. **Demonstrated capacity** is the average recent output actually achieved. This should *slightly exceed* the required capacity, which is usually understated.

4. **Effective capacity** is the portion of demonstrated capacity applied to making the correct items. This must be very close to 100%.

Theoretical capacities are rarely achieved; there is constant attrition to prevent this. Demonstrated capacity is the easiest to measure. Capacity utilized to make the wrong things reduces the effective total which must equal the required amount.

Principle 46. Capacity is wasted when used to make unneeded items.

Complete, integrated planning and control of capacity in all kinds of manufacturing plants requires a hierarchy of plans as shown in Figure 9-15. The principal differences lie in the length of the planning horizon and in the level of detail.

As in forecasting, ordering materials and any other function, selection of the proper technique to suit the planning requirements is the key to effective control of operations. These are indicated in Figure 9-15. No one technique is best and a complex, sophisticated one should be selected only if it is clear that the costs involved will be offset by significant tangible benefits. More precise data are rarely more accurate in capacity requirements planning.

Inventory control techniques focus on priorities (dates and quantities of specific items wanted) and cannot control manufactured inventories by themselves; such techniques are designed to *cope* with lead time changes but not to *control* them. Control of lead times is dependent on control of backlogs which in turn requires some means of planning and controlling capacity and production rates.

The control of production rates requires more than machine loading—which is basically only a measurement of the amount of work at machine centers. True control requires knowing the **throughput rate**. With increasing pressures to ship ''from the shelf'' and provide shorter lead times as well as a mounting need to provide more stable levels of employment, it is necessary to plan production rates based on *forecasts* rather than *backlogs*. The need for long planning horizons and the lack of specific, accurate data for many important factors make rough-cut capacity planning techniques more practical than voluminous detailed calculations. While machine loading techniques are useful in planning production rates in some companies, their principal value is in showing where temporary overloads, underloads and bottlenecks exist, as covered in Chapter 10. For most companies, some form of production plan by broad product groups that are meaningful in terms of manufacturing capacity can be developed to provide for capacity changes based on the forecast rather than backlogs. Since lead times are largely dependent on backlogs, a production plan is necessary to plan and control production rates and to provide a regulator to control order input so that work-in-process levels can be controlled. Orders are then put into production on regular weekly or even daily schedules to replenish those items required by the customers, aiming at just-in-time response.

The idea of assuming more responsibility for projecting capacity requirements and then controlling input to meet planned rates is not difficult to understand and accept; it is, however, very difficult to implement in a specific plant. For planners who have gained their experience through order release and expediting, the idea of assuming more responsibility for smooth plant operation is foreign. Capacity planning methods must be tailored to the individual plant and must be based on

Planning Horizon	Extent	Time Periods	Decisions	Techniques
Resource planning (long range)	Beyond one year	Monthly Quarterly Yearly	Plant construction Equipment procurement Manpower planning	Gross calculations Bill of labor
Operating horizon plan (medium range)	Up to one year	Weekly	Manpower transfers Work plan adjustments (hours, shifts) Alternate routing Make/buy Subcontracting	Capacity requirements planning
Execution (short range)	One to four weeks	Daily Weekly	Order release Overtime Alternate routing Order overlapping	Operation sequencing Input/output control (See chapters 10 and 11)

Figure 9-15 CAPACITY MANAGEMENT.

master schedule projections rather than existing work queues. As more pressures for lower inventories, stabler plant production rates and improved customer service continue to make themselves felt, there will be increasing development and application of techniques to plan and control production rates based on forecasts rather than backlogs.

## CHAPTER TEN

CONTROLLING INPUT

The Role of Input Control
in Effective Manufacturing Control

Up to this point we have developed the methods of planning inventory levels, order-ing materials and planning production rates. The control of orders input to manufac-turing facilities and suppliers must be a function of both the inventory requirements and the available capacity if work-in-process, backlogs and lead time are to be con-trolled. Input control can be broken into several factors:

1. **Selecting** the right orders to feed into the plant, based either on the materials control system or customer orders and at a rate matching the planned production rates

2. **Scheduling** the orders—assigning desired starting and/or completion dates to the operations that must be performed on each manufacturing order

3. **Loading** the orders—developing a total of the hours required in each time period for all operations scheduled in each work center and comparing this total to the center's capacity to handle it

The techniques of capacity planning covered in Chapter 9 establish the needed overall flow rates through the production facilities, often in fairly crude form, pro-viding a means for controlling capacity, total work-in-process levels, and resultant lead times. The input-selection process chooses individual manufacturing orders in the sequence that best balances the requirements of the inventory system and the capabilities of the plant or vendor. Scheduling provides a basis for following job progress through the succeeding manufacturing operations and machine loading is a short-term priority-control technique that highlights day-to-day bottlenecks and underloads that result from attempting to meet schedules on specific orders.

The control of input naturally precedes the plant controls needed to meet schedule dates in the factory. In practice, input control has received far too little consideration. Its absence causes excessive replanning, dispatching and tracking of jobs—including, sometimes, searching for lost jobs; this reduces the production-control function to a group of expediters working extremely long hours, trying desperately to answer a constant barrage of questions relating to late jobs and interrupted schedules raised by both sales and manufacturing personnel. When some production control effort is channeled into better planning and control of input, conditions improve substantially. When better input control is achieved, less time and effort are required for job location, expediting and dispatching; far more important, however, are the positive benefits obtained through *getting more jobs completed on schedule.*

Selecting the Proper Input

All inventory control techniques used in manufacturing companies generate random peaks and troughs in the rate of release of shop orders, even where master production schedules are leveled. The flow of these orders into the plant must be regulated in order to control lead times of plants and vendors. To complete orders on time requires a *smooth input* of orders for the right items *at the rate needed to meet the planned production level.* The temptation to release excess orders seems irresistible; overzealous planners usually overload the factory principally, it seems, from a desire to insure meeting required dates by getting jobs started on time or early. The overwhelming desire to avoid idle- and down-time also results in a substantial cushion of orders being maintained in every work center.

The penalties of such actions far exceed the benefits. These penalties include large investments in work-in-process, excess required plant space, long and erratic lead times, high component inventories and shortages. These are easily avoided by feeding orders into plants and vendors *at the rate they can handle them.* The mechanics of this are simple.

Figure 10-1 shows a simple production plan developed by a company making several models of lamps. This production plan covers the final assembly operation; other similar production plans cover the component manufacturing sequences. Note that this plan calls for level production over a 5-week period and a 10% reduction of inventory.

Figure 10-2 shows the weekly production scheduling report for the lamp models included in the production plan of Figure 10-1. This report has many of the elements found in a standard **stock status** report. It shows data on incoming business for each item, net stock available, the amount currently on order with the factory and the order point and economic ordering quantities. However, other features of this report are specifically designed to make it useful in generating orders to meet a planned production rate.

All figures in pieces			Sales	Production	Inventory
Week 8 (Actual starting inventory)					22,000 pieces
Week 9	Planned		5200	6000	22,800
	Actual				
Week 10	Planned		6200	6000	22,600
	Actual				
Week 11	Planned		6200	6000	22,400
	Actual				
Week 12	Planned		7200	6000	21,200
	Actual				
Week 13	Planned		7200	6000	20,000*
	Actual				

Figure 10-1 PRODUCTION PLAN—ALL MODELS OF LAMPS.

In this report, the exponential smoothing technique explained in Chapter 4 has been used to update a weekly weighted average of incoming business to serve as a forecast of demand for each item, so that the latest sales trends can be identified. The order point itself has been recalculated each week for the new demand forecast, using an updated calculation of the mean absolute deviation (explained in Chapter 5) to revise the reserve stock portion. The total inventory (the sum of on hand stock and quantities on order with the factory) and the order point are both expressed as weeks of stock by dividing them by the latest forecast of incoming business for each item. The scheduler uses this report in selecting lamps to fill the starting schedule to meet the planned production rate.

The total inventories of all lamps shown on the production scheduling report in Figure 10-2 are above their order points. This is a fairly normal situation when inventories are being built up in anticipation of seasonal sales or a vacation shutdown. Nevertheless, this production scheduling report can be used to choose the proper items to be scheduled in order to meet the planned production rate of 6000

Lamps	Weekly incoming business	Year to date incoming business	Net stock available	Factory order	Order point	Weekly weighted average incoming business	Total weeks of stock	Order point expressed as weeks of stock	Economic ordering quantity
#7W	341	17,933	1739	3078	2730	485	10	5.6	2250
#7D	288	9837	1224	832	1436	274	7	5.2	1500
#9W	894	35,329	4007	1956	4242	924	6	4.5	2000
#9D	251	10,120	2189	662	1386	259	11	5.3	1500
#9P	1187	46,690	8371	----	6250	1290	6	4.8	2500
#11D	1332	47,078	2844	7050	6768	1345	7	5.0	2500
#11P	598	21,896	778	3302	3346	639	6	5.2	2000

Figure 10-2 WEEKLY PRODUCTION SCHEDULING REPORT.
(Figures in pieces and weeks)

lamps per week shown in the production plan. To do this, the scheduler selects those lamps closest to their order points—those with the lowest total weeks of stock—and schedules them so that inventories are kept in balance. There are three items that have a 6-week inventory level: The first is the no. 11P (pinup lamp), which is closer to its ordering point than any other; the next is the no. 9P (pinup lamp); and the third the no. 9W (wall lamp). Scheduling normal orders for these would release a total of 6500 lamps for assembly production. While this is slightly in excess of the planned production rate of 6000, the scheduler would release these this week and compensate for the small excess in the next week's starting schedule. Precision in adjusting order quantities to equal the planned rate exactly is neither necessary nor justified.

Such a production scheduling report provides one technique for generating a starting schedule to meet a planned production rate, much superior to having order points generate orders at random with widely varying demands on the plant's production capacity. Another extremely valuable feature is that it also eliminates the need to recalculate order points when inventory levels need to be built up in anticipation of periods of high sales or low production. The production plan indicates the total needed to raise the inventory and the scheduling report shows *which items* to start in order to produce the right mix of products. Tinkering with order points is unnecessary.

The production scheduling report would be easier to use if all the items were ranked, so that the scheduler could readily see which were closest to their order points. Figure 10-3 shows such a ranked weekly production scheduling report with the items arranged in order of increasing total weeks of stock and decreasing order point weeks. This technique can be applied manually but a large number of items will require a computer to do the sorting and listing. This type of ranking can speed up and eliminate errors from the work of preparing a schedule.

Principle 47. Ordering techniques should be used simply to rank orders in priority sequence before selection for release.

Lamps	Weekly incoming business	Year to date incoming business	Net stock available	Factory order	Order point	Weekly weighted average incoming business	Total weeks of stock	Order point expressed as weeks of stock	Economic ordering quantity
# 11P	598	21,896	778	3302	3346	639	6	5.2	2000
# 9P	1187	46,690	8371	- - - -	6250	1290	6	4.8	2500
# 9W	894	35,329	4007	1956	4242	924	6	4.5	2000
# 7D	288	9837	1224	832	1436	274	7	5.2	1500
# 11D	1332	47,078	2844	7050	6768	1345	7	5.0	2500
# 7W	341	17,933	1739	3078	2730	485	10	5.6	2250
# 9D	251	10,120	2189	662	1386	259	11	5.3	1500

Figure 10-3 RANKED WEEKLY PRODUCTION SCHEDULING REPORT.
(Figures in pieces and weeks)

The production scheduling report provides the link between inventory control and production control. It provides the tool the scheduler needs to do an effective job of selecting the items that must be included on the starting schedule to feed work to the plant to meet planned production rates. This eliminates the need for large paper order backlogs in the plant that inevitably result when orders are generated without regard to the plant's production capabilities.

There is great reluctance among schedulers and their managers to deviate from the start dates for orders highlighted by ordering techniques, both order point and MRP. It is widely believed that releasing orders earlier will result in generating excess inventory and holding orders until later will jeopardize on-time deliveries. Standard lead times used by ordering techniques are viewed as fixed, not as the *averages* they really are.

When schedulers are responsible only for releasing orders on time, erratic loads, large work-in-process levels, and long and variable lead times inevitably result. Schedulers must also be responsible for *a smooth, level release of work* matching the capacity of work centers and suppliers to handle it.

Other factors must often be considered in addition to the overall capacity of the manufacturing facility when preparing schedules. When scheduling press work, a screw machine department or automatic insertion of printed circuit board components, for example, the ability of the department to perform the required number of setups is as important as its total of available machine hours. For this situation, a periodic view of all the parts made in the department (using a scheduling report such as Figure 10-4, weekly schedule review—turret lathes) will make it possible to schedule to both a total of machine hours and a limiting maximum number of setups.

First, a target of hours must be set, based on the forecast rate of usage of all the parts, adding or deducting the effects of any desired changes in inventory levels of these parts. This is identical to preparing a production plan as discussed in Chapter 9, except that hours of machining time or other capacity measures are used instead of pieces or dollars.

Next, a maximum limit is established for setups, based on the number of setup people available or the number of machine-hours that can be devoted to setting up without cutting into needed capacity for making parts.

Using these two factors, total hours and setup hours, the planner or scheduler can review the inventory position of all items, as shown in the column headed "Next planned order release" of Figure 10-4. As an example, a review of the report indicates that components 21, 30, and 46 should be started in the next week. If these were scheduled, the scheduler would release:

Component	Order quantity hours	Setup hours
21	22	5
30	31	3
46	15	5
Totals:	68	13

Week ending _____ 12-10

Week no. _____ 48 _____   70 planned weekly schedule hrs.

Dept. _____ 84 _____   10 maximum setup hours

Machine center #1700   110 total hrs. in machine center

Part no.	A B C	Description	Used on	Annual use	Next planned order release	Order qty	Order qty cost	Order qty hours	Setup hours
21	A	2nd-spindle	"A" motor	3000	Week #47	200	1222	22	5
30	A	Upr. spg. carr.	"A" motor	6000	Week #48	700	281	31	3
59	A	Piston	"A" motor	6000	Week #3	400	298	31	2
64	B	Lwr. spg. carr.	"A" motor	6000	Week #50	1000	235	40	3
18	C	Pack washer	Gear box	1000	Week #51	500	41	12.5	2
27	B	Roller	Gear box	2400	Week #51	400	138	20	2
29	C	Spg. guide	Coupling	200	Week #50	500	25	50	3
34	C	Adj. screw	Coupling	2400	Week #50	2300	85	77	3
54	C	Ball seat	Emerg. relse.	275	Week #50	150	37	30	2
55	C	Spg. plug	Coupling	275	Week #51	250	29	25	3
56	C	Floor plate	"B" motor	92	Week #2	100	82	9	3
46	C	#3-1st, #5-2nd – lens holder	Control box	850	Week #49	450	131	15	5

Figure 10-4 WEEKLY SCHEDULE REVIEW—TURRET LATHES.

This would be close to the planned weekly schedule of 70 total hours but would exceed the maximum of 10 setup hours. Consequently, the shop could not run to this schedule.

By reviewing other items in the group near their release dates, the scheduler would find component 27 would soon have to be reordered. Substituting this for component 46, which would be delayed less than either 21 or 30, the schedule would be:

Component	Order quantity hours	Setup hours
21	22	5
30	31	3
27	20	2
Totals:	73	10

This would be practical for the shop. The scheduler would then have to be sure to schedule component 46 the following week and might even have to expedite subsequent operations on this part to cut the normal lead time and get it in stock on time. While greatly oversimplified, this example illustrates a very useful technique for scheduling to meet two limitations on production capacity.

The techniques just described for selecting a satisfactory mix of orders to match a planned production rate apply directly to starting (gateway) work centers, the first (important) center performing operations on orders released from a planning system. Typical of these are machining operations like turning, boring, milling, blanking and forming. In process plants, these include blending, mixing, calendaring and fractionation. Subassembly and final assembly operations are also starting operations, however, because they involve work on orders released from the system. Purchased material orders should likewise be scheduled by such techniques; vendors are truly starting work centers (a possible exception is one subcontracted operation in the middle of a sequence done in-house). Such work centers can be operated with very smooth input, small queues of orders and short lead times, approaching just-in-time production. Secondary or downstream work centers are not so easy to smooth out.

Scheduling Secondary Work Centers

Secondary work centers usually receive work from several others in functionally organized plants where all similar operations and equipment are grouped. To smooth these requires identification of orders that follow *similar paths* through the facilities. Most intermittent, semiprocess and even so-called job shops have a definable flow of work for families of items through the plant. While even the crudest attempt to control work-in-process will result in some improvement, any time that flow lines of reasonably sequenced operations can be identified, specific scheduling techniques can be adopted to enable the scheduler to reduce work-in-process dramatically without risking excessive downtime. Where such flow lines can be identified, operations can be greatly improved by having the scheduler look beyond the first operation to subsequent operations that are real or potential bottlenecks because of limited capacity or because the operation is inflexible. Releasing work into a starting operation that will be backlogged later is self-defeating.

In many plants, it is quite practical to generate a weekly schedule to meet the planned production rates and then have the scheduler release individual orders to the plant on a daily basis. Consider, for example, the Pattern Panel Company, making control panel housings. The general sequence of operations is

1. Shear—press department
2. Blank—press department
3. Form—press department
4. Deburr—subassembly department
5. Insert bushings—subassembly department
6. Subassemble fasteners—subassembly department
7. Plate or paint—finishing department

8. Inspect—quality control department

9. Pack—shipping department

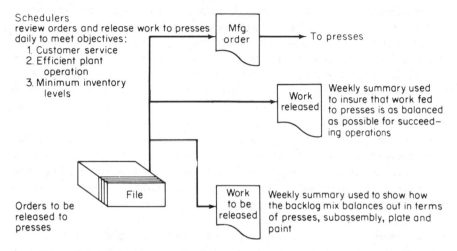

Figure 10-5 PATTERN PANEL COMPANY—PRODUCTION SCHEDULING SYSTEM.

The Pattern Panel Company, following the simple production scheduling system shown in Figure 10-5, releases a balanced load into this sequence of operations each week using techniques like those described in the preceding section. Their emphasis is on rapid flow. They receive many individual orders, most of them requiring fairly short processing times. Figure 10-6 shows the weekly release summary used for scheduling all operations.

		Week #14
Load center	Hours released	Weekly capacity
Press department	20 48 108 168 180	240 hours
Subassembly	40 60 105 115	120 hours
Plate	5 11 24 28	80 hours
Paint	10 18 36	40 hours

Figure 10-6 PATTERN PANEL COMPANY—WEEKLY RELEASE SUMMARY.

For each major load center, the scheduler has a target number of cumulative hours to be released per week. Orders ahead of the press department are reviewed daily. As new orders are released, the scheduler tries to select orders that provide a load within the capacity of subsequent departments. For example, based upon the information in Figure 10-6, the planner would try to release orders totaling as near as possible to 240 hours to the press department, without exceeding 120 hours in the subassembly department, 80 hours in plating or 40 hours in painting. This approach insures rapid flow through the sequence of operations if the capacity of the work centers is adequate to handle the total load.

An adjunct to the weekly release summary is a weekly analysis of orders to be released showing how much work is about to be generated for the press, subassembly, plating and painting departments. Thus any drastic change in the mix of hours to be sent out into the plant can be seen ahead of time and plans can be made for additional or reduced capacity. Particularly where there are some make-to-stock products manufactured along with make-to-order items, it is sometimes possible to see a temporary drop-off in plating load coming because of the mix of make-to-order business. This can be offset by generating more make-to-stock orders, which will help level the load on the plating facility. This *input load balancing* is a most effective technique for controlling semiprocess flow operations characteristic of many of the plants that call themselves job shops.

Figure 10-7 shows this type of load balancing for a series of three of the most critical operations in a metal-fabricating plant: the second, eighth and tenth operations, respectively. Prior to the actual order scheduling, the machine load has been projected weekly to estimate the required capacity. This was a capacity planning function and actual orders were generated separately using a materials plan. It is reasonable to expect that adequate average capacity should be available at each operation but it is known that just releasing orders into production at random would cause temporary overloads and underloads on the factory floor. Orders are rechecked weekly to put them in the latest proper priority (designated alphabetically, with order A being highest). These manufacturing orders are put in a "hold for release" file and reviewed weekly by a planner, whose objective is to get the needed orders into process while generating the best balanced load on the facilities.

Schedule 1, containing orders A, B, C, D, E and F would generate overloads at operations 2 and 8 over the 10% excess allowed in this company. Removing job F from the proposed schedule—since it has the lowest priority and a high percentage of its hours in operations 2 and 8—gives an underload at all operations. From the next lower priority jobs in the unreleased file, choosing jobs H, J, and K results in a better-balanced schedule that does not exceed the 10% allowance for overloads or underloads. Job G (there is no I) is left out because it would generate the same unbalanced conditions that job F did.

Obviously, jobs F and G will have a very high priority on next week's schedule. This approach really just keeps backlogs on the scheduler's desk rather than out on the factory floor, but the result is to avoid releasing work to a starting operation that will simply get bogged down at a succeeding operation.

Scheduling a balanced load means that work flows more smoothly so that plant backlogs are kept to a minimum and the lowest level of work-in-process is maintained while keeping all operations working. This type of approach is often difficult to sell to a scheduler who has been in the habit of releasing work into

Running time in hours			
	Operation 2	Operation 8	Operation 10
Job *A*	– – – – –	2.22	3.99
Job *B*	2.76	4.96	6.00
Job *C*	– – – – –	– – – – –	6.75
Job *D*	0.63	0.50	1.30
Job *E*	8.75	7.80	8.75
Job *F*	13.52	11.84	12.64
Job *G*	7.64	6.56	7.24
Job *H*	1.46	– – – – –	3.26
Job *J*	2.52	2.00	5.20
Job *K*	4.38	4.44	8.04
Job *L*	7.30	8.00	14.00
Job *M*	16.90	13.80	13.40
Schedule #1 = Jobs *A, B, C, D, E, F*			
Schedule #2 = Jobs *A, B, C, D, E, H, J, K*			
Planned Cap.	Operation 2 20 hr/wk	Operation 8 20 hr/wk	Operation 10 40 hr/wk
Schedule #1	25.66	27.32	39.43
Schedule #2	20.50	21.92	43.29

Figure 10-7 BALANCING INPUT FOR SEQUENCED OPERATIONS.

the factory when the ordering technique says to start. The advantage of holding backlogs in the office is easier, faster reaction to changing priorities, engineering changes, etc. When they are out in the plant, an expediter has to try to select the proper orders with little information to go by.

Load balancing is an organized approach to controlling shop input that can be used in conjunction with conventional scheduling and loading techniques. If work does not usually follow the same path, it may be necessary to take time periods into account when balancing the load. A painting operation, for example, might be the fifth operation on one job or the twelfth operation on another job. Under these circumstances, it would be important to take arrival times into account when loading these jobs. This approach becomes practically identical to the *finite-capacity loading* technique described later in this chapter.

Load balancing techniques have been shown in their simplest form in order to explain the concept, but where more than two operations have to be balanced, the calculations can become very tedious. This logic can be programmed and a computer can select the optimum starting schedule.

Actions for Shop Input Control

The techniques for selecting input and load balancing do not keep customer requirements and ordering techniques from creating uneven demands on the shop; they merely try to smooth out the random ups and downs in the demand in a controlled manner rather than by having large inventories on the plant floor.

Principle 48. Backlogs can be controlled better in the office than on the factory floor.

Principle 48 is indeed one of the most important principles of shop input control. The following actions are important if work-in-process is to be controlled:

1. *Select the proper input* using techniques like the production scheduling report (Figure 10-2) or the weekly schedule review (Figure 10-4) to meet the planned production rate. If the plant is not actually producing to meet this plan, the amount of work released into starting operations *should not exceed* actual output. This is a difficult point to make to the scheduler who knows that the output is needed. Learning to use the production plan rather than backlogs of work-in-process to control capacity may require a considerable education program for schedulers, supervisors, and even many managers.

Principle 49. Input should be less than or equal to—but never more than—output.

2. *Keep backlogs off the shop floor,* since backlogs on the shop floor
   a. Are more difficult to control
   b. Make engineering changes more expensive to implement
   c. Generate more expediting
   d. Create physical problems (newer jobs pile up in front of older work that gets pushed back into corners).
   One of the most difficult things for any scheduler to resist is the temptation to get orders started. It is comforting for the scheduler to get everything on order with the factory and to emphasize this point when the factory is not meeting schedules. Unfortunately, the more work there is in the factory, the more expensive it becomes to control the actual job selection. Excessive backlogs on the factory floor can compound seriously the problems of getting the right items through production and it is precisely when capacity is tight or the plant is behind schedule that job selection becomes most critical.

3. *Sequence orders based on latest requirements* rather than on release dates established when the order was first generated. When some backlog of orders must be kept in the production control office and there is a demand forecast involved in establishing the release dates, the production control system should be designed so that planners or schedulers release orders based upon dates established at the last possible moment. Even

when other requirements make files of "To be released" orders useful, the availability of computers (which can compare changing inventory requirements for many items with production requirements) and the introduction of such techniques as Critical Ratio, described in Chapter 11, make it possible to review desired schedule dates periodically to be sure that orders are released to the factory based only upon the latest possible information on requirements.

4. *Schedule only items the factory can make.* In generating orders to meet a planned production rate, it is meaningless to release orders if they cannot be run during the scheduled period. One of the first steps that should be taken to improve manufacturing operations is to force planners or schedulers to hold up releasing all orders for which raw materials, components, tools or other necessary materials are not available. This practice will define clearly where the basic problems lie in getting work completed. It will be evident immediately if the inability to meet production rates results from the failure of materials control to provide purchased materials, tools, shop paperwork or similar items for manufactured parts or from the factory having insufficient workers or equipment to produce at the desired level. Another benefit—which should not be underrated—is that releasing firm orders representing real work for the factory increases the respect of plant-operating people for the abilities of planning and control people and also develops confidence in the latter's decisions, leading to better cooperation and resulting in greatly improved operation of the plant.

There are some exceptions to the rule that orders should not be released until all necessary materials are available. If a finished product takes 3 weeks to assemble and the only component missing is one that is added at the last operation, assembly orders can be issued to the plant to start work immediately if the scheduler is confident that the missing component will be available by the time it is needed. There are other exceptions based on unique situations in the drug, electronic and similar state-of-the-art industries where it is impossible to determine before a schedule is released whether the product *can* actually be produced. In such operations involving custom-built products it is not certain exactly what component materials will be required.

5. *Schedule to a short cycle* weekly or even daily. This not only helps to get the latest and most accurate requirement dates on the orders scheduled, but it also assists in controlling the orders flowing through the factory. The point was made very well by John F. Magee (7) who said,

the more frequently scheduling is done, i.e., the shorter the scheduling period, the lower the in-process inventory can be, and the faster can material be processed through the departments. For example, in the case described, a change in the scheduling period from one day to one week would mean increasing the total processing time from roughly 13 days to roughly 6 weeks.

In the typical manufacturing operations having a semiprocess flow and with many intermittent operations, generating a monthly schedule for the department performing most of the starting operations gives that department a broad choice of items to run on any particular day. They normally run those items that suit their own convenience and performance measures; the load flowing into subsequent departments probably does not match their capacities. The result is to have large backlogs of work ahead of these departments in order to maintain their production at the level rate. Moreover, if a department can be considered on schedule if a job is manufactured on the first day of the month or on the 30th day of the month, quoted lead times will have to be exceedingly long in order to give customers realistic delivery dates.

An interesting fallacy that has gained wide recognition among production control and manufacturing personnel is that the schedule period must equal the lead time. The question, How can a product possibly have a weekly schedule when it takes 1 month to produce the product? is frequently heard. Although it sounds perfectly rational, there is no reason why schedule periods must be equal to the total lead time. Even in the extreme example of a company with a 6-month lead time required for a sequence of 50 different major operations, someone must make a decision practically on a daily basis as to which items will be started in each operation. A firm 6-month starting schedule is *not* required. It is certainly more sensible to issue a weekly starting schedule based on the latest available information on customer requirements, the inventory status and the plant workload. Only in this way can a factory be kept flexible enough to meet changing demands in an economical manner. These principles help to control the flow of work into the plant at the first operation. Scheduling techniques then provide a basis for keeping jobs flowing into succeeding operations.

Scheduling Techniques

Scheduling is the activity of assigning dates to important steps in the process of manufacturing products. It is part of planning and control, not execution. Its purpose is to provide milestones against which to compare execution to get early-warning signals that corrective action is needed. There are three levels of scheduling:

1. Master production schedules, showing quantities and dates for products
2. Order schedules, giving starting and completion dates for batches of raw materials and components purchased and manufactured in making products
3. Operation schedules, providing starting and finishing dates (or times) for each significant operation needed to process a component order in the plant.

Master production and order schedules are linked together by the bills of materials of the products planned. Parent and component order schedules are similarly linked. These are all revised and updated in concert by MRP replanning.

Operation schedules should be coupled to order due dates and kept valid by rescheduling when such due dates change significantly. Unfortunately, this is often neglected and plant priorities are driven by inaccurate data as a consequence.

One of the important steps that can be taken by any company to improve its delivery performance is to establish schedule dates by operations. In companies where production control is basically expediting, even this does not often begin until orders have failed to meet their shipping dates. The next step is to review jobs that are due to ship in the current and next weeks, as well as those that are past due, to determine what problems are causing delays. Figure 10-8 shows this type of production-schedule review. This can be a very effective report if used in conjunction with both order and operations schedules to make sure that no slip-ups have occurred and also as a means of keeping the sales department informed.

Customer	S.O.	Past due	This week	Next week	Nearest lot		Next lot		Remarks
					Loc.	Qty.	Loc.	Qty.	
Stalco	17624	577			D-32	1150	---	---	Will ship next week
Chambers	11318			40	D-40	94	---	---	On salvage (?)
Trild Inc.	10628		1100		D-29	1000	---	N.A.	Call complete
Morton	10959		1780	2500	D-32	5200	---	---	Balance 6040 stock
Padsing	11003		7000		D-22	7500	---	---	O. K.
Pennbush	11004			20,000	D-22	10,750	D-2	10,750	Will ship 10M, balance 3/26
Stalco	11008			7000	D-40	8240	---	---	O. K.

Figure 10-8 PRODUCTION SCHEDULE REVIEW—WEEK 27.

The production schedule review can be sent to personnel in the sales department so that they know which jobs will be shipped on time and which will not, thus providing them with the means of telling the customer ahead of time if a job will not be shipped out as promised—a very important element in customer service. Earlier warning signals of potential trouble are needed, however, and these can be provided by operation scheduling.

Figure 10-9 lists the steps in operations scheduling. The first is, of course, to provide the data for scheduling which must include the *operations sequence or factory routing.* Figure 10-10 is a typical manufacturing order, including the operations sequence and showing the *setup hours and running time* required. On this factory order, the running hours for this lot have been calculated by multiplying the quantity on the order (expressed in thousands) by the time figure shown in the column headed "Running hours/1000". This manufacturing order is designed to travel with the work through the factory, so that each operator can note time and quantities directly on it. Routings are maintained typically in a computer file. When an order needs to be generated, the manufacturing order is printed

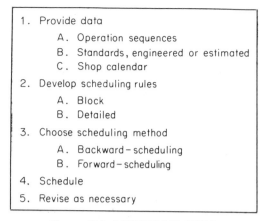

1. Provide data
    A. Operation sequences
    B. Standards, engineered or estimated
    C. Shop calendar
2. Develop scheduling rules
    A. Block
    B. Detailed
3. Choose scheduling method
    A. Backward–scheduling
    B. Forward–scheduling
4. Schedule
5. Revise as necessary

Figure 10-9 SCHEDULING STEPS.

out, along with a punched card for each operation which can be used by the worker to report work done.

Time standards for setup and running times, either engineered or estimated, are essential to any scheduling system. Since there will always be orders for new items that have to be scheduled into production before fully engineered standards have been developed, some means of estimating these standards will have to be provided. Accuracy is not vital, but consistency in estimating these standards is important. It is not necessary to schedule every operation on all routings, of course. Groups of operations on the same or similar machines can be handled as one operation. Minor operations (deliver from stock, cut off, weigh out, deburr, sort, in-process inspection, etc.) can be lumped into major operations or covered by a standard time allowance for all such operations.

Figure 10-11 shows a **shop calendar** of the type used by many companies to facilitate automated scheduling. Each **working day** is numbered consecutively—in the case of a 1000-day calendar, the consecutive numbering covers a period of 4 years. This enables scheduling programs to establish dates easily and directly without correcting for weekends, plant shutdown periods or holidays, since these have been omitted from the shop calendar.

Some **simple scheduling rules** are shown in Figure 10-12. These are oversimplified when compared to the rules needed in most companies but they illustrate the type of rule that must be developed before scheduling can begin. The intent is to provide means for calculating or estimating each of the elements of lead time. (See Chapter 9.)

Principle 50. Scheduling rules must develop allowances for all elements of lead time.

An alternative to the detailed scheduling rules shown in Figure 10-12 is use of general rules, such as the **block-scheduling rules** shown in Figure 10-13. Large increments of time are used to estimate roughly the amount of time required for each operation. Block scheduling saves computation time but usually results in extremely long lead times.

The next step is to choose one of the two principal scheduling methods:

Part name	Drawing no.	Used on	Date	Order	Qty.
Pinion spindle	E-17352	Frame assembly E-0014	wk.21	2950	5000

Material
: Steel bar stock – 0.500" Spec. #A-407

Remarks
: Note thread is left-hand

Dept.	Mach. group	Op. no.	Operation description	Set-up hr.	Run. hr./1000	Run hr. this lot	Oper. no.	Qty. comp.	Qty. scrap	Qty. salv.	Insp. no.
#040	Truck	10	Draw bar stock from stores	—	—	—					
#517	#14	20	Make pinion spindle on screw machine	14.5	3.1	15.5					
#319	#18	30	Mill slot to B/P	1.3	9.5	47.5					
#771	#42	40	Tumble for burrs	—	—	2.0					
#624	#06	50	Drill hole for pin	0.2	4.0	20.0					
#771	#40	60	Degrease	—	—	0.5					
#771	#43	70	Plate – dull zinc	—	—	4.7					
#009	#04	80	Inspect	—	—	AQC 403					
#040	Truck	90	Deliver to stock	—	—	—					

Figure 10-10 TYPICAL MANUFACTURING ORDER.

JUNE

WK#	SUN	MON	TUE	WED	THUR	FRI	SAT
22	MAY 24	25 347	26 348	27 349	28 350	29	30
23	31	JUNE 1 351	2 352	3 353	4 354	5 355	6
24	7	8 356	9 357	10 358	11 359	12 360	13
25	14	15 361	16 362	17 363	18 364	19 365	20
26	21	22 366	23 367	24 368	25 369	26 370	27

JULY

WK#	SUN	MON	TUE	WED	THUR	FRI	SAT
27	JUNE 28	29 371	30 372	JULY 1 373	2 374	3	4
28	5	6 375	7 376	8 377	9 378	10 379	11
*29	12	13	14	15	16	17	18
*30	19	20	21	22	23	24	25

*Vacation weeks are subject to change

AUGUST

WK#	SUN	MON	TUE	WED	THUR	FRI	SAT
31	JULY 26	27 380	28 381	29 382	30 383	31 384	AUG. 1
32	2	3 385	4 386	5 387	6 388	7 389	8
33	9	10 390	11 391	12 392	13 393	14 394	15
34	16	17 395	18 396	19 397	20 398	21 399	22

Figure 10-11 SHOP CALENDAR.

1. Multiply hours per thousand pieces by number of thousands on order. Add setup time.

2. Round up to nearest 16 – hour day (2 shifts) and express time in days; round down to nearest day when excess hours are less than 10 % of total; minimun 1 day for operation.

3. Allow two days to withdraw stock from stockroom.

4. Allow one day between successive operations within the same departments.

5. Allow two days between successive operations in different departments.

6. Allow one day for inspection.

7. Allow one day to move and record material into stock.

Figure 10-12 SIMPLE SCHEDULING RULES.

1. **Backward scheduling** is used to schedule components needed before parent item orders can be started. It starts with the date on which the order is required in the stockroom, on the assembly floor, or to be shipped and calculates the schedule backward through the routing to determine the proper release date for the order. Backward scheduling assumes that the finished date is known and that the start dates must be computed for each step in the manufacturing sequence.

2. **Forward scheduling** is applied to scheduling a series of orders through a major processing step or machine. It starts either with today's date or the first open time on the equipment and computes schedule dates for each subsequent order to determine its completion date.

Forward scheduling is most frequently used in companies such as steel mills and process plants where jobs are manufactured to customer order and delivery is usually requested soon. One characteristic of plants where forward scheduling

1. Allow one week for releasing order and drawing material from storeroom.

2. Allow four weeks for screw machine operations.

3. Allow one day for each 400 pieces in the Milling Department; round upward to next full week.

4. Allow one week for drilling and tapping, burring and similar operations using minor equipment.

5. When operations are especially short, combine within the same week.

6. Allow one week for inspection and delivery of completed material to stock.

Figure 10-13 BLOCK SCHEDULING RULES.

is used is that the product is usually *not* an assembly requiring a great many components. Even when forward scheduling is used, the scheduler must check the customer's requested date before doing the scheduling. If the required date is far enough away, the order is not scheduled immediately so that, in effect, the scheduler is really combining backward scheduling with forward scheduling.

Backward scheduling is typically used where components are being manufactured to go into an assembled product. Components usually have different lead times, some considerably shorter than others. After determining the required starting dates for major subassemblies, the scheduler uses these as the required dates for each component and works backward to determine the proper release date for each component manufacturing order. If the scheduler were to schedule forward, all orders would be released at the same time and a good many of the components would be on hand long before they were required. More important than this, parts for urgent orders would be competing in the factory for the same production facilities required for orders that would actually be needed later.

Figure 10-14 shows two ways of scheduling the manufacturing order shown in Figure 10-10. In both cases, the order has been scheduled backward from the required date (week 51 or day 445). Block scheduling is done according to the rules listed in Figure 10-13 with scheduled completion dates expressed by week numbers. This method results in a total of 12 weeks' lead time.

The operation time scheduling starts with the required date expressed as a day number and works backward using the day numbers of the shop calendar to

Operation number	Block scheduling		Operation time scheduling	
	Time allowed	Week	Time allowed	Day
	Release date = #39			420
10	1 Week	#40	2 days	422
20	4 Weeks	#44	2 days	424
			T^*= 2 days	
30	3 Weeks	#47	3 days	429
			T = 2 days	
40	1 Week	#48	1 day	432
			T = 2 days	
50	1 Week	#49	2 days	436
			T = 2 days	
60	} 1 Week	#50	1 day	439
			T = 1 day	
70			1 day	441
			T = 2 days	
80	} 1 Week	#51	1 day	444
90			1 day	445
Date required =		Week #51		Day #445

$^*T$ = transit time

Figure 10-14 COMPARISON OF SCHEDULING TECHNIQUES.

compute the required completion date at each operation. This schedule requires 25 working days or 5 weeks, to complete. In Figure 10-14 the setup time has also been taken into account. For example, in operation 20 one extra operating day is included because of the setup time required on the screw machine. Notice in the computation that the transit time is more than is required normally to move material. **Transit time** in this example is really a very loose term that is used to cover the following elements:

1. The time the job spends waiting to be picked up for movement out of the department—*wait time*

2. The time the job spends actually in transit—*move time*

3. The time the job spends waiting to be started at the next machine center—*queue time*

Very few companies attempt to use precise estimates of wait and move times; most depend on simple estimates. The real problem in developing rigorous schedules is determining the standard queue time for each work center. There are three methods for doing this:

1. Making pragmatic estimates

2. Using recent history of loads

3. Calculating future loads

Random observations using work sampling techniques are an easy but effective way to estimate pragmatically the average queues in work centers. Some measure of load that is easy to determine visually (number of pieces, orders, boxes of work, etc.) is selected and tallies are made during each observation of the actual load in work centers. After a sufficient number of observations (10 to 20) spread over a period deemed representative of normal operations, average queues are determined for each work center and used in the scheduling rules.

Essentially similar but more precise is keeping a log of actual loads for a representative period. The data used are standard hours taken from orders actually in the work centers. The average over the period is calculated and used as the standard queue. Periodical recalculations are then made to detect significant changes. Shorter queues replace the previous standards; longer ones trigger corrective actions in input cuts or output increases to reduce them.

Powerful computer programs tempt many well-meaning people familiar with techniques but inexperienced in their applications in real plants to attempt to calculate future loads and use these to develop rigorous, precise schedules. This is an attempt to simulate exactly how orders would be handled. It is possible but not worth doing. It assumes that a **model** of the factory can be set up in the computer and the flow of orders calculated from it. It is far more effective and much less work to set up estimated standard queues, measure actual queues and compare them to the standard and *take corrective action* when deviations are significant. Well-run plants continuously strive for lower levels of work-in-process and shorter lead times. This subject, including the vicious cycle initiated by increasing planned queue times and the lead time syndrome thus generated is covered in depth in Chapter 5 of the second volume (10).

Operation-time scheduling is even more complex than block scheduling and requires considerably more data and computations. The lead times determined by block scheduling, however, are considerably longer than those required by operation scheduling (7 weeks less in the example in Figure 10-14). One additional advantage of operation-time scheduling is that it provides input data for the machine load report. Details are covered in the next section of this chapter, along with the modifications to schedules needed when capacity limitations interfere with running orders in the desired sequence.

Sample schedule calculations of only a few orders will show that the proper sequence of working on operations in any work center is very often different from the sequence of due dates for completion of the orders. Operation schedules, therefore, provide a better basis for determining priorities of work in individual work centers.

It is generally agreed that dates should not be shown on shop orders because

1. They are impossible to change as schedules are replanned.

2. Erroneous conclusions about true priorities can be reached with them.

3. Past due dates suggest the existence of crises, which may not be real.

4. Factory people really need to know only the *proper sequence* in which to work on orders.

The effectivity of scheduling is improved greatly by running small, uniform lot-sizes requiring short setups, by having small loads in important work centers and by having orders follow a common processing sequence. These subjects are discussed at greater length in the second volume (10).

The ABC concept applies to scheduling as well as to many other areas of production and inventory control. If the orders going through any work center are classed A, B or C according to the work hours they generate, even though there are many of them and the total product mix is extremely varied, the 80-20 relationship is almost always apparent. A very few of the items going through the center generate the bulk of the work hours required. Controlling the input of only these items can effectively level the production rate, reduce the work-in-process and, consequently, reduce lead time.

Most purely make-to-order plants have customers who place repeat orders for some regularly scheduled items which can be used as buffers to absorb the ups and downs in incoming business for a product group. When total orders fall below the anticipated rate, these regularly scheduled items can be run at something higher than the normal rate in order to make up the deficit in the production level. This approach requires ingenuity and work but it reduces the amount of backlog required and can pay off very handsomely in reduced lead times and better customer service.

The important point to remember in using scheduled items as inventory buffers or using a reduced backlog is to *set up some controls.* It is not unusual to find that this type of approach has been tried at some previous time in a make-to-order plant but that the inventories of scheduled items used as buffers went completely out of control or the backlogs were not controlled properly. *When decision rules are set up ahead of time and when action is taken properly* on the basis of these rules either to reduce or increase the production level, these techniques can be used with a great deal of success. Like all forecasting, planning future capacity in a make-to-order plant must recognize explicitly that no incoming order rate is likely to be fixed for a very long period of time.

Work Center Loading

Figure 10-15 shows the steps in work-center loading. The first of these is to *choose the load centers*. Some companies load by department only. If all the machines in a department are interchangeable, this simplified approach can be justified but when different machine centers within the department have different capabilities (as in a general machining department), loading the total department does not really accomplish much. Separate process units, assembly and packaging lines, of course, must be scheduled individually. The next refinement is to subdivide the equipment into similar machine groups. All 24-inch boring mills, for example, might be included in the same group if jobs are interchangeable among the machines. In the case of a screw machine with a side milling cutter attachment but otherwise identical to other machines in the group, for example, individual machine coding should be set up in order to single out that particular machine if a job can be done only on that machine. Thus a machine group might be designated as group 2400 containing a specialized machine, designated 2407. All jobs that could go on any machine would be loaded into machine group 2400, while a job that could only be done on that particular machine would be designated as being loaded for machine 2407. It is important to group as many machines or work centers together as possible, however, since this will reduce the work required, generate a smaller report and tend to stabilize the load. Trying to load individual

```
1. Choose load centers
2. Choose load period
3. Choose loading method:
   Infinite
     • Schedule work orders
     • Load work centers in any sequence
     • To update, remove finished work,
       add new orders
   Finite
     • Schedule work orders
     • Set priorites on orders
     • Set work center capacity limits
     • Define alternatives
     • Load work centers in priority sequence
     • Select alternative
     • Reschedule overloads
     • To update, start over
```

Figure 10-15 LOADING STEPS.

machines when there is considerable interchangeability is poor practice and will result in very erratic loads.

Next the *load period is selected;* it is usually weekly because it is rarely useful to load shorter intervals. The load period cannot be shorter than that used for scheduling.

The next setp is to *choose the actual loading method.* In the previous section, for example, it was noted that 20 hours of drilling time would be added to the machine load in the week in which this drilling time was scheduled to be done to meet the finished product schedule. This type of loading is called **infinite**, meaning loading to infinite capacity; the load is shown in the week in which it is scheduled, without regard to the current load already existing in that week. If the department were loaded only to the limit of its present capacity, called **finite loading** or loading to finite capacity, scheduling cannot be done in one continuous calculation and the loading steps are considerably different as shown in Figure 10-15.

Prior to infinite loading, orders are scheduled by operation on the assumption that *ways will be found to hold the schedules.* Such orders can be loaded in any convenient sequence without regard to priority. If the operation can be completed and is scheduled in one load period, it is shown in the load in that interval. If the schedule covers more than one load period, however, some loading rule is necessary. This can be

1. Place all the load in the first period scheduled.
2. Place all the load in the last period scheduled.
3. Spread the load over the periods evenly, in proportion to days scheduled or on some other basis.

For the example in Figure 10-14, operation 30 spans 5 days including 2 days for wait, move and queue (transit) times and 3 days for machining to be accomplished on days 425 through 429. If day 425 falls on Thursday of week 49 and 429 falls on Wednesday in week 50, the load (setup plus running time standard hours) can be placed

1. All in week 49
2. All in week 50
3. Half in each week or two-fifths in week 49 and three-fifths in week 50

Work center loads can be developed for released orders only or for both released and planned orders. Released orders show "real loads" in the sense that work has been (or soon will be) started. It is still only a plan, however, and only a small fraction of the orders in the load will be in any work center at any time; some will not arrive as scheduled. For best control of priorities—the primary use of work center loads—such true loads should be distinguished from planned amounts.

Load data used as the basis for capacity requirements planning does not need such distinctions, of course, and both released and planned orders must be included. The second volume has an extensive discussion of the application of work center loading to capacity requirements planning and the differences between these techniques, supplementing the material in Chapter 9.

Consideration must also be given to the selection of the *unloading* technique. When manual systems were used, it was necessary to take shortcuts such as considering a job to be completed when the first time card was turned in. This saved posting many production lots and recalculating load balances but resulted in a load that was always understated by the number of hours remaining on each job that had been unloaded from the system. Another shortcut approach uses the last time card on a lot to relieve the load. This results in a load constantly overstated by the hours completed on each job but not yet removed.

With computers and data collection equipment, it is possible to deduct hours as they are completed and show the true number of hours remaining in the load. This should be attempted only when *there are real tangible benefits* from the extra work and expensive equipment. One point sometimes overlooked is that the number of hours to be unloaded for any job must be equal to the number of hours loaded for that job. Work center loads always use standard hours. For example, if an estimated time standard of 12 hours has been set on a job but the job is completed in 9 hours of actual time, 12 hours must be relieved from the load in order to state correctly the work remaining in the load. This is done by multiplying the number of pieces that are reported to be completed by the standard rather than deducting actual elapsed time from the load.

As Figure 10-15 shows clearly, finite loading is considerably more complex than infinite loading. Since capacity limitations are to be recognized, orders must be loaded in proper priority sequence so that high-priority orders have first claim on available capacity. When capacity constraints are defined, it is possible to identify acceptable alternatives such as overtime (up to some predefined limit), selection of an approved alternate operation, reduction of the order quantity by some permissible amount, and so on.

When loads are developed in the finite technique, overloads are not permitted. Orders causing such overloads are then rescheduled into periods having available capacity, either

1. Earlier, if materials, tooling, etc. are available

2. Later, in periods when capacity is adequate

Updating finite loads usually requires starting over since the priorities of individual orders will have changed. Contrast this with infinite loading, which can be maintained indefinitely simply by adding new orders and deleting completed orders.

Figure 9-11 shows a typical work-center load. As stated in Chapter 9, it is very easy to draw completely erroneous conclusions from such data. This is covered thoroughly in Chapter 5 of the second volume (10). Briefly, here are some considerations on each of the features:

1. "Late" simply means not completed as scheduled. Whether or not there is a real problem depends on how load is dropped into weekly periods,

how much queue time still remains in the schedule and the load conditions in downstream work centers.

2. The load in the near future includes the hours associated with the planned queue, which are not intended to be completed.

3. Unless deliberately smoothed, work does not flow evenly because of lot-sizing and coincidental arrival of two or more orders in the same period.

4. The load shows *how much* work is scheduled to be in the work center, not the *rate* at which it will be arriving and should be completed.

Considerable confusion has resulted from popular references to a display like Figure 9-11 as a capacity requirements plan. It is not. The differences were shown in Chapter 9. It can lead to development of capacity requirements plans if two major adjustments are made:

1. Standard queue hours must be deducted. The plan does not intend that these be completed in any close-in time period.

2. Unplanned demands on capacity must be added. These include scrap replenishment, rework and many other factors. (See Chapter 5 in the second volume (10) for thorough coverage of these topics.)

Load and capacity are clearly differentiated in the analogy of the bath tub: Load is the depth of water; capacity is the rate water is running in and out.

Work-center loading is a good technique for showing where short-term overloads or underloads will result if orders are processed according to current priorities.

Principle 51. Loading is a priority control technique, useful only if the data represent reality.

Loading is not a satisfactory means for long-term capacity planning. Some form of production or capacity plan based on a simulation of anticipated requirements is necessary in almost every company, since few have enough firm orders upon which to plan capacity and the pressures for stabilizing the labor force have become very strong. Scheduling and loading are effective techniques only when applied with a full understanding of the problems of controlling the flow of individual production orders and the objectives and principles to be observed. Frequently, orders are generated at random by an inventory control system, schedules are sent down to the plant and backlogs are measured in a machine load report without any attempt to control the rate of flow of these orders into the plant and without any recognition of the fact that the required dates may change before the orders are completed. This problem of reacting to changes in requirements that occur after orders have been released will be discussed in the following chapter.

Controlling Input to Vendors

Distributors who do not manufacture anything generate an input of orders to their vendors. Most manufacturing companies purchase a large percentage of their components from outside vendors. Relations between the materials control and purchasing functions within many companies are perpetually strained because of the problems involved in getting the right items in from these vendors. Some of the most significant of these problems are:

1. **Quantity discounts:**

   Purchasing is usually measured on price variances and appears to perform better when purchasers can take advantage of quantity discounts or larger buys. If the materials control system does not recognize quantity discounts in ordering purchased materials, purchasing will often increase the quantities on the requisitions sent to them and this will, of course, increase inventories. These quantity discounts can be handled in the materials control system as described in Chapter 8. Policies on what constitutes an acceptable discount should be established, considering the aggregate effects on costs and inventory. These ordering rules should then be built into the materials control system.

2. **Buyer delays in placing orders:**

   A good purchasing department concentrates much of its efforts on buying—the actual negotiation of prices and placing orders. This is an extremely important function since—in most companies—the cost of purchased material *exceeds the direct labor cost* by significant amounts. To the planner, however, the objective of reducing costs seems rather shortsighted when a missing component holds up delivery of a customer order because the requisition sent to purchasing was held up by the buyer to negotiate better prices. This problem cannot be eliminated but it can be handled better if

   a. Fewer vendors and longer-term contracts are used.
   b. Purchasing is advised of anticipated yearly requirements of standard components and negotiations are handled on a planned basis, not as requisitions are received.
   c. Purchasing receives requisitions generated well in advance of the time orders need to be released to vendors, using the forward visibility of time-phased order point and MRP techniques.

3. **Long purchased-component lead times:**

   It is not unusual to hear purchasing tell a vendor, "We aren't too concerned about your long lead times as long as you meet your delivery promises." Unfortunately, longer lead times on the vendor's part will impair its ability to meet delivery promises as well as adding more uncertainty to the customer's knowledge of its needs. A program to educate purchasing people to understand some of the fundamental relationships in planning and control can generate many tangible benefits via reduced lead times.

4. **Lack of follow-up:**

   Nothing generates more friction between materials control and purchasing people than late deliveries of purchased items. Techniques for improving control over a vendor's output are discussed in Chapter 11.

Frequently, however, poor vendor deliveries—such as plants that are always behind schedule—can be overcome more by improving control over input rather than by concentrating solely on better control over output.

The most significant step that can be taken to improve a vendor's output, especially where a significant fraction of total output goes to a customer, is to plan production rates and then feed a matching amount of work on a weekly basis. Many purchasing people are repelled by this idea, which they associate with scheduling the vendor's plant, a task they do not want to undertake. Similarly, many materials control personnel feel that if they generate orders and show where the overloads are, it is then the factory's responsibility to get work out on time. A vendor is really running a manufacturing facility which can be considered to be another work center in the customer's plant; using some of the techniques described in this book to help plan production levels and control input to meet this plan will improve vendor performance substantially. Far from being an altruistic gesture, this approach will result in shorter, more dependable deliveries of purchased parts. *It is the proper approach to just-in-time deliveries.*

Principle 52. For on-time deliveries, treat vendors exactly like plant work centers.

Scheduling Assembly Operations

In many plants assembly times are short, assemblers are very flexible and assembly scheduling is straightforward. The assembly department can often be broken down into a few major flow lines that can be loaded to finite capacity. In other companies that have complex assembly operations, such as those manufacturing sophisticated electronic equipment, detailed scheduling of assembly operations can become very important indeed. Where this is true, the scheduling and loading job often becomes as detailed as scheduling component manufacturing operations, and schedules for assembly can best be planned operation by operation, using the techniques described earlier in this chapter.

In repetitive manufacturing, like automotive, home appliance and office equipment plants, where a distinct assembly-line flow exists, it is necessary to balance the workload on the line so that each worker has a reasonable amount of work to perform as the product moves down the line. While line-balancing, in terms of defining what work will be done at each station, is usually done by the industrial engineer, the scheduler must then feed work into the balanced line.

The basic steps in line balancing are:

1. Establish time standards for all operations on all products to be assembled in as small elements as possible.

2. Determine by assembly line zone which operations must be done in each and which operations can be done there if desired.

3. Work backward from the finished-product end of the line to get the optimum balance among jobs, considering all products to be run. This is usu-

ally done using a trial-and-error approach and is most effective when a computer can be used for simulating all the possibilities that exist.

4. Make up the production schedule that will give the most flexibility in production mix with the best utilization of available manpower.

No scheduling technique can generate production from an assembly line that is short of components and, in many plants (especially where the assembly department is being fed by many functional departments), chronic parts shortages always seem to exist. This is an excellent example of the interactions in any manufacturing control system and illustrates clearly the need for a disciplined system that is really used to control. Too often, lack of good, basic discipline of systems generates problems and attempts at "quick-and-dirty" solutions merely compound the problems.

Many companies have been through this cycle:

1. Because inventory records are inaccurate, parts shortages occur at assembly (since parts that were shown by the system to be available are not).

2. This causes serious disruptions in the assembly line and someone suggests that kits of parts for assembly be laid out or *staged* farther in advance. If the procedure has been to make up these kits 1 week in advance of the assembly schedule, the suggestion is often to increase it to 4 or 6 weeks. The reasoning is that the additional time will then be available to expedite parts through manufacturing to fill the shortages revealed by kitting.

3. Staging components farther in advance then generates these problems:
   a. Generating an extra 4 or 5 weeks of components laid out against future assembly schedules requires substantial increases in component inventory, which usually are not readily available. This is the equivalent of writing this inventory off the records, since this 4- or 5-week supply of components will no longer be available to be used on new assembly requirements, yet it will not be available in the form of an assembled product either.
   b. Increasing the advance layouts to determine parts shortages earlier places a peak load of real magnitude on stockroom personnel to pull the required components faster than they are being assembled.
   c. More advance layout requires more space.
   d. A layout shortage record file must be developed and maintained, indicating which components are short in each of the layouts. Work on this file by itself can become extremely cumbersome and time-consuming.
   e. Typically, where there is multiple use of components, the advance-layout technique results in components being improperly allocated. A component laid out for an assembly that cannot be made for lack of other components will be found to be the only part missing from another layout.

f. Shifting components from one layout to another is inevitable and increases with the layout period. As a result, record accuracy is more difficult to maintain and usually decreases.

g. The work of putting away excess components is increased tremendously. The original quantity of each component pulled from stock to make a given assembly is based upon the desired finished assembly lot-size. When the component in shortest supply finally comes in—typically, in less than the desired quantity—it must be distributed among several assembly layouts, at least one of which cannot be assembled in the desired lot-size. Consequently, the leftover components must be put back into the stock bins. Design changes can have the same impact.

h. When the advance layout technique is used, control over the sequence of assemblies run in the assembly department by default is left to line people. In times of extensive parts shortages, any product for which components are available is seized upon and run by the assembly department. This adds to the shortages by using up scarce interchangeable components.

The "quick and dirty" solution of staging components usually generates far more problems than it solves and the result is poorer utilization of the limited supply of available components and a further deterioration in accuracy of the inventory records which was the original cause of kitting.

Too frequently, inaccurate inventory records are only one of many deficiencies in the system that cause problems at assembly. Component shortages may also be due to poor reordering practices or poor discipline in priority control. Shortages may also result from too low a level of component production, resulting from poor capacity planning.

Good control over the flow of components to support assembly operations requires

1. Accurate inventory records that are checked by regular cycle inventories rather than by an annual physical inventory and which are supported by the education of all personnel entering the system so that they understand the proper techniques for handling each transaction and realize the importance of following the proper procedures. For more on this topic, see Chapter 1 and Appendix I, both in the second volume (10).

2. A reorder system that bases component requirements on anticipated assembly schedules—rather than average past usage—and reacts to changes in these assembly requirements by changing the requirements shown in the materials plan.

3. Means to plan the rate of component production in advance of desired changes in the assembly department production rate.

4. Smooth input of work matching actual capacity.

Scheduling component manufacture, component purchasing and assembly are the important elements in controlling input to most plants. The techniques described in this chapter can be implemented manually, graphically or on a computer. There are also specialized manufacturing situations for which specific techniques have been developed. The following sections cover one popular graphic method and some project scheduling approaches.

Loading and Scheduling Devices

The Gantt chart, developed by Henry L. Gantt at Frankford Arsenal in 1917, is one of the oldest planning tools known to production control. Figure 10-16 shows a Gantt chart used to plan a project in which a large purchased motor, a housing fabricated on a frame, and a machined casting are to be assembled, inspected, packed and shipped. The scheduled dates for each activity, starting and finishing, are shown by the short vertical lines at the ends of the light horizontal lines. Each project activity has its own set of lines and the chart shows the full period from start to finish of the project. The caret mark above the date headings shows the present time (end of week 9).

At the end of the 9th week, the heavy horizontal lines (representing actual progress) show that the motor was ordered on time, that the frame steel was ordered, received and fabricated and that the housing is now being fabricated around the frame. The chart also shows that the base casting has been ordered but has not been received and, in fact, is behind schedule, thus threatening the desired delivery date in the 17th week if corrective action is not taken at once.

In this example, the Gantt chart is used to show a project schedule only. It can also be used in a slightly different form to show machine loads by labeling the rows to represent machine centers and drawing lines within the columns to represent the amount of capacity that is loaded.

There are many commercial devices available today that are really mechanical Gantt charts. Some of these use strips of paper to represent the amount of work that has been loaded into a particular department and then combine these strips of paper with colored signals to show where critical overloads have occurred. Other mechanical devices are perforated boards with pegs attached to strings that can be manipulated to make a Gantt chart, showing either project plans, machine loads or work center backlogs.

Mechanical Gantt charts can be of assistance in presenting information in visual form. By themselves, they are not a manufacturing control system. They are successful only if the system used to generate the information presented is sound, if there are relatively few elements in the project and if changes are few. These techniques present some problems in recording, duplicating and transmitting their messages. A Gantt chart made on paper can be duplicated readily and sent to all personnel who require information. A mechanical Gantt chart can be duplicated only by taking photographs of it, by summarizing the information manually on paper or by bringing people to the information display.

Such mechanical Gantt charts have little place in planning and control today. They have been supplanted by computer graphics, which do not have the

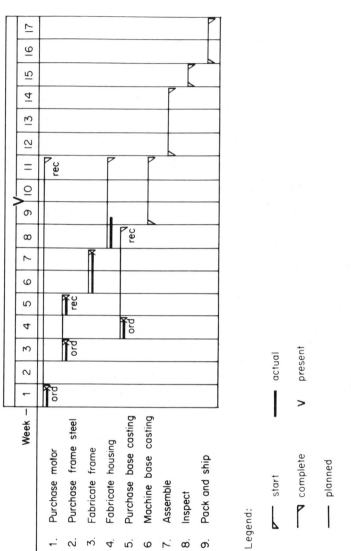

Figure 10-16 PROJECT GANTT CHART.

Week —

| | 1 | 2 | 3 | 4 | 5 | 6 | 7 | 8 | 9 | 10 | 11 | 12 | 13 | 14 | 15 | 16 | 17 |

1. Purchase motor
2. Purchase frame steel
3. Fabricate frame
4. Fabricate housing
5. Purchase base casting
6. Machine base casting
7. Assemble
8. Inspect
9. Pack and ship

Legend:

start ——— actual

complete ⌐ present ∨

planned ——

274

limitations of reproduction and transmission of the Gantt charts and can handle large numbers of project elements.

Project Planning and Control

Since the introduction of the Gantt chart, there have been some dramatic innovations in project planning, brought about by the need to plan and control complex projects involving many elements and working groups. The critical path method (CPM) or critical path scheduling (CPS) is a form of project planning called **network planning**. Network planning involves setting up a chart of the elements and activities making up a complex project, showing the necessary sequences and interrelationships and determining the critical path or longest sequence of events that really determines when the project can be completed. Additional resources applied to these activities would be effective in reducing the project time span.

Figure 10-17 shows the project covered by the Gantt chart in Figure 10-16 as it would be handled by CPM. It is presented as a series of events (shown by the circles) and activities (shown by the lines that connect the circles). Event 1, for example, is to place requisitions and the activity is "purchase," which requires 4 weeks for the casting, as shown on the chart by the notation 4W. Once the critical path chart has been made up, the total time required to complete the activities that follow any path can be determined. In Figure 10-17, for example, the critical path is 1-5-8-9; this determines the ultimate completion date for the project. If the base casting happens to be received 1 week late, for example, this would not affect the final project completion date. There are 3 weeks' slack time available since path 1-4-7-8 requires 10 weeks, as compared to 13 weeks for 1-5-8. The critical path method has been applied to many complex projects and an entire science of network planning has been developed.

Perhaps the most publicized network planning technique is PERT (Project Evaluation and Review Technique). This is a refinement of the critical path method in which estimates of optimistic, most likely and pessimistic times are made for the completion of each element in the project. These data are introduced into a computer where the statistical probabilities of completing the various paths are calculated and the critical path is determined. The computer also prints information on those activities that have slack time and can tolerate delays, so that effort, labor, machines and money can be diverted from slack to more critical activities, if possible, reducing the total project time at no extra cost. This analysis also shows the earliest and latest start and completion dates for each element in its proper sequence with other elements.

These project planning techniques can also be used in project control but just making the original plan can do a great deal to insure that important elements are not overlooked and to help get the project started properly. Once a PERT chart is established, progress of the project can then be reviewed periodically and the chart can be updated. Frequently, substantial changes will be noted in the critical path as some events are completed ahead of schedule and some fall behind. Maintenance of the updated information necessary to use project planning as a control

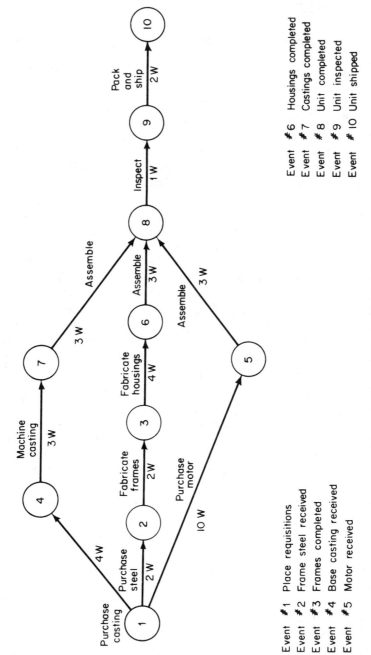

Event #1 Place requisitions
Event #2 Frame steel received
Event #3 Frames completed
Event #4 Base casting received
Event #5 Motor received

Event #6 Housings completed
Event #7 Castings completed
Event #8 Unit completed
Event #9 Unit inspected
Event #10 Unit shipped

Figure 10-17 CRITICAL PATH PROJECT PLAN.

technique requires a considerable effort as time passes and changes occur in the project. Nevertheless, the effort is considered worthwhile by many companies involved in highly complex project type manufacturing. Typical examples are bridge and building construction, new aircraft design, testing and construction and new product line development and introduction.

Production control practitioners should be familiar with network planning techniques and should know where to apply them to advantage. They should be very much aware that these techniques do not replace the normal production control functions of materials planning, scheduling, dispatching, etc.

Most project planning techniques treat the project elements as if they were entities without recognizing that each element is itself a series of activities. A project to deliver 100 completed units, for example, might require fabricating or purchasing components at a rate of 10 per week to meet the specified delivery. There are projects that require this type of monitoring and the line-of-balance (LOB) technique was used in the past to handle them. It used graphical techniques to extend a project plan into a series of stepped lines representing quantity requirements for components or subassemblies at any point in time. This line of balance was the objective against which bar charts showing actual completions were plotted. When the bars did not come up to the line, the component involved was shown as behind schedule. Where the bar extended above the line of balance, it indicated that deliveries of this component were ahead of schedule. LOB was more valuable as a monitoring technique than as a planning technique. It has been supplanted by computer-based MRP. Such programs are also being applied to project planning. Note that the elements and activities in Figure 10-17 could be represented in a bill of activities and a list of process sequences (routings) which could then be planned, monitored and revised just the same as manufactured and purchased components in a product.

Linear Programming and Queuing Theory

Linear programming is a name given to a family of techniques that solve linear equations simultaneously through a systematic routine that typically involves many repetitions (iterations) of the basic routine. Having received much publicity a few years ago, linear programming is probably the best known and most characteristic of the *operations research* type of techniques used in manufacturing.

Linear programming can be applied to problems having the following general characteristics:

1. There are definable objectives (such as profit, cost and maximum possible production within a time period).

2. There are alternative solutions available. For example, a job could be run on one production unit or on another at different costs or warehouse-replenishment orders could be filled from separate manufacturing plants at different manufacturing and freight costs.

3. Resources are limited. For example, the capacity of the lowest-cost facility is not sufficient to make all the product required and less profitable units must be used.

4. The relationships among important cost and performance variables can be expressed in linear (first-order) algebraic equations.

Linear programming methods have been applied to several production problems, principally in process plant scheduling of refineries, chemical, paint and glass plants and, most recently, in flexible machining centers. Such techniques are in limited use in practice in manufacturing plants at the present time. Simpler and more effective techniques have made these sophisticated mathematical approaches unnecessary.

Similar mathematical analyses have been made of waiting line or queuing situations, and queuing theories have developed. A *service facility* (work center, machine, store checkout clerk, bank teller, etc.) performs some work on arrivals (people, manufacturing orders), which have some pattern of arrivals and which,

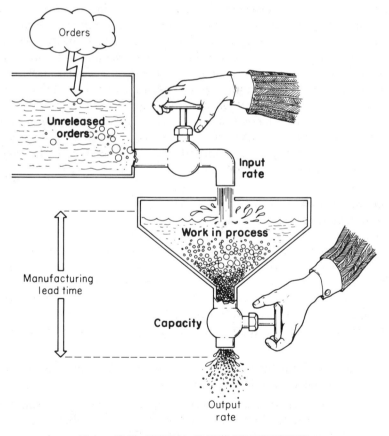

Figure 10-18 TYPICAL PLANT ENVIRONMENT.

it is to be hoped, are described adequately by some convenient statistical distribution (like the Poisson, normal or exponential). The technique predicts the size and variability of the queues for assumed rates at which arrivals can be serviced. Like linear programming and even MRP techniques, queuing theory describes what will occur if the environment is as it is described. Excellence in operations concentrates on *changing the environment* to reduce problems. More on this will be found in Chapter 12 and also in Chapter 9 of the second volume (10).

Practical Considerations

The typical plant environment is shown in Figure 10-18, which indicates the compelling need to control both input and output. For the practitioner, here are some practical considerations in controlling input:

1. When a finished product is being assembled, it is important to avoid committing components to a particular product until the last moment. The use of MRP to reschedule the purchased or manufactured components and techniques for handling rescheduling in the plant are discussed in Chapters 6 and 11, respectively.

2. Component manufacturing facilities can be scheduled as effectively as assembly facilities. Someone is deciding—practically on a daily basis—which items should be started. Firm commitments to long-range schedules should be avoided in both cases.

3. Control over input to the factory is essential. This can be as elaborate as holding components in a central storeroom between operations and releasing them only as directed by schedulers, in order to have complete control of all items. Frequently, however, functional work centers (such as plating or painting) work on many components and detailed control of all items input to these is impossible. It is quite feasible, however, to use an ABC classification to determine the parts that generate the bulk of the hours of work in these secondary centers. Most companies will find that these will be a small percentage of the total parts going through them. If this small percentage of items is scheduled carefully, a balanced load and smooth flow can be maintained in these secondary operations.

4. The same approach applies to the components that make up a particular assembly. It is normal to find that only a few components have long lead times, while the majority take considerably less time to get. Demand for these components with long lead times is difficult to predict; it may be worthwhile to maintain an inventory in order to obtain flexibility with a minimum investment. The components with short lead times can be controlled more tightly.

5. Manufacturing costs associated with setting up machines can be substantially reduced if items are scheduled in family groups. With screw machines, for example, only minor setup changes are required between items

in a family that uses stock of the same diameter. Substantial economies can be realized by having the scheduler review all products within a family group and order all when any one of them is ordered. Economic lot-sizes calculated for each item in a family using the technique discussed in the section, "Major and Minor Setup" of Chapter 3 will aid this also.

6. Determining the proper shop input in a seasonal business is extremely difficult. During the inventory building period the particular mix of items run is rather unimportant since excesses are available to meet unexpected demand. As the peak selling season approaches, the actual demand should be used to indicate what the best product mix should be. Typically, a greater amount of setup time and flexibility will be required during the peak season than during the off season. Many companies handle this by having skilled personnel perform both setup and manufacturing operations during the off season, bringing in relatively unskilled personnel for manufacturing operations during the peak season and letting the skilled personnel handle only changeovers.

There are many scheduling and loading techniques. The mark of the novice is to learn only a few and try to apply them everywhere. Part of this problem has been generated by articles that discuss specific techniques without relating them to others and without presenting application criteria. Even worse are proprietary programs advertised as panaceas without adequate description of how techniques are handled. Such "magic" should be avoided. Criteria for the selection of scheduling and loading techniques revolve around the amount of lead time (and consequent backlog) available and desirable and the plant manufacturing configuration. Companies can be classified as

1. **Distributors**, who purchase materials, maintain inventories and resell but do not manufacture

2. **Make-to-order companies**, which manufacture many products but maintain very little finished product inventory, if any

3. **Make-to-stock companies**, which manufacture many products and maintain inventories in one or more locations.

Distributors are concerned only with inventory management and make-to-order companies are concerned primarily with planning and controlling production while, in a make-to-stock company, both inventory and production planning and control functions must be meshed together very carefully to get optimum results. The student should recognize that, in practice, most manufacturing companies usually have some make-to-stock and some make-to-order products but this classification of their activities is still helpful in determining the proper techniques to use. In considering input criteria, it is helpful to think of one other type of make-to-order company: the project-oriented company manufacturing areospace products, computers and other complex products, where long engineering and manufacturing lead times have made long delivery times traditional and acceptable to the customer. The techniques that are most appropriate for each general manufacturing classification are

1. **Project-type make-to-order products:**
   In this situation, the amount of delivery time available usually provides the planner with a reasonably firm backlog of orders to use for scheduling and loading. Backward scheduling and infinite loading are appropriate, the latter providing information for detailed capacity planning. For broad scheduling of project elements, techniques like CPM and PERT can supplement the regular detail scheduling and loading.

2. **Short-lead-time, make-to-order products:**
   If the amount of backlog normally available is less than the time required to make a capacity change, rough-cut CRP is used, based on forecasts of customers' orders, together with backward scheduling, revised as MRP replans orders. Infinite loading is used only for showing temporary overloads and bottlenecks which must be eliminated to stay on schedule. Assembly schedules are based on actual customers' orders.

3. **Make-to-stock products:**
   Rough-cut CRP based on family forecasts is used to provide capacity when it is required. All detailed schedules are driven by the MPS via MRP and are updated frequently. Input is controlled using the techniques as described in this chapter to regulate the level of work-in-process and control lead times.

The choice of specific scheduling and loading techniques should recognize that the better the input can be controlled to level out the flow of work through the plant, the lower in-plant backlogs will be. This, in turn, means shorter, more reliable lead times and more valid plans. The plant manufacturing configuration (within any of the service classifications above) could be further broken down into several classes:

1. **Intermittent production**, where products are largely one of a kind. Examples of this type are die-making and shipbuilding.

2. **Semiprocess flow**, where some departments are set up functionally (with similar equipment segregated by department rather than lined up in the sequence on which it will be used) but many follow the same general series of operations and there is much repetitive manufacture.

3. **Process flow**, such as automotive assembly, chemical process units or textile finishing, involving dyeing and finishing cloth.

For a process flow type of plant, control over input determines control over output since every job will go through all operations in the same sequence in which it was started. Capacity can usually be planned in terms of total output (cars per day, yards of cloth, etc.). Line balancing techniques can help to define the constraints on the scheduler to get optimum use of labor. There is no need for operations scheduling, since each job flows through the same series of operations and there is no real need to follow job progress. Load reports are only of value in showing the amount of unreleased backlog since, once in process, jobs do not stop long enough for a load report to be meaningful.

In most plants, there is a great deal of semiprocess flow (even if it exists only within certain product lines). Wherever this type of flow exists, forecasting in terms of broad product groups that go through similar manufacturing sequences can be very useful in planning production rates. Control over input can be refined to the point of load balancing for series of operations, as explained earlier in this chapter. Operations scheduling provides a basis for following job progress and machine loading shows where short-term bottlenecks and overloads are occurring.

In a genuinely intermittent production type of factory (most plant people think of their factories as job shops), effective capacity planning can be done only in rough-cut approaches but is essential in controlling work-in-process. Control over input cannot usually be done precisely and sometimes can be done only in starting operations. The machine load and input/output reports are the prime documents in controlling priorities and capacity. These are broad guidelines for selecting from among the available techniques.

Principle 53. The more input is controlled, the less output has to be controlled.

Most plants tend to concentrate on output control, neglecting input. Some control over plant output is necessary in any plant that is not pure process flow. The principles and techniques for controlling output are the subject of the following chapter.

CHAPTER
ELEVEN

CONTROLLING OUTPUT

The Elements of Control

Control over any function requires these four elements:

1. Norms or plans against which to measure actual data to know when the function is on target

2. Feedback, reporting actual performance to be compared to plans

3. Some tolerance limits so that the system does not react to minute variations that will eventually be canceled out by offsetting variations but which will allow the system to recognize significant changes promptly and call for corrective action.

4. Specific corrective actions to be taken to get back on plan when the function is out of control or, as a last resort, revisions to the plans.

In output control, the norms are the capacity plans discussed in Chapter 9 and the scheduled dates are developed as covered in Chapter 10. The tolerance limits are set by managers using judgment on acceptable limits, modified by experience or management policies. The feedback involves reporting actual performance for the same facilities included in the plan and the specific corrective actions include hiring, layoff, overtime, subcontracting work, changing priorities, etc.

Some of the effects of poor manufacturing control and its impact on the national economy were discussed in Chapter 1. The need for control over production rates in order to control backlogs and lead times and the techniques of capacity planning were discussed in Chapter 9. Scheduling and loading techniques to set valid start and finish dates on orders were covered in Chapter 10. This chapter is concerned primarily with using the capacity plans and schedules to control production in both plants' and vendors' facilities.

Principle 54. Output control must cover both capacity and priority.

The Need for Control Over Capacity

If the fluctuations in production level for the average company were compared with the fluctuations in demand, it would be apparent quickly that most manufacturing executives tend to wait too long before deciding to change production levels and that they overreact when they do change. The root of this problem is usually the information—or lack of it—on which they base their decisions. The manufacturing executive is basing this type of decision on loads and also on uncertain information (i.e., forecasts) about the future. When this uncertainty is not measured so that managers can at least play the averages, they tend to let changes in overall demand accumulate into large inventory overstocks or deficits before making a change in production rate. Since in most companies no one has established what size inventory deficit or overstock justifies a change in production rate, the decision is postponed while the changes in demand accumulate week after week—building up to a genuine crisis which then forces a decision. In make-to-stock companies the inventory may decline far below the level required to give good customer service, while in make-to-order companies the delivery lead times quoted to customers may lengthen until business is lost because these times are uncompetitive. If, on the other hand, capacity ought to be cut, inventories build up higher and higher while the decision is postponed. A good planning and control system should focus attention on the unpleasant decisions that must be made, the alternatives that are available (usually unpleasant) and the consequences of not making a decision.

Principle 55. Effective capacity control is a prerequisite for priority control.

Input/Output Control

As discussed in Chapter 10, planning and controlling the input rates of work to suppliers and plant work centers is at least as important as achieving the correct output rates. Input and output rates must be kept tightly linked to control work-in-process levels and lead times for both purchased and manufactured items. The technique for doing this is the input/output control report shown in Figure 11-1. Work center 54 is a secondary center receiving materials from several other facilities. A program to smooth the flow of work in the plant has begun to take hold and the input fluctuations are less than they had been. If this were a gateway work center receiving orders suggested for release by the materials planning system, a scheduler could match planned rates of input even more closely as was described in Chapter 10.

Work center 54
(All data in standard hours)

- Input:

Week number	32	33	34	35	36	37	38
Planned	900	900	900	900	900	900	900
Actual	1033	817	836	992	847	974	811
Cumulative deviation	133	50	(14)	78	25	99	10

- Output:

Planned	900	900	900	900	1100	1100	1100
Actual	922	895	915	911	1076	1087	1093
Cumulative deviation	22	17	32	43	19	6	(1)

- Queue:

Planned (900)	1800	1800	1800	1800	1600	1400	1200
Actual (1821)	1932	1854	1775	1856	1627	1514	1232

Figure 11-1 INPUT/OUTPUT CONTROL REPORT.

A significant increase in output was planned to begin in week 36, but the plant is having some difficulty hitting the higher rate. Note that the plan does not include raising the rate of input during the period illustrated; output from feeder departments will be increased later. This will reduce the queues from the present level of about 2 weeks work toward the ultimate planned level of less than 1 week. This in itself is just another step in the continuous process of cutting work-in-process and lead times. Both the planned rates, input and output, are derived from capacity requirements planning techniques described in Chapter 9. Actual input data are determined by adding up the work content of orders arriving each week. In the absence of data collection on the plant floor, this can be a major clerical chore. A good approximation can be obtained by posting the hours on orders as they are released in all work centers for which input/output control is operating *as if they arrived* in all centers the week released. Actual output is measured in practically every company; the data used by input/output control, of course, are *standard*, not elapsed hours. No credit should be given for scrap, rework or significant overruns. Actual queues are represented by orders in the work center; while a running total can be maintained by adding input and deducting output, periodic checks of actual orders are good insurance against the accumulation of errors. Where it is impractical to tally actual receipts, this number can be derived from actual data on output and a physical check of the queue.

The input/output control report is one of the most powerful tools any manu-facturing company can have in its planning and control system. It is the key to

1. Insuring that capacity is adequate to support the plan
2. Keeping input and output rates balanced
3. Controlling queues of work and reducing lead times
4. Providing early-warning signals of the need for corrective action in chang-ing capacity
5. Integrating priority and capacity planning and control activities.

The report can be very effective even when based on rough-cut capacity re-quirements plans, estimated work standards or other capacity measures like pieces, tons or gallons. No system is complete and no company can operate under tight control without it. Such a report is also the technique vitally necessary to getting just-in-time deliveries from vendors. A more complete discussion of its applica-tions is included in Chapter 5 of the second volume (8).

Effective capacity planning and control are necessary to avoid the pitfalls of overcompensation for business changes by requiring that production rates change *only enough during the planned period* to get the inventory back to the planned level. Figure 11-2 shows a production plan for a seasonal product with actual ac-tivity for the month of July posted with the plan. This is a make-to-stock plan, and the budgeted inventory level (believed adequate to give the desired level of customer service) is 1400 units.

In July, in spite of the fact that cumulative production totals were ahead of plan, sales were even further ahead, so that the inventory was then at the base level of 1400 units. If this base inventory level is to be maintained during the peak sales month of August, production will have to be 1500 units instead of the 1120 units previously planned.

Sales				Production		Inventory	
Month	Weeks	Month	Cumulative	Month	Cumulative	Month	Remarks
July Planned Actual	2	1000 1120	8600 9400	448 470	9184 9600	1784 1400	At Budget
August Planned Actual	5	1500	10,100	1120	10,304	1404	
Sept. Planned Actual	4	900	11,000	896	11,200	1400	

Figure 11-2 MAKE-TO-STOCK PRODUCTION PLAN.

This is typical of the decision making facing management; they have only two alternatives:

1. Do nothing, have inventories drop below the budgeted level and have customer service go below the planned level.

2. Make a fairly substantial change in the production rate, although this change will only last a short period of time since the peak sales period is over.

It is possible to make a production plan that includes additional inventory in the form of **stabilization stock** in order to reduce the probability of having to change the plan too frequently. It is important, however, to determine how much stabilization stock must be included in order to accomplish the purpose without excessive amounts of inventory. This problem is analogous to that of determining the amount of reserve stock to carry for an item in order to reduce the possibility of a stockout. Unfortunately, the costs associated with these alternatives are not well defined and readily available.

A similar problem can occur in a make-to-order business. Figure 11-3 shows incoming business stated in machine hours for a small company selling turret-lathe work as a subcontractor. The forecast called for 1000 hours per week and sales have varied quite widely around this forecast for the 3 months shown. One way to handle this incoming business would be to produce the 1400 hours received during the week of 5-1 the following week, reduce production to 700 hours the next week to handle orders received during the week of 5-8, increase it once again to 920 hours for orders received in the week of 5-15 and continue to change production weekly to meet incoming sales rates. When production levels can be changed cheaply and easily (by shifting workers and equipment to other products, for example), this is certainly feasible and will give the best customer service. Unfortunately, changing production levels in most plants incurs heavy extra costs due to overtime, hiring, training, lost production, higher scrap rates from inexperienced operators and many other factors.

Forecast = 1000 hr/week	
Week	Incoming business
5 – 1	1400 hours
5 – 8	700
5 – 15	920
5 – 22	700
5 – 29	850
6 – 5	1060
6 – 12	425
6 – 19	950
6 – 26	1300
7 – 3	1060
7 – 24	856
7 – 31	502

Figure 11-3 INCOMING BUSINESS— TURRET LATHE WORK.

Figure 11-3 shows that the original forecast of 1000 hours per week now seems high when compared to the actual incoming business average. If the weighted average forecasting technique discussed in Chapter 4 were applied to this particular set of data, a regular weekly updated forecast could be maintained. Figure 11-4 shows such a forecast, based on the actual incoming business, which could be used as the production rate for the following week if fairly small changes in production were feasible and acceptable.

Comparing Figures 11-3 and 11-4, using the weighted average forecast as a means of controlling the production rate would reduce the weekly high rate from 1400 hours to 1080 hours and increase the low from 425 hours to 840 hours. By passing the full fluctuations in business level back to the plant, the production rate would have to vary almost 1000 hours (from a high of 1400 to a low of 425

New forecast = α x incoming business + $(1-\alpha)$ x old forecast

Using weighting factors: $\alpha = 0.2$
$(1-\alpha) = 0.8$

Week	Incoming business	0.2 x Incoming business	Old forecast	0.8x Old forecast	New forecast
5−1	1400	280	1000	800	1080
5−8	700	140	1080	865	1005
5−15	920	185	1005	805	990
5−22	700	140	990	791	931
5−29	850	170	931	745	915
6−5	1060	212	915	731	943
6−12	425	85	943	755	840
6−19	950	190	840	672	862
6−26	1300	260	862	690	950
7−3	1060	212	950	760	972
7−24	856	170	972	778	948
7−31	502	- - -	948	- - -	- - - -

Figure 11-4 WEIGHTED AVERAGE FORECAST—INCOMING BUSINESS—TURRET LATHE WORK.

hours), while use of the weighted average technique reduces this variation to just over 200 hours. It is apparent, however, that this second approach requires some order backlogs (not shown in Figure 11-4) because full fluctuations are *not* passed back to production.

In a make-to-order business, backlogs of orders are commonly used to absorb the fluctuations in incoming business. Our previous examples assumed that there were no backlogs of orders and that all production was handled the week after the orders were received. In actual practice, most companies find that it is not practical to change production rates frequently because such changes are expensive and take considerable time to accomplish.

The question that must be answered if backlogs are to be used to stabilize production is, How much backlog must be maintained? In Chapter 9 this decision was made very roughly by observing deviations from the forecast of incoming business hours (Figure 9-12). A more accurate method is to use the statistical techniques explained in Chapter 5 to analyze the variations in incoming business and to determine the amount of backlog normally required to keep production fairly level. Figure 11-5 shows the calculation of mean absolute deviation for the first 5 weeks of incoming business. The individual weekly deviations are calculated and the MAD is found to be 247 hours.

Week	Incoming	Forecast	Deviation
5 – 1	1400	1000	400
5 – 8	700	1080	380
5 – 15	920	1005	85
5 – 22	700	990	290
5 – 29	850	931	81
			Total = 1236
		MAD = 1236/5 = 247 hours	

Figure 11-5 MEAN ABSOLUTE DEVIATION OF INCOMING BUSINESS—TURRET LATHE WORK.

In the table of safety factors for the normal distribution, Figure 5-7, the values are given for variations *above* the average only. Reserve stocks must protect only against *excessive* demand during the lead time. Since demand during the lead time will be *less* than the forecast approximately half of the time, no reserve stock will be needed to give 50% customer service. Therefore, the values given in Figure 5-7 are those for service levels above 50%.

In determining how much backlog is needed to stabilize manufacturing operations, a different table must be used since backlogs will go down when incoming business is less than anticipated and will go up when incoming business is higher. In other words, while only plus variations must be considered in setting reserve stock levels, both plus and minus variations must be accounted for in determining backlog requirements for a production plan. Figure 11-6 is the table to use for both plus and minus variations.

Figure 11-7 shows the results of level production at 900 hours per week with backlogs starting at 617 hours ($2\frac{1}{2}$ mean absolute deviations) in the week of 6-5. Figure 11-6 shows that this should protect against changing capacity more than 95% of the time (47.72% for plus and 47.72% for minus deviations), meaning only one change about every 20 weeks. With a backlog of 617 hours and a production rate of 900 hours equal to the average incoming business forecast, the backlog would drop whenever incoming business was less than the forecast and rise whenever the forecast was exceeded. The backlog could then go as low as zero (at which point production would have to be decreased) or as high as 1234 hours (at which

Probable % of occurrences	Standard deviation	Mean absolute deviation
0 00 %	0.00	0.00
25.00 %	0.67	0.84
30.00 %	0.84	1.05
34.13 %	1.00	1.25
35.00 %	1.04	1.30
39.44 %	1.25	1.56
40.00 %	1.28	1.60
43.32 %	1.50	1.88
44.00 %	1.56	1.95
44.52 %	1.60	2.00
45.00 %	1.65	2.06
46.00 %	1.75	2.19
47.00 %	1.88	2.35
47.72 %	2.00	2.50
48.00 %	2.05	2.56
48.61 %	2.20	2.75
49.00 %	2.33	2.91
49.18 %	2.40	3.00
49.38 %	2.50	3.13
49.50 %	2.57	3.20
49.60 %	2.65	3.31
49.70 %	2.75	3.44
49.80 %	2.88	3.60
49.86 %	3.00	3.75
49.90 %	3.09	3.85
49.93 %	3.20	4.00
49.99 %	4.00	5.00

Figure 11-6 TABLE OF SAFETY FACTORS FOR NORMAL DISTRIBUTION.

point production should be increased). Figure 11-8 shows the turret lathe backlog graphically and shows the upper and lower control limits in a control chart to indicate when to change production rates.

This backlog of hours at the turret lathes is like stabilization stock. The greater the stabilization stock, the less frequently production level changes will have to be made. Figure 11-9 shows the amount of stabilization stock required for various numbers of production level changes during the year. The calculations are clear in Figure 11-9, but it should be remembered that these are based on the assumption that variations are normally distributed. In examples like these just given, the choice of how many changes are desirable will depend on the economics of carrying the backlogs of inventory versus the costs of changing the production rate. Like all statistical techniques, the calculations can be rigorous but the data needed are guesses at best and the assumptions may be invalid. It is far more effective to work

Week	Incoming business	Production	Backlog hours
6−5	1060	900	617*
6−12	425	900	142
6−19	950	900	192
6−26	1300	900	592
7−3	1060	900	752
7−24	856	900	708
7−31	502	900	310
*2.5 x 247 (MAD) = 617			

Figure 11-7 BACKLOG HOURS WITH LEVEL PRODUCTION−TURRET-LATHE WORK.

closer with at least the major customers to assure more uniform receipt of orders and more timely adjustments of capacity. The second volume (8) covers this in detail.

Practical Considerations in Capacity Control

The following are some practical considerations to improve control of capacity:

1. **Seasonal production:**
   Controlling the level of production to meet a seasonal production plan provides some interesting problems. During the off-season, when produc-

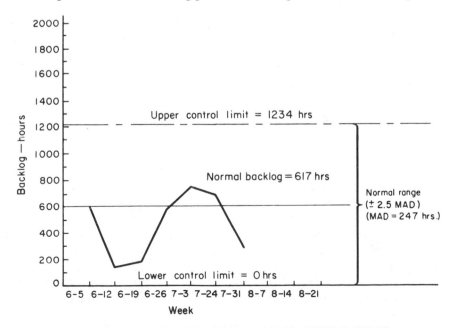

Figure 11-8 TURRET LATHE WORK BACKLOG-CONTROL CHART.

Production changes per year	Fraction of weeks without a change	% of weeks without a change	No. MAD* ± required (MAD = 247 hrs.)	Stabilization stock
1	49/50 =	98 %	2.91	1440 hrs.
2	48/50 =	96 %	2.56	1265 hrs.
4	46/50 =	92 %	2.19	1080 hrs.
6	44/50 =	88 %	1.95	964 hrs.
8	42/50 =	84 %	1.74	860 hrs.
10	40/50 =	80 %	1.60	790 hrs.
12	38/50 =	76 %	1.48	730 hrs.
14	36/50 =	72 %	1.36	670 hrs.
16	34/50 =	68 %	1.25	617 hrs.
18	32/50 =	64 %	1.15	568 hrs.
20	30/50 =	60 %	1.05	519 hrs.

*From Figure 11-6

Figure 11-9 STABILIZATION STOCK VERSUS PRODUCTION RATE CHANGES.

tion is being maintained at levels that will build up inventories (which act as stabilization stocks) there is little need for fast reaction to deviations from the production plan. The required reaction becomes increasingly crucial as the end of the peak selling season approaches and inventories are down to their lowest level.

During the inventory building season, the actual inventory can vary from the planned level by as much as a month's supply without causing any immediate problems as long as corrective action can be taken in time to meet the target set for the end of the peak selling season. It is often practical, for example, to maintain a monthly production plan during the inventory-building period and then switch over to a weekly production plan during the peak selling season.

2. **Inertia in changing production:**
There is a tendency in most plants for production levels to have tremendous inertia. As previously mentioned, it is frequently difficult to get line managers to change production levels since they are far more conscious of the costs and difficulties involved in changing rates than they are of the potential customer-service problems involved in not changing. This, of course, is the very reason for having decision rules—delays in changing the production rate can make the amount of change required so large as to be almost impossible to attain.

If, for example, it is found that the actual inventory level is the equivalent of 1500 units (hours, dollars worth, etc.) below target 20 weeks before the planned low point of the inventory, this situation can be corrected by raising the production rate over the planned level by only 75 units per week (1500 divided by 20). If this decision is postponed and the production rate is not changed until 5 weeks before the inventory is to be at its lowest point, the production rate will have to be changed by 300 hours per week (1500 divided by 5). Such a change will be very much more expensive and making it may be beyond the ability of the organization. Customer service will suffer over the longer period needed to restore the proper inventory levels.

This inertia exists when the production rate is cut back as well as when it is increased. Companies with incentive systems often find that they can produce as much after a reduction in hours (for example, from a 5- to a 4-day week) as they could on regular time because the workers on incentive plans increase their paces in order to earn their normal wages even though hours have been shortened.

3. **Average production rates:**
   Line manufacturing people often tend to look at planned production rates as ceilings rather than as averages. The fear of idle time strongly tends to keep worker levels low. Production losses caused by such factors as holidays, unexpected equipment breakdowns and absenteeism tend to be overlooked if the planned rates are being attained during periods of full output. Close attention to the *cumulative* production totals on the production plan will avoid serious effects resulting from the sum of many small losses and, even more important, will give early-warning signals about the need for corrective action to combat the inertia in changing capacity.

4. **Sequence of changes:**
   In manufacturing assemblies, conventional wisdom states that any change in the assembly production rate can be made only in the proper time sequence, following changes in plans to purchase raw materials, manufacture components and put together subassemblies. The belief is that there is no practical value in increasing the assembly production rate if components are not available to meet the planned increase in the rate. This is true, of course, if available levels of component inventories are very low. In most assembly plants such inventories are usually too high and reducing inventories *will not increase* the number of shortages. However capacity is increased, every precaution must be taken to avoid increasing work-in-process levels.

   Decreases in the production rate, on the other hand, can be instituted simultaneously at all stages of production. If they are expected to be long-term decreases, the purchasing and production rates should be set low enough to reduce the intermediate inventories of work-in-process, components and semifinished inventory.

Whether increasing or decreasing capacity, sharp increases in a short period should be avoided if at all possible. The balance of operations among work centers is practically impossible to maintain in such quick adjustments. Equally difficult to handle well are capacity changes to meet simultaneous increases (or decreases) in total demand and aggregatge inventories. Both require *overcorrection*, thus requiring two adjustments in capacity.

5. **Overtime versus increased work force:**
One debate that frequently occurs in a manufacturing firm concerns the relative value of overtime. Some companies try to enforce a rule that no overtime will be allowed while others feel that overtime is an extremely economical way to manufacture and, therefore, normally include overtime in their production planning.

The real question is, Will the production increase be of a long enough duration to justify hiring people (assuming sufficient equipment is available) or should it be handled with overtime? The answer to this question could be obtained readily if approximate costs were available. The costs involved are those of overtime (including any additional overhead, which goes up proportionately with overtime) versus the costs of increasing production to the new level and bringing it back down again. For example, if overtime costs for a change in the production level of a given magnitude were expected to total $200 in overtime premium per week and the costs of hiring and training people, plus the consequent layoffs to make this same change, were estimated at $1000, the following rule could be used: Whenever the anticipated increase in the production level will last for more than 5 weeks—the break-even point, or the point at which the total weekly overtime premium would equal the hiring and training costs—then people should be hired.

Like any attempt to assign costs to decision alternatives, this one must be handled with the practical recognition that the costs involved are not readily available and that managers mistrust making decisions by inserting numbers into a formula. There might also be other intangible considerations—such as the company's reputation for employment stability—that should be considered. As with any decision alternatives, the proper approach is to gather the best available cost information, show the probable costs of the alternatives and point out the intangibles involved to assist management in making a decision.

6. **Integrating capacity and priority planning:**
Significant capacity changes must be integrated with master production schedule revisions so that the material planning programs will furnish the proper priorities. The only exception to this occurs when additional capacity is needed to handle *unplanned* upsets, such as unusual scrap losses or interruptions in production.

Interrelated Elements
in Output Control

One of the characteristics of production and inventory control that has caused practitioners great problems is the interrelationship of the elements involved. Capacity planning cannot be effective until there is an inventory control system that generates realistic requirements. On the other hand, the inventory control system that merely generates orders and releases them to the plant without regard for capacity usually generates its own excessive lead times and resultant higher inventories and shortages. If the planning system has not been provided with controls, it is inevitable that production will eventually go out of control and that changes in the production level will occur too late to avoid crises.

It is essential that the production control system include some decision boundaries and it is important that these be spelled out so that anyone might recognize when a change in production level is required. Such tools as the service versus investment curve (Figure 8-8) can then be used to show the potential impact on customer service if production levels are not changed. In a make-to-order company, the impact on future delivery lead times can be projected to help other managers recognize the real alternatives involved.

The need for some decision rules or boundaries is so essential to control that these rules should be implemented in any production control system, even if they must first be developed according to tolerances established by judgment (later refined, using some of the techniques discussed in this chapter). Even if these control limits are less than scientific to start with, they are better than none. Establishing the boundaries only once provides far more rational control than having to debate continuously where the boundaries should be and postpone corrective action until a crisis makes it obvious that action was indeed required.

Control over the level of production is necessary in order to insure that the right items come through production. If sufficient capacity does not exist, techniques such as expediting will get only some of the items through. It is folly to increase expediting efforts when the real problem is lack of capacity, since expediting only robs Peter to pay Paul. If the requirements generated by the inventory control system are realistic, yet a great deal of expediting is required in a particular plant, the chances are that this is merely a symptom of the real problem: *lack of control over production capacity.*

Aggregate production rates are also needed for purchasing plans (and to the purchaser, the most meaningful total is often dollars). The use of the bill of labor for rough-cut planning of vendors' capacity requirements, together with more detailed techniques, was covered in Chapter 9. Another method for making a purchasing plan is to determine the total number of components that will be needed to meet a planned production rate over some long horizon and then to extend each of the aggregate totals for the individual components by the unit cost so that a meaningful total in dollars results. In most respects, the purchasing plan is identical to the production plan and its use as a control instrument is exactly the same.

Cost accounting systems must be able to give cost information immediately after activities occur; this requires that they be integrated with the production systems. This similarity in the information required by all members of the organization is what makes an integrated management information system imperative. The idea is to develop and present the basic information necessary for running the plant in a standardized form that can be used by all departments on a timely basis, so that it is of real value as control information.

The Objectives of Control
of Priorities

In addition to capacity control, effective control of priorities is necessary. Manufacturing plants must make enough total product and work on the right items; both are necessary. The following functions must be handled properly:

1. **Shop planning,** to be sure that everything required to start work is available
2. **Job selection and assignment,** to make the actual choice of which job at a work center should be done next and by whom
3. **Feedback,** to enable plant performance to be measured against plan and corrective action to be generated when required
4. **Lot control,** to provide data on job location, means of auditing the counts reported by machine operators and accumulation of costs against the manufactured lot
5. **Rescheduling,** the jobs in process to meet changing requirements

Shop planning is a most important function, designed to include the responsibility for coordinating arrival of necessary paperwork and materials, insuring the availability and preparation of tooling and equipment and any other items required to start work. *These are properly the responsibility of planning and control personnel,* not line supervisors. Shop planning can also generate savings by seeing that jobs that require similar setups are run together or by overlapping lots, starting work on the next operation before the entire lot has been completed at the previous operation which can very significantly shorten lead times. It can also provide useful information to supervisors on jobs requiring unusual tolerances, special machine adjustments or unique worker skills.

Proper **job selection** on the shop floor increases in difficulty as the number of orders at a machine center increases. The more shop input can be controlled to minimize queues, the less problem job selection becomes. Nevertheless, in a plant with intermittent batch operations and functional manufacturing departments, some provision must be made for job selection on the factory floor. Too often, there is conflict between line supervisors and planning personnel over who should have the primary voice. Choosing the job that best balances shop and customer requirements is best handled by close cooperation between supervisors and the dispatchers or shop planners assigned to the manufacturing department. This choice often involves deciding whether a job that can follow in the setup currently in a machine should run next or whether a job urgently needed to meet service requirements should be run. Such decisions determine the customer service that will result and many costs as well. Assignment of a particular machine operator to the job is usually the supervisor's responsibility because it involves knowledge of operators' skills and a fair distribution of the more difficult or less desirable jobs.

Good shop control requires timely and accurate **feedback** tracking the progress of orders. This permits generating variance reports, like delay reports indicating which jobs are not moving and why. Such feedback is essential to good control since it is the basis for warning signals that action is needed and where.

Lot control involves assigning an identification (order) number to a particular manufacturing batch to accumulate data relating to it. These data include piece counts which machine operators report so that the accuracy of labor claims—the basis for the operator's pay—can be verified. In companies using standard costing, actual material and labor costs are accumulated for each manufacturing lot. In most companies, tracking the movement of this lot is the basis for updating job location records so that job progress and adherence to schedule can be monitored.

The following section on priority rules discusses techniques for **rescheduling** jobs once they are in the plant, so that when there is a choice of jobs to be run, this choice can be based on the latest requirements. In most companies, the required dates on orders issued to the plant are subject to change once the job is in process. In a make-to-stock company some items will sell faster than forecast and the inventory position will change significantly in a few weeks' time. Ability to react promptly to these changing requirements can be a real asset in improving customer service.

Several of these functions are selected for additional discussion in the next sections of this chapter. Additional in-depth coverage is included in the second volume (8).

Expediting

Expediting is probably the best-known technique for shop control and the one with the longest and widest use in industry. Expediting consists principally of finding and rushing "hot" jobs through the production facilities by pushing them ahead of other jobs competing for the same facilities. The simplest type of expediting consists of locating (among the work-in-process) items that are out of stock or those past due and getting immediate attention to moving these items through production. It begins to function after trouble has occurred. Modern expediting attempts to prevent trouble by identifying potential shortages or troubles early enough to prevent them from interfering with planned production.

Expediting has fallen into disrepute because it is frequently overdone, generates high costs and often does little for the factory except creating confusion and undermining confidence in planning and control activities. Nevertheless, some "firefighting" will always be necessary; interruptions and upsets cannot be predicted accurately, and there is often a gap between planned and actual results. Some companies claim that they don't have expediters, but this simply means that they call them something else; there is someone or a group in every company conscious of the customers' requirements and with the responsibility for troubleshooting and solving problems so that schedules are met. A valid comment frequently made is that the expediter just urges other people to do what they should have known enough to do by themselves.

The qualifications of expediters are important factors in their success. Expediters should be highly energetic and resourceful people. They must be forceful and effective in getting supervisors, inspectors, engineers and others to face their problems and solve them quickly. In practice, expediters' activities are usually poorly organized and much of their time is wasted. This condition can be improved by having a supervisor work with them to plan the expediters' daily activities so that their time is spent effectively and so that some measures of accomplishment may be used to evaluate the expediters' results.

Expediting consists of picking one job out of the queue at a work center and running it ahead of all others. It reaches the point of diminishing return as soon as two orders are competing for position at the head of one queue. As expediting efforts are increased, the number of selected rush jobs increases. If the real cause of the excessive backlogs is not eliminated, all jobs soon become rush jobs and a special designation must be developed for those with top priority. These become special rush jobs. It isn't long before only the special rush jobs seem to come through on schedule. All jobs then become special rush and the vicious cycle continues. This is the history of all informal priority systems operating under continuing shortages. Expediting can be effective only as an exception technique. It works well only when a very few jobs are given priority over others, regardless of the number and caliber of the expediters.

Principle 56. The less expediting there is, the more effective it will be.

Dispatching

Dispatcher is the title commonly used for control people working closely with workers in a manufacturing department. Their function is to help choose the correct sequence of jobs to be run from a file of orders representing jobs released to each work center. Dispatchers also have access to copies of all manufacturing orders generated by the material planners, whether released or not, on which each work center has operations. Unreleased orders are known as the **dead load file;** they are used for shop planning, to initiate action to get the tools, fixtures, gauges, etc., needed to run the job. When the material arrives at each work center, the order moves into a **live load file** with other jobs already waiting to be run. When a job is released to be run, some form of authorization is given to the production floor, frequently accompanied by specifications, blueprints, time cards and related paperwork. This is usually called the **order packet.**

Commercial equipment is available to assist the dispatcher. The simplest aids are load boards, mechanical devices to represent jobs in the backlog. These are discussed in Chapter 10. Such cumbersome manual dispatching techniques have been replaced largely by communication hardware, such as data collection terminals and other data transmission equipment. This equipment makes practicable a centralized dispatching function without dispatchers located in individual work centers. Centralized dispatching can be more practical because it helps solve two of the major problems of dispatching:

1. It requires fewer people than having a dispatcher in each department.
2. It provides for ready communication among dispatchers so that they can all be aware of the latest job requirements and shop status.

However, centralized dispatching requires that some form of communication equipment be used to report job progress to the central location (such as data collection terminals) where the operator reports via the terminal and the open order data files are updated immediately and continuously or periodically in batches. The actual job assignment is usually handled by discussions with supervisors or set-up people who place job assignment cards in the proper sequence in a rack at the input station on the shop floor where they are given or are available to the operator assigned to the work.

A typical centralized dispatching control center handles several work centers each represented by an order file, usually in a rack. Jobs being worked on are represented by order packets of cards in the proper slots at the front of the racks and jobs in backlog or queue are placed in corresponding slots on the backs of the racks.

Notification of job activity comes via data collection on the plant floor. This data collection can be by manually posted and hand carried documents, voice transmission to central dispatch stations or sophisticated electronic equipment. Data collection terminals vary widely in function and cost from simple remote reproduction devices handling both fixed data (order and part numbers, operation numbers and descriptions, etc.) and variable data (date, time, quantities completed, worker identification, etc.). They can be simple or complex to operate; some of the latter have tutorial displays which guide people along every step of the reporting process.

Terminals offer several benefits:

1. Less time involved in reporting and recording
2. More timely updating of system data
3. Fewer errors with editing (for instance, comparing order and part numbers for compatibility) and less human involvement

Notice that the second and third benefits may be intangible unless real savings can be made as a result. Expensive data collection equipment should be justified only on the basis of *tangible* benefits. Benefits such as better decisions, faster response and higher productivity are not legitimate; these can all be achieved with simpler, less expensive data transmission.

Flow Control

Beginning in the mid-1950s, a simple system for controlling plant production in semiprocess flow operations was applied very successfully in several companies. This type of operation exists whenever families of parts follow the same sequence of operations, even though different machines or equipment are used. Called **flow control,** it was based on the principle that jobs started through a semiprocess flow will progress with a minimum of paperwork and formality if work-in-process levels are kept low. There are six basic elements of flow control:

1. **Planned production levels of major activities:**
   Planned production rates for every operation or every product line are not necessary; the ABC classification applies here as it does in so many other areas of production control. There are a few products that require the bulk of available work hours in a given manufacturing process. By controlling the rate of input in these few areas closely, production rates can be maintained at a fairly even level.

2. **Well-defined "In" and "Out" stations for material:**
   Clearly marked In and Out locations should be available in each department so that all work coming to a work center is easily recognized as new and all work completed at that center is immediately brought to the attention of the material handlers, who will move it to the next "In" station.

3. **Clearly visible dating and identification of work-in-process:**
   Flow control emphasizes visual control of work-in-process. As each operation is completed, the work identity and completion date are marked on a tag on each move-lot of material so that anyone concerned can tell how long each job has been at each operation.

4. **Delay reports on slow-moving work:**
   At regular intervals (usually twice each week), lists are made of those jobs that have been in any machine center more than a stated period of time (usually 1 or 2 days) without actually being processed. This report is used to bring delayed jobs to the supervisor's attention so that action can be taken to get them moving.

5. **A priority system:**
   A simple priority system is sometimes needed, but the short lead times and rapid flow of work through machine centers resulting from Flow Control techniques usually reduce the importance of priorities on individual orders.

6. **Good housekeeping and shop floor discipline:**
   Since Flow Control is a visual way to control material on the factory floor, it depends heavily on good housekeeping and discipline in handling, arranging and locating shop containers so that material is in its proper location and is readily identifiable.

Flow Control is a thoroughly practical method for applying the principles of work-in-process control discussed in this chapter. It applies when there is a semi-process flow of work— practitioners should be sure this is true of their plants before attempting to use Flow Control. This technique places on schedulers the responsibility for sending out to the factory only those jobs actually required and for gearing input very closely to actual plant capacity. It leaves the burden of shop planning to the department supervisor and does not, by itself, provide for lot control. Job location and auditing of counts must, therefore, be handled by a separate system.

Rescheduling and Priority Rules

Since the problems introduced by long lead times have been discussed so frequently and since their effects are so important in designing a shop control system, a characteristic example of the type of schedule changes encountered is worth consideration. Figure 11-10 shows the results of a study of a sample of 17 items ordered to arrive in week 21. The order system indicated that these items would be required during week 21, based on lead times of 13 weeks. Subsequent experience showed that five of these items were actually required before week 19 and an equal number were required later than week 23. One item was actually needed in week 14 and another item, for which sales had slowed, was not needed until week 26. This may seem like an extreme example, but those in industry who work with long lead times will agree that it is quite typical of actual experience.

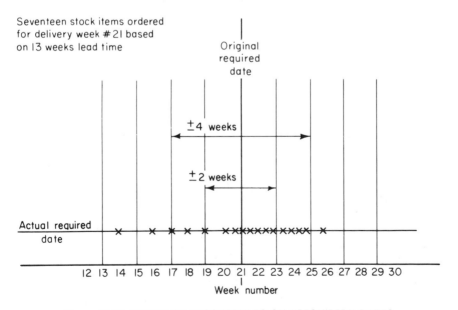

Figure 11-10 EFFECT OF RESCHEDULES ON "REQUIRED" DATES.

A good material control system provides the means for reviewing required dates periodically so that the proper items are started based on the latest possible information. It also provides the means for reviewing required dates for any items already started so that these can be rescheduled if changes in requirements make revisions to required dates necessary or desirable. This is covered in detail in Chapters 5 and 6.

Most priority techniques simply use the dates, either required (due) or start dates, for orders and operations. A second important factor is the amount of work remaining to be done. One technique for including both dates and work content is called **"Critical Ratio."**

The Critical Ratio technique was developed by Arnold O. Putnam and his associates at Rath & Strong (12). For items ordered using order points, this technique compares the rate at which inventory of the item is being depleted to the rate at which manufacturing lead time is being used up. The stock depletion rate is the numerator and the manufacturing lead time rate is the denominator of the Critical Ratio, which is then used to set priority for jobs in the plant or in the hold-for-release file. It should use the latest information on actual requirements—jobs with high ratios are not urgently required, while those with low ratios should be expedited.

To calculate a Critical Ratio, accurate data are needed on

1. Reorder points for each item in inventory
2. Inventory of each item on hand and available at any given time
3. The total manufacturing lead time required by each item
4. The remaining manufacturing lead time required by each item (in process in the factory or in the hold-for-release file at the given time)

Using these data, two factors are then determined:

$$\text{Stock-depletion factor } A = \frac{\text{available stock}}{\text{reorder-point quantity}}$$

This factor will usually be less than 1.00 since another lot would not be ordered if the available stock were above the order point. Customer returns or order cancellations would increase the available stock and could cause this factor to be more than 1.00, of course.

$$\text{Lead-time factor } B = \frac{\text{standard lead time remaining}}{\text{total manufacturing lead time}}$$

This factor will also usually be less than 1.00 since some part of the total lead time will have been used up if the part is in process. The Critical Ratio is determined from the following relationship:

$$\text{Critical Ratio} = \frac{\text{stock-depletion factor } A}{\text{lead-time factor } B}$$

For example, suppose the order point of an item is 2000 pieces. Three weeks after a new lot is ordered, only 1000 pieces are available in the storeroom. The stock depletion factor A is

$$A = \frac{1000}{2000} = 0.5$$

The total time required to complete one lot of this item is 6 weeks, of which 3 weeks remain. The lead time factor B is

$$B = \frac{3}{6} = 0.5$$

Thus

$$\text{Critical Ratio} = \frac{A}{B} = \frac{0.5}{0.5} = 1.00$$

By its magnitude, the Critical Ratio indicates that an order is in one of three general conditions:

1. Good ratio: A/B is between 0.80 and 1.20.

Available stock is being used up about as fast as lead time and the replenishment lot should be completed about on time. No action is needed on such jobs. The example above is in this condition.

2. Expedite ratio: A/B is less than 0.80.

For example, $A = 0.2$ and $B = 0.5$ (giving a Critical Ratio of $0.2/0.5 = 0.4$) indicates that the remaining stock has been reduced to 20% of the order point— yet 50% of the total lead time remains to complete the order now in process to replenish the inventory. With this condition, the job will have to be expedited or a stockout will occur.

3. Slack ratio: A/B is more than 1.20.

Such ratios indicate that the rate of consumption of the available stock is less than was anticipated when the order point was established and/or the manufacturing order has moved through the plant faster than normal. Regardless of the cause, replenishment of this item can be delayed without risking a stockout. If it is not delayed, the new lot will come into inventory while there is still a substantial quantity on hand and inventory carrying costs will increase.

This technique, although it involves handling a large volume of data and calculations in most companies, is an extremely effective one for reviewing and revising schedule dates for work-in-process and orders held in the release file or for directing effective action to control work-in-process.

This type of ratio can also be used where order due dates are generated from a materials requirements plan. Consider two jobs in a work center on day 105, both originally scheduled to be run on day 104. Both of them seemingly should have the same priority but job A is due to be shipped on day 106 while job B has more operations remaining and is not due to be shipped until day 110. Apparently job

A should be assigned a more urgent priority because it has so little time left to get back on schedule. The relative work content is important, however, and a priority ratio can be developed as follows:

$$\text{Critical Ratio} = \frac{\text{Required date} - \text{today's date}}{\text{Required date} - \text{operation schedule date}}$$

$$\text{For job A:} \quad \frac{106 - 105}{106 - 104} = \frac{1}{2} = 0.50$$

$$\text{For job B:} \quad \frac{110 - 105}{110 - 104} = \frac{5}{6} = 0.83$$

The calculations for Critical Ratio must be modified when work is overdue. The ratio will be negative for such orders. An order 1 day late with 1 day's work remaining has a ratio of -1, as will an order 10 days late with 10 day's work left to do. To determine proper priorities in past due situations, the two critical Ratio factors are multiplied, not divided. In this manner the two jobs just discussed will have ratios of -1 and -100, respectively, giving a truer relative priority.

An effective priority technique should be

1. **Definitive**, giving different relative priorities with few "ties" (jobs with identical priority)
2. **Factual**, based on accurate, timely information
3. **Dynamic**, reacting to both customer-driven (actual sales or changes in order quantities or dates) and plant-driven (interruptions in processing) changes
4. **Simple**, easily understandable by all those needing information on order priorities

The applications of various methods of assigning priority and other factors than date and work content are covered in detail in Chapter 6 of the second volume (8).

Two variations of the Critical Ratio technique have had some use:

1. **Queue ratio:**
   The nonworking time remaining divided by the original total queue planned for the balance of the operations
2. **Slack ratio:**
   The nonworking time remaining divided by the number of operations yet to complete

Both require more data analysis than Critical Ratio and have no real advantages over it.

A dynamic system of this type can be used to generate a daily dispatch list such as the one shown in Figure 11-11. Here jobs are ranked in priority sequence starting with the lowest (most urgent) number for the ratio. This can be of aid to advance planning in a shop by showing not only the jobs that are in a work center but also those that are expected to arrive during the next few days. This

			(In priority sequence)		

Work center #4010   Date   3/21
                                                           Shift   1

Job #	Part #	Op. #	Operation description	Ratio	Remarks
71823	7123X	030	Blanchard grind	.55	Hopper feed
30756	1937A	070	Grind	.68	To B.P. 23789
63117	6424B	040	Rough grind	.82	
92318	7702X	060	Finish grind	.94	Commercial tolerance
94413	6866M	050	Rough grind	1.60	Remove case harden only

Figure 11-11 DAILY DISPATCH LIST.

approach provides advance notice, so that tool preparation, sequenced setups and overlapped operations can be planned more effectively.

The importance of accurate, up-to-date information to the success of this type of reporting cannot be overemphasized. Dispatch lists are best when issued daily because of constant changes in shop status—their value to the shop will be very low if the status represented on the report is more than a few hours old.

The use of data collection terminals in the plant was mentioned in connection with dispatching and it is important to note that most companies using dynamic priority rules for shop rescheduling do use some mechanized system for shop feedback. The terminals solve one technical problem related to a mechanized system. When prepunched time cards are sent to the plant along with the shop order, only one card need be sent out for each operation, no matter how many times work is reported on that operation, since the card can be inserted in the terminal over and over again. Without terminals, the prepunched reporting cards—usually called a shop packet—must be supplied in sufficient quantity so that there will be a card available to be returned to the dispatch office at the end of each shift (or other period for reporting labor) as well as at the time the operation is completed.

Kanban

In Japan, the word KANBAN means card, tag or ticket. From this specific meaning, however, the term has been applied to everything relating to control of work on plant floors, even including a production control system. The proper meaning is *an execution technique* to generate replenishment of products, subassemblies or components both purchased and manufactured.

The technique was developed at Toyota Motor Car Company in Japan as part of their Toyota Production System (13) and has application only where certain conditions prevail:

1. Production schedules are leveled. Items are produced regularly, if not every day, although some variation is possible. Smoother production requires less work-in-process. To do this
   a. Master production schedules must be valid and firm for 3 to 4 weeks.
   b. Production runs must be very small (i.e., setups must be very short).

2. Capacity is flexible and can be increased in very short time to handle small excess loads.

3. Flow of production is carefully planned and disciplined, with clearly defined "In" and "Out" stations.

4. Standard sizes of containers are used, each containing a fixed number of each item.

Two types of KANBAN tickets are used: move cards and production cards. Production cards authorize in each work center the making of one container quantity of an item to replace a container taken from the work center's Out station. Typical of the information on these cards is

Part number and description

Card number

Container quantity

Source work center number

Other information may be included, such as bills of material, tooling, etc. Where only a few items are made, the card may be replaced by colored balls or some other simple means of telling the source work center which item is to be manufactured. Some cards are very sophisticated, using bar coding and serving as a vendor's invoices for delivered materials.

Move cards authorize the transfer of one container of an item from a source to a user work center. They contain essentially the same information as the production card. They are attached to the container when items are being moved into and stored in the user work center area. Both types of cards move from user to source areas (by hand, usually) and are held in a rack while moves or production are being prepared. Figure 11-12 schematically shows the movements of the two cards.

The KANBAN technique focuses on making *only what is needed* to replace items soon after they are used. Use of any items from their containers triggers the delivery of the move card on that container to the source work center's Out station. This, in turn, initiates movement of one container to the user work center's In station. Elapsed times may range from 5 minutes to a few hours maximum.

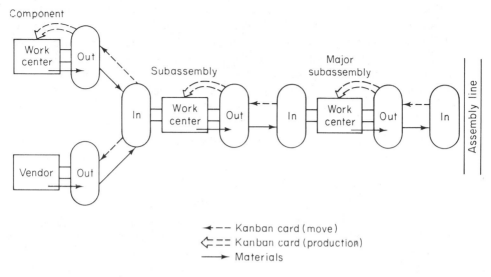

Component

Figure 11-12 KANBAN CARD MOVES.

Removal of a container from its Out station releases a production card to the source work center and another lot is produced to fill one container. This is delivered to the Out station when completed, usually within 1 to 3 days. Use of components in this work center's In station to make the lot in turn triggers move cards and production cards in upstream work centers. Thus all production is geared to making *only what is used.* Hence the technique has been called a **pull system.**

KANBAN may be used on one or all of a sequence of production activities. Most of its application has been made on final assembly and the replacement of major components from vendors or in-plant operations. The amount of total inventory of an item in the whole process flow depends on

Container quantities of each item

Variability of demand anticipated

Variability of supply tolerated

In the best run plants, the number of containers in the whole operation (equal to the number of KANBAN cards) is being reduced constantly. This, of course, requires a constant attack on problems interfering with a smooth, rapid flow of work.

Purchasing Follow-Up

Many hours of discussion concerning follow-up of purchased materials take place in most companies. Materials control people usually maintain that if purchasing would only follow up each order to make sure it came in on schedule, most of the problems would be solved; purchasing people argue that there aren't enough hours in the day to follow up on all items, particularly since there are so many new rush orders and that if *all* the material came in on schedule, there would be no room to store it. The problems of controlling output from vendors revolve largely around the rescheduling problem discussed earlier. The real objective of purchasing follow-up is to make sure that material arrives in time to meet *real requirements.* This can be done effectively only if vendors' produce *at the needed rates* and specific orders are placed with short lead times. This is covered in Chapter 9 and 10 and is discussed further in the second volume (8).

As expected, many purchased material requirements will change after the orders have been placed and it is more important to relay these changes to the suppliers and have them try to effect them than it is to insist on adherence to original scheduled dates. If material for which requirements have dropped off is received later than the original due date, no harm will result.

One technique applying the correct principle of getting enough in total and identifying the specifics at the last moment, also used by many purchasing departments, is the blanket order calling for delivery of a portion of the order at a particular weekly rate. Contracting in advance for a large amount (usually either 6 months' or a year's supply), the vendor gets information needed to plan capacity and the customer is able to take advantage of quantity discounts. Because of the long-range commitment, accuracy of the specific deliveries is a serious problem and it is important to review actual required dates frequently.

Figure 11-13 shows a weekly report issued by the materials control group reviewing blanket orders (in this case, for the components required to manufacture the lamps discussed in Chapters 6 and 10). The "Projected average weekly use" is taken from MRP data, as are the "Required this week" data.

The inventory in weeks on the blanket order review form is intended to cushion the variability in demand anticipated for these components. The no. 4107 cord set, for example, is used on all lamps and its actual total weekly demand will be equal to the planned production level. Thus an inventory target of 1 week should be sufficient. The no. X27 switch is used on only two lamps and its demand might be expected to fluctuate rather substantially from week to week; consequently, an inventory of 3 weeks is considered desirable. At the present time, the inventory is considerably above this level because material has been purchased in anticipation of a price increase.

The no. X18 switch inventory target is 2 weeks since it is used on the majority of the lamps and demand for it—while not as stable as that for the no. 4107 cord set—should still be considerably steadier than the demand for the no. X27 switch.

The basic purpose of the blanket order review is to provide control over a schedule originally set up with the vendor according to long-range estimates of future demand and to allow a tolerance for adjusting it when actual requirements turn out to be considerably different from the original estimates. The principle involved is fundamental to all purchasing follow-up systems: The production control department is responsible for supplying information regarding any changes in requirements—advances or deferments—and a tolerance must exist in the system so that it will not overreact to small changes in requirements.

Week ending __2/25__

Week number __8__

Part no.	Part name descr.	Used on	Proj. avg. wkly. use	Req'd this week	Inv. range in wks.	On* hand	Past due	Scheduled delivery						Remarks
								Due Wk.8	Due Wk.9	Due Wk.10	Due Wk.11	Due wk.12	Due later	
X18	Switch	7W,7D 9W,9D,9P	3,700	4,500	2	7,105	—	5,700	4,000	4,000	3,000	4,000	42M	—
X27	Switch	11D,11P	2,000	2,300	3	15,423	—	3,400	—	—	—	—	34M	Bought against for. incs.
X4107	Coil set	All	6,000	6,500	1	6,400	8,000	7,200	6,000	6,000	6,000	6,000	40M	P.D. prom. for Fri.

*Note — If out of range more than one week's use, reschedule next release.

Figure 11-13 BLANKET ORDER REVIEW.

Modern materials-requirements planning programs can be operated with very frequent (even real-time) replanning and very precise (even daily) time periods. These give an illusion of accuracy which is false. They can also, however, generate a constant flood of notices of the need to change due dates on purchase orders. Relaying such notices promptly and efficiently to vendors can be counterproductive. Until actual work is started on the material, it is sufficient that the vendor know the week it is needed. When delivery nears, the customer can then specify whether it is wanted on Monday, Tuesday or Friday. This subject is discussed in greater detail in Chapter 6 of the second volume (8).

Lead Time Control

As discussed in Chapter 9, controlling lead time requires controlling both capacity and priority. Before attempting a program aimed at reducing lead time, practitioners should analyze a sample of actual orders completed recently to determine the actual elements of lead time, such as setup, running, move and queue times as well as the time for customer order processing. Customers consider lead time to start when they send in their orders. Delays of 10 or more days may occur in some companies before orders clear the order entry process. Standards are usually established or good estimates are easily made of setup and running times. Move times can be estimated quite closely. Queue times can be calculated by subtracting all other elements from the total time the plant was operating while the order was in process. Usually this is found to be more than 90% of the total.

There are three major areas of improvement in seeking a reduction in lead time:

1. **Order-processing time:**
    The time that elapses from the moment an order leaves the customer's hands until the material is actually pulled from storage in a make-to-stock plant or until it is being scheduled into production in a make-to-order plant.

    Actual delivery time of orders from customer to vendor rarely comprises an important fraction of this element of lead time. If it does, the use of teletype equipment, telephone or modern data transmission equipment can cut this very substantially. Most long order-processing times result from two basic causes: Every order is handled as an exception or all paper-work operations—order entry, updating sales records, inventory adjustments, invoicing, etc.—are completed before the order is released for processing. In many companies, the credit manager must look at each order that comes in, rather than merely checking credit risks, because the sales department wants someone to look at each order received to pick out unusual ones. If these people handle orders in sequence, even if they do their review promptly, this order handling time can require several days; with some delays it can take weeks.

    While order processing is a complex system beyond the scope of this book, it is important to recognize its contribution to lead time and to control it as well as factory lead times. Ingenuity in reducing paperwork lead time can improve a company's performance as much as new processing equipment or improved production control systems. For example, copying machines make it possible to get a customer's order to schedulers promptly in order to start factory work before beginning the required formal paper work (type the order, edit it and check it through engineering, credit and sales). In most plants, the order will not have progressed far if there is reason to stop it because of poor credit or engineering questions.

2. **Scheduling:**
Backlogs constitute the largest portion of total lead time in most companies. As discussed in Chapter 10, some method of leveling production is required and, if this method is not provided by planning, it will be achieved by maintaining backlogs ahead of the starting operations. In a make-to-order plant, incoming business fluctuations make starting backlogs inevitable. If there is no effective capacity control, these backlogs may add weeks of unnecessary lead time.

Controlling input as described in Chapter 10 can assist in reducing scheduling lead time by keeping total production geared closely to total demand and feeding individual orders into production according to the latest customer requirements. Lead time can also be reduced by scheduling to the shortest possible cycle.

3. **Reduced work-in-process:**
In most intermittent operations, analysis of the lead time will indicate that the greatest gains are to be made by reducing waiting time at individual operations.

Control of lead time is not well understood in most manufacturing companies. Many believe that their actual lead times are appropriate. Unfortunately, if lead times are expected to be long, they will be as long as expected. The vicious cycle of rising business activity, stepped-up ordering, lengthened lead times, additional ordering and further increases in lead time, described in Chapter 5 in the second volume (8), will generate severe shortages and unnecessary increases in inventory of both purchased and manufactured items. A major educational program is needed to convince all the personnel involved that by planning and reducing backlogs and controlling input and output, a department that could not meet its requirements with an average 15 weeks lead time will now be able to give correct deliveries with an average of 2 weeks lead time!

Figure 11-14 is a memorandum sent by a purchasing agent to her company's materials control manager. This illustrates a not-uncommon reaction by a purchasing agent, Ms. Seagar, to increased pressure when suppliers get so busy they cannot give good deliveries. In this case, Mr. Jones' company is the only supplier of bearing inserts to the Fairville Division and the question of what Mr. Moss should do now is an interesting one. The only way to increase inventory is to place more

Fairville Division
of Johnson – Fairville
Interoffice Correspondence

To: Mr. J. R. Moss. Materials Control   Date: 7/23

Subject: Lead times

> I called Mr. R. Jones in reference to Bearing
> Inserts which we wanted at once.
> Mr. Jones said their bearing insert department
> is now operating on a six – week delivery time.
> He suggested we increase our inventory to take
> care of future delays.
>
> J. Seagar. (Ms.)
> Purchasing Agent

Figure 11-14 THE VICIOUS CYCLE STARTS.

orders on Mr. Jones' company, which inevitably will result in quotes of longer delivery lead times. Mr. Moss' estimates about which bearing inserts he needs and when he needs them will become less and less accurate as he tries to predict further in advance. Even if the supplier's service did not deteriorate as in-plant backlogs increased (which is not likely), the ability of the Fairville Division to give its customers good service would certainly deteriorate since customers would be less able to predict actual requirements over the extended lead time.

Earlier ordering is requested of their customers by suppliers who imply that they will then reserve enough capacity to meet the customers' needs. Poorer plans to meet customer requirements projected over the longer lead times, however, actually result in wasted vendor capacity. Reserving vendor capacity in terms of machine hours, tons of castings or some other meaningful total units and committing this capacity to specific customer items at the latest possible time avoids this waste. Generating larger backlogs will only aggravate the problem of inadequate capacity.

The essence of lead time control is control over work-in-process through planned production rates and controlled input. Many of the problems on plant floors are caused by inattention to control over *total amounts* of work-in-process. In most intermittent production plants, it is necessary to have some work ahead of each work center to smooth out the flow of production and to insure that there is a minimum of idle time caused by lack of work. Nevertheless, most manufacturing people do not recognize the great effect that the level of work-in-process has upon lead time, output control and, consequently, customer service. Missing this, they fail to exert sufficient efforts toward keeping work-in-process to a minimum.

The basic relationship between the level of work-in-process and the control of mix output has been receiving an increasing amount of emphasis in the literature of production and inventory control. This is not a newly discovered subject. One of the earliest published items on this subject is a most interesting article titled "The Case of Management Versus Excessive Inventories," which tells of a company that made a very drastic reduction in work-in-process inventory and thereby reduced average lead time from 5 months to 2 weeks. Their approach was simple: They tagged all work on the floor and removed all material that was not actually being worked on. This insured that the right jobs would go through production. This article appeared in the **September 1930** issue of *Factory and Industrial Management*. Unfortunately, its message seems to have gone almost unheeded in the many decades that have followed its publication.

The benefits of reducing work-in-process are much easier to recognize than to attain. The real problem is teaching the value of lower floor stocks to people such as

1. *The supervisor,* who wants more work on the floor before adding labor to meet rising demand.

2. *The inventory controller,* who is concerned only with generating orders to replenish stocks without concern for planned production levels and proper scheduling.

3. *The expediter,* who feels that with "just 2 more weeks" every job could be completed on schedule.

4. *The scheduler,* who wants to get the jump on important jobs by getting them on order with the factory as soon as possible, believing that extra lead time will insure getting orders through on schedule. This puts the scheduler in the very comfortable position of being able to say, "It is on order with the factory!" when asked the status of a particular job.

5. *The dispatcher,* who recognizes that work-in-process is too high but is too busy trying to get the right job shipped out on schedule to do anything about it.

6. *The setup person,* who delays starting one job so that its run can be combined with that of another expected soon.

The education job is a major stumbling block in reducing work-in-process, but the necessity for this effort is obvious in most plants. It is important that the effects of excess work-in-process inventory throughout the system be emphasized to all concerned and that they recognize the results that can be attained by reducing it. These benefits include

1. Shorter lead time—decreases as backlogs decrease

2. Better plans—more likely to be accurate as lead time shortens

3. Simpler dispatching and communication—easier as backlogs are reduced.

4. Better utilization of people—increases as the need for expediting and dispatching decreases

Reducing work-in-process requires major adjustments by both materials control and manufacturing people. Taking the responsibility for keeping work flowing in the factory at a smooth rate requires a new perspective by materials control practitioners who have historically depended upon large factory backlogs to do this. Factory operating people will be deeply concerned when they see in-process inventory levels decreasing—a reasonable time period should be allowed for building everyone's confidence in the availability of work. Learning to use the control system to detect out-of-control backlogs before they occur, coupled with fast reaction to prevent them, works real wonders!

During this transition period, line and planning personnel will have to work together very closely to iron out the problems causing excess queues. A machine operator may occasionally run out of work when work-in-process levels are first reduced. If this is investigated objectively, ways can usually be found to prevent it; for example, better scheduling might have avoided this situation. To make a work-in-process reduction permanently effective, managers will have to check every reported case of machine downtime or operator idle time, determine what caused it and try to insure that it does not happen again.

One legitimate reason for having inventory is to provide insurance against breakdowns of equipment and plant people often cite this as a primary reason for having high levels of work-in-process. Unfortunately, most companies' work-in-process inventories provide very little protection against breakdown because they have not been planned properly. If a critical machine is subject to breakdown, spare parts should be available, preventive maintenance should be used and repair actions should be taken quickly to get this machine back into operation when it breaks down. If, in spite of the best planning, it is still necessary to have inventory ahead of this machine, the inventory should be chosen so that it represents a balanced load on subsequent operations and should be physically removed from process so that it will not interfere with normal operations but will be available when a breakdown occurs.

For most companies, work-in-process can be reduced drastically with no ill effects. Any work-in-process reduction program, however, should begin by determining the amount of worker and machine downtime that exists with current factory backlogs so that direct comparisons can be made with downtime that occurs with lower levels of in-process inventory. Unless this comparison is available, excessive downtime will be cited as the principal result of reducing work-in-process. Such a reaction is understandable. It is a major change for plant operating personnel who have been used to large banks of work ahead of each operation to watch these banks dwindle and to have to learn to work today without having tomorrow's material on hand. In spite of such difficulties, more and more practitioners are recognizing that reducing material in the shop is the most effective means of lowering lead times and is fundamental to real control over output.

Job Shop Simulation

Simulation is a useful tool when there are so many variables that a direct mathematical solution is impractical. Many problems involved in intermittent or job shop scheduling obviously fit this description and, since the advent of the computer, considerable time has been spent on **job shop simulation**.

In the typical job shop simulators, numerical data—the language of the computer—are used to describe how many machines of each type are available, how many shifts each one is manned and how many productive hours can be expected from each work center. Each of the jobs to be studied is described along with each work center in the manufacturing sequence, setup time and running time for every job. With this information, the computer is programmed to simulate actual factory operations and print out the results, showing such information as starting and finishing dates. The equivalent of months of experience can be developed in a few hours of computer time.

Several firms and universities have used computer simulation to test dispatching rules that could be used when deciding which job to run next. Many dispatching rules have been applied, but four fairly typical and frequently used ones are:

1. **First come, first served:**
   The oldest job at each machine center should be run first.

2. **Value priority:**
   Preference is given to the A items (those having the highest dollar value for the lot) so that work-in-process dollar inventory investment is kept low.

3. **Critical machine:**
   Those jobs are run first that must later go through critical machines of limited capacity. The rule was designed to get jobs to bottleneck machines sooner, permitting the highest utilization of critical equipment and reducing the likelihood of delays.

4. **Least processing time:**
   The next job to be run is the one requiring the least time to complete the lot at the machine center (the easiest job to get done).

Published results would appear to show that the best all-around dispatching rule is the least processing time rule. This rule typically results in

1. The most jobs completed—this makes sense, since by picking the easiest jobs first, the dispatcher will be able to help the shop complete more jobs within a given period.

2. The lowest in-process inventory.

3. The shortest average lead time.

4. The best machine utilization.

5. The fewest late jobs—this is particularly interesting since this dispatching rule pays no attention to job schedule dates at all.

Using this rule over a long period of time, however, might mean that jobs with long processing times never get done. They will be worked on only when there is no other work at the machine center requiring less time and this might never happen! Simulation study of dispatching rules in a job shop has not yet come up with the answer to the problem of finding the best dispatching rule but it has demonstrated one point that has been emphasized throughout this book: Any technique that keeps work-in-process low—this is the principal effect of the least process-ing time rule—will improve plant performance by almost every measure.

One of the most popular applications of the computer has been simulating the flow of work through factories to study shop flow (especially delays and inter-ruptions) and to develop optimum schedules for complex operations. Schedules based on computer simulations can take cognizance of sequences of operations and balance the input to provide uniform loads for secondary as well as for starting operations. Unfortunately, several such programs have been sold as panaceas, tempt-ing managers to avoid the tedious, hard work of getting systems and plants in or-der. Until the "model" of the factory represented by these programs is more than "a small imitation of the real thing," their real value will be negligible. It is not likely that they will ever find practical use over more than a short horizon into the future.

In well-controlled plants, Raymond L. Lankford and Stephen D. Smith (6) have implemented successfully a technique they call **Manufacturing Resource Simula-tion**. In one program this simulates master production scheduled items, MRP for the components, production-order scheduling and final assembly scheduling. It tests when materials will be available to support the capacity plan and when capacity will be available to support the materials plan. It shows how items being simu-lated will compete for materials and capacity with existing orders already in the plant. It develops realistic completion dates based on the simulated flow of work.

Such programs have great potential power. They can give early warning sig-nals on orders that will be delayed by bottleneck work centers *before they are late*—while there is still time to take corrective action. They can indicate whether or not orders can be *brought back on schedule* in the tme remaining to complete unfin-ished operations. They can link together components of products so that scarce re-sources of materials and capacity can be utilized best to improve shipments and customer service. They can provide a sounder basis for customer order delivery prom-ises. Such techniques are available. The real question is, Is the environment suitable?

Effective Shop Floor Control

True control over work on any plant floor must begin long before the work gets to the floor. Here is the sequence of activities which must precede dispatching, priority techniques, simulation and expediting:

1. Shorten lead times—essential to making sound plans and being flexible and reactive

2. Reduce setup times and lot-sizes—to avoid overcommitment of resources beyond immediate needs

3. Simplify bills of materials—to permit making products in smooth progres-sion in fewer steps

4. Use firm, valid schedules—to minimize the nervousness of replanning and still insure accurate priorities

5. Smooth input—to feed facilities a rate and mix of orders that they can handle promptly.

Done properly, this sequence of activities will insure a minimum number of orders on plant floors; these can then be more tightly controlled. With small queues, however, the effects of interruptions become more immediate and serious. Diligent efforts must be made to reduce or eliminate

1. Poor quality materials

2. Record errors

3. Defective tooling

4. Equipment breakdowns

5. Vendor delays

6. Scrap and rework

Improved control of the plant environment is fundamental to control of work moving through it.

Principle 57. The best method of controlling work on plant floors is to prevent it from getting there too soon.

Selecting Output Control Techniques

One of the most challenging tasks for student and practitioner alike is to sort out the various output control techniques and to recognize where they apply properly. Much literature has been devoted to one particular technique or another but relatively little has been written about how they work together in a system in a real manufacturing firm. Both this book and the second volume (8) have stressed these interactions. Guidelines for selecting the proper output control techniques should be considered with a particular application in mind.

One of the first points to determine is whether output control (essentially capacity control and job selection) is the real problem or whether problems that appear to revolve around output control are just a result of poor planning or lack of input control. This question can be answered by checking actual elapsed lead time for a sample of manufactured items. If average lead times are reasonable but some items take very long to complete while others are manufactured well ahead of schedule, then job selection is the problem. If, on the other hand, average lead times are extremely long, it should be recognized that no amount of expediting or dispatching is likely to improve this average and the problem is inadequate capacity.

If job selection is the real problem, the proper technique to apply must be chosen. When many jobs follow similar patterns of flow in production, techniques like Flow Control should be considered. Here again, it is important to keep techniques in perspective. The general elements of Flow Control (such as planned rates, well-identified in and out stations and delay reports) make sense in any system and do not necessarily have to be used in conjunction with a visual follow-up if the visual approach is not appropriate. The general concepts of Flow Control are being applied using electronic data collection terminals. Any system used in a plant that has some degree of flow should focus the greatest attention on control of input to the plant and keeping jobs moving.

If work flow is truly intermittent, formal dispatching can best handle job selection and might be introduced only in bottleneck centers. When dispatching is to be used in many departments, a centralized approach is better. It is sometimes worth having an output-control person assigned to the manufacturing department when job selection is not particularly critical just to handle shop planning. This type of department is characterized by the need for considerable planning of details to coordinate all factors needed to start work. These include

1. Raw material and component requisitioning and delivery
2. Documentation, including drawings, specifications, routings, shop cards and numerical control tapes
3. Material containers and handling facilities
4. Tooling, gauges, fixtures and testing equipment
5. Coordination with supervision, quality assurance, maintenance and cost accounting

In a plant where the actual requirements may change considerably after jobs have been sent into the plant, dynamic priority techniques like Critical Ratio will be very effective in reflecting these changing requirements to the plant. The application of techniques of this type should improve customer service by helping to move the right items through production.

When purchased components are particularly important, consideration should be given to the use of better follow-up techniques. This follow-up should be based on latest requirements rather than required dates set when purchase orders are issued. Insisting that the purchasing department bring all material in on time and still bring the rush jobs in ahead of time does not recognize the fact that for every rush job, there should also be one that can be rescheduled to a later date. Knowing this will help reschedule vendors more effectively. Close attention to vendors' delivery lead times (using summaries such as that shown in Figure 11-13) can help to spot trouble before it is highlighted by excessive shortages or inventory increases.

The job of selecting the proper technique for controlling output requires a knowledge of the techniques available and where each best applies. Beyond this, however, design of output control systems requires an understanding of the way the elements of a good system must interrelate. Shop control can be very expensive and sophisticated yet achieve very little if lack of attention to planning and controlling capacity has let work-in-process levels build up too high. Even the most dynamic priority system decreases in effectiveness as shop backlogs get out of control. One the other hand, if the materials control system does not truly reflect requirements or changes in these requirements, efforts to get items through production according to unrealistic schedules will be largely wasted. Output control is a vital part of any production control system, but it should be remembered that it can only function as part of a well-designed overall production control system.

## CHAPTER TWELVE

FEEDBACK AND CORRECTIVE ACTION

Feedback—the Basis for Control

By definition, control means measuring actual performance (called **feedback**), comparing to plan, detecting significant deviations and initiating corrective action. As illustrated in Figure 1-1 in Chapter 1, a manufacturing-control system has two feedback loops, one for priority (material) and one for capacity.

Using the production plan to control production levels was discussed in Chapter 9 as an example of effective feedback to compare execution progress against plan. A forecast of demand and the desired change in inventory level was used to determine the production rates. Actual incoming business, production, and inventory status were then compared periodically with the plan. When the inventory was outside the acceptable range, some corrective action was necessary. Control of input also requires feedback of sales and inventory information to indicate exactly which items should be started into production. Output control, involving shop planning, expediting and dispatching, requires regular feedback of information about what has been produced, the location of jobs in process and the problem areas that require attention. Corrective action can mean getting back on plan (preferable), revising the plan (the last resort) or some combination of both.

> **Principle 58. Getting back on plan is tougher—but far better—than replanning.**

Manufacturing control is primarily operation of an information system. This does not mean that it should be a passive function merely turning out reports, but it does mean that the basis for control is *information* and that the department has the responsibility for generating the proper information so that the plant can be managed to meet established goals. This is not a simple task—the job of establishing the goals for operating the plant, tracking progress against these goals and recommending proper corrective action is an extremely challenging one. Information is not data; producing information requires analyzing—sifting data to extract the important facts that managers and other people need to know.

Principle 59. Sound planning and effective control involve information, not data.

Materials managers frequently find themselves in difficulty because customer service, inventory levels or plant operating expenses are out of control. Since they have no direct authority over the manufacturing operations that can correct the conditions, they sometimes feel that it is unfair to place the blame on them. Unfortunately, in many instances, this is exactly where the blame should be placed since the basic cause of the problems is that not enough information was presented to management soon enough to show them the real problems and the alternatives available in solving these problems in time. It is the materials manager's job to distill constantly the data the system provides and to provide guidance to plant management in making operating decisions.

There are three links in the chain of manufacturing control. All must be present and work together effectively in order to have good control. They are

1. A planning and control system—a discipline for handling information that is complete, integrated and accurate

2. Use of the system by qualified planning and control personnel to generate timely information

3. Use of this information by competent plant operating personnel to manage manufacturing operations effectively.

The system should be designed to be an effective control panel for the manufacturing manager. All activities must be directed toward solving the most important problems in order to correct a situation that is out of control. The system should be designed to present information in terms meaningful and useful to those responsible for taking action.

For example, a quality problem that is hindering delivery should be reported immediately to quality control or line personnel who can generate corrective action. The information should be reported objectively, briefly and with the best recommendations that the planning and control person can make for resolving the problem. This relationship also exists with other organizational groups, such as industrial engineering, product design engineering, maintenance, etc. Any problems that are not solved promptly and effectively should then be reported to the next higher level of management. Good control and fast action are synonymous.

Developing timeliness in a control system is one of the most difficult problems. In some plants, for example, it often appears economical to use payroll transactions to report job progress in the plant. This employs common source data already in machine language for two important jobs. In most companies, payroll has higher priority than plant data collection; adjustments required before processing payroll delay work on job location reports, so that these reports may sometimes be 2 or 3 days old before they are delivered to those who need them. These personnel then find that many jobs have moved and soon come to look upon the reports as useless. Electronic data collection terminals on the factory floor can collect this information for both payroll and job status at the point of origin so that it will be more accurate and timely. This has great impact on improving feedback.

Inventory reports that show the stock status as it existed 2 or 3 days earlier are another common violation of the principle of timeliness. Control cannot be exercised over things that have already happened, only over things that are going to happen. Outdated control information is not control information at all.

Principle 60. For control, timeliness is more important than accuracy, although both are necessary.

Once a sound manufacturing control information system has been set up, getting personnel to use it properly requires an effective education program. Planning and control personnel who have not had a good information generating system consider that their principal jobs are expediting and trouble-shooting, and they often resent the discipline that a system imposes. They are too busy drowning to take time to learn to swim. They find it difficult to comprehend that the routine of reviewing items that require reordering and generating replenishment orders properly, for example, is really far more important than expediting an individual job that has fallen behind schedule. Many action-oriented trouble-shooters never do learn to come to terms with the routine paperwork, detailed planning and difficult thinking ahead that is required in operating with a good planning and control system. Consequently, they always have plenty of trouble-shooting problems to occupy their time.

Education of management is needed to avoid emasculating the system by cost-reduction programs that save the pay of one or two clerks at the expense of poor customer service, excess inventories and upsets in the factory. The system itself must be based on information provided by up-to-date routings and bills of material. Penny-pinching in the maintenance of this basic information can be very costly in the long run.

The existence of a well-designed information system and its effective use by planning and control personnel accomplishes nothing, however, *until line personnel take action.* Top management frequently look for changes in their systems to cure an out-of-stock problem, for example, when the present system has already pointed out quite effectively that plant output levels are not high enough to support the desired level of customer service—yet no real action is being taken by plant management to increase capacity. The most effective system and the most competent planning and control personnel cannot succeed where the third link in the chain of production control is not provided. The business of production control is *information,* information that must be presented promptly, briefly and frequently in such a fashion that the required action will result. The business of line manufacturing people is *execution* of the plan, making enough high quality products at the proper cost.

Feedback and Corrective Action in a Make-To-Order Plant

While more planning is possible in a make-to-order plant than is usually done, it is usually not possible to preplan activities as well as in a make-to-stock plant. It therefore becomes extremely important to report problems more promptly and react faster to solve them in a make-to-order shop. The orders being run (even though there may be repeat orders from customers) require more engineering, tooling and supervision because they are run less frequently than those in a make-to-stock plant. For this reason, personnel are not as familiar with the individual jobs and there tend to be more manufacturing problems. In a make-to-order plant, the emphasis must be on prompt reporting and quick reaction to solve the problems in tooling, materials, schedule changes and the like.

Many make-to-order plants do a large percentage of their business in new orders, which must start with individual engineering and special tooling for each job. In such situations, it is mandatory to schedule carefully the engineering and tooling required. If these elements proceed on schedule, it will not be necessary to make up for the time lost in engineering and tooling by reducing manufacturing lead time. Since fewer people are involved, it is much more economical to use extra help or overtime in the engineering department to meet the original schedule or to work some overtime in the tool room rather than to disrupt other schedules and work many overtime hours trying later to make up the time lost in earlier phases of the project. Project planning techniques outlined in Chapter 10 can be used to monitor activities against check points set up for each major element in the project.

Establishing check points by operations scheduling is one of the first improvements usually made in a make-to-order operation. Most companies progress from having expediters chase only those jobs that have appeared on the **past due list** (jobs still in the plant beyond the shipping date promised to the customer) to a system that establishes a date when critical operations should be completed and takes action to get intermediate operations completed on time in order to meet a promised completion date. Up-to-date job location records are, of course, essential.

The next step is to report unavoidable schedule changes to the customer promptly so that no surprises result. While this requires an amount of courage that is often hard to muster, it generally results (over the long run) in far better customer relations than telling customers nothing unless they ask, even after the order is late. Having the customers initiate the call to find out why a job is late and hearing, "We'll check and call you back" gives them the clear impression that their orders have been forgotten and that there is little control over production in this supplier's plant.

Most make-to-order companies can gain a considerable competitive advantage by having shorter lead times and by meeting promised dates. For this reason, it is important to develop a management team within this type of company that is fast on its feet and quick to react to changes. This requires a good feedback system so that management attention can be focused quickly on delays and the alternatives available to correct them. For example, as the backlog ahead of starting operations increases, the alternatives open to management are relatively few and are all unpleasant:

1. Either:
   a. Quote longer lead times—and start the "vicious cycle."
   or:
   b. Turn away some business (many companies which haven't changed their quoted lead times as their starting backlog increase lost their reputation for service because they did not meet the delivery promises they made).
   or:
   c. Increase the production level.

2. If it is decided to increase the production level, this means
   a. Working overtime
   b. Adding personnel
   c. Subcontracting
   d. Some combination of these

3. The decision to work overtime or add personnel hinges principally on predicting the duration of the increase in business, which must come from sales or marketing personnel and which would indicate either:
   a. The increase is short-term and should be handled with overtime or subcontracting.
   or:
   b. The increase is long-term and should be handled with added personnel.

Unfortunately, few manufacturing control departments are effective in pointing out these alternatives quickly enough. Management personnel are themselves frequently guilty of not facing the real alternatives available and of not insisting upon assistance from control personnel in pointing out these alternatives. The final result is customers who are disappointed in the service they are receiving and a general manager who is thoroughly disappointed in the management team because service deteriorates and costs go up.

Providing the information to permit management to weld the sales and marketing personnel, plant operating personnel, engineering, quality control and other major elements of the business into an effective operating team is one of the challenges that faces the planning and control function in any plant. An effective planning and control manager must be able to show management its real decision alternatives in specific terms such as which orders will suffer when rush orders are forced through the plant. In fact, a good manager will be able to advise management considering a newly booked customer order how that order might jeopardize service on others. Organizing information effectively enough to point out the rational basis for making this type of decision is an extremely challenging job requiring a great deal more skill than the expediting that usually occupies so much of the manager's time in a make-to-order operation.

Principle 61. Operations control involves picking the least worst choice from available alternatives.

Feedback and Corrective Action in a Make-To-Stock Plant

In a make-to-stock plant, there must be more emphasis on planning production levels, controlling input and output and planning the total production of individual parts requiring substantial investments in tooling or equipment. While it is a mistake to release orders any further in advance than necessary, it is possible to plan tooling, machine capacities and the like by viewing requirements for a stock part well ahead of the time individual orders are generated.

In a make-to-stock business, such standard techniques as forecasting, MRP and time-phased order points, CRP, input/output control, work center loading, daily dispatch reports and job progress feedback are used. Inventories provide a cushion against demand and supply changes, making make-to-stock operations less sensitive than make-to-order businesses. The most difficult problem to overcome in controlling any make-to-stock operation arises when all planning is based on forecasts translated into master production schedules. No matter how much effort is devoted to improving the MPS, many operating changes are needed to meet changing demand. Most line operating and output control personnel have a natural aversion to working with uncertainty—they try to develop fairly rigid approaches with firm plans made far in advance to overcome this uncertainty. As these usually fail, such people then blame the failure on lack of a reliable forecast. Since the reduction of lead time helps make the whole planning process more accurate, short lead times are every bit as important in a make-to-stock business as they are in make-to-order firms.

A considerable improvement in customer service can be made if flexibility is introduced into both the planning and execution activities and it is recognized that the planned schedule dates are subject to change when customer demand becomes real orders. This requires some form of dynamic priority system and the means for revising these priorities; periodic MRP replanning (see Chapter 6) and critical ratio (see Chapter 11) are very practical techniques for revising priorities. It should be kept in mind, however, that the necessity for revising plant priorities is reduced as the level of work-in-process and (consequently) the plant lead time are reduced.

In most make-to-stock companies, customer demand is quite effective in calling the attention of the production control department to those items that are selling at a higher rate than forecast since they will go low in inventory or out of stock and therefore require special attention. MRP provides equally good information on the items that are *not* selling up to forecast rates and can therefore be rescheduled in order to get more urgently needed parts through. It is at least as important to have timely feedback information on the stock status of individual items as it is to know where their replenishment orders stand in production.

The requirement for schedule flexibility can be especially trying in a plant that has partly make-to-stock and partly make-to-order business and where stock items and make-to-order items compete for the same facilities. It is very tempting and, in fact, usually the practice in such companies to give make-to-order items priority over make-to-stock items. This persists until the service rendered to those customers who buy stocked items from inventory deteriorates to such a low level that considerable sales department pressure is exerted to improve it.

The usual reaction is a management dictum that states that schedule dates on make-to-stock orders are just as important as those on make-to-order items and that both must be observed religiously. This policy usually stays in effect until an individual case comes up where a stock item is run in accordance with its originally scheduled date and pushes aside a make-to-order item competing for the same manufacturing facility. Someone then finds out that the stock item was not really needed on that date because actual sales were below the rate forecast at the time the manufacturing order was scheduled. This customarily results in make-to-order items being assigned higher priority than stocked items and the cycle begins anew.

What is actually required in combined make-to-stock and make-to-order businesses is some means of assigning an adequate *share of materials and capacity* to both types of products. Input/output control is then used to insure that each receives its proper share. Stocked items, of course, provide cushions to make possible short-time diversions of material and capacity to make-to-order items. These must then be *replaced* promptly.

Feedback in a make-to-order operation is concerned principally with job progress and the effects of problems in the plant. Since there is not likely to be a high percentage of repetitive operations and new problems arise constantly in a make-to-order plant, emphasis must be placed on good feedback to find out what the problems are and to report them to someone who can take corrective action. In a make-to-stock plant, on the other hand, manufacturing tends to be routine, with the same items processed over and over again. In order to have an efficient operation and to get the best customer service for the inventory investment, feedback is needed both from the plant (to report job progress) and from the inventory so that significant changes in the stock status of finished goods can be reflected in up-to-date manufacturing priorities.

Feedback From Purchasing

The more a company depends upon purchased components in the manufacture of its product, the more important it is to have good feedback from suppliers. In a make-to-order business, following up vendors to be sure that all material is received as close to required date as possible is of particular importance. This responsibility is usually assigned to purchasing but more and more companies are placing it with materials control (such people are called **planner-buyers**), freeing purchasing for more work finding better sources. Each vendor should be rated according to delivery performance and quality as well as price. All must be major considerations in the selection of vendors. Also valuable are delivery performance reports showing the percentage of jobs delivered from vendors on time as compared with the total number of jobs required in any given week. This type of performance report should emphasize the number of orders requested within shorter-than-usual lead times. Really professional purchasing personnel recognize the advantages of exerting as much pressure as possible *to reduce vendors' lead times.* They will spend their time working with vendors to do this rather than simply reporting vendor lead time changes frequently.

Most important, though, is the need for purchasing to set up feedback arrangements whereby vendors can tell purchasing in advance of anticipated late deliveries so that materials control can also be advised and all can work together on actions possible to counteract this situation. Such problem solving requires well-designed systems and people skilled in determining the least worst solution. This is discussed in detail in Chapter 8 of the second volume (5).

The relationship between materials control and purchasing and the amount and type of feedback information required between them is also a function of the type of operation. In a make-to-order operation, delivery dates tend to be more firm once established; in a make-to-stock operation, they are more likely to change and more emphasis must be placed on the vendors' ability to react to changes in schedule.

Likewise, in a make-to-order business, soliciting bids on individual items typically starts when a requisition is written for that item and it may only be purchased for one order or for a particular customer. Delays in placing purchase orders are frequent; an acceptable period for this delay should be agreed upon ahead of time. In a make-to-stock business, on the other hand, where items are purchased repeatedly, there is no reason for waiting until the ordering technique signals that it is time to reorder. In modern systems, the forward visibility of planned orders permits negotiating prices with present suppliers or seeking new vendors before orders need to be placed for replenishment of materials.

As with internal operations, on-time deliveries of purchased materials requires insuring that a vendor's capacity will be adequate, feeding orders smoothly and deciding on specific items at the last possible moment. Feedback should measure the output rate by period and also the adherance to schedule on individual orders.

Principle 62. On time vendor deliveries depend on adequate capacity and short lead times, not on customer ownership, closeness and clout.

Some Feedback Techniques

In some companies, the out-of-stock list or the past-due list is used to trigger an analysis of the causes of these delays. An interesting relationship usually exists between the problems that cause delays in meeting schedules and the number of falldowns they generate. This is the same relationship that is the basis for the ABC classification of inventory. Generally, in analyzing schedule upsets by cause, it is found that approximately 20% of the causes generate 80% of the problems. With this information, corrective action can be directed where it will do the most good.

When individual departments or work centers are set up as checkpoints at which the status of each job is compared to its scheduled completion date at the particular checkpoint, it is practical to maintain a performance report for each department showing how well it is able to meet schedules. This report is of value principally as a means of comparing present performance against past performance, since departments farther along in the manufacturing sequence are likely to receive more jobs *already* behind schedule and thus have a more difficult time completing jobs on schedule. Whether or not the report can be adjusted for this handicap is of secondary concern. The important point is to measure improved departmental performance in giving better service and to consider this measure of performance to be as important as the supervisor's ability to meet the budget. Many line managers profess concern over the difficulties in getting supervisors to be customer service oriented but they persist in measuring a supervisor's performance against other goals and really consider customer service to be primarily the responsibility of the materials control and sales departments.

A very effective feedback device from any plant is a regular **delay report**, similar to the one discussed under Flow Control in Chapter 11. The daily delay report shown in Figure 12-1 is made out by the department dispatcher, indicating jobs delayed on the shop floor and the reasons for their delay as well as the action being taken. Since it is extremely important that this information be up-to-date and since only those jobs delayed are listed, the information can often best be handled by the dispatcher as a visual review of all work on the floor ahead of each machine center, listing only jobs delayed beyond some acceptable interval.

An essential element of feedback that is often neglected is a regular report that capsulizes plant activity and problems in order to direct management attention to the important problems to be solved. Figure 12-2 shows a weekly summary of activity and problems summarized by the materials manager and addressed to manufacturing and other individuals concerned with operating the plant. It contains a general summary of activity for the week, a listing of the major problems and the recommendations of the materials manager. Space is provided to indicate the action being taken by the manager responsible. In Figure 12-2, for example, major problem 2 concerns delivery of some switches from a vendor and the purchasing agent has advised of the action being taken in the right-hand column. This type of summary serves many functions:

1. Preparing the summary forces the materials manager to think through the plant's problems each week, put them in perspective, organize the knowledge of plant activity and problems and condense this for the manufacturing manager.

2. The summary serves as the agenda for a weekly production meeting of the people most concerned. When managers tend to postpone making

| | | | | | Dept. _Sub-Assembly_ |
| | | | | | Date ___10/20___ |

To:
Dept. foreman:

To:
Supv. of dispatchers:

From:
Dept. dispatcher:

| _C. Brown_ | | _S. Tobias_ | | | _J.C.T._ |
| Name | | Name | | | Name |

Part no.	Part name	Order no.	Qty. delay	Days delay	Problem and action
10-1762	X-Type Panel	4321	1200	4	Jig being repaired – promised 10/21
17-1105	Switch Assy.	4004	2500	2	Q.C. 100% Insp.

Figure 12-1 DELAY REPORT.

decisions, its use will quickly point out the effects of such inaction. The report gives the chief manufacturing executive a means to follow up decisions and insure that needed actions are taken promptly.

The principal requirement of a weekly summary of activity and problems is that it be brief. Some companies set an arbitrary rule, limiting the number of problems that can be listed in any one week to 10 or 12. A long catalogue of problems, however genuine, serves little useful purpose. The normal management team of six or seven can take effective action on only a few problems each week; listing any more will only cause confusion, discouragement and dilution of effort.

The proper presentation of this type of information to manufacturing management is an essential function of the materials manager. Developing this information properly is far more important than trouble-shooting out on the factory floor (although one useful way of obtaining good feedback from the factory is a regular

From: Materials Manager	To: Manufacturing Manager	Week no. 13

cc: Chief Industrial Engr.
General Foremen (4)
Quality Control Mgr.
Purchasing Agent
Production Planners (2)

Summary of activity:

1. Current finished goods inventory = 56,000 pcs. – one week below 72,000 pcs. goal.

2. Service level last week = 96% vs. 98% goal.

3. Incoming business 22% ahead of forecast for 1st quarter. Marketing revising forecast; due Monday.

Summary of major problems	Recommendation	Action
1. New people in Elect. Subassembly not producing acceptable product.	Continue overtime to meet prod. reqt's. Q.C. aid foreman in finding specific operators responsible and retraining.	Replacing one girl. Adding temporary super-vision. J.P.V.
2. Popco switches still one month behind scheduled deliveries.	Second source.	Buyer to visit Popco weekly. 3 potential suppliers bidding this week. F.W.W.

Figure 12-2 WEEKLY SUMMARY OF ACTIVITIES AND PROBLEMS.

tour of the plant to see how operations are progressing). Nevertheless, there must be a balance between close contact with factory operations and the desk work required to operate a satisfactory management information system. Regular meetings of planning and line people in individual work centers to discuss more detailed problems should be timed to permit problems they cannot solve to come to the attention of the materials manager before preparing the summary report.

The materials manager starting a formal report of this type may find initial reaction to it negative since it points out problem areas for which other managers are responsible. Its preparation requires a great deal of objectivity on the part of the materials manager—this individual should be very careful to be objective (though factual) and to be honest in pointing out failures within the materials department. Other managers must know in advance of the weekly meeting the problems to be listed. This avoids generating resentment at being "put on the spot" and gives managers time to decide on corrective actions. In practice, this type of report (when it is developed effectively) brings real problems to the attention of the managers and almost always results in getting solutions to these problems.

Performance Measures

At the beginning of Chapter 1, the three major objectives of manufacturing companies were stated as

1. Maximum customer service
2. Minimum inventory investment
3. Efficient (low cost) plant operation

Performance measures are needed for each of these to insure that continued, steady progress is being made in improving them. There are many performance indicators available for each objective. One of the most important is customer service. Statistical measures of customer service were discussed in Chapter 5. Other measures in a make-to-stock business can be based on the number of items stocked, the total number of line items backordered as a percentage of the total line items on incoming orders or the percentage of the total number of orders on which a backordered item occurs.

Figure 12-3 shows one type of report of service from finished goods inventory in a make-to-stock business. For this company, the measure used is demand filled as a percentage of total demand and the goal is 95% service. An upper limit of 97% has been set, based on the understanding that service at a higher level will require more inventory than can be justified by the improved customer relations. It has also been decided that 92% is a low limit of customer service and that service below this level will jeopardize their position as a vendor to many of their customers. The comments made by the materials manager indicate that inventories have been reduced in this particular product line, and, as a result, service has come back down to about 95% from a range that was considered too high to be necessary or economical.

In a make-to-order business, service is usually measured by how well orders are shipped to customers in relation to scheduled dates. Figure 12-4 shows a delivery performance report of a product for a make-to-order company. There were 20 jobs due to be shipped in the first week of the fourth quarter and all were shipped on schedule; delivery performance was therefore 100%. Note that this report also shows delivery performance on orders with revised promises.

The problem in developing a suitable measure of customer service is that a great many factors are involved. In a make-to-stock company, the *number* of items out of stock affects customer service—but frequently more important is *which* items are out of stock and *how long* they remain out of stock. A very popular item generates a great many back orders while a less popular item may not even be missed by most customers. In companies where records are kept of back orders, the total number at any particular moment is a fair measure of performance.

Nevertheless, critics can point out that this still does not measure the *duration* of the back order. Some items may stay out of stock for extremely long periods, causing customer dissatisfaction that cannot be measured by merely counting the back orders. Even if this factor were included in a more complex system for measuring customer service, it could still be pointed out that it is often desirable to give some customers preference—because they are new and have a high potential business or because they are old, loyal customers providing a good share of business.

This rationale can lead to the development of highly complex methods for measuring customer service that require more effort than they are worth. Measures

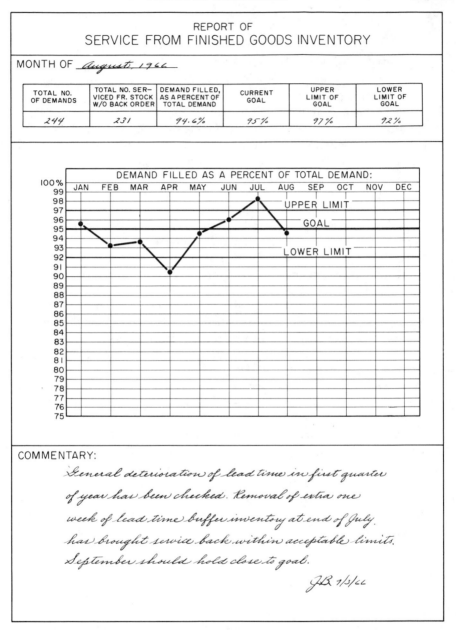

Figure 12-3 REPORT OF SERVICE FROM FINISHED-GOODS INVENTORY.

of customer service should be as simple as possible—their prime value consists in showing that customer service either has or has not been improved. Discussion about whether or not any particular measure of service is fair or unfair is wasted effort which might better be devoted to improving the company's performance under

	Last 13 wks	Week #1	Week #2	Week #3	Week #4	Week #5	Week #6	Week #7	Week #8	Week #9	Week #10	Week #11
		10/16	10/23	10/30	11/6	11/13						
Jobs due to ship		20	23	23	22	17						
Jobs shipped		20	22	23	22	15						
Delivery perform. %	91%	100%	96%	100%	100%	88%						
Repromised jobs due to ship		0	0	1	0	0						
Repromised jobs shipped		0	0	1	0	0						
Repromised delivery performance %	97%	0	0	100%	0	0						
Number of jobs past due		0	1	0	0	2						

Figure 12-4 PQR COMPANY PRODUCTS DELIVERY PERFORMANCE.

simpler measures. There is no one best method; different measures should be applied to suit the particular interests of management at the moment.

The second major area for measuring performance is inventory control. This is most effectively measured by aggregate trade-off curves like the customer service versus investment relationship developed by the techniques explained in Chapter 8. Once a production plan has been introduced, level production may result in building some inventory with seasonal demand as discussed in Chapter 9. Consequently, inventory-control performance should be measured against this production plan rather than against some fixed target that does not recognize desirable inventory fluctuations.

Inventory turnover is a performance measure that has some real meaning but is abused more often than not. Many practitioners refuse to use an inventory turnover measure because they are aware of these abuses. In some companies, where inventory turnover has been used as a performance measure without balancing it against related costs, some managers have forced inventories down by holding back deliveries until the first of the following month, bringing in small quantities toward the end of the month and using other approaches that generate excessive costs in other areas which must handle the flood of material that arrives in the first few days of the new month. These tactics do not reflect on the validity of inventory turnover as a performance measure but they do underscore the fact that it cannot be used effectively unless related costs and customer service are considered at the same time.

Like many other performance measures, inventory turnover has little meaning when used to compare the activities of one company with those of another. It can be used for comparison of one company with averages for an industry if used with restraint. Two companies in the same business may have extremely different rates of turnover, depending upon the degree of manufactured versus purchased material contained in the end product, whether the business is make-to-stock or make-to-order or both, consignment stocking policies, distance from suppliers, the number of warehouses maintained and many other considerations that very substantially affect the companies' ability to turn inventory.

Far more important than attaining a certain turnover is establishing reasonable inventory levels to give desired customer service and then measuring a company's performance over the short term in meeting these inventory levels and over the long term in improving the service attained with a given amount of inventory. Inventory turnover has most meaning as a measure of improvement in inventory control performance.

The common formula for determining inventory turnover is

$$\text{Turnover} = \frac{\text{cost of sales in period}}{\text{cost of average inventory on hand}}$$

Turnover figures are often obtained from published data in profit and loss statements and balance sheets; the most common data given are the inventory at year end (at cost) and annual sales (at net selling price). Turnover calculated from inventory value and sales figures for annual sales activity gives much less realistic data for comparison. Although industry wide comparisons have to continue to use available data, each company should measure improvement of its own performance using cost data for both inventory and sales which gives the most meaningful results and is unclouded by pricing policies, profit policies, administrative costs and other irrelevant factors.

Inventory turnover, like all performance measures, must be used judicially. It should be thoroughly understood by those applying it and comparisons within companies between divisions and even between departments should be made with extreme caution and with full knowledge of all the elements that affect their abilities to perform.

Most materials control departments have been slow in recognizing their responsibilities for keeping the plant operating efficiently and, consequently, very few companies measure such performance. This requires measures that relate overtime, machine down time, employee idle time and the number of hirings and layoffs during the year to the validity of the plans developed. Since materials control is concerned with balancing customer service, minimum inventory investment and efficient plant operation, any effective set of performance measures must include measure of plant operations against such goals, just as any measure of a line supervisor's activities should include performance in meeting scheduled delivery dates and total output as well as expense goals.

Finally, one objective implicit in running any staff department is to have the smallest number of people consistent with good performance. Devising a means of measuring the amount of work turned out by planning and control personnel and the number of personnel required is extremely challenging and probably not worth the effort. Modern computer-based systems have eliminated most low-level clerical labor. The remaining decision making and problem solving activities are difficult to measure. One simple, effective technique is to compare planners, schedulers and dispatchers on the number of items, products or work centers handled, assuming they all have the same degree of difficulty. A comparison of the number of people in planning and control and the department budget with plant activity measures should be made on a regular basis. Note that higher rates of output of the same products need not require increases in planning personnel. On the other hand, lower volumes with more diversity of products, materials and processes will probably take more people to plan and control properly.

Most planning and control departments have increased their functions and have required more and more personnel over the years. Whether or not this is justified, it is more often than not true that inefficient use is being made of the personnel now available. Each additional person requires a greater percentage of the group's time in communicating among personnel—and nowhere is this more evident than in a planning and control department. In a small plant, it is relatively easy for a few people to know what other personnel are doing but, in a large plant, communication among planning and control personnel and with purchasing or manufacturing people becomes a formidable task.

Measures of performance are extremely important in any company. Before any improvement program is started, measures of performance should be established to show how future performance will compare with the present situation. It is always easy to see today's problems while forgetting how big yesterday's problems were. If measures of performance are not started before the improvement program begins, few people will remember how bad the "good old days" really were. Measures of performance are by themselves one of the best ways of improving performance and thus should be one of the fundamental elements of any production control system. It is a recognized fact that performance measures in any field of activity tend to generate a healthy spirit of competition and that people will work hard to meet or better a realistic goal that they have accepted.

Principle 63. Select performance measures carefully; people perform to look good on them.

Neophyte materials manager (particularly if they are under the pressure of criticism within their companies) are usually anxious to get performance information from other companies. These managers ask other materials control managers how many people they have in their departments, how good their customer service is, how much inventory they carry and similar questions, hoping that some of these figures can be used to convince the boss that their performance isn't really so bad after all.

More experienced materials managers recognize that performance comparisons between companies are not meaningful. These managers devote their attention to improving their own performances rather than justifying a poor showing by trying to find someone who is a little bit worse.

Operating Controls

Well-designed manufacturing planning and control systems are capable of generating reports containing information on performance against plan for several important operating measures. These include

1. **The master production schedule**

   Since the MPS represents the basic manufacturing plan, measuring actual performance against it is vital to good control. Figure 12-5 shows one report format. Several features are worth noting:

   a. The report shows individual weeks and monthly totals. The latter are also compared with the production plan to insure that detailed plans are kept in step with broader, family totals in the higher level, longer range aggregate plan.

   b. Such direct comparison of actual versus planned production is not easy (and may be impossible) where modular planning bills of material are used with the MPS for products with many options. Chapter 6 of this volume and Chapter 4 of the second volume (5) have detailed discussions of such bills and their use.

   c. Family totals for weekly production may be even more significant than output of individual products. Last-minute reaction to actual demand may shift the mix significantly but totals must be adequate.

   d. The Rollover shows quantities uncompleted in the past, a very real experience in most companies. The important thing about this figure is that it not be increasing steadily either positively or negatively. Both are signs of real production problems.

2. **Aggregate inventory input/output**

   The details of this are shown in Figure 8-2 in Chapter 8. It permits monitoring on one report actual versus planned data on purchased ma-

		Rollover	23	24	25	26	June	27	28
12 A 341	MPS		50	–	50	–	100	52	–
	Actual	–	48	–	52	–	100		
12 B 423	MPS		610	610	610	610	2440	610	610
	Actual	(10)	603	601	610	625	2439		
12 C 246	MPS		340	360	380	400	1480	420	440
	Actual	(12)	342	355	373	400	1470		
12 D 318	MPS		180	180	180	180	720	170	170
	Actual	5	185	176	178	180	719		
12 E 416	MPS		15	–	–	–	15	15	–
	Actual	–	–	15	–	–	15		
12 F 195	MPS		205	205	205	205	820	210	210
	Actual	8	206	202	203	207	818		
12 Family	Planned		1400	1355	1425	1395	5575	1477	1430
	Actual	(9)	1384	1349	1416	1412	5561		
Production plan							5600		

Figure 12-5 MPS VERSUS ACTUAL PRODUCTION.

terial and direct labor (input) and shipments (output) which in balance determine the aggregate inventory.

3. **Work-center output**

   Practically every company has detailed reports of production output but too rarely do these show actual versus planned data. Popular reports show labor efficiency, percentage of work covered by standards and machine utilization, all easy to record but only of minor importance. Reports should be generated to show aggregate output by time period; Figure 9-10 in Chapter 9 is one example. Adherance to schedule should also be measured for individual orders handled in work centers in each time period. Comparisons should be made only with the latest due date, not the date on the order when it was released. Daily dispatch lists like Figure 11-11, in Chapter 11 provide a convenient basis for tallying late, on-time and ahead-of-schedule jobs to use as performance measures.

4. **Vendors**

   Techniques for following up purchased materials are covered in Chapter 11. These can generate very adequate reports of both total vendor output rates (for the company's needs, of course) and on-time delivery. Quality and price are usually traced by quality control, purchasing and cost accounting.

5. **Lead time**

   The importance of managing lead times was stressed very heavily in several chapters in both volumes. Periodic samples should be made of both purchased and manufactured items to develop *actual average* lead times to compare to planned lead times. This is one of the most important performance measures. Equally important is the cumulative lead time (see Figure 7-6 in Chapter 7) for products; it should be checked regularly by samples of actual vendor and plant performance. While not easy to get, lead time measures are well worth the effort required.

6. **Record accuracy**

   Reports for assessing the changes in levels of record accuracy of inventories are presented in Appendix VI of this book, and others are given in Appendix I of the second volume (5). The key measure is *number of items with no significant errors*. This should be developed by sampling *all* important records, which include

   a. Customer orders

   b. Bills of materials

   c. On hand inventory

   d. Open purchase orders

   e. Open manufacturing orders

   f. Processing data (methods, routings, standards, tooling, etc.)

   g. Costs

System Health Diagnostics

Well designed systems also are capable of producing reports indicating real or potential problems within themselves. Like body temperature, blood pressure, swelling and tremors, these measures can point to "diseases" needing attention:

1. Volume and type of action notices or exception messages
2. Data omissions and errors
3. Unplanned transactions

These are discussed fully in Chapter 7 of the second volume (5) along with systems design and installation topics.

Generating Corrective Action

The three links in the chain of production control discussed earlier in this chapter were

1. A system for generating information
2. Use of the system to generate the proper information
3. Action on the part of plant operating personnel to react to the information generated

The weekly summary of activity and problems shown in Figure 12-2 is a good example of the type of information that planning and control must provide to the manufacturing manager. This information must be generated on a timely basis—control can be exerted only over events that have not yet occurred. A good index of the success of this effort is the number of times the manufacturing manager has to ask about a problem rather than having first been informed of it. An effective materials manager tells the plant manager about upcoming problems *ahead of time* and recommends actions to keep them from becoming serious interferences to good customer service or efficient plant operation.

Principle 64. The difference between excuses and control information is simply timing.

The true function of planning and control is to generate the information required in managing the plant in order to keep out of trouble rather than just handling the day-to-day activities required to get out of trouble. The manufacturing control system is a discipline for handling information; it requires that specific activities take place at specific times. Materials managers, like managers of other functions, find that they can best organize their activities by making up a daily list of things that require their attention and following this list in doing the most important jobs first.

Since no manager can give attention to all existing problems, it is extremely important to sort out these problems and handle the more important ones first. A checklist such as the one shown in Figure 12-6 helps to insure including in this

	11/23	11/30	12/7	12/14	12/21	12/28	1/4	1/11	1/18
Schedules prepared									
Production plans posted									
Production plans revised	X		X	X	X	X		X	X
MRP output reviewed									
Out-of-stock report prepared									
Percent out-of-stock graph updated									
Work center loads updated									
Raw materials inventory report issued									
"C" stock review made									
Finished goods card inventory audit	X		X	X	X	X		X	X
Summary of activity and problems prepared									
Mfg. areas delay report compiled									
Purch. comp. delay report compiled									
Lead time reviews made	X	X	X	X	X	X	X		X

Figure 12-6 PLANNING AND CONTROL CHECKLIST.

daily list those routine activities that require regular attention in order to keep the system running effectively. This particular checklist shows that schedules must be made out weekly, that production plans must have actual activity posted against planned activity weekly and that schedules must be reviewed and revised (if necessary) on a monthly basis.

Some materials managers use a manufacturing control calendar which lists the major activities that must take place during the year, including such regular chores as reviewing ABC classes and order policy codes, preparing for physical inventory, reviewing personnel performance, making up lists of obsolete material for disposition and the many other activities that take place only infrequently but must be handled promptly in order to perform the job properly.

Managing the Planning and Control Functions

It has been mentioned frequently in this book that the primary function of the planning and control group is managing an information system. It is important to emphasize that this management cannot be done passively. The materials manager *must take the initiative* in the presentation of alternatives to management, along with estimates of the costs and results of these alternatives. In a company with seasonal sales, the materials manager should develop alternative production plans to show how much extra inventory would be carried if production were leveled completely, what added capacity would be needed if production were geared directly to sales, how many times manning levels would have to be changed during the year, etc. The materials manager should estimate the costs of these various plans, recognizing that most of them will not be in the cost-accounting chart of accounts, recommend one plan to management and assist in making the basic decision. Once this decision has been made, the job of the materials manager is to generate control information to keep the plant on course. Since there will be many deviations from plan along the route, this will require constant corrective action.

Ironically, a manufacturing control system is rarely considered successful when the line people have not taken the proper corrective action. *A system is necessary but not sufficient.* Merely generating the proper information—even going to great effort to show line managers what needs to be done—does not guarantee that the proper action will be taken. Timid materials managers are most vulnerable when they permit their performances to be judged by the actions of others. Even if the system indicates that additional capacity is required and this estimate of increased capacity has been given to them sufficiently in advance, but plant operating people postpone adding this capacity, the planing and control group is usually blamed when customer service deteriorates as a result. Almost everyone recognizes poor customer service but few can identify the true causes. By the way they manage information, materials managers should be able to generate action. If they do their job of handling information expertly, it will be obvious to all concerned what actions are needed and who is responsible for taking them.

The information generated by the manufacturing control system often puts a great deal of pressure on a line manager, even on the manufacturing manager, who is often the materials manager's boss. If materials managers do not have confidence in the system and if they do not take the initiative and identify problems vigorously and courageously, they may become the "nice guys" who are blamed for someone else's failure to take the proper action. The manufacturing control system must be able to stand up to considerable back pressure and nit-picking from line managers who try to postpone taking action by challenging the information generated by the system and requesting exhaustive reviews or further analysis. There is a limit to the amount of skepticism that can be justified or tolerated. At this point, the capable materials manager deserves the solid support of his or her seniors in overcoming passive resistance and getting effective action without further demands that the system justify itself.

Keeping the initiative requires courageous managers with a good system and competent people to operate it. It also requires that the managers remember that their jobs look easy to other people. Every day, materials managers and their staffs must make hundreds, even thousands, of decisions about the future. Inevitably, hindsight will show some of these decisions to be wrong and critics will be able to point out the mistakes that were made in the planning process. Beyond this, many other managers with whom the materials manager must work may be sub-optimizing—working toward objectives different from those of the overall business. They may feel that materials managers do not understand the true situations when they disagree with these objectives. This situation is aggravated in companies that practice to extremes the *unique-accountability* theory of organization, in which the sales manager is solely responsible for sales, the chief engineer is solely responsible for product function, and so forth.

Effective manufacturing control requires an objective approach, which recognizes that firefighting is necessary but that fire prevention is preferable. One of the most serious temptations in manufacturing control is to become a firefighter—to come in each morning prepared to charge out at every telephone call and handle most of the expediting personally. This is undoubtedly satisfying to action-oriented people; it creates the impression of great activity and of a manager who has his or her finger on the pulse of the factory and knows what is going on all the time. Unfortunately, such firefighting activity indicates clearly that the unromantic—but vital—task of fire prevention is being neglected. The work of finding the anticipated life of major tools and whether or not they are being replaced on time to meet the needed volume or analyzing the facilities of the proposed new product line to see where bottlenecks might occur and what can be done to avoid them can appear prosaic and dull indeed. The materials manager who neglects fire-prevention activities can be sure that tomorrow will bring bigger and better firefighting opportunities.

Materials managers must expect trouble. Murphy's law, "What can go wrong will go wrong at the least opportune time," was invented in a factory. Materials managers should be happy pessimists who recognize that problems are a way of life and that tomorrow's troubles are undoubtedly brewing today. Crises in plants very seldom develop overnight—they usually grow over a long period of time and are frequently the result of continued inaction. The materials manager has the responsibility for pointing out ahead of time where troubles are likely to occur, showing what the alternatives are and doing everything possible to insure that operations continue as planned or are quickly corrected to prevent crises.

One of the most important characteristics of effective manufacturing control information is timeliness. As stated in Principle 64, this is the difference between giving excuses and presenting information soon enough so that someone can take action to prevent problems. If the materials manager's boss asks why a particular product is out of stock and, after some investigation, is told that it was caused by a bottleneck in the plating department last week, the materials manager has given only an excuse. If, on the other hand, the materials manager had pointed out the bottleneck ahead of time, made positive recommendations to overcome it and predicted that, if it were not overcome, the product would be out of stock, control information was generated. The simple difference is timeliness—information supplied in time for plant operating people to take the necessary corrective action *in advance of trouble.*

To continue to be effective, materials managers must use their power of information and knowledge in an objective, constructive way. They should be realistic and avoid the wishful thinking of optimists who hope that troubles may not occur or will go away if ignored. Since they are constantly calling attention to existing and potential troubles, however, they must do this in a positive way, avoiding accusations and implications of incompetence in others and resisting the temptation to prove they are always right.

Since the materials manager's success will be largely dependent on the accuracy and promptness of the information system, the use of simple techniques to insure that things are being done on time can do much to insure that the requirements of the system for attention and activity are met. Frequently, some of the most important but routine activities (reviewing the materials plan or lead times) are postponed because of the pressure of urgent interruptions. It is sometimes difficult to associate the poor results that show up later with the actual cause. A check list like Figure 12-6 to insure that important routines are being followed regularly and on time can be of great assistance in the proper organization of activities in the production control department.

A vital mental exercise for materials managers should be to sit down regularly (at least once a month) and do an ABC analysis of known and anticipated problems in the next 6 months, sorting out the biggest ones and insuring that activities are projected to handle or prevent these problems. A good habit to form is the preparation of a daily "to-do" list of the activities to be performed in priority sequence. Half an hour spent before each working day getting this list prepared will result in much better direction of activities and higher productivity.

The materials manager should set aside some time each day to visit major or critical production areas in the plant. Often, a quick tour through the plant will detect potential problems a great deal faster than even the most up-to-date information system. A materials manager also must set aside some time—and this will probably have to be after regular plant hours when the telephones have stopped ringing—to do the thinking and planning that is essential to the department's future performance. This is the time when fire preventing projects are conceived and when long-range programs to improve the department's performance are developed. A good materials manager has to strike a balance between action to solve today's problems and planning to prevent tomorrow's. While the weight of their office is needed in solving many daily crises, they must avoid getting directly involved in too much expediting. This must be counterbalanced with a disciplined program of preparing for the future.

One of the most important steps in preparing for the future is education. A complete discussion of this subject is beyond the scope of these books; additional coverage is provided, however, in Chapter 8 of the second volume (5). Included must be education in the development and use of new techniques, new systems, more modern equipment and a broadening of scope through participation in professional societies and attending special courses to gain exposure to areas of business management outside of the field of manufacturing control.

This education should include in-house programs as well. In the beginning, most people got into planning and control work without study or preparation in the field. Not only did they not know much about production control, they frequently did not realize that there was very much to know. Such people frequently became expediters and firefighters and developed little ability to control production effectively. Since then, the field has become a true profession with a unique body of knowledge, language, techniques and applications. Examinations are available through APICS, whereby an individual can be certified as technically qualified. This requires education and, since it involves adults, this education must be as practical as possible. Adults must see the practical applications of the material if the education program is to be effective. Studying economic lot-sizes is a waste of time for people in a make-to-order plant, where most lot-sizes are dictated by order size. If people can see specifically how each technique applies to their companies and how the failure to use these techniques properly has caused problems in the past, they will respond enthusiastically. Almost everyone has some desire to become more proficient at work.

The need for education related to manufacturing-control activities, however, goes well beyond planning and control personnel. In many companies, other department supervisors have been able to use the planning group as a whipping boy, challenging any information that was produced and thus reducing their need to take action based on this information. Getting these supervisors to understand what a manufacturing control system really is, how they must work with it and use it and how they affect its performance through the information they supply and the action they take is vital to the success of any company. Top management people often have little understanding of the true role of manufacturing control. They do not recognize the limited alternatives available to them in managing inventories and production and are not always aware of the need to balance the conflicting objectives in day-to-day operations. Manufacturing control must accept the responsibility for pointing these out. An extensive education program can justify its very high costs if it results in developing full awareness of the functions of manufacturing control and its contribution to all facets of the business.

A very effective program of self-development can be undertaken by any manufacturing-control department conducted by the senior members of the department—both for training the junior members and for providing orientation programs for marketing personnel, line supervisors, purchasing people and others who must work effectively with production control. In this way, the latter group learns what to expect and what not to expect from planning and control activities.

In the final analysis, though, success in the job of selling manufacturing control to management and others in the company will rest on results. The manager who is willing to risk setting ambitious goals, who works hard to improve the operation of his or her department and who succeeds in developing and administering programs that improve the performance of the plant as a whole in the areas of inventory control, customer service and profitable plant operation will have little difficulty convincing management of the importance and value of his or her work.

Reducing Inventories

Excess inventories of most items accompanied by shortages of many has been and will continue for a long time to be the rule, not the exception. Inventory has been accepted as a necessary evil by top management (even listed as an asset), viewed as a necessity by middle managers and workers and used by educators, consultants and other thinkers to develop a body of theory based on higher mathematics. Such theories were based on the assumption that the environment of manufacturing and distribution has certain characteristics that *could not be changed*. These included

1. Inaccurate forecasts and unreliable supply, requiring finished goods in excess of expected demand
2. Unreliable vendors and long, uncertain procurement times, making excess raw materials and purchased components necessary
3. Long setups, erratic flow, poor quality, scrap and rework, faulty tooling and equipment and Murphy's law, necessitating high levels of work-in-process.
4. Changes causing obsolete inventory

Modern approaches refuse to accept such conditions as inevitable.

Principle 65. Problems interfering with planned operations can and must be solved.

Constant pressure by management to reduce inventories is sound. The "right" amount of inventory in any company is less than now exists in many firms and much less in most firms. The following is the proper procedure:

1. Set a challenging target for reduction (such as 25%) in a defined period (for example, 6 months).

2. Develop targeted input (purchased material and productive labor) and output (shipments) rates and monitor these monthly. Act promptly and aggressively to correct deviations.

3. Attack problems in the environment, including
   a. Forecast errors—shorten lead times, group products
   b. Record errors—cycle count
   c. Poor quality, scrap and rework—eliminate causes
   d. Shorten setups—engineering-production team
   e. Smooth flow—control input, set up cells
   f. Reduce queues—starve input, speed up output

4. Make inventory reduction a company-wide program. All departments have some role to play.

All classes of inventory must be attacked including obsolete. Too often such inventory is deemed to be the price of progress; there is some truth in this—it may be more practical and economical to throw some material away than to postpone introducing a change. Most is avoidable, however. The key is identification of potential obsolete materials *before they become so,* by highlighting items with inventory and no planned requirements, items with more than a specified number of weeks' supply, items with no transactions since a specified date and items whose average usage rate has dropped by a specified percentage. Several means of disposal are available:

1. Return items to the vendor for some or full credit.
2. Apply the items in new designs as temporary or permanent use.
3. Keep items for service-parts demand.
4. Rework items to a usable state.
5. Find a market for the items in other divisions or outside the company.
6. Scrap the items.

Principle 66. Significant cuts in inventory come only from finding and fixing the causes of excess.

Shortening Lead Times

No more important work needs to be done than developing shorter and shorter lead times. This runs counter to the ideas held by many people in manufacturing operations; they believe that more time allowed will insure better performance. Their experience usually supports this belief: Shortages require more time to overcome, excess load takes more time to handle and delays are proof that insufficient time was allowed.

Cutting lead times, proven to be possible, relatively easy and most effective, will first require overcoming these fallacies. An effective program is

1. Prepare people:
   a. Who? Line manufacturing, manufacturing planning and control, design and manufacturing engineers, managers
   b. How? Education in external and in-house courses
2. Select work centers:
   a. Vendors with long erratic lead times supplying significant amounts of product
   b. Gateway starting operations with large paper backlogs handling significant amounts of work
   c. Secondary operations with erratic loads and high levels of work-in-process
3. Engineer shorter setups:
   a. Modular tooling
   b. Running families with similar setups
   c. Reengineer work stations, equipment
   d. Train setup personnel
4. Implement input/output control:
   a. Plan queues
   b. Develop rough-cut CRP, refine to set input/output rates
   c. Manage capacity tightly
5. Keep materials moving
6. Brace for criticism but keep the faith.

Manufacturing Control: The Future

Manufacturing control originally was a paper-work function: maintaining inventory and order records, issuing shop orders and handling other necessary record-keeping functions. From there, it developed to include stock chasing and some departmental machine loading—but most techniques were crude and functions were highly decentralized, to the point of separating inventory control from production control in many companies.

Decentralization was the solution that most companies tried to use as problems of increasing size and complexity arose. While it often offered some improvements, it also introduced its own problems (such as duplication of effort and considerable suboptimization), with each group tending to concern itself with limited goals rather than overall company objectives. Some companies went so far as to have separate production control functions for each major manufacturing area within a plant. This trend toward decentralization compounded the control problems since it made more difficult the task of getting financial, manufacturing and sales managers to work toward common goals.

There have been three major developments: operations research, also called scientific management; the computer, providing means for handling economically the masses of data involved; and APICS, providing a means for practitioners to develop and exchange knowledge. The result has been a revolution in less than three decades as workable techniques and the means for implementig them have become known.

In the 1960s, practitioners sought the right amount of safety stock to buffer operations against variations in demand and uncertainties in supply in an extremely hostile environment. They were thankful for statistical techniques to update forecasts and reevaluate amounts of buffer inventories needed. In the 1970s, it became clear that valid schedules were possible even with demand changes and that up-to-date priorities could be used to vary replenishment lead times to get urgently needed items on time. The powerful MRP technique made this possible and dominated all others in practitioners' thinking and actions.

In this decade, all the needed techniques were developed and tested. The future will see only refinements. In the early 1980s, it became clear that all the techniques in the most sophisticated systems were practically powerless in the chaotic environment of most manufacturing plants. The compelling need for short lead times was recognized and work began in earnest in successful companies to eliminate record errors, improve quality, reduce batch sizes and smooth out the flow of materials in plants. Real success was spectacular, if spotty.

The elements of a complete system were identified in the 1970s, but few companies developed complete systems for themselves. Preoccupation with a few techniques—MRP and daily dispatching—resulted in fragmented systems, most lacking capacity planning and control. Effective use of such systems was plagued further by lack of integration with financial, engineering, purchasing and quality control systems. This can be and is gradually being overcome by mini- and microcomputers used in a network of integrated programs. The technology and economics of computer hardware and software will support this in the future. As the environment is cleaned up and lead times are reduced, however, the trend will be toward simpler, less sophisticated systems.

Modern manufacturing control has created an organized body of knowledge that can be passed on from those practitioners who have demonstrated the practical application of modern techniques to those who need them via educators, consultants and APICS. Much of the early progress was in developing techniques but only later were they related satisfactorily to one another or to specific applications. The development of a practical body of knowledge that can be taught readily offers the best encouragement to the further use and development of scientific techniques. These statistical and mathematical techniques (queuing theory, linear programming, mathematical scheduling) will be at best fine-tuning devices useful only after the real bases for control are in place and operating effectively.

The demand for improved manufacturing control has also created a growing demand for qualified people, professionals who understand the body of knowledge, are familiar with the strengths and weaknesses of the techniques and know how to apply them in their companies. Strong educational programs have proliferated in academia, consultants' offerings, internal company programs and APICS seminars. APICS certification will continue to grow as a condition for employment and for holding managerial rank in this field. Compounding the problem of getting and keeping competent personnel is management recognition that this field develops a manager's perspective and understanding of the major segments of the business and many successful practitioners will be promoted into higher levels of management.

New organizational forms will continue to be seen. A strong trend will continue to combine the efforts of accounting and inventory control functions since they deal basically with the same information and are the staff functions most concerned with management controls. The problems and the resulting benefits of such an approach are illustrated in companies when they set up standard cost systems. Typically, design and installation of the standard cost system is initiated by the financial department and suffers recurring problems. Almost every year, major inventory adjustments are necessary because of errors in data in the systems. If the standard cost data are used also by the materials manager in planning and controlling production, the system is always more successful; discrepancies become quickly apparent when data that do not make sense are used daily. Detecting errors at the source eliminates decisions based on incorrect data and prevents wasted time incurred by chasing down the reasons for such errors long after they have taken place. Efforts will continue to increase to generate cost data needed for decision-making by the players, not just for keeping score and recording history.

Undoubtedly, the same influences that focused management attention on manufacturing control in the past will make it increasingly important in the future. Product complexity and variety will continue to increase dramatically along with ever stronger pressures to level production. Most companies must continue to reduce inventories in order to free scarce, expensive capital for other profitable investment opportunities. Above all, competitive pressures for better customer service will increase from domestic and foreign firms. This field provides the most fertile area for profit improvement as well as the basis for increased market penetration against competition. Improvement must be sustained, not be an isolated spurt intermittently. Unquestionably, the greatest influences on the field of manufacturing control will come from a growing professionalism, better education and the wider application of modern integrated systems.

Traditional organizational forms will continue to change drastically. The primary roles assigned to each group will be modified as necessary to produce a working team rather than the more typical collection of all-stars seen in the past. The Materials Department will disappear in favor of one recognizing that the function is equally concerned with money, machinery and people. The title of the function is really of secondary importance—no matter what it is called, the basic information required to manage a manufacturing operation in the face of intensive competition will become more and more vital to every company. This planning and control function will not only become more important in the operation of the company but will become a vital training area for higher levels of management. Top managers must learn how to operate manufacturing companies as well as how to manipulate them in financial markets.

Growing awareness of these facts, coupled with intense foreign competition and successive sharp recessions, has focused more attention on better integration of planning and more effective execution of the plans. These two subjects comprise the bulk of the material in these two volumes. Successful companies demonstrating the rewards from excellence in these operational controls have fed the fires of interest. The importance of manufacturing as the generator of real wealth (along with agriculture and extractive industries) places a heavy burden of responsibility on managers to use this knowledge to the fullest benefit for their companies and countries and, not incidentally, for themselves.

PROBLEMS

Chapter 1

1-1 (a) What are the principal reasons why effective inventory and production control are vital to the successful operation of a manufacturing firm?

(b) What effects can one company's inventory and production control activities have on another company? On the national economy?

1-2 Why are the functions of inventory and production control receiving increasing recognition and attention from business management and educators?

1-3 Explain why the activities of sales, financial and manufacturing people are not likely to meet the objectives of customer service, inventory investment and plant operation if each group concerns itself only with its own function.

1-4 (a) What are the major policies management should establish for balancing customer service, inventory control and plant operation objectives?

(b) Give specific examples of some unrealistic management policies and point out the problems these cause.

1-5 (a) Does the electronic computer contribute to achieving better balance among conflicting objectives?

(b) Is the introduction of a computer to the inventory and production control system likely to achieve this balance?

1-6 Sketch a flow chart including the major departments and the basic elements of an inventory and production control system as you would imagine it, showing the flows of information for

(a) An auto-parts distributor

    (b) A machine-tool builder of special-purpose automated equipment

    (c) A manufacturer of electric razors

1-7 (a) Why are inventory control and production control separate functions in many companies?

    (b) What are the disadvantages of such separation in a manufacturing company?

1-8 Visit a local industrial firm. Outline how it provides the elements of the production control system and how it recognizes the balancing of the conflicting objectives.

1-9 What problems would you expect with a control system that lacked any of the principal elements? (Take each element in turn.)

1-10 What differences would you expect to find in the application of computer programs to inventory and production control activities in a make-to-stock plant, as compared to a make-to-order factory.

Chapter 2

2-1 How does capital invested in inventory earn a return? Answer separately for raw materials, work-in-process, finished goods, supplies, lot-size material, safety stocks, transportation goods and anticipation material.

2-2 Make up a company, indicating its major product and manufacturing departments. Classify its inventories by condition and then indicate how each inventory function exists for inventory in each condition.

2-3 (a) Divide the various costs associated with ordering and carrying inventory into fixed, variable and mixed (fixed or variable) classes.

    (b) Why do accounting systems rarely develop such costs directly?

2-4 What kind of inventory-control technique is best adapted to

    (a) High-usage rivets totaling $25,000 worth annually?

    (b) A $250 casting with 15 pieces used per year?

2-5 How does the application of a computer to inventory control affect the techniques used to control C items?

2-6 What factors might account for recent indications that proper inventory management is reducing the effects of inventory fluctuations on the business cycle?

2-7 How would you expect the ABC curve to differ in shape for a discount department store, a specialty camera supply shop, a hand tools manufacturer and a steel casting foundry?

2-8 Make an ABC analysis for all the items in the inventory of a local business.

Chapter 3

3-1 Name at least three situations in which the EOQ concept does *not* apply.

3-2 (a) What factors might account for the reluctance or failure of many companies to apply EOQ's, in spite of substantial potential benefits?

    (b) What should be done to correct or overcome each factor?

3-3 (a) What specific savings can result from using EOQ's?

    (b) What intangible benefits can result?

3-4 (a) If an item passes through several successive operations in different machines having short and long setups, how would you calculate setup costs to be used in the EOQ formula?

(b) Standard unit costs usually include a prorated amount of setup in burden or overhead. Should such costs be used in calculating EOQ's?

3-5 Why might the cost of carrying inventory be different
(a) In two successive years?
(b) For two different inventory items?

3-6 What approach would you use to calculate EOQ's for
(a) A blanket order for an annual requirement to be delivered in weekly lots?
(b) 50 items shipped weekly to a branch warehouse?
(c) A highly seasonal item?
(d) A part purchased as a casting, put in a raw material inventory, machined in an automatic chucking machine, held in semifinished component inventory, finished in milling, boring, drilling, tapping and grinding machines, kept in finished component inventory and used continuously on an assembly line?

3-7 (a) Calculate EOQ's from the following data:

Fixed ordering cost   = $7.00

Inventory-carrying cost = 15%

Annual demand   = $1500, $3000, $6000, $12,000, $18,000

(b) Repeat (a) for inventory carrying costs of 10% and 20%.
(c) Repeat (a) for fixed ordering costs of $5.00 and $10.00.
(d) Repeat (a) using requirements data for Part no. 418 in Figure 6-13 and the Least Total Cost formula in this chapter.
(e) Calculate the Period Order Quantity using data in (a).
(f) For a $3000 annual demand, would you buy twice the EOQ if a discount of 2% were offered? (Use costs in (a).)

3-8 Contact the materials control or controller's department in three local companies and determine
(a) What inventory carrying-cost is used
(b) How it was determined
(c) Where it is used

3-9 Requirements and replenishment orders for a parent item and one component are as follows:

Week No.

	1	2	3	4	5	6	7	8	9	10	11	12	13	14	Total
Part No. 1513	L.T. = 3 wks.														
Required				10	6		10	6		10	6		10	6	64
Ord. Due				10	6		10	6		10	6		10	6	64
Ord. Rels.	10	6		10	6		10	6		10	6				64
Part No. 4785	L.T. = 6 wks.														
Required	10	6		10	6		10	6		10	6				64
Ord. Due	20			20			20				20				80
Ord. Rels.	20				20										

The lot-size rule for the parent item (1513) is lot for lot; the component (4785) has a lot-size of = 20. What are the effects of changing the parent order quantity to 20 on:

(a) Total ordered in 14 weeks?
(b) Average inventories of both?
(c) Action notices on released orders?

3-10 When order quantities are set intuitively, why are they usually far from the economical lot-size calculated by formula?

Chapter 4

4-1 (a) Under what general conditions would a forecast based only on statistical analysis of past history be reliable?

(b) When would a prediction made without reference to history be preferred as a forecast?

4-2 Is the demand forecast (incoming business) or is the sales forecast (shipments) of more importance to inventory and production control?

4-3 What factors would determine whether or not a company should spend more money on improving its forecasts?

4-4 What do you think are the underlying causes of forecast characteristics leading to greater accuracy for larger groups of products and for shorter periods?

4-5 Actual incoming orders (in units) for a product for 3 years are:

	1st year	2nd year	3rd year
Jan.	200	220	250
Feb.	290	310	350
Mar.	350	370	430
Apr.	410	430	500
May	450	470	520
June	500	530	580
July	850	860	900
Aug.	920	940	990
Sept.	730	760	810
Oct.	520	550	600
Nov.	310	340	380
Dec.	230	260	300

Using exponential smoothing, calculate and plot forecast versus actual orders for year 3, assuming a starting forecast of 230, using each of the following.

(a) First-order smoothing with α = 0.1, 0.2, 0.3
(b) Second-order smoothing with α = 0.1 and β_{old} = 200
(c) First-order smoothing (as in (a)) plus seasonal index based on years 1 and 2.
(d) Second-order smoothing (as in (b)) plus seasonal index (as in (c)).
(e) Comment on the quality of each forecast.

4-6 Using an available computer and software program for exponential smoothing, test the various combinations of simple, trend and seasonal forecasting techniques for assumed data showing random, increasing, decreasing, seasonal, rising seasonal and falling seasonal characteristics. How could mathematical tests for accuracy of fit be applied?

4-7 Visit a nearby manufacturing company and determine the source, number and type of forecasts prepared. What units are used for forecasts needed by the following departments?

> Sales
> Marketing
> Treasurer (controller)
> Engineering
> Manufacturing (production)
> Purchasing

How are forecast revisions handled?

Chapter 5

5-1 (a) Distinguish between *order point* and *order quantity*.
(b) What factors are common to both?

5-2 What important factors are usually overlooked when reserve stocks are determined intuitively? Give examples.

5-3 (a) Using the first-order smoothing forecast with seasonal index for year 3 in Problem 4-5 and a starting MAD of 100 pieces, calculate the MAD for each period.
(b) What MAD would be used to calculate the order point as of October 1 if the lead time were 2 months? 4 months? 2 weeks?

5-4 The number of pieces of an item sold in the last 26 two-week periods (replenishment lead time is 2 weeks) were:

18	21	5	14
12	13	11	6
9	12	17	13
7	13	10	15
14	15	12	19
13	8	11	13
	7	4	

Totals: 73   +   89   +   70   +   80   = 312

(a) Assuming a fixed forecast of 12 pieces per period, sum up the deviations to determine MAD.
(b) With an EOQ of 40 units, how many orders will be placed per year?
(c) What order points are required to give the following service?
   1. 2 stockouts per year
   2. 1 stockout per year
   3. 1 stockout every 2 years
   4. 1 stockout every 5 years
   5. No stockouts

(d) What is the average total inventory required for each service level in (c)?

(c) Lay out a time-phased order-point display for 26 weeks.

(f) What benefits would the time phased order point display of (e) provide?

5-5 (a) What are the similarities and differences between the fixed quantity–variable cycle (order point) and the fixed cycle–variable quantity (periodic review) systems?

(b) What types of businesses would use each?

5-6 What service level would be obtained for item X on pages 110–114 if reserve stock were set at 1 week's supply? Two week's supply? One month's supply? What are the corresponding average inventory totals?

5-7 What are the advantages of order points?

5-8 Can order points be used effectively on items with truly dependent demand? Cite any required conditions.

Chapter 6

6-1 In addition to design engineering and planning, what other departments require data from bills of material? Give specific uses.

6-2 How is MRP affected by poor control of engineering changes?

6-3 Where in manufacturing is the logic of MRP used besides ordering materials?

6-4 What are the advantages of time-phased material requirements planning?

6-5 How do statistical concepts of forecast error pertain to a material requirements plan?

6-6 Assuming an average finished product demand for one year of 200 units per month and fixed order points and order quantities as shown below, which approach gives the best results?

(a) The finished product and components are controlled by order points.

(b) The finished product is controlled by order point as above and components are ordered by MRP. These parts are used in this assembly only. The following data apply:

	Finished product	Part A	Part B	Part C	Part D
Unit cost	$20.00	$1.00	$5.00	$1.50	$0.50
Lead time	4 weeks *	4 weeks	4 weeks	8 weeks	8 weeks
OQ	1200	1400	800	1000	6000
Inventory cost	12%	12%	12%	12%	12%
Setup cost	$250.00	$75.00	$25.00	$11.25	$135.00
OP	1000	1000	1000	2000	2000

*Assembly, testing and packaging time included.

Assume that manufacturing rates can be varied each month to meet the demand (leveling not necessary) and that starting inventory of finished product is 2000 units and of each part is zero.

6-7 Calculate the EOQ's for the four parts making up the finished product in Problem 6-6 if they are manufactured to an MRP plan. Use square root and period order quantity techniques.

6-8 What factors should be considered when determining the frequency of replanning with MRP?

Chapter 7

7-1 (a) Give at least four specific applications (capital needs, machinery procurement, scheduling purchase orders, etc.) of each of the major plans in the planning hierarchy.

(b) What specific problems could arise if they are not consistant?

7-2 When tracking actual production and comparing it to the MPS which is more important? Why?

(a) Make the individual items planned

(b) Make the total output planned

7-3 Give at least two advantages and disadvantages of using percentage bills of material with master schedules.

7-4 Trace the sequence of possible events if the sales forecast of an item is changed significantly but the MPS is not.

7-5 What are the important considerations in changing the MPS frequently or holding it fixed in the near future? Further out?

7-6 Are there any significant sources of demand in addition to those determined by the MPS on

(a) Capacity

(b) Materials

7-7 If modular-planning bills of material are used with the MPS set one or two levels below that of the end product, how can final assembly, test and packaging capacity be planned?

7-8 Describe specifically the sequence of events which will occur when the MPS is:

(a) overstated.

(b) understated.

7-9 It has been said that a 5% variation in retail sales can be amplified to 10% at the assembly plant, 20% at the parts-manufacturing level and 40% for raw-material demand. How can better production planning help reduce this type of amplification?

7-10 What control benefits are obtained by having sales, production and inventory data shown together on a production plan?

Chapter 8

8-1 Trace the actual sequence of events which might occur if orders for EOQ's were released to a department which lacked the capacity to handle the required number of setups.

8-2 If EOQ's are introduced where they have not been used formerly and lot-sizes change substantially, what are the specific sources of savings

(a) If inventories increase

(b) If inventories decrease

8-3 A department has three people engaged in setting up machines. These setters also perform in-process quality control inspections. The superintendent wants to double the amount of time these setters spend on this inspection to improve quality. What data are needed and how would you solve the problem of how many more setup people would be needed if order quantities are kept the same?

8-4 Will reducing finished product inventory always result in poorer customer service?

8-5 Why is it usually impossible to guarantee 100% customer service?

8-6 What classes of inventory do not lend themselves to customer service versus investment calculations?

8-7 In making customer service versus investment calculations:
(a) What items should be grouped together?
(b) How frequently should the calculations be updated?

8-8 What actions should management investigate if it wishes to improve customer service without increasing inventory investment?

8-9 Could the application of LIMIT result in a need to recalculate reserve stocks for the items included?

8-10 How would you use LIMIT to assist in deciding whether or not to add capital equipment?

8-11 Four items are made on one machine. Pertinent data on these items are as follows:

	1	2	3	4
Annual use	1000	40,000	1500	1000
Unit cost	$1.00	$0.25	$2.00	$3.00
Setup cost	$2.00	$2.00	$12.00	$25.00
Inventory cost	20%	20%	20%	20%
Present order quantity	250	10,000	375	250

(a) By means of LIMIT, calculate the individual lot-sizes that will keep the annual setup cost the same as for the present order quantities.
(b) Show the average cycle stock inventory for present, LIMIT and theoretical EOQ and the corresponding total setup cost.

8-12 There can be only one real cost to carry inventory. Why calculate various LIMIT order quantities?

Chapter 9

9-1 In making a production plan, how is forecast error taken into account?

9-2 How does production planning provide for reducing the backlog of unshipped orders?

9-3 (a) Prepare a production plan for a 13-week period for Widgets based on this year's calendar and working days as in Problem 9-6(a).

Forecast incoming business = 105 pieces per week

Starting inventory = 855 pieces

Closing inventory = 920 pieces to meet sales promotion

(b) Revise the plan to meet a closing inventory goal of 600 pieces.

9-4 Rank the four kinds of capacity in order from largest to smallest (indicating equalities, if any) for effective operation.

9-5 (a) What cost factors must be considered when making a production plan?
     (b) Which costs would be highest using level production?
     (c) Which costs would be lowest using level production?

9-6 Monthly forecasts of incoming orders for a product group are:

Jan.	220	Apr.	430	July	860	Oct.	550
Feb.	310	May	470	Aug.	940	Nov.	340
Mar.	370	June	530	Sep.	760	Dec.	260

(a) Make an annual production plan for level production: Starting inventory = 900; ending inventory = 500; plant vacation shutdown last 2 weeks in July, no other official holidays throughout the year.
(b) Make an annual production plan, changing the production rate only twice and minimizing inventory buildup.

9-7 Why is introducing production level planning frequently the most rewarding systems improvement in a company experiencing difficulty in maintaining customer service?

9-8 If lead times average 15 weeks and it requires 10 to 12 weeks to accomplish a change in production capacity, would rough-cut or detailed capacity requirements planning give better results? Why?

9-9 What difficulties may result if an order point–order quantity inventory control system is allowed to generate orders for assembled products without any planning of production levels?

9-10 Visit a company in your area and determine
      (a) Who sets capacity levels? How? How are they changed?
      (b) What unit of measure best expresses capacity in each major department?
      (c) Does the company use work center loading? If so, how is it related to capacity planning?

9-11 (a) How large a backlog of incoming orders would have to be permissible to permit level production during the year if no inventory was maintained for the product in Problem 9-6?
      (b) What backlog level would you recommend for the following year to limit random changes in production level to one change? (Note that these sales data are the same as year 2 in Problem 4-5).

Chapter 10

10-1 In addition to improved customer service, what benefits can be expected from effective scheduling?

10-2 (a) How do the time elements (setup, running, move, inspection, etc.) used in scheduling relate to the lead times used in calculating order points?
      (b) What is the effect of using ''comfortable'' move and delay times in scheduling on

      1. Work-in-process inventory levels
      2. Finished component inventory levels
      3. Finished product inventory levels

10-3 List the advantages and disadvantages of using detailed operations-scheduling rules versus block scheduling.

10-4 Compare and contrast loading to infinite capacity and loading to finite capacity.

10-5 What are the limitations of work center loading as a means of controlling production capacity?

10-6 (a) Discuss the effects of effective scheduling on an inventory control system using floating order points and economic order quantities.
     (b) Are these effects the same if MRP is used?

10-7 Justify the statement: There is no reason why schedule periods must be equal to the total lead time.

10-8 Visit a local process plant, a repetitive manufacturing plant and a batch production plant and report on
     (a) Scheduling techniques used
     (b) Sources of scheduling data
     (c) Reliability of lead times

10-9 Justify the statement that releasing orders early for smooth input does not increase work-in-process inventories.

10-10 If the ordering technique should simply rank orders to facilitate selection for release, is there any need for precise (daily) start dates?

Chapter 11

11-1 Which is more important, control of capacity or priority?

11-2 Distinguish between load and capacity.

11-3 What three alternatives are available to companies to use in reducing work-in-process?

11-4 What specific effects does inability to determine actual input have on the effectivity of input/output control reports?

11-5 Why is it true that the amount of work-in-process on a factory floor usually expands to fill the space available?

11-6 (a) What are the basic functions of shop floor control?
     (b) Which are addressed by dispatching, expediting and Flow Control?

11-7 Discuss the statement: There will always be a need for expediting. Do you agree? Does it apply to all businesses?

11-8 What system elements are needed before you can use Critical Ratio?

11-9 Taking the basic elements of Flow Control, discuss the effect of omitting each on the control of work-in-process.

11-10 (a) Analyze the lead time in a local company, from receipt of a customer's order to shipment of the material or rendering the service.
     (b) What should be done to improve service to customers by reducing lead times?

Chapter 12

12-1 How can the organizational level at which control is located affect the performance of the feedback and corrective action elements of the system?

12-2 What differences in inventory and production control activities in make-to-order versus make-to-stock plants affect the level of organization to which the materials manager should report?

12-3 What actions would you recommend if the first issue of a daily delay report for a milling machine department contained over 100 items?

12-4 In addition to delays to specific components of finished products, what classes of problems might appear on a production manager's weekly summary?

12-5 What are the advantages and disadvantages of using more than one measure of customer service at one time?

12-6 Give reasons why timeliness of feedback is more important than accuracy.

12-7 Can the necessary education for effective planning and control be accomplished by individuals studying alone with tutorial programs? Why?

12-8 Give at least five examples of information (as contrasted to data) generated by a manufacturing planning and control system.

12-9 What specific benefits would result if follow up of purchase orders were handled by materials planning people?

12-10 Study the manufacturing-control system of a local manufacturing company.
   (a) Identify specifically each of the control system elements used for control of the level of production.
   (b) Repeat (a) for the level of customer service.
   (c) Make detailed recommendations for any missing or deficient elements.

CASE STUDIES

Case Study 1: Inventory Control

The companies described in this case are all having serious problems with their inventories. Customer service is poor and factory operations are frequently upset by shortages, even though inventories are very large. Inventory losses due to obsolescence, loss and deterioration are high.

Company A manufactures drill bushings. The product begins as rod or tubing and moves through screw machines, milling, grinding, heat treating, plating and packaging. A total of 3500 different, single-piece, finished products are maintained in stock made from 150 different items of raw material. The company tries to maintain a 45-day supply of raw material and a 60-day finished stock level.

Company B manufactures small electrical appliances, including accessories. Demand for their products seems to fluctuate rather widely and the company therefore maintains a very high level of component inventories. Finished goods inventories of the 100 products and the component stocks of several thousand parts and subassemblies are all controlled using statistical order points. Their most serious problem is that components never all seem to be available when an assembly is to be started on the line.

Company C makes composition friction material for clutches, brakes and similar applications. Finished goods inventories of several hundred items are maintained by statistical order points. These consist of cut shapes of material, some riveted and some bonded to metal backing plates.

The total lead time from raw material to finished stores is 6 to 8 weeks, with only 1 to 2 weeks required for the final operations that convert a basic piece of material into a specific item. For this reason, a semifinished inventory larger than the finished stores is maintained from which a given piece of material can be processed quickly to make any one of several different items.

The total of semifinished and work-in-process inventory for each item is maintained at 3 months' supply by ordering 1 month's replenishment lot when the semifinished total drops to a 2 months' supply. These inventories are very high but needed items are often in short supply, particularly when business is picking up. There are also many very slow moving items in the semifinished stores.

Company D produces a limited line of specialized machine tools comprised of 11 basic machines with many optional features. They normally have a backlog of 12 to 18 months of customer orders on hand. Each month, a manufacturing planning group consisting of the president and the vice-presidents in charge of sales, manufacturing and finance review the order backlog and develop a firm production schedule for the ninth month in the future.

Production control uses this authorization (usually for 20 to 25 finished machines) to order purchased materials and release orders to the plant. The 8-months lead time is adequate to cover all except a very few critical materials.

The most critical problem is that customers request many changes in the optional features from those on the original order, often several months after placing the order. Production control finds difficulty in working these changes into the firm schedules already issued. The shop spends much time working on components for items no longer needed, while many other needed items are short.

Questions: Answer the questions for each company individually. State any assumptions you believe necessary.

1. What is your opinion of the strengths and weaknesses of the present inventory control system?

2. What changes would you recommend to improve the system's performance? Justify each recommendation.

3. What problems would you anticipate in making the changes? What timetable would you follow and what actions would you take to resolve these problems?

4. What specific improvements would you expect? Give reasons and some means to measure the amount of improvement.

Case Study 2: Lead-Time Simulation

The length and variability of lead times measure the effectiveness of any production control system. Long lead times lengthen the forecast period over which the inventory control system must predict the requirements and accuracy decreases as this period grows longer. Variability of lead times prevents setting dependable delivery dates. Both necessitate carrying higher reserve stocks or giving poorer customer service.

An important factor in the control of lead times is the size of backlogs of work-in-process. This can be verified by a simple manual simulation using small cardboard boxes to represent shop boxes, each containing a different job. In this simulation, there are two work stations—both drill presses—the first one doing a drilling operation and the second a tapping operation. Each job goes into the drilling operation first, requiring 1 day to complete. It then goes into the tapping operation, which also requires 1 day to complete. These operations are perfectly balanced—a day's work at the drilling operation also represents a day's work at the tapping operation. Once a job has been tapped, it is completed.

The shop boxes consist of two groups, those without any markings and those numbered 1 through 10. The objective of the simulation is to start with a given shop workload, represented by a number of unmarked boxes and try to run jobs 1 through 10 through in the proper sequence with *no scheduling, dispatching or expediting*. Running the simulation requires four people:

1. A production control manager who sends the jobs down from that office in the proper sequence. (That is, job 1 goes out on the factory floor to the drilling operation on day 1, job 2 on day 2, and so on.)

2. An operator at the first drill press who looks only at the back of each shop box in the queue at the machine and cannot see the number on the front so that a random choice is made, work is done on the job chosen and it is then passed to machine center 2.

3. An operator at the second drill press who takes each job that has been drilled and taps it. The numbers on the front of the boxes cannot be seen and a random choice is made from the total workload ahead of the machine.

4. A record clerk who watches the jobs coming out of the second operation and posts the order in which they are completed, noting both numbered and unnumbered boxes.

As the jobs are completed, they are recorded on the form shown in Figure CS-1. The spaces in Figure CS-1 numbered 1 through 30 represent completion days. The X's in these squares represent unnumbered jobs that were completed on that day. A number in the square indicates that one of the numbered jobs was completed on that day. Total lead time is easy to calculate. In the example shown in Figure CS-1, an unnumbered job came through on each of the first three days and job 2 came through on the fourth day. Since job 2 started on the second day, its total lead time was 2 days.

Data in Figure CS-1 are typical of the lead times obtained when this simulation is run with two jobs ahead of each machine center. Jobs 1 through 10 are released by the production control manager in their proper sequence. In order to insure that the operator always has two jobs ahead of his or her machine center from which to choose, the production control manager also released blank jobs into production once the ten numbered jobs had all been started. Because the operators choose jobs at random out on the factory floor, the jobs are not completed in the same sequence in which they are started.

Figure CS-2 shows the lead-time summary for the simulation with two jobs in backlog or queue at each machine center. The shortest lead time for any job was 2 days, the minimum possible. The longest lead time was 6 days (and three

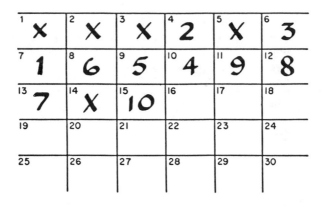

Figure CS-1 JOB-COMPLETION SEQUENCE

jobs required this long to complete). The average lead time for the ten numbered jobs was 4 days—as might be expected when there are 2 days of work already in process ahead of each machine center.

After this first simulation has been completed, a second can be run with just one change—this time there are five unnumbered jobs ahead of each machine center at the start. As before, the production control manager releases in sequence the ten numbered jobs to be worked at random. Also, the production control manager releases unnumbered boxes after Job 10 to keep the queues full.

Figure CS-3 shows a typical job-completion sequence with five jobs in queue at each machine and Figure CS-4 gives the lead-time summary for this simulation together with the previous one.

Job no.	2 Jobs in queue	5 Jobs in queue
1	6	
2	2	
3	3	
4	6	
5	4	
6	2	
7	6	
8	4	
9	2	
10	5	
Total	40	
Avg.	4.0	

Figure CS-2 LEAD-TIME SUMMARY

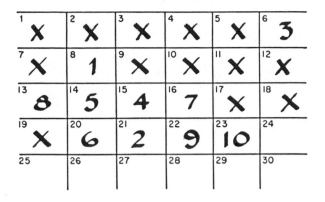

1 X	2 X	3 X	4 X	5 X	6 3
7 X	8 1	9 X	10 X	11 X	12 X
13 8	14 5	15 4	16 7	17 X	18 X
19 X	20 6	21 2	22 9	23 10	24
25	26	27	28	29	30

Figure CS-3 JOB-COMPLETION SEQUENCE

Questions:

1. What two conclusions regarding the effects of backlogs on lead time can be drawn from this demonstration?

2. How could this demonstration be modified to illustrate the effect of expediting on lead times?

3. What effects do backlogs have on dispatching? Machine loading?

4. (a) What actions would be necessary to reduce the backlogs from five jobs to two in controlling this oversimplified manufacturing operation?

Job no.	2 Jobs in queue	5 Jobs in queue
1	6	7
2	2	19
3	3	3
4	6	11
5	4	9
6	2	14
7	6	9
8	4	5
9	2	13
10	5	13
Total	40	103
Avg.	4.0	10.3

Figure CS-4 LEAD-TIME SUMMARY

(b) How would you accomplish this reduction if the backlogs were still on paper instead of in physical parts?

5. What reaction toward small backlogs would you expect from:
   (a) An expediter
   (b) An inventory control supervisor
   (c) A shop supervisor
   (d) A machine operator
   (e) The company controller (treasurer)

Case Study 3: The Black Pot Company

The Black Pot Company manufactures small electrical home appliances such as toasters and coffee pots. The basic components of these appliances are stampings manufactured in their press department, purchased electrical subassemblies, plastic bases, to which the heating units, switches, and other components are assembled at the plant and cord sets which are purchased from a single vendor.

Sheet metal components start in the stamping department, move into the forming department, where secondary operations are performed, and then go through the plating department and into finished component stores. Electrical parts are subassembled in a separate department and sent to finished component stores. These electrical subassemblies, the sheet metal subassembly and the cord set are withdrawn from finished component stores, assembled into finished products, inspected, packed and shipped.

The principal participants in this case study are:

General Manager, Mr. J. F. Black

Sales Manager, Ms. R. B. Forsythe

Plant Manager, Mr. Fred Atkins

Controller, Ms. R. C. Braken

Production Control Manager, You

History: Before World War II, the Black Pot Company was a small appliance firm concentrating principally on one model of a 6-cup coffee pot and a standard toaster. The coffee pot was very well accepted as a low-priced yet dependable appliance and was purchased by many retailers and private-brand outlets who marketed it under their own names.

During World War II, the company made minor electrical subassemblies, particularly those employing stampings, for military use. When World War II was over, they had a large number of orders in backlog for the standard coffee pot and toaster which carried them into 1953. In the meantime, some new model appliances were introduced.

The production control system was a very simple one. Since the order backlog was never under 6 months, it was standard procedure to make out a quarterly schedule, which was firm for the assembly department. It was also divided into required electrical subassemblies, stampings and purchased parts ordered by the production control department from the supplying department and vendors to meet the scheduled assembly dates. This ordering sytem worked very well as long as the order backlog existed.

Late in 1953, the order backlog had diminished to approximately 4 weeks of production and the quarterly ordering system became increasingly difficult to work since there were not enough firm orders to make up a schedule for the next quarter. Recognizing the seriousness of the situation, the company hired a marketing manager, who set up forecasting procedures in order to develop a quarterly forecast to be used by the production control department for planning production. She was also instrumental in urging new ventures in small appliances. Consequently, many new products were added after 1953, including drip-type coffee makers, large coffee urns in 20- to 100-cup capacities, many different models of toasters, toaster-broilers, waffle irons and, most recently, an electric plug-in bean pot in three different sizes and a dozen different canister sets.

While the marketing manager was highly capable in new product-development and introduction, forecasting ability was somewhat less enviable. The production-control department's records showed that 50% of the forecasts for individual items were off by plus or minus 25% over a 13-week period. With such inaccuracy the quarterly ordering system could not work very well and, in fact, a great deal of expediting was required to get the proper items through the plant. The plant people complained that the production control department always wanted something extra in addition to the quarterly schedule given to them. The production control department in turn complained that the forecasts were inaccurate and they had to spend the necessary time and effort in expediting, not only to get the proper assemblies made but to get the needed components through manufacturing and purchasing.

One of the most serious problems was the fact that the requirements for components were reviewed only quarterly, when the quarterly assembly schedule was drawn up. At this time, the assemblies were exploded into component requirements and component orders were scheduled throughout the plant. While this system was intended to generate a fairly level amount of work for the plant, the degree of forecast inaccuracy caused some very serious lumps in the production schedule. Each time production control reviewed their quarterly assembly requirements, they found that these had changed drastically from the last review and that many components were required immediately. This meant that demands on supplying departments (in particular, the stamping department) tended to crowd into the first month of the quarter and there was a decided bulge in the workload at the beginning of the quarter.

Management was very concerned about these problems, particularly since inventories had increased steadily and substantially since 1953 and customer service was still very poor by industry standards. The sales department maintained that the service given by the Black Pot Company factory was among the very worst in the appliance industry.

In 1965, Mr. Black, under heavy pressure from his sales manager, called in a management consultant to recommend improvements in the production control system that would solve the customer service problem. This consultant recommended applying computer-calculated economic order quantities and order points to control manufacturing and inventory, and these recommendations were adopted. The EOQ's resulted in larger lot-sizes, but these were accepted because of Mr. Black's understanding that this larger investment in inventory would be economical. Order points were established for all assemblies, manufactured and purchased components and many raw materials.

Present Situation: After running this system for more than 8 years, many problems still existed in 1974. The inventory had increased steadily and the level of work in the plant was very unstable and was more erratic than it had ever been in the past. Customer service—far from improving—had grown poorer and the pressures were so great that the production control manager left the company. Three successors had no appreciable success for another 5 years.

Mr. Black recently called together his executive group and discussed the problem. They talked about calling in another consultant but agreed that their past experience did not justify the expense. They have decided to hire a materials manager (you) and to act as a task force to assist you in analyzing the problem. Each member of the task force wrote a memorandum outlining his or her analysis of the problem and made specific recommendations for solutions.

As the new materials manager, you are to review the memos submitted by the other members of the task force and develop a program embodying any of their recommendations you find pertinent along with your own improvements. Your presentation should contain specific comments on all the task force recommendations. Your program should include specific techniques to be used in

1. Developing and utilizing forecasts, together with recommendations for improving them
2. Planning and controlling inventory levels and capacity rates
3. Preparing for and implementing a modern computer system
4. Improving procurement of purchased items
5. Leveling the load on the factory, particularly the plating department
6. Reducing and controlling work-in-process
7. Measuring and improving customer service

Include a timetable and comments on the required time to install any recommended system changes.

As a separate assignment, discuss this company's approach to the use of a management consultant.

Interoffice Memorandum

THE BLACK POT COMPANY

To: J. F. Black, General Manager

From: R. B. Forsythe, Sales Manger

SUBJECT: The production control problem

If we are going to resume the rate of growth in the future that we had in the past (you'll note that sales peaked out 2 years ago), we have to provide competitive customer serivce. We're supposed to be a make-to-stock company and we're supposed to have our appliances on the shelf when our customers ask for them. Unfortunately, we don't seem to be able to do this consistently.

We in the sales department are constantly in the position of trying to push our new products to our customers who tell us that they're interested in the new products but don't want to order until we demonstrate we can deliver our existing ones. We have more ideas for new products but see no sense in suggesting these when our factory seems to be completely incapable of handling our present business properly.

Reviewing the situation from a common sense point of view, I can make two observations:

1. When we recently got in trouble with our major private brand account, we added an expediter who concentrated his efforts on this account. Since that time, we have had very few complaints about service to this customer. I believe that it would be well worth the expense to add more expediters to the payroll so that we could improve our service to our valued customers.

2. We constantly emphasize the need to improve inventory turnover at Black Pot. Instead, it would be a good idea to invest the needed funds in more finished goods inventory before it is too late.

I am not qualified to tell you how to run a factory but I can tell you about sales: You can't sell from an empty wagon!

R. B. Forsythe

Interoffice Memorandum

THE BLACK POT COMPANY

To: J. F. Black, General Manager

From: F. Atkins, Plant Manager

SUBJECT: The production control problem

     In my opinion, our switch from a quarterly ordering program to an order point–order quantity system years ago simply aggravated our problems at Black Pot and cured almost none of the basic ills. The other approaches we tried also did not work. As I see it, we have the following problems:

1. The order point system tends to generate many orders for parts and products that are not really needed and exaggerates the ups and downs in our business cycle. When business picks up, a lot of orders are generated and sent out to the plant. Unfortunately, we don't know how to recognize this flood of orders as a true pickup in business because the order point system seems to cause a high degree of variability, even under normal circumstances. Typically, there will be 1 week of heavy orders, followed by 2 weeks of light orders and then another week of very heavy orders generated and sent down into the plant. It is impossible for plant operating people to determine from the size of the order backlog when to add workers or when to lay them off.

        It is easy for the production control department to say that we should increase or decrease production rates but this is a long, slow process. We can't get press operators hired and trained overnight and once we lay them off, we never seem to see them again. Until we see a 10- to 12-week buildup of work ahead of our manufacturing departments, we do not feel justified in adding workers or increasing production other than by occasional overtime.

        For example, at the present time, we know that sales are down (judging by the dollar incoming business reports), yet there is a very substantial backlog out in the plant. Would you feel that we would be justified in adding people to work off the backlogs of work in the plant?

2. The system for generating orders in materials control doesn't seem to be connected to actual requirements. We have many orders now in the plant that were released 4 and even 6 months ago, yet no one has asked us to run them. Specifically, our colonial coffee pot that is made for the Ace Premium Company only twice a year was assembled for the Christmas order and the components were immediately reordered from the stamping department and the electrical subassembly department in January. These components are not used on any other product and could not possibly be needed before the next Ace vacation promotion order in August. This work just lies around on the floor until some expediter comes down to push it.

3. Expediting concentrates on putting pressure upon our factory people but it does not seem to exert as much pressure on people outside our company. We are doing rush jobs every day of the week and getting blamed for missing the schedule on our regular work, yet we find many orders in the plant for which there is no material and the expediters don't seem to know when the vendors are going to ship the material. In fact, a recent survey of the orders in the stamping department indicated that, while we had a 12-week backlog, only 6 weeks of this could be worked on since material was not available for about half the orders ahead of the department.

4. There have been very heavy surges of work in the plating department. All plating work seems to come at one time with everything wanted at once. We simply cannot hire and train new plating people to do the quality work that Black Pot expects quickly enough to keep up with these surges. This department is a constant bottleneck because the materials control department does not feed a level rate of work into the plating department.

In my own opinion, the following actions are needed to solve our immediate problems:

1. Lengthen the lead time allowed on components. The lead time for press parts was lengthened from 6 weeks to 8 weeks recently, but right after that we received a flood of orders from materials control which bogged the department down so badly we haven't recovered yet. We need to increase the lead time on these parts to a minimum of 12 weeks. If the materials department could plan further ahead, it would certainly be of assistance in keeping this department operating smoothly and on schedule.

2. We are in constant trouble in final assembly because we have sets of parts laid out for assembly with one or two parts missing. I feel that we should be laying out at least 4 weeks in advance of our scheduled assembly date instead of just 2. If we did this, we would find out earlier which components were short and the expediters could use this shortage list for effective and timely expediting of critical parts rather than expediting everything through the plant.

3. I don't see why the purchasing department can't institute a regular follow up procedure to get purchased materials—particularly special steels for the stamping department, plastic bases for the subassembly department and cord sets—in on time.

4. We used to have a firm quarterly schedule that worked out very well. When we lost our order backlog, our biggest problem was that we could no longer get a good quarterly forecast. An improvement in forecasting by the marketing department and some discipline and restraint on the part of the sales department (so that we could have a firm quarterly forecast with which to work) would make substantial improvements in plant economy and in service to customers.

5. Our sales department is constantly asking for new and different products. From a small company making two or three products when I first joined

it as a press operator, we have expanded to where we are now making 60 different assemblies, averaging ten components each, and the sales department is still clamoring for more. It must be recognized that we are basically a job shop and that we cannot turn out the volume of production in the variety required by the sales department.

A return to our quarterly ordering system with reliable forecasts is probabaly the best solution available to the current problems at the Black Pot Company. I will certainly do everything I can to cooperate with those parties who will participate in this or any other program.

Fred Atkins

Interoffice Memorandum

THE BLACK POT COMPANY

To: J. F. Black, General Manager

From: R. C. Braken, Controller

SUBJECT: The production control problem

Recognizing the very serious problems in our company in the areas of inventory control and customer service, I have had an audit group working in the plant during the last few months. Listed below are their findings and recommendations:

1. Economic order quantities were installed long ago and resulted in larger lot-sizes. So far, there have been no offsetting economies in setup or ordering cost. *Recommendation:* These EOQ's should be reviewed, using an inventory carrying cost approved by the controller.

2. Orders are all over the plant with old, incorrect dates for completion. I have heard that MRP can keep such data timely. *Recommendation:* We should buy and install quickly an MRP program on our computer.

3. The amount of work in the plant is excessive; there is far too much work-in-process. One of the serious problems this causes is a last-in, first-out effect in front of machine centers. The work is piled so deeply ahead of these machine centers that the oldest jobs are ignored because they get pushed so far in back and the more recent jobs get done first. *Recommendation:* Reduce the amount of work-in-process.

4. Our audit group has found that many orders are lost in the plant. Materials control expects these orders to come through when, in fact, the orders cannot be found. Occasionally, they assume that these orders have been completed and adjust inventory records accordingly. This results in large

inventory write-offs at year-end. *Recommendation:* A reduction in work-in-process would help solve this problem also.

5. The inventory records were checked and found to be inaccurate in over 30% of the items. These records are now prededucted when orders are sent out to the assembly floor and, consequently, they cannot be reconciled with the physical inventory. *Recommendation:* A permanent, roving audit team should be checking inventories of components against stock records and these component inventory records should be kept on an actual rather than a prededucted basis.

6. There are lots of inventory for specific orders all over the assembly floor, with practically every lot lacking in some required components. Productive time is often spent borrowing components from order A to use on order B, even though order A was laid out first. *Recommendation:* More accurate records would help in avoiding this type of waste of time and money.

7. There are indications of loose control in materials control. Their personnel accept as complete an order with 90 to 95% of the material delivered against it rather than checking to find the balance of the order. Other basic disciplines seem to be lacking in materials control. *Recommendation:* Such well-recognized devices as data collection terminals should be installed throughout the plant. (This ties in with my next recommendation.)

8. Too much time is spent expediting various orders in the plant. Since job location records are frequently 2 to 3 days late, most of the expediters' time is spent in actually looking for the job. Black Pot has grown enough to require and be able to afford a data collection system and the latest electronic computer equipment to keep our job location records up-to-date. *Recommendation:* A computer could be used to print out job location records on a day-to-day basis for production control. Such a computer could also handle inventory control and machine loading—a function sadly lacking in our present production control system.

R. C. Braken

BIBLIOGRAPHY

Chapter One

1. Harris, F. W. *Operations and Cost* (Factory Management Series). Chicago: A. W. Shaw Co., 1915, Chapter 2.
2. Kanter, Rosabeth M. *The Change Masters.* New York: Simon and Schuster, 1983.
3. Peters, Thomas J., and Robert H. Waterman, Jr. *In Search of Excellence,* New York: Harper & Row, 1982.
4. Plossl, George W. *Production and Inventory Control: Applications,* Atlanta, GA: George Plossl Educational Services, 1984.
5. Plossl, George W., and Oliver W. Wight. *"You Can't Eliminate Expediting, But. . . ." APICS Quarterly Bulletin,* 5, no. 2 (April 1964).
6. Scheele, Evan D., William L. Westerman, and Robert J. Wimmert. *Principles and Design of Production Control Systems,* Englewood Cliffs, NJ: Prentice-Hall, 1960.
7. Taylor, Sam G., Samuel M. Seward, Steven F. Bolander, and Richard C. Heard. "Process Industry Production and Inventory Planning Framework." *Production and Inventory Management,* APICS (First Quarter 1981).
8. Wilson, R. H. "A Scientific Routine for Stock Control." *Harvard Business Review* 13, no. 1 (1934).

Chapter Two

1. Brown, Robert G. *Statistical Forecasting for Inventory Control.* New York: McGraw-Hill, 1959.

2. Dickie, H. F. "ABC Inventory Analysis Shoots for Dollars." *Factory Management and Maintenance* (July, 1951).

3. Kobert, Norman. "Inventory Outlook: ABC Analysis." *Purchasing* 89, no. 6 (September 1980).

4. McCoard, Frank G. "Proposed Objectives for Production and Inventory Control." *The Quarterly Technical Bulletin,* APICS 1, no. 1 (January 1960).

5. Plossl, George W. *Production and Inventory Control: Applications.* Atlanta, GA: George Plossl Educational Services, 1984.

6. Rivers, David L. "ABC and Finished Goods." *Production and Inventory Management,* APICS, (Second Quarter 1982).

7. Sims, E. Ralph, Jr. "How Material Control Aids Your Company's Operation." *Material Handling Engineering,* (March 1961).

Chapter Three

1. Axsater, S. "Economic Order Quantities and Variations in Production Load." *International Journal of Production Research* (May-June 1980).

2. Banks, Jerry, and C. L. Hohenstein. "Simplification of the Economic Order Quantity Equation." *Journal of Purchasing and Materials Management* (Summer 1981).

3. Harty, J. D., G. W. Plossl, and O. W. Wight. "Management of Lot-size Inventories." *APICS Special Report* (September 1963).

4. Heard, R. C. "Cyclical Production Scheduling." *Process Industries Seminar Proceedings,* APICS (April 1981).

5. Lowerre, William M. "Lot-size Rules, A One Act Play." *Production and Inventory Management,* APICS (Second Quarter 1975).

6. Plossl, George W. "How Much Inventory is Enough?" *Production and Inventory Management,* APICS (Second Quarter 1971).

7. Plossl, George W. *Production and Inventory Control: Applications.* Atlanta, GA: George Plossl Educational Services, 1984.

8. Theisen, Earnest C. "New Game in Town—The MRP Lot-size." *Production and Inventory Management,* APICS (Second Quarter 1974).

9. Welch, W. Evert. *Tested Scientific Inventory Control.* Greenwich, CT: Management Publishing Co., 1956.

10. Zimmerman, Steven M., and Leo M. Conrad. "Combining Break-Even Analysis and Economic Order Quantity." *Industrial Engineering* (August 1982).

Chapter Four

1. Brown, Robert G. *Statistical Forecasting for Inventory Control.* New York: McGraw-Hill, 1959.

2. Brownell, Donald R., and Mark S. Miller. "Model-based Service Parts Forecasting." *APICS 1983 Conference Proceedings.*

3. Edelman, Martin P. "Basic Forecasting Workshop." *APICS 1982 Conference Proceedings.*

4. Ling, Richard C. "Demand Management." *APICS 1983 Conference Proceedings.*

5. MacCombie, Frank. "Managing the Forecast." *APICS* 1975 *Conference Proceedings.*

6. Monroney, M. J. *Facts From Figures.* London: Penguin Books, 1957.

7. Muir, James W. "The Pyramid Principle." *APICS* 1979 *Conference Proceedings.*

8. Plossl, George W. "Getting the Most from Forecasts." *Production and Inventory Management,* APICS (First Quarter, 1973).

9. Plossl, George W. *Glossary of Manufacturing Control Terms,* Atlanta, GA. George Plossl Educational Services, 1980.

10. Smith, Bernard T., Focus Forecasting. *APICS* 1976 *Conference Proceedings.*

11. VanDeMark, Robert L. "How to Get Along Without a Sales Forecast." *APICS* 1964 *Conference Proceedings.*

Chapter Five

1. Brown, Robert G. *Advanced Service Parts Inventory Control.* 2d. ed. Norwich, VT: Materials Management Systems, 1982.

2. Burbridge, John L. *The Principles of Production Control.* 3d. ed. London: MacDonald and Evans, 1971.

3. IBM General Information Manual. *IMPACT,* Publication E20-8105, 1962.

4. Mather, Hal F. *Are We Taking Independent/Dependent Demand Too Seriously?* News Note #28. Atlanta, GA: George Plossl Educational Services, 1979.

5. Monroney, M. J. *Facts from Figures.* London: Penguin Books, 1957.

6. Plossl, George W. *Production and Inventory Control: Applications.* Atlanta, GA: George Plossl Educational Services, 1984.

7. Plossl, George W. "Safety Stock—Snare and Delusion" *Newsletter #17.* Atlanta, GA: George Plossl Educational Services, 1974.

8. Plossl, George W., and Oliver W. Wight. "Determining Order Points Using the Poisson Distribution." *APICS Quarterly Bulletin* (April 1963).

9. Putnam, Arnold O., Robert E. Barlow, and Gabriel N. Stilian. *Unified Operations Management.* New York: McGraw-Hill, 1963.

10. Silver, Edward A. "The Use of Programmable Calculators in Inventory Management." *Production and Inventory Management,* APICS (Fourth Quarter 1979).

11. Wilson, R. H. "A Scientific Routine for Stock Control." *Harvard Business Review* 13, no. 1 (1934).

Chapter Six

1. APICS. *Material Requirements Planning Training Aid,* 1979.

2. APICS. *Material Requirements Planning, Certification Program Study Guide,* 1980.

3. Greenshields, R. V. "MRP: A Solution to Scheduling Problems." *Manufacturing Engineering and Management* (January, 1976).

4. Orlicky, Joseph A. *Material Requirements Planning.* New York: McGraw-Hill, 1975.

5. Orlicky, Joseph A. "Closing the Loop With Pegged Requirements and the Firm Planned Order." *Production and Inventory Management*, APICS (First Quarter 1975).

6. Plossl, George W. *Production and Inventory Control: Applications*. Atlanta, GA: George Plossl Educational Services, 1984.

7. Plossl, George W. "MRP—Has Its Time Really Come?" *News Note #1*. Atlanta, GA: George Plossl Educational Services, 1973.

8. Plossl, George W., and Oliver W. Wight. "Material Requirements Planning by Computer." *APICS Special Report*, 1971.

9. Rucinski, David, and Fred Woodman. "Use of the Firm Planned Order." *Production and Inventory Management*, APICS (Fourth Quarter 1977).

10. Welch, W. Evert. "MRP—Its Time Has Come." *APICS 1973 Conference Proceedings*.

11. Wight, Oliver W. *Production and Inventory Management in the Computer Age*. Boston: Cahners Publishing Company, 1974.

12. Wilkerson, David A. "Materials Requirements Planning and Manpower Planning." *Production and Inventory Management*, APICS (Second Quarter 1976).

Chapter Seven

1. APICS. *Master Planning, Certification Program Study Guide*.

2. Bacigalupo, Paul F. "Master Production Planning and Scheduling for the '80's." *APICS 1982 Conference Proceedings*.

3. Berry, William L., Thomas Vollman, and D. Clay Whybark. *Master Production Scheduling Principles and Practice*. APICS, 1979.

4. Drucker, Peter F. *Management: Tasks—Responsibilities—Practices*. New York: Harper & Row, 1973.

5. Everdell, Romeyn, and Judith A. Ryde. "The Production Plan—The Top Management Interface." *APICS 1982 Conference Proceedings*.

6. Ling, Richard C. "The Production Planning Process—Top Management's Role." *APICS 1982 Conference Proceedings*.

7. Mather, Hal F. "The Master Production Schedule—Stuff It At Your Peril." *News Note #13*. Atlanta, GA: George Plossl Educational Services, 1974.

8. Mather, Hal F., and George W. Plossl. *The Master Production Schedule*. 2nd ed. Atlanta, GA: George Plossl Educational Services, 1977.

9. Orlicky, Joseph A. *Material Requirements Planning*. New York: McGraw-Hill, 1975.

10. Plossl, George W. *Production and Inventory Control: Applications*. Atlanta, GA: George Plossl Educational Services, 1984.

11. Plossl, George W. *Manufacturing Control: The Last Frontier for Profits*. Reston, VA: Reston Publishing Company, 1973.

12. Plossl, George W. "The Master Production Schedule—Servant of All Managers." *Newsletter #18*. Atlanta, GA: George Plossl Educational Services, 1975.

13. Plossl, George W., and W. Evert Welch. *The Role of Top Management in the Control of Inventories*. Reston, VA: Reston Publishing Company, 1979.

14. Wight, Oliver W. *MRP II—Unlocking America's Productivity Potential.* Brattleboro, VT: The Book Press, 1981.

Chapter Eight

1. Ballou, Ronald H. "Estimating and Auditing Aggregate Inventory Levels at Multiple Stocking Points." *Journal of Operations Management,* (February 1981).
2. Brown, R. G. "Use of the Carrying Charge to Control Cycle Stocks." *APICS Quarterly Bulletin* (July 1961).
3. Harty, James D., George W. Plossl, and Oliver W. Wight *Management of Lot-size Inventories.* APICS Special Report, 1963.
4. Mather, Hal F. *How to Really Manage Inventories.* New York: McGraw-Hill, 1984.
5. Plossl, George W. "How Much Inventory is Enough?" *Production and Inventory Management.* APICS (Second Quarter 1971).
6. Plossl, George W. *Production and Inventory Control: Applications.* Atlanta, GA: George Plossl Educational Services, 1984.
7. Plossl, George W. *Manufacturing Control: The Last Frontier for Profits.* Reston, VA: Reston Publishing Company, 1973.
8. Plossl, George W., and W. Evert Welch. *The Role of Top Management in the Control of Inventories.* Reston, VA: Reston Publishing Company, 1979.
9. Shaughnessy, Thomas E. "Aggregate Inventory Management." *Journal of Purchasing and Materials Management* (Fall 1980).
10. Taylor, Paul A. "Aggregate Inventory Management." *APICS* 1975 *Conference Proceedings.*
11. VanDeMark, R. L. "Hidden Controls for Inventory." *Proceedings of the* 1960 *APICS Annual Conference.*
12. Welch, W. Evert. *Tested Scientific Inventory Control.* Greenwich, CT: Management Publishing Company, 1956.

Chapter Nine

1. APICS Certification Program Study Guide. "Capacity Planning and Master Production Scheduling." *Production and Inventory Management* (Second Quarter 1979).
2. Clark, James T. "Capacity Management—Part 1." *APICS* 1979 *Conference Proceedings.*
3. Clark, James T. "Capacity Management—Part 2." *APICS* 1980 *Conference Proceedings.*
4. Lankford, Raymond L. "Capacity Management in the 1980's." *News Note #33.* Atlanta, GA: George Plossl Educational Services, 1981.
5. Lankford, Raymond L. "The Crisis in Capacity Management." *News Note #47.* Atlanta, GA: George Plossl Educational Services, 1983.
6. Mather, Hal F., and George W. Plossl. "Priority Fixation vs. Throughput Planning." *Production and Inventory Management,* APICS (Third Quarter 1978).
7. Plossl, George W. "Classical CRP—What's It Worth?" *News Note #15.* Atlanta, GA: George Plossl Educational Services, 1977.

8. Plossl, George W. *Manufacturing Control: The Last Frontier for Profits*. Reston, VA: Reston Publishing Company, 1973.

9. Plossl, George W. *Production and Inventory Control: Applications*. Atlanta, GA: George Plossl Educational Services, 1984.

10. Plossl, George W. "Planning Safety Capacity Instead of Safety Stock." *News Note #29*. Atlanta, GA: George Plossl Educational Services, 1980.

11. Osgood, William R. "How to Plan Capacity Using the Bill of Labor." *APICS* 1976 *Conference Proceedings*.

12. Warren, Charles R. "Capacity (not Materials) Planning." *APICS* 1980 *Conference Proceedings*.

Chapter Ten

1. APICS Training Aid. *Types of Schedules*. 1982.

2. Gue, Frank S. "Control Capacity and Priority—Part I." *Inventories and Production* (May/June 1981).

3. Gue, Frank S. "Control Capacity and Priority—Part II." *Inventories and Production* (November/December 1981).

4. Heard, Richard C. "Cyclical Production Schedule." *APICS Process Industries Seminar Proceedings*, 1981.

5. Lankford, Raymond L. "Job Shop Scheduling." 1982 *APICS Conference Proceedings*.

6. Lankford, Raymond L. "Scheduling the Job Shop." 1973 *APICS Conference Proceedings*.

7. Magee, John F. *Production Planning and Inventory Control*. New York: McGraw-Hill, 1958.

8. Mather, Hal F. "Reschedule the Reschedules You Just Rescheduled." *Production and Inventory Management*, APICS (First Quarter 1977).

9. Orlicky, Joseph A. "Rescheduling with Tomorrow's MRP System." *Production and Inventory Management*, APICS (Second Quarter 1977).

10. Plossl, George W. *Production and Inventory Control: Applications*. Atlanta, GA: George Plossl Educational Services, 1984.

11. Spencer, Michael S. "Scheduling Components for Group Technology Lines." *Production and Inventory Management*, APICS (Fourth Quarter 1980).

12. Taylor, Sam G. "Scheduling with Run-Out Lists." 1982 *APICS Conference Proceedings*.

Chapter Eleven

1. Belt, Bill. "Integrating Capacity Planning and Capacity Control." *Production and Inventory Management*, APICS (First Quarter 1976).

2. Gue, Frank S. *Increased Profits Through Better Control of Work in Process*, Reston VA: Reston Publishing Company, 1980.

3. Hoyt, John H. "Dispatching in 'Real Time' in the 'Real World.'" *APICS Operations Scheduling Seminar Proceedings*, 1979.

4. Johnson, Bruce P. "Controlling Capacity is the Only Thing." *APICS Process Industries Seminar Proceedings,* 1981.

5. Lankford, Raymond L. "Input/Output Control: Making it Work." *APICS* 1980 *Conference Proceedings.*

6. Lankford, Raymond L., and Stephen D. Smith. "The Beginning of the Post-MRP Era." 1984 *APICS Conference Proceedings.*

7. Mather, Hal F., and George W. Plossl. "Priority Fixation vs. Throughput Planning." *Production and Inventory Management,* APICS (Third Quarter 1978).

8. Plossl, George W. *Production and Inventory Control: Applications.* Atlanta, GA: George Plossl Educational Services, 1984.

9. Plossl, George W. "The Semiconductor Story." *Newsletter #20.* Atlanta, GA: George Plossl Educational Services, 1976.

10. Plossl, George W. "The Semiconductor Story—A Sequel." *News Note #49.* Atlanta, GA: George Plossl Educational Services, 1983.

11. Plossl, George W. "Small Backlogs = Big Control." *Executives' Bulletin #228* (1965).

12. Putnam, Arnold O., Robert E. Barlow, and Gabriel N. Stilian. *Unified Operations Management.* New York: McGraw-Hill, 1963.

13. Shingo, Shigeo. *Study of Toyota Production System.* Tokyo: Japan Management Association, 1981.

14. Wight, Oliver W. "Input/Output Control, A Real Handle on Lead Time." *Production and Inventory Management,* APICS, (Third Quarter 1970).

15. Young, Jan B. "Practical Dispatching." *APICS* 1981 *Conference Proceedings.*

Chapter Twelve

1. Bittel, Lester R. *Management By Exception.* New York: McGraw-Hill, 1964.

2. Chantlos, Robert F. "Management Decision Rules." *APICS* 1982 *Conference Proceedings.*

3. Fogarty, Donald W., and Thomas R. Hoffman, "Customer Service." *Production and Inventory Management,* APICS (First Quarter 1980).

4. Grieco, Peter L., Jr. "Monitoring Performance Levels." *Production and Inventory Management,* APICS (Fourth Quarter 1980).

5. Plossl, George W. *Production and Inventory Control: Applications.* Atlanta, GA: George Plossl Educational Services, 1984.

6. Plossl, George W. "Execute the Plan—Don't Just Revise It." *News Note #16.* Atlanta, GA: George Plossl Educational Services, 1977.

7. Prather, Kirk L. "Analyze Service Objectives, Maximize Results." 1981 *APICS Conference Proceedings.*

8. Smith, Leighton F., and Roy L. Harmon. "Closed Loop Systems in Japan." *APICS* 1981 *Conference Proceedings.*

9. Voss, Christopher A. "Measuring Make To Order Delivery Performance." *Production and Inventory Management,* APICS (Second Quarter 1980).

10. Wight, Oliver W. "MRP Outlook: Making Performance Measures Work." *Purchasing* (November 5, 1981).

APPENDICES

APPENDIX I   TABLE OF SQUARE ROOTS

No.	√	No.	√	No.	√	No.	√	No.	√	No.	√
1	1.0	30	5.5	300	17.3	3,000	54.8	30,000	173.2	2,000,000	1,414
2	1.4	35	5.9	350	18.7	3,500	59.2	40,000	200.0	3,000,000	1,732
3	1.7	40	6.3	400	20.0	4,000	63.2	50,000	223.6	4,000,000	2,000
4	2.0	45	6.7	450	21.2	4,500	67.1	60,000	244.9	5,000,000	2,236
5	2.2	50	7.1	500	22.4	5,000	70.7	70,000	264.6	6,000,000	2,450
6	2.4	55	7.4	550	23.5	5,500	74.2	80,000	282.8	7,000,000	2,646
7	2.6	60	7.7	600	24.5	6,000	77.5	90,000	300.0	8,000,000	2,828
8	2.8	65	8.1	650	25.5	6,500	80.6	100,000	316.2	9,000,000	3,000
9	3.0	70	8.4	700	26.5	7,000	83.7	150,000	387.3	10,000,000	3,162
10	3.2	75	8.7	750	27.4	7,500	86.6	200,000	447.2	12,000,000	3,464
11	3.3	80	8.9	800	28.3	8,000	89.4	250,000	500.0	14,000,000	3,742
12	3.5	85	9.2	850	29.2	8,500	92.2	300,000	547.7	16,000,000	4,000
13	3.6	90	9.5	900	30.0	9,000	94.9	350,000	591.6	18,000,000	4,243
14	3.7	95	9.7	950	30.8	9,500	97.5	400,000	632.5	20,000,000	4,472
15	3.9	100	10.0	1,000	31.6	10,000	100.0	450,000	670.8	25,000,000	5,000
16	4.0	110	10.5	1,100	33.2	11,000	104.9	500,000	707.1	30,000,000	5,477
17	4.1	120	11.0	1,200	34.6	12,000	109.5	550,000	741.6	35,000,000	5,916
18	4.2	130	11.4	1,300	36.1	13,000	114.0	600,000	774.6	40,000,000	6,325
19	4.4	140	11.8	1,400	37.4	14,000	118.3	650,000	806.2	45,000,000	6,708
20	4.5	150	12.2	1,500	38.7	15,000	122.5	700,000	836.7	50,000,000	7,071
21	4.6	175	13.2	1,750	41.9	17,500	132.3	750,000	866.0	60,000,000	7,746
22	4.7	200	14.1	2,000	44.7	20,000	141.4	800,000	894.4	70,000,000	8,367
23	4.8	225	15.0	2,250	47.5	22,500	150.0	850,000	922.0	80,000,000	8,944
24	4.9	250	15.8	2,500	50.0	25,000	158.1	900,000	948.7	90,000,000	9,487
25	5.0	275	16.6	2,750	52.5	27,500	165.8	1,000,000	1,000	100,000,000	10,000

FORMULA DERIVATION:
ECONOMIC ORDERING QUANTITY

This derivation covers the formula for determining the most economic ordering quantity (EOQ) for one item carried in inventory, whether the item is purchased or manufactured. The term *received* is used to cover delivery into inventory; the word *issued*, for usage out of inventory. All assumptions are written in boldface type.

The daily rate of receipt of the item is p and the daily rate of issue is u. **Both are assumed to be uniform over the whole cycle of receipt and issue.**

To produce one lot of q pieces requires q/p days.

The rate at which pieces will be added to inventory is $p - u$, and the maximum quantity added to inventory is

$$\left(\frac{q}{p} \right) (p - u) \tag{1}$$

The reserve stock inventory is R, **assumed constant over 1 year.** The maximum total inventory is

$$R + \left(\frac{q}{p} \right) (p - u)$$

Assuming that the **storage space and handling charges are directly proportional to the maximum inventory and are measured by w dollars per year per piece,** the annual cost of storage is:

$$w[R + \left(\frac{q}{p} \right) (p - u)] \tag{2}$$

Assuming uniform rates of receipt and issue, the **average** value of the lot-size inventory is one-half the maximum given by equation (1), or $(q/2p)(p - u)$.

The average total inventory also includes all the reserve stock R and is then

$$R + \left(\frac{q}{2p}\right)(p - u) \tag{3}$$

The unit cost per piece is C and includes labor, material and that portion of the overhead that varies with the size of the lot produced but does not include ordering charges associated with each lot procured.

The ordering cost is S and includes all **preparation charges**, such as writing orders, setting up machines, inspecting the setup and other charges **incurred each time one lot is procured.**

The total cost of one piece is $C + (S/q)$, and the total cost of a year's requirement with daily issue rate u and with N working days based on using lot-size q throughout the year is

$$Nu[C + \left(\frac{S}{q}\right)] \tag{4}$$

Applying this total cost per piece to the average total inventory, as given by equation (3), the value of the inventory is:

$$[C + \left(\frac{S}{q}\right)] \times [R + \left(\frac{q}{2p}\right)(p - u)]$$

The cost of carrying this inventory (expressed as I dollars per dollar of inventory) includes elements for **cost of money, obsolescence, deterioration, taxes, insurance and other factors not included in this derivation as separate costs.**

The total annual cost of carrying the average inventory is

$$I \times [C + \left(\frac{S}{q}\right)] \times [R + \left(\frac{q}{2p}\right)(p - u)] \tag{5}$$

The grand total T of the costs for 1 year's operation is the sum of

1. The storage cost, equation (2)
2. The direct cost, equation (4)
3. The carrying cost, equation (5)

$$T = w[R + \left(\frac{q}{p}\right)(p - u)] + Nu[C + \left(\frac{S}{q}\right)] + I[C + \left(\frac{S}{q}\right)]$$
$$\times [R + \left(\frac{q}{2p}\right)(p - u)]$$

This expands to:

$$T = wR + \left(\frac{wq}{p}\right)(p - u) + NuC + \left(\frac{NuS}{q}\right) + ICR$$
$$+ \left(\frac{ICq}{2p}\right)(p - u) + \left(\frac{ISR}{q}\right) + \left(\frac{IS}{2p}\right)(p - u)$$

By definition, the minimum value of T results when the lot-size **q** is set at the most economic size, the EOQ. This is determined by differentiating this equation with respect to **q** and setting this equal to zero:

$$\frac{dT}{dq} = \left(\frac{w}{p}\right)(p - u) - \left(\frac{NuS}{q^2}\right) + \left(\frac{IC}{2p}\right)(p - u) - \left(\frac{ISR}{q^2}\right) = 0$$

Combining terms gives

$$\frac{NuS + ISR}{q^2} = \left[\frac{IC + 2w}{2}\right] \times \left[\frac{(p - u)}{p}\right]$$

from which:

$$q^2 = \frac{2(NuS + ISR)}{(IC + 2w)(1 - u/p)}$$

The final step is

$$EOQ = \sqrt{\frac{2NuS + 2ISR}{(IC + 2w)(1 - u/p)}} \tag{6}$$

In practical use, the annual usage is expressed as a single factor, A, instead of the daily rate, u, times the number of days, N. Also, the **storage charge, w**, is not handled as a separate factor but **is considered part of the inventory-carrying cost I**. This reduces equation (6) to

$$EOQ = \sqrt{\frac{2AS + 2ISR}{IC(1 - u/p)}} \tag{7}$$

If reserve stock is a relatively small factor whose influence does not justify the complication of including it in the calculations, the **reserve-stock factor, ($2ISR$)**, can be omitted and equation (7) reduces to:

$$EOQ = \sqrt{\frac{2AS}{IC(1 - u/p)}} \tag{8}$$

This is the common form used where the rate p at which the item is received is not large when compared to the rate issued u, called the **noninstantaneous receipt case**.

Where the ratio of these rates, u/p, is small enough to be considered negligible (which is often true in practice) the most frequently used form of the EOQ equation results:

$$EOQ = \sqrt{\frac{2AS}{IC}} \tag{9}$$

Summarizing, the symbols used are:

EOQ = economic ordering quantity, in pieces
A = annual total issues, in pieces
S = total ordering cost for one lot, dollars
I = inventory-carrying cost, in dollars per dollar of inventory
C = unit cost, not including setup, in dollars per piece.

THE LIMIT TECHNIQUE

The LIMIT (Lot-size Inventory-Management Interpolation Technique) is designed to handle a family of items that passes over common manufacturing facilities. All the parts that pass through a screw machine department or a milling machine department or all parts purchased by one buyer are logical groups to be handled with LIMIT.

The LIMIT calculations can be made manually or on a computer. These calculations are simple and straightforward—even if a computer is available, they should be made manually by the practitioner on a sample number of items to insure complete understanding of the concept. For large numbers of items, a computer program is the practical day-to-day way to apply this technique.

LIMIT is a two-phase technique: In the first phase, trial economic lot-sizes are calculated for each item in the chosen group using the standard EOQ equation. The total setup hours required for these economic lot-sizes is then compared with the total setup hours required for the present lot-sizes. New LIMIT order quantities are then calculated, which result in a total of setup hours equal to the present total. The result is usually to reduce the total inventory very substantially without changing total setup hours. Thus benefits from reduced inventory investment are obtained with no change in operating conditions.

In the second phase, a series of alternatives is presented for the family of items, showing the effect on the lot-size inventory when more orders are placed or more time is spent on setting up machines. The number of alternatives can be varied to suit any desired conditions. This phase of the program shows the alternatives available if it is desired to move in controlled steps from present conditions toward operations that result in lower total costs or investment.

LIMIT Manual Technique

For purpose of illustration, an example involving ten parts is used. These are all of the items machined on a group of four milling machines. The following data are required for each item in order to perform the LIMIT calculations:

1. Annual usage in units
2. Unit cost
3. Present order quantity
4. Setup hours per order
5. Setup cost per hour, including paperwork costs

Figure III-1 shows the data for the ten items that have been chosen for this example. In addition, a setup cost of $2.80 per hour (not intended to represent real costs but for example purposes only) is assumed to be the same for all ten items. The first series of calculations is then made to determine the present annual setup requirement for each part and the total setup for all ten items. The setup require-

			0.20		Inventory carrying charge				
			$2.80		Setup cost per hour				
(1) Item no.	(2) Annual usage	(3) Setup hrs. per ord.	(4) Unit cost	(5) Pres. order qty.	(6) Yearly setup hrs. pres.	(7) Trial order qty.	(8) Yearly setup hrs. trial	(9) Limit order qty.	(10) Yearly setup hrs. LIMIT
1 A	3000	5.5	6.12	600	27.5	274	60.0	391	42.3
2 B	2000	6.0	2.85	350	34.3	343	35.0	490	24.4
3 C	8000	7.0	0.56	1500	37.4	1673	33.6	2389	23.4
4 D	1100	4.0	2.26	400	11.0	233	18.9	333	13.2
5 E	600	4.0	4.08	300	8.0	128	18.8	183	13.1
6 F	1200	2.0	0.91	950	2.5	271	8.9	387	6.2
7 G	300	4.0	3.09	150	8.0	104	11.6	149	8.1
8 H	2000	2.0	0.42	1000	4.0	516	7.7	737	5.4
9 I	275	8.0	2.05	275	8.0	173	12.7	247	8.9
10 J	615	6.0	0.79	310	11.8	361	10.2	516	7.2
Total	19,090	---	----	5835	152.5	4076	217.4	5822	152.2

Figure III-1 LOT-SIZE INVENTORY-MANAGEMENT INTERPOLATION TECHNIQUE (LIMT) CALCULATIONS

ments are determined by dividing the annual usages by the present order quantities to find the number of setups and then multiplying by the setup hours per order.

For example, the calculation for item 1A is

$$\left(\frac{3000}{600}\right) \times 5.5 = 27.5 \quad \text{hours yearly}$$

Figure III-1 shows the annual setup hours for each item calculated in this manner and the total for the family under the heading, "Yearly setup hrs. pres."

The next step in the LIMIT analysis is to calculate trial order quantities. This is done using the standard EOQ formula (3-6) from Chapter 3 and the data from Figure III-1

$$EOQ = \sqrt{\frac{2US}{IC}} \tag{3-6}$$

where

U = annual usage, pieces

S = setup cost per setup (setup hours per order × setup cost per hour)

I = inventory carrying cost expressed as a decimal fraction

C = cost per piece

Some reasonable value of the inventory carrying cost should be used in the formula to calculate the trial order quantity. The specific value of the inventory carrying cost used in this first calculation is not of great significance because the order quantities eventually obtained as LIMIT order quantities will be the same regardless of the value selected. Using a reasonable value of I, however, shows what would result if the standard approach to EOQ calculations were adopted and the trial order quantities were used directly.

For item 1A, the following answer is obtained for the trial order quantity (TOQ) using the EOQ formula and a carrying cost, I, equal to 0.20:

$$TOQ = \sqrt{\frac{(2 \times 3000 \times 5.5 \times 2.80)}{(0.20 \times 6.12) = 274}}$$

An order quantity is similarly calculated for each item and is entered in the column headed "Trial order quantity," as shown in Figure III-1.

The yearly setup hours resulting from the use of the trial order quantities are then determined in the same manner used to calculate the yearly setup for the present order quantities. Item 1A is calculated as follows:

$$TOQ = \left(\frac{3000}{274}\right) \times 5.5 = 60.0$$

This trial setup is calculated for each item and entered in the column headed "Yearly setup hours, trial." The column is then totaled, as in Figure III-1. Note that the order quantities calculated using an inventory carrying cost of 20% would give a 30% decrease in the order quantity but would cause a 43% increase in setup hours over the present order quantities.

The next step is to determine the order quantities that will result in the same total annual setup hours as the present order quantities. Having calculated the total setup hours that would result from the present order quantity (152.5 hours) and the total yearly setup hours that result from the trial order quantities (217.4), the LIMIT formulas can now be applied to calculate LIMIT order quantities. The derivation of these formulas is shown later in this appendix.

$$\text{LIMIT formula 1:} \quad I_b = I_a \left(\frac{H_b}{H_a} \right)^2 \tag{1}$$

and

$$\text{LIMIT formula 2:} \quad M = \left(\frac{H_a}{H_b} \right) \tag{2}$$

where

H_b = total setup hours resulting from present order quantities, which will be equal to the total for the LIMIT order quantities, since this is the limiting factor

H_a = total setup hours resulting from trial order quantities.

I_a = inventory carrying cost used to calculate trial order quantities.

I_b = The implied inventory carrying cost used in calculating the LIMIT order quantities.

LIMIT formula 1 is used to determine the implied inventory carrying cost that is used in the EOQ formula to calculate LIMIT order quantities so that the total setup hours associated with these lot-sizes are approximately equal to those resulting from present lot-sizes. LIMIT formula 2 provides a multiplying factor M to convert trial order quantities simply and directly to LIMIT order quantities, eliminating the need to recalculate these using the square-root formula with the implied inventory carrying cost. LIMIT order quantities are identical in both cases and are the most economical lot-sizes that can be used while staying within the present setup-hour limitation.

The following illustrates the calculations of the LIMIT order quantities and the resulting yearly setup hours in Figure III-1. Using LIMIT formula 1 and LIMIT formula 2, the implied inventory-carrying cost and the multiplier factor are determined as

$$I_b = 0.20 \left(\frac{152.5}{217.4} \right)^2 = 0.098$$

$$M = \left(\frac{217.4}{152.5} \right) = 1.428$$

Using the multiplier factor, the LIMIT order quantity for item 1A is calculated as follows:

Trial order quantity × multiplier factor = LIMIT order quantity

$$274 \times 1.428 = 391$$

Similarly, the order quantity is calculated for each item and entered in the table as shown in Figure III - 1.

The yearly setup hours resulting from the use of the LIMIT order quantities are calculated as before. For item 1A, for example, the calculation is

$$\left(\frac{3000}{391}\right) \times 5.5 = 42.3$$

This setup hour calculation is then made for each item and entered in the column headed "Yearly setup hours, LIMIT"; this column is then totaled. Note that the total yearly setups are equal for both the present and LIMIT order quantities, which is the desired result. There is apparently no reduction made in the total number of pieces in the order quantities by the LIMIT calculations. Extending these ordering quantities by the unit costs, however, will show that there has been a substantial reduction in the total *value* of the average lot-size inventory.

A comparison of the three sets of order quantities is shown in Figure III - 2 for both pieces and dollars. The average lot-size inventory (one-half the total) for the LIMIT order quantities is actually $767 less than it was with the present order quantities. This is a reduction of 15% in inventory investment with *no* increase in operating expense. In the preceding steps, the LIMIT order quantities were calculated to obtain the most economical order quantities possible within the present setup limitation.

Illustrating the second phase of the LIMIT calculations, Figure III - 3 shows the total lot-size inventories that result from various alternative setup limitations calculated using LIMIT formula 2. For example, the minimum average lot-size in-

	Pieces				Dollars		
No.	Present	Trial	LIMIT	Unit cost	Present	Trial	LIMIT
1A	600	274	391	$6.12	$3672	$1677	$2393
2B	350	343	490	2.85	998	977	1396
3C	1500	1673	2389	0.56	840	937	1338
4D	400	233	333	2.26	904	527	753
5E	300	128	183	4.08	1224	522	747
6F	950	271	387	0.91	864	246	352
7G	150	104	149	3.09	464	321	460
8H	1000	516	737	0.42	420	217	309
9I	275	173	247	2.05	564	354	506
10J	310	361	516	0.79	245	285	407
Total	5835	4076	5822		$10,195	$6063	$8661

Figure III-2 AVERAGE LOT-SIZE INVENTORY VALUE

Implied inventory cost (%)	Total setup hours	Total setup cost (at $2.80 per hour)	Total avg. order qty. inv. ($)	Mult. factor
(Present)	152.50	$ 427	$ 5097.50	— — —
4.2 %	100.00	$ 280	$ 6660.00	2.2
9.5 %	150.00	$ 420	$ 4550.00	1.5
9.8 % (LIMIT)	152.20	$ 426	$ 4330.50	1.4
17.0 %	200.00	$ 560	$ 3340.00	1.1
20.0 % (Trial)	217.40	$ 609	$ 3031.50	1.0
26.5 %	250.00	$ 700	$ 2730.00	0.9
38.0 %	300.00	$ 840	$ 2120.00	0.7
52.0 %	350.00	$ 980	$ 1820.00	0.6
68.0 %	400.00	$ 1120	$ 1515.00	0.5

Figure III-3 ALTERNATIVE TOTAL LOT-SIZE INVENTORIES

ventory for this family of items using only 250 hours of setup time is determined as follows:

$$M = \left(\frac{217.4}{250}\right) = 0.87 \quad (\text{or } 0.9)$$

The corresponding value of the total trial order quantity in dollars (from Figure III-2) is $6063. The total lot-size inventory for a 250-hour setup limitation is therefore

$$\$6063 \times 0.9 = \$5460$$

and the average lot-size inventory is

$$\frac{\$5460}{2} = \$2730$$

Figure III - 3 shows the average order quantity inventory for various alternative setup levels for this family of items. It also shows the data for present conditions and for the trial and LIMIT calculations. As stated previously, it is possible to reduce the present inventory level without increasing the setup cost. Inspection of Figure III - 3 shows it is also possible to reduce the total setup requirement without increasing the average inventory level. A setup total somewhere between 100 and 150 hours yields the same total average order quantity inventory as the present $5097.50. Both of these result in savings with no offsetting increases in cost.

The data in Figure III - 3 can also be presented as a curve such as the one shown in Figure III - 4. The present condition is shown as point A and the LIMIT situation is point B. Holding inventory constant and reducing setup costs is illustrated by point C. The trial order situation is represented by point D. The curve shows the *lowest total average order quantity inventory* that can be obtained by operating with the setup hours shown.

The example used here involved a family of items with a setup limitation.

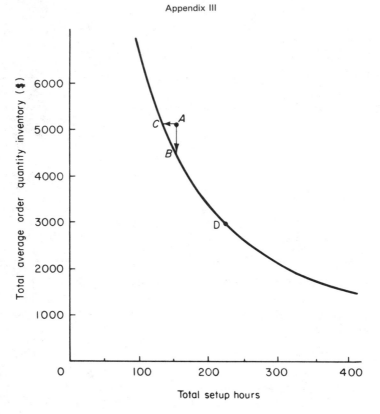

Figure III-4 CURVE OF LOT-SIZE INVENTORY VS. SETUP

The technique can be used equally well to solve a problem for purchased parts where the limitation is based on the number of orders. In this case, the items would be grouped according to vendors or buyers. When worthwhile discount schedules are involved, the LIMIT discount program covered later in this appendix should be used.

Advantages of LIMIT

The standard approach to economic ordering quantities assumes that a precise value for the inventory carrying cost can be determined. The LIMIT concept makes it possible to realize substantial savings through the use of lot quantities obtained by applying the EOQ principles without the need for determining a precise value for the inventory carrying cost.

In addition, LIMIT has the following advantages:

1. It is simple to understand and easy to apply.

2. It points the way to immediate gains—either decreased inventory investment or lower ordering costs—without any offsetting increases.

3. It shows real-life economies of EOQ as they apply to a specific situation and what action must be taken to attain these economies.

4. LIMIT presents information on *total* inventories, *total* ordering costs and *total* inventory investment costs and is not restricted to individual item considerations.

5. LIMIT is on management's wavelength. It shows the alternative of increasing investment versus reducing operating costs in the familiar terms that management needs to manage the lot-size inventory.

Applications of LIMIT

One of the first applications of LIMIT was in a large screw machine department. Standad EOQ calculations had been used to generate lot-sizes and, as a result, far more setup time was required than could be handled by the available setup people in the department. There were no additional setup people to be hired in the area and training operators to set up machines would have required a very long time. The EOQ's generated by the formula were, as a consequence, not at all economical. In fact, the company had to purchase screw machine parts from outside sources because their machine utilization decreased substantially as a result of the additional setups required by the EOQ's. The LIMIT formulas were used to recalculate lot-sizes for all the parts made in the screw machine department, so that setups stayed within the setup hour limitation that existed—these were the most economical lot-sizes for the existing circumstances. LIMIT also showed the management of this company the overall economics of the application of EOQ's and how to reduce the lot-size inventory by increasing setup hours as more trained people were added.

Plant management people whose experience has been primarily in manufacturing are frequently disturbed by the amount of setup time that is needed. They feel that too many setup hours are being generated to allow the most economical operation of the plant. Use of the LIMIT program shows the total setup hour requirements with the present lot-sizes and the revised lot-sizes, using whatever inventory carrying cost is considered appropriate by the company. Thus it shows the range of alternate decisions. After reviewing these alternatives in one plant, management personnel who were previously concerned about having too much setup time decided to increase the amount of setup. The fact that LIMIT showed them the inventory costs implied by their decisions aided them in establishing more rational policies that balanced better the real alternatives in lot-size inventory management. The LIMIT calculations show the total lot-size inventory versus total setup cost decision in terms familiar to management, accustomed to making decisions involving additional investment balanced against decreased operating costs.

While the LIMIT concept was developed around the philosophy of varying the inventory carrying cost to suit management policy, it can be used as a simulator even if management has known inventory carrying cost which they believe to be correct for their circumstances. One of the two possible results of the application of EOQ's is to increase the lot-size inventory. Using the LIMIT calculations, the amount of this increase can be predicted and even planned in practical steps. Plans can then be made to have the necessary capital and space available to handle this increase. Since the corresponding reduction in setup hours is also shown, definite plans can be made to realize the setup savings that should result from increases in the lot-size inventory.

With the standard approach to EOQ's these savings are seldom known definitely in advance and are therefore seldom achieved. A reduction in setup hours of 15% or 20% among a group of setup people would rarely result in a proportional savings to the company, unless management knew about this reduction ahead of time and had made specific arrangements to capture these savings. This is also true of reductions in clerical costs associated with preparing purchase or manufacturing orders.

LIMIT is also of great value to materials control and manufacturing managers when the addition of automated equipment is being considered. Most companies are constantly exploring applications of automated equipment which is complex and usually requires long and expensive setups. This results in larger lot-sizes and very substantial increases in the lot-size inventories of the parts made on the new equipment. The LIMIT technique can be used to show the increased inventory investment and space requirements with the new equipment in comparison with the present situation. The result is a far more practical and satisfactory application of automated equipment, since all related factors will have been considered.

The idea of using the inventory carrying cost as a management policy variable rather than a fixed-cost factor enables the practitioner to cope with changing real-life conditions in industry. It frees him or her from dependence on faith in a formula and provides some valuable tools in managing the lot-size inventory.

LIMIT-Discount

The standard EOQ calculation or the LIMIT program can be used to arrive at the optimum ordering quantities for manufactured parts. When material is purchased, however, there is frequently a discount schedule offering a reduction in unit price for larger purchases.

The normal method for handling discounts was covered in Chapter 3. Basically, calculations are made to determine whether the added inventory carried because of the larger lot-size costs more or less than the amount saved by taking advantage of the discount. Once again, the entire decision hinges upon the inventory-carrying cost used to determine what the added inventory will cost. This cost is then balanced against the total savings from the discount and from the fewer number of orders being placed.

One of the most serious problems for the practitioner arises because practically every discount appears attractive. If every discount were taken, however, the inventory could be increased beyond the company's financial capacity or beyond the available storage space. It is not a novelty for a materials manager to wonder where to store material ordered to obtain savings from an attractive discount schedule.

The standard method for handling discounts is very much like an individual asking a stockbroker what he or she recommends as an attractive rate of return on an investment in common stocks. The broker indicates that 7% to 8% is a good figure and recommends several stocks presently earning at this level. It is obvious that the investor is limited in regard to the number of shares of stock he or she can buy by the capital available for investment, regardless of how many attractive opportunities are available. An investor begins by determining how much capital there is to invest and then picks the investments that should yield the greatest return. Discounts should be handled in the same way, recognizing that funds and space are limited, rather than basing all investment decisions solely upon an inventory carrying cost, which is, at best, only an approximation and which ignores the fact that some discounts yield higher returns than others.

How can this be done? **LIMIT-discount** is a technique for evaluating many discounts simultaneously. Using LIMIT-discount, the amount of money saved by the discount and the reduction in orders (because of larger order quantities when the discount is accepted) is expressed as a percentage of the required increase in the lot-size inventory level. This percentage is called the **discount preference ratio** and is really an expression of the rate of return on investment that each discount opportunity will yield. Using the discount preference ratio, each possible discount (there are often several available for a given item) is ranked according to its rate of return on investment. This shows the manager the most preferable discounts, listed in order of their attractiveness and also shows the added investment required in order to obtain the discount. The manager can now set a limitation on the amount of extra money that will be put into inventory and can be sure that the maximum savings within that limitation are being realized.

The steps in using LIMIT-discount are:

1. Choose a group of purchased items (these may be product, vendor or buyer groupings).
2. Calculate EOQ's for each item.
3. Obtain the discount schedule for each item from the vendors.
4. For each possible discount, calculate what will be saved by the discount, what will be saved by placing fewer purchase orders per year and the added investment that will be required in order to attain this saving.
5. Express the savings as a percentage of the added investment to obtain the *discount preference ratio.*
6. Rank each available discount according to the discount preference ratio, with the highest ratio item first.
7. List all available discounts showing savings for each versus investment and cumulative discount savings versus cumulative inventory investment.

Item #	Annual forecast	EOQ ($)	Orders per year
1342	$ 18,350	$ 1720	10.7
1343	5700	920	6.2
1434	4480	825	5.4
1460	2480	775	3.2
1469	2450	775	3.2
1471	1090	408	2.7
1620	926	368	2.5
1633	840	362	2.3
1635	565	296	1.9
1701	485	272	1.8
Totals		$ 6721	39.9
Average total lot-size inventory		$ 3360	

Figure III-5 LIMIT—DISCOUNT—ECONOMIC ORDERING QUANTITIES BEFORE CONSIDERING DISCOUNTS

The following example illustrates the technique. Figure III-5 shows the basic data concerning EOQ's before considering discounts for 10 items. All of the annual figures and lot-sizes are expressed in dollars for simplicity of calculation. Figure III-6 lists the available discount schedule. All the percentages are the amounts to be saved by going to the first discount order quantity. For example, item 1342 has a present lot-size of $1720, and a 2% discount is available if item 1342 is ordered in lots of $10,000 or more. A further 1.6% discount is available (this 1.6% is a percentage that can be saved on the *already* discounted price used with the previous lot-size) if item 1342 is ordered in lots of $20,000 or more. *Each discount is handled as if it were a separate item* (and, in fact, in the final ranking, the two available discounts for item 1342 rank in positions 5 and 9, respectively).

Item #	First discount at minimum % order qty.		Second discount at minimum % order qty.	
1342	2.0 %	$ 10,000	1.6%	$ 20,000
1343	12.0 %	$ 10,000		
1434	11.0 %	$ 5000	10.0%	$ 10,000
1460	7.0 %	$ 5000		
1469		None available		
1471	7.0 %	$ 3000		
1620		None available		
1633	5.0 %	$ 1000	3.0%	$ 2000
1635		None available		
1701	5.0 %	$ 1000		

Figure III-6 LIMIT—DISCOUNT—THE DISCOUNT SCHEDULE

Figure III-7 shows the calculation of the discount preference ratio. The first five columns are taken from Figures III-5 and III-6. The suffixes 1D and 2D refer to first and second discounts. The annual discount is calculated by multiplying the discount percentage rate by the annual forecast and represents the amount of money to be saved annually because of the lower unit cost. Note that the annual forecast for the second discount for item 1342 is different from that for the first. The *discounted annual usage* is the total annual forecast minus the value of the annual discounts taken. It is the net cost of 1 year's supply at the discount price. The LIMIT-discount program assumes that the first discount has already been taken or the second one would not even be under consideration.

The eighth column in Figure III-7 shows the number of orders per year that would be placed if each discount were accepted. The ninth column shows the number of orders per year saved by taking each discount and is obtained by subtracting the figure in the eighth column from that in the fourth. To keep this example simple, it has been assumed that the cost of placing orders is negligible and no annual savings is included because of the reduction in number of orders placed. In a real application, this savings would be added to the annual discount (column 6) to calculate the preference ratio.

The tenth column lists the discounted order quantities and the eleventh shows the average added inventory resulting from accepting the discount. This calculation is made by subtracting the order quantity before discount from the discount order quantity and dividing the answer by two to determine the average extra inventory investment. Here is an example for item 1342-ID:

Discount order quantity	= $10,000
Order quantity before discount	= $1720
Increase in order quantity	= $8280
Increase in average lot-size inventory	= $4140

The discount preference ratio is now calculated by expressing the annual discount savings (column 6) as a percentage of the average added inventory investment (column 11). An example for item 1342-ID is shown:

Annual discount	= $367
Average added inventory	= $4140
Discount preference ratio	$= \dfrac{\$367}{\$4,140} = 8.9\%$

The items under consideration are then ranked in order of their discount preference ratio, the highest one first, and Figure III-8 is drawn up showing the discount versus investment situation in perspective. Some important points should be noted:

1. Before the discounts were considered, there were 39.9 orders placed per year and the average lot-size inventory was $3360 (see Figure III-5).

2. If all the available discounts were taken, the number of orders would be

(1) Item	(2) Amount forecast $	(3) O.Q. before disc.	(4) Ord. per year	(5) Disc. %	(6) Ann. disc.	(7) Disc. annual usage $	(8) Disc. ord. per year	(9) Ord. saved per year	(10) Disc. O.Q. $	(11) Avg. added inv.	(12) Disc. pref. ratio	(13) Rank
1342–1D	$18,350	$ 1720	10.7	2.0%	$ 367	$17,983	1.8	8.9	$10,000	$ 4140	8.9	5
1342–2D	17,983	10,000	1.8	1.6	286	17,697	0.9	0.9	20,000	5000	5.7	9
1343	5700	920	6.2	12.0	685	5015	0.5	5.7	10,000	4540	15.1	3
1434–1D	4480	825	5.4	11.0	494	3986	0.8	4.6	5000	2087	23.6	1
1434–2D	3986	5000	0.8	10.0	399	3587	0.4	0.4	10,000	2500	15.9	2
1460	2480	775	3.2	7.0	174	2306	0.5	2.7	5000	2113	8.2	6
1471	1090	408	2.7	7.0	76	1014	0.3	2.4	3000	1296	5.9	8
1633–1D	840	362	2.3	5.0	42	798	0.8	1.5	1000	319	13.2	4
1633–2D	798	1000	0.8	3.0	24	774	0.4	0.4	2000	500	4.8	10
1701	485	272	1.8	5.0	24	461	0.5	1.3	1000	364	6.6	7

Figure III-7 LIMIT—DISCOUNT—CALCULATING THE DISCOUNT PREFERENCE RATIO

Item	Disc. pref. ratio	Orders/ year saved	Cum. orders saved	No.of orders left	Disc.	Cum. disc.	Added inv.	Cum. added inv.
Present totals				No.of orders 39.9				Average lot-size inv. $3360
1434-1D	23.6	4.6	4.6	35.3	$494	$494	$2087	$2087
1434-2D	15.9	0.4	5.0	34.9	399	893	2500	4587
1343	15.1	5.7	10.7	29.2	685	1578	4540	9127
1633-1D	13.2	1.5	12.2	27.7	42	1620	319	9446
1342-1D	8.9	8.9	21.1	18.8	367	1987	4140	13,586
1460	8.2	2.7	23.8	16.1	174	2161	2113	15,699
1701	6.6	1.3	25.1	14.8	24	2185	364	16,063
1471	5.9	2.4	27.5	12.4	76	2261	1296	17,359
1342-2D	5.7	0.9	28.4	11.5	286	2547	5000	22,359
1633-2D	4.8	0.4	28.8	11.1	24	2571	500	22,859

Figure III-8 LIMIT—DISCOUNT—DISCOUNT VS. INVESTMENT

reduced to 11.1 orders per year but the inventory would have been increased by $22,859 to a new average lot-size inventory of $26,219. The savings resulting from a reduced number of orders was neglected in this example. The cumulative discount of $2571 would require an increased inventory investment of $22,859.

3. A good manager would undoubtedly move very slowly in considering a total investment increase of this magnitude for these few items. Using LIMIT-discount, the manager can go back over the individual discounts offered and determine which ones to accept. For example, item 1434-ID has a first discount that is quite attractive at $494 and would require an additional inventory investment of only $2087. The manager can now go through item by item, determine how much to invest and see what the corresponding savings will be.

LIMIT-discount can be done manually (as illustrated in the previous example). It requires only a simple computer program but is far more practical on the computer for a large number of items. The basic calculations can be varied to suit a particular company's situation. For example, if the manager wished to assign a cost of $5.00 for each purchase order placed, the savings from placing fewer orders could be added to the discount savings in calculating the discount preference ratio.

The basic advantage of LIMIT-discount is that it presents the results of ordering quantity decisions in terms that are familiar to management. The manager can see how much extra money must be invested and what savings will result from this investment. If the manager chooses to take all the savings possible, he or she will know how much extra investment to make and will also have a basis for estimating the amount of extra space required.

Unless funds and space are unlimited, the standard approach to discounts presents many problems to the practitioner. The LIMIT-discount approach removes such risks.

Derivation of LIMIT Mathematical Formulas

The following symbols are used—with lowercase letters applying to individual items and capital letters to totals—for all items in any group:

$$a, A = \text{annual usage, in dollars}$$
$$q, Q = \text{EOQ, in dollars}$$
$$s, S = \text{setup or procurement cost, in dollars}$$
$$I = \text{inventory-carrying-cost fraction}$$
$$h, H = \text{setup or ordering time, in hours}$$
$$c = \text{setup or ordering cost, per hour}$$

Subscripts 1, 2, 3, . . . , n are used to designate symbols applied to individual items. The setup cost, c, and the inventory carrying cost fraction, I, are assumed constant for all items and hence carry no subscripts.

The EOQ is given by the basic equation from Chapter 3, equation (3-1):

$$q = \sqrt{\frac{2as}{I}} \tag{3-1}$$

The number of orders needed per year for each item to produce the annual total demand is

$$n = \frac{a}{q} \tag{3}$$

Each item will require h setup hours at c dollars per hour, so that the total annual setup cost for each item is

$$nhc = \frac{ahc}{q} \tag{4}$$

For an inventory of n items, the total annual cost of setup is

$$S = \left(\frac{a_1 h_1 c}{q_1}\right) + \left(\frac{a_2 h_2 c}{q_2}\right) + \cdots + \left(\frac{a_n h_n c}{q_n}\right) \tag{5}$$

Equation (3-1) can also be written:

$$q = \sqrt{\frac{2as}{\sqrt{I}}} \tag{6}$$

Substituting equation (6) in equation (5) for each item gives

$$S = \frac{c\sqrt{I}\, a_1 h_1}{\sqrt{2a_1 s_1}} + \frac{c\sqrt{I}\, a_2 h_2}{\sqrt{2a_2 s_2}} + \cdots + \frac{c\sqrt{I}\, a_n h_n}{\sqrt{2a_n s_n}} \tag{7}$$

A basic assumption of this derivation is that I, the inventory carrying charge, is equal for all items in the group. Also, c, the cost of a setup hour, is assumed equal for the group of items. Equation (7) can then be rearranged:

$$S = c\sqrt{I}\left[\left(\frac{a_1 h_1}{\sqrt{2a_1 s_1}}\right) + \left(\frac{a_2 h_2}{\sqrt{2a_2 s_2}}\right) + \cdots + \left(\frac{a_n h_n}{\sqrt{2a_n s_n}}\right)\right] \tag{8}$$

Squaring both sides gives

$$S^2 = c^2 I\left[\left(\frac{a_1 h_1}{\sqrt{2a_1 s_1}}\right) + \left(\frac{a_2 h_2}{\sqrt{2a_2 s_2}}\right) + \cdots + \left(\frac{a_n h_n}{\sqrt{2a_n s_n}}\right)\right]^2 \tag{9}$$

Solving for I yields

$$I = \frac{S^2}{c^2}\left[\frac{1}{(a_1 h_1/\sqrt{2a_1 s_1}) + (a_2 h_2/\sqrt{2a_2 s_2}) + \cdots + (a_n h_n/\sqrt{2a_n s_n})}\right]^2 \tag{10}$$

The total annual setup hours, H, is equal to the total annual setup cost, S, divided by the cost per hour, c, or

$$H = \frac{S}{c} \tag{11}$$

Substituting equation (11) in equation (10) gives

$$I = H^2 \left[\frac{1}{(a_1 b_1 / \sqrt{2a_1 s_1}) + (a_2 b_2 / \sqrt{2a_2 s_2}) + \cdots + (a_n b_n / \sqrt{2a_n s_n})} \right]^2 \tag{12}$$

For simplification, let the quantity in brackets equal T, so that

$$T = \frac{1}{(a_1 b_1 / \sqrt{2a_1 s_1}) + (a_2 b_2 / \sqrt{2a_2 s_2}) + \cdots + (a_n b_n / \sqrt{2a_n s_n})} \tag{13}$$

Note that T is constant for a group of items and is independent of I. Equation (12) then becomes

$$I = H^2 T^2 \tag{14}$$

If the lot-sizes of individual items, q, are calculated for a family of n items using the best estimates available for the cost factors S, c and I, a corresponding value of total setup hours, H, for the group can be obtained from equations (4) and (10). This can be repeated for different values of I.

Each value of I yields one value of H. Let subscripts a, b, c, . . . designate corresponding values of I and H and from equation (14):

$$I_a = H_a^2 T^2 \quad \text{and} \quad I_b = H_b^2 T^2, \text{ etc.}$$

The total setup hours, H_a, resulting from EOQ's calculated in the usual manner (using estimated costs) may be impractical to attain immediately or beyond the capacity of the manufacturing facilities. This total of setup hours can be adjusted to any predetermined desired value by determining the proper value of I to use in the individual EOQ calculations. This is found by taking the ratio of the two equations:

$$\frac{I_a}{I_b} = \frac{H_a^2 T^2}{H_b^2 T^2} = \left(\frac{H_a}{H_b} \right)^2 \tag{15}$$

or, solving for I, the desired value of the carrying cost:

$$I_b = I_a \left(\frac{H_b}{H_a} \right)^2 \tag{16}$$

Equation (16) gives the "apparent" value of I to use in equation (3-1) when calculating each item's EOQ so that the resulting total setup hours will equal the desired value H_b.

To simplify the calculations for a family of items and avoid recalculating the square roots for each item, note from equation (6) that for I_a,

$$q_{na} = \sqrt{\frac{2a_n s_n}{I_a}} \tag{17}$$

and for I_b,

$$q_{nb} = \sqrt{\frac{2a_n s_n}{I_b}} \qquad (18)$$

Dividing equation (18) by (17)

$$\frac{q_{nb}}{q_{na}} = \sqrt{\frac{2a_n s_n}{I_b}} \div \sqrt{\frac{2a_n s_n}{I_a}}$$

or

$$\frac{q_{nb}}{q_{na}} = \sqrt{\frac{2a_n s_n}{I_b}} \times \sqrt{\frac{I_a}{2a_n s_n}}$$

and

$$q_{nb} = q_{na}(\sqrt{I_a/I_b}) \qquad (19)$$

Equation (15) can be restated as

$$\frac{H_a}{H_b} = \sqrt{\frac{I_a}{I_b}} = M \qquad (20)$$

Therefore, order quantities of individual items can be adjusted by the multiplier M (a constant for all items) calculated from equation (20) by:

$$q_{nb} = M \times q_{na} \qquad (21)$$

Equation (21) will adjust order quantities of individual items to give the least total inventory and hold the setup total for the family to any predetermined level H_b.

APPENDIX
IV

EFFECT OF CHANGES IN ORDER
QUANTITY ON TOTAL INVENTORY
INVESTMENT

When calculating economic lot-sizes, it is frequently assumed that a reduction in the lot-size portion of the inventory will reduce the total inventory by the same amount. This is not exactly the case. Reductions in the order quantity result in more frequent exposure to stockout and require larger reserve stocks for the same level of customer service. Figure IV-1 shows a series of possible order quantities for an item with an annual forecast of 96,000 units. The service level desired is one stockout in 2 years and the MAD is found to be 1680 units. The sixth column shows how reserve stock will have to increase as order quantity decreases in order to maintain the same service level.

Figure IV-2 shows a graph of the average lot-size inventory and the average total inventory, including reserve stocks, showing that reductions in lot-size inventory are not reflected in their full amounts in the total inventory because reserve stocks have to be increased.

Figure IV-1 shows that an extremely small order quantity (in his case, one that represents considerably less than a 1-week supply) actually results in a slightly higher total inventory than that for the next larger quantity. This is, of course, because the increase in reserve stock due to the additional exposures more than offsets the decrease in the average lot-size inventory for the smaller order quantity.

When lot-sizes are calculated independently of reserve stocks, there is no assurance that the total inventory that results will necessarily be the lowest inventory for the specified level of service. Frequently, a slightly larger lot-size results in a lower total inventory because reserve stock requirements are reduced. Without using fairly complex mathematical approaches, the best technique is an iterative trial and error approach.

Annual forecast = 96,000 units
Desired service level is 1 stockout in 2 years
Lead time = 4 weeks
Mean absolute deviation = 1680 units

Order quantity	Exposures per year	Service factor	Service ratio	Required number of MAD[1]	Reserve stock	One-half order quantity	Total inventory
96,000	1	1/2	50.0	0	0	48,000	48,000
48,000	2	3/4	75.0	0.84	1,410	24,000	25,410
32,000	3	5/6	83.3	1.20	2,020	16,000	18,020
24,000	4	7/8	87.5	1.43	2,400	12,000	14,400
16,000	6	11/12	91.7	1.74	2,920	8,000	10,920
12,000	8	15/16	93.8	1.93	3,240	6,000	9,240
8,000	12	23/24	95.8	2.16	3,630	4,000	7,630
4,000	24	47/48	97.9	2.55	4,280	2,000	6,280
2,000	48	95/96	99.0	2.91	4,890	1,000	5,890
1,000	96	191/192	99.5	3.20	5,380	500	5,880
500	192	383/384	99.7	3.44	5,770	250	6,020

(1) From Figure 5-7, Chapter 5, interpolated where neccessary.

Figure IV-1 EFFECT OF CHANGES IN ORDER QUANTITY ON TOTAL INVEN-
TORY INVESTMENT.

In practice, so many other factors can affect inventory investment that this effect is of little importance. The student should be aware of it and the practitioner should consider iterative calculations only on the very high value items, where the inventory savings would justify the additional computations.

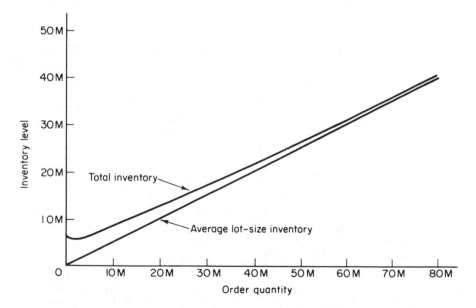

Figure IV-2 EFFECT OF CHANGES IN ORDER QUANTITY ON TOTAL INVEN-
TORY INVESTMENT (DATA FROM FIGURE IV-1)

STOREROOM TECHNIQUES

In many companies, the responsibility for storeroom control is assigned to the materials control group. Even where it is not, this group has a vital interest in these functions. It is good practice to have one manager responsible for operation of the storeroom and the accuracy of the inventory records used to control the storeroom.

One of the problems present in every storeroom is limited space. When space is inexpensive and the design life of parts fairly long, each item in inventory can have space permanently assigned to it and storeroom personnel will not need a location index to find it. This is called **fixed-location storage** and saves considerable time. The maximum number of parts to be stored using any type of storage usually approximates the economic lot-size plus two times the reserve stock. Reserve stock is intended to cover above average demand but it is reasonable to expect that demand will be below average just as often. If normal reserve stock for an item is equal to 100 units then, on the average, there should be 100 units on hand when the new supply arrives. When demand has been lower than normal, there might be as many as 200 units still in storage bins when the new lot arrives.

With each storage space assigned to a part, no advantage can be taken of bins or shelves that are empty or partially filled because the items normally stored in them are nearing the replenishment time. Storage space must be provided for the maximum expected quantity.

Because such a system does require more space, very few companies use a pure fixed location or reserved space storage system. Even those theoretically using this system find that many items of stock are actually juggled from one location to another as part of the normal operating procedure.

Another alternative is to have **random location storage**, where parts are assigned to available empty space when they reach the storeroom. This requires a location index telling the storeroom personnel which spaces are empty and available and where each item is stored. Random storage is more economical in terms of space since the total required need handle only the average inventory on hand (approximately one-half the economic lot-sizes plus the reserve stock). The clerical work of maintaining the locator file can be time-consuming if done manually, but it does lend itself to computerized information control.

A compromise system frequently used with either fixed or random location storage is called **zone storage**. Using this approach, all related components (for example, all those that go into a particular assembly) are located in the same general zone within the storeroom. This reduces the amount of back-and-forth traveling by the material handlers in collecting related components and reduces the time required.

Space requirements and the material handling effort in a storeroom can be greatly reduced by keeping working stocks of low-value items on the assembly floor and maintaining in the storeroom only the minimum or order point quantities equivalent to the maximum anticipated demand during lead time. When more low-value items are needed on the assembly floor, the required quantity is sent out and a replenishment lot is ordered at the same time.

Locator records in the past consisted of a simple 3-by-5-inch file or wheel index for each item listing its bin location. In some systems, material handlers report where they put the materials to a clerk who handles the locator file. In others, the space is preassigned and the material handlers are dispatched from central locations and told where the materials should go. The low cost of data transmission and computer storage and ability to use the data for other purposes has made manual records obsolete.

Locator files duplicate inventory records to the extent, at least, of part number and description and, at most, of where-used information and issues, receipts and balance-on-hand quantities. They must also be searched and updated each time a receipt or issue of parts is handled. A question that must be decided when using manual records is whether the inventory records should be kept in the stockroom or in the inventory office. They are generally more accurate and up-to-date if kept in the stockroom, where people find it easier to understand their function and to relate stockroom activity to the information on the records and where mailing delays affecting requisitions can be eliminated. Unfortunately, this makes it difficult to get the information required to those who need it to plan production, makes it harder for the supervisor of inventory control to review the records and uses space for an office function in an area needed for physical storage.

The ideal system makes it possible for both stockroom personnel and production and inventory control office personnel to have simultaneous accesss to the records. This is possible with modern computer and terminal systems accessible by both storeroom and planning office people. Other modern devices, such as electronic counting scales, optical character recognition and bar coding with light pencils are speeding up recording of storeroom transactions and improving their accuracy.

The number of storerooms and their locations should be of primary interest to materials control people. Whenever new storerooms are being considered, these people should be deeply involved in the question of whether there should be one storeroom or many, and they should simulate the amount of activity in the storeroom—the number of withdrawals and receipts—to help in deciding on labor, layout and equipment needs. They should recognize that the needs for accurate storeroom control must be balanced against the extra material handling cost that can be easily generated by too rigid a system.

One of the basic problems faced by materials control managers in maintaining records of storeroom inventories is that of assigning responsibility in the storeroom for record accuracy. Almost all but purely clerical errors in the inventory records can best be eliminated in the storeroom. There are many sources for these errors:

1. Extra material withdrawn from the storeroom to replace material that is lost, scrapped or, for other reasons, is not available on the assembly floor without making the necessary corrections in the records.

2. Withdrawal of material from the storeroom by unauthorized personnel—night-shift operators, department supervisors, sales or service people, etc.—without informing the records. Some companies handle the night-shift problem by giving a storeroom key and the responsibility of filling out the proper paperwork to a guard.

3. Direct delivery of urgently needed parts from manufacturing departments to assembly departments without going through inspection or the storeroom and having the proper paperwork made out. Handling this problem requires discipline and a clear understanding of each individual's responsibilities and of the benefits to be realized from maintaining accurate records. Rigid enforcement of materials movement into storerooms avoids this problem but adds extra material handling cost and delays the movement of urgent parts, so that it is rarely justified or enforceable. The combination of data collection terminals in fabrication departments informing computer-stored inventory records when work is completed permits developing a system that can determine whether or not there are any emergency requirements, deducting these from the records properly and delivering the components directly to the area that requires them.

4. Misidentification of parts, particularly if the same part is stored in various stages of manufacturing that are not easily recognized. One solution to this is to have the order number and part number transmitted to the inventory records clerk so that he or she can verify the identification by referring to the original manufacturing or purchase order.

5. Inaccurate piece counts, compared with requisitioned quantities, caused by human error or deliberate delivery of shop box quantities that are different from the ordered amounts. This causes additional work because some components must be returned and put away again. The use of counting scales and standardized shop boxes helps to ease this problem but the only real solution is good storehouse discipline.

6. Delayed flow of paperwork between material handling personnel and the inventory records, plus loss of some copies of important receipts or requisitions. One technique that can be of some assistance in being sure that all paperwork is getting into the inventory records is to have serially numbered forms for all documents that affect the inventory control records so that missing documents can be traced.

Undoubtedly, most problems in controlling storeroom inventories can be traced to poor education and lax discipline. Personnel whose activities have the most effect on record accuracy frequently have a poor understanding of their duties or of the results of their failures to follow the proper procedure. Manufacturing, material handling and other shop people seem to have a disdain for paperwork that can be overcome only by training and enforcing the rules. The introduction of sophisticated computer systems can hardly be expected to generate real improvement until tight control of information flows at all levels has been attained.

Standardizing on a few sizes and shapes of containers can be of great help in storeroom control. Plastic bins or pans and wire baskets are easily cleaned, nest well when empty, protect their contents from damage and maintain a constant tare weight for scale counting. Developing and insisting on the use of standard patterns for nesting components in the proper container aids greatly in accurate counting. There is no substitute for good housekeeping.

APPENDIX
VI

PHYSICAL INVENTORY TECHNIQUES

Taking the Annual
Physical Inventory

Many companies take an annual physical inventory which is intended to satisfy the auditors that the inventory records represent the value of this major asset accurately. Of more direct interest to planning people is the use of the data from the physical inventory to correct any inaccuracies that may have occurred in their records during the year. The responsibility for taking physical inventory usually falls upon the materials manager who should be sure that sound techniques are used to get the greatest benefits from the substantial costs incurred in such inventory taking.

Taking an inventory is very much like painting; the results depend principally upon the effort put into preparation. Preparation for physical inventory involves four phases:

1. **Housekeeping**
   Getting materials arranged and located properly so that they can be inventoried easily.

2. **Identification**
   The quality of the inventory depends on the accuracy of parts identification and there are only a limited number of people who can identify them. *All identification work should be completed prior to taking the physical counts.*

410

3. **Instruction**

   Letting everyone know what to do in taking the inventory: Which things are to be inventoried and which are not and the control disciplines that must be observed.

4. **Training**

   Actual training in counting and checking must be given to those people who will do the counting. Since physical inventory is usually taken on a yearly basis, even experienced personnel need to have their memories refreshed.

In taking the inventory, four basic steps are usually involved:

1. Count the goods and record the count on a ticket left on the material.

2. Verify this count either by recounting or by sampling.

3. List the inventory items in each department from the tickets.

4. Adjust the inventory records for differences between record and physical quantities and dollars. Recounts should be made of items with large discrepancies. Materials managers cannot take a passive approach to the annual physical inventory, even if it is not directly assigned to them. Their planning personnel should be active in organizing the inventory and supervising its taking. They should also be available to answer questions on procedure or identification during the actual inventory. Materials managers should also have checking teams available so that, as inventories are reported and posted against the records, obvious discrepancies can be checked immediately before production is resumed and recounts are made impossible.

Some general pointers that will help make a successful annual physical inventory are

1. Auditors will usually agree to a physical inventory of low-value items less frequently than once a year. Inventory records, if available, may be used. Many companies are determining by review of past data the value of low-value items as a percentage of other inventory totals and using this percentage to calculate the inventory for low-value items each year.

2. In choosing inventory teams consisting of inventory counters, checkers and an inventory writer, one individual should be able to identify material so that he or she can catch and correct misidentified items in the plant. This is the greatest single cause of errors *put into the records* by annual inventories.

3. Serially numbered inventory identification tags provide a method of insuring that all items counted have been accounted for in the records.

4. Prepunched tabulating cards can assist greatly in processing inventory data since they can have the correct item identification number, description, price, etc. punched into them from master records, eliminating hand-

writing and other human errors. The problems with prepunched cards are in determining how many of each card to prepare in advance for each item and in finding the correct card quickly while identifying material. If the number of prepunched cards is based on high-volume items, there will be far too many cards for most items, creating a very bulky file of cards to be searched. Preventing physical damage to cards (which makes them unfit for machine processing) is another serious problem. Nevertheless, the tremendous gains in increased accuracy and speed of processing make the use of prepunched cards a necessity for inventories of a large number of items. Bar-coding packages and items for identification and light pencils for recording the identities are a significant improvement over cards.

5. The most important concern in reconciling inventory records with the physical inventory data is the establishment of cutoff dates so that paperwork in the system is accounted for properly. An inventory of all parts on paper records, receiving reports, scrap tickets, requisitions, shipping orders, etc. is just as important as the physical inventory of the parts. Input and output papers should be posted properly to inventory records so that a valid comparison of record balances and physical counts is possible.

6. Inventory records should be updated and verified during the inventory if possible and always before physical inventory information is passed on to accounting. This permits rechecking physical counts and clearing up other questions immediately so that the inventory data are purified and so that production can be resumed based on accurate records. It can be extremely helpful to have duplicate inventory information available so that both physical and financial inventory records can be posted simultaneously.

One of the most helpful techniques to improve physical inventory taking is a post-inventory review. This is usually the time when people are least inclined even to think about physical inventory but this is also the time when problems that occurred during physical inventory taking are freshest in everyone's mind. If the people most directly involved are assembled in the post-mortem briefing, problems can be reviewed and specific program revisions can be developed for improving physical inventory taking procedures for the coming year. This is also the time to determine which items should be written off the inventory records. All companies, particularly fast-moving industries where obsolescence is a real problem, should have a policy for writing off unsalable items so that their financial statements accurately reflect the value of materials in inventory.

There are many disadvantages in taking a yearly physical inventory and many companies are getting away from this time-honored procedure. The greatest problem is that more errors are introduced into the records than are eliminated. Taking a physical inventory usually involves shutting the plant down and losing production. The labor and paper work can be very expensive. Since it is usually done under pressure, there is much hurrying to complete the inventory and it is frequently done poorly. Under any circumstances, using a large number of people who are not used to the job of taking inventory almost always results in waste and errors. Not the least of the disadvantages of an annual physical inventory is that it results in correcting record errors only once a year for the great majority of items. Because of these disadvantages, many companies are turning to periodic cycle inventories.

Cycle Counting

Cycle counting involves taking inventories on a sample of specific items at regular intervals so that records can be verified regularly rather than on an annual basis. Cycle inventory avoids the costly shutdown of production facilities and the high labor costs and overtime premiums that almost always result from the pressure to complete the annual physical inventory in minimum time. In addition, it can usually be handled by stockroom personnel during the off-peak hours and these employees can be trained to be far more accurate counters than the factory personnel who only take an inventory once a year.

Cycle inventories should be conducted in three phases: Phase I is designed to identify and eliminate the *causes* of errors; phase II is intended to verify the high levels of accuracy to the satisfaction of management and auditors; and phase III is intended to detect and correct new sources of errors and measure continuing accuracy levels. These and other aspects of cycle counting are covered in detail in Appendix I of the second volume.

There are disadvantages as well as advantages to cycle counting. The problem of establishing paperwork cutoff dates is difficult enough for an annual physical inventory but it becomes extremely challenging to handle effectively for cycle counts made while normal factory activity is going on. Picking up the paperwork in the system so that the inventory can be reconciled properly to the records requires considerable ingenuity and discipline. The most serious disadvantage of the cycle count system is that it is often done by people hired specifically for this purpose. These people are "overhead" and are highly visible for layoff when cutbacks occur. Cycle counting is performed also by regular stockroom personnel who normally have sufficient time to handle it. When activity in the factory picks up, however, there is always great reluctance to add more personnel in the stockroom. In order to permit stockroom personnel to handle stores' receipts and issues during periods of heavy activity, cycle counting is too often discontinued. More cycle count systems have failed for this reason than have been successful in spite of the obvious advantages of cycle counting. Accurate record keeping must be viewed as a vital part of the work content of all those involved in handling data.

Annual physical inventories or cycle counts are not a substitute for good records and discipline in handling paperwork. Many companies recognize their failure to maintain accurate records because of the resulting problems generated in the plant (such as shortages or overstocks), but they often depend solely on the physical inventory to straighten out their records. Unless the failures that caused the records to go wrong are corrected, the records will always be in error.

APPENDIX VII

CONTROLLING BRANCH WAREHOUSE INVENTORIES

The Basis for Successful Branch Warehouse Inventory Control

Increasing competition to provide better service to customers has resulted in heavy management pressures to spread distribution of the products more widely. Many large cities such as Atlanta, Chicago, Dallas, Los Angeles, New York and San Francisco have branch warehouses representing practically every major manufacturer in the country. They provide the customer with an extension of the factory in his or her own city, reducing delivery time to a minimum.

Unfortunately, many companies have been extremely disappointed with the results of their warehouse programs. Part of this disappointment has resulted from a lack of understanding of the fundamentals of inventory management. Managers have frequently been surprised to discover that the freight savings from carload and truckload versus LCL (less than full carload) and LTL (less than truckload) shipments are largely offset and often exceeded by the costs of running the warehouse and the added inventory required. This added inventory might well be justified to achieve the increase in customer service but it has too often come as a distinct surprise to the managers concerned. The surprise has become increasingly more unpleasant as interest rates and inventory-carrying costs increase.

In Chapter 5, the problem of splitting inventory among several locations was discussed and a general rule was formulated, which stated that the total inventory level increases as inventories are divided. A manufacturer in the Chicago region who decided to set up branch warehouses in New York, Atlanta, Dallas and San

Francisco would find that the total inventory required to maintain the same level of customer service would increase. With the total inventory now divided among a number of locations, the number of demands on individual locations of the inventory would be only a fraction of that on the original single location. Thus there would be a higher degree of variability and, necessarily, more reserve stock required in total.

In addition to this higher reserve stock inventory, there is also a transportation inventory that must be maintained—material in transit to the warehouses. Before the warehouses existed, this inventory belonged to the customers—since the shipment was en route to them—but now the transportation inventory belongs to the company.

Figure VII-1 shows the amount of transportation inventory that results from weekly shipments with a transit time of 4 weeks. In the first week, a truckload

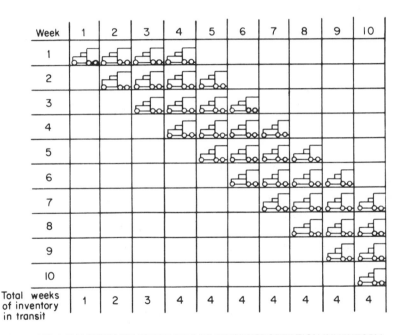

Figure VII-1 WAREHOUSE REPLENISHMENT TRANSPORTATION INVENTORY
TRANSIT TIME 4 WEEKS

of material is dispatched to the warehouse; in the second week, another truckload is dispatched—but the first truckload has not yet arrived. By the third week, there are three truckloads of material in transit and by the fourth week the system stabilizes with four truckloads of inventory in transit.

Thus when warehouse inventories are maintained at constant levels with deliveries replacing shipments, the simple rule can be applied that the transit inventory is equal to the transit interval times the selling rate. Written as an equation;

$$Q = T \times R$$

For example, a warehouse with a 3-week transit time and average sales of $30,000 per week would have an average in-transit inventory of:

$$Q = 3 \times 30,000$$
$$= \$90,000$$

Even when increases in warehouse inventory have been expected, results in the accompanying customer service have frequently been disappointing. Many companies have taken the approach that the warehouse inventories are part of the distribution system and, therefore, belong either to a separate distribution department or to the sales department. The result is that the responsibility for balancing service, inventory and efficient plant operation is no longer assumed by one person or department and much wasteful internal competition develops. Instead of having a great many customer orders coming in at a fairly even flow, the plant finds itself trying to react to very erratic demands from a few large warehouses. Since the personnel at these warehouses feel little or no responsibility for inventory levels back at the plant or for maintaining plant operations at efficient levels, their orders will be based only on their own evaluations of future demand.

The result is almost always to amplify the effects of changes in the rate of actual customer demand on the production level. This adds very drastically to the costs of operating the manufacturing facilities because of the frequent and substantial changes in production rates. Customer service results are frequently just the opposite of what the sales or distribution people intended. When each warehouse controls its own inventories, it is almost certain that production levels cannot be controlled to respond properly and that the inventory will not be distributed efficiently.

These facts can be verified by using the following approach: Warehouse demand on the factory can be compared with actual customer demand on the warehouses to see how much the warehouse demand amplifies customer demand. Then, all warehouse inventories can be checked for the items that are currently out of stock at the factory. It will almost always be found that some warehouses have a very good supply of these items. In addition, there will be some items on order with the factory that would not have to be manufactured at all if the inventory were properly distributed. This not only means that unnecessary inventory is being produced, it also means that *production capacity vitally needed to manufacture out-of-stock items is being used to produce items that are not needed.*

The warehouse problem is one of the best examples of what the language of operations research calls *suboptimization*. This simply means that different groups within the company pursue their own limited objectives rather than the overall company goals. When each warehouse is responsible only for its own inventory, the warehouse manager's chief concern is to fulfill his or her imagined needs without regard to the effects these demands will have on the other warehouses or the main plant. The manager also feels no responsibility for helping the plant maintain operating efficiency. I know of instances where branch warehouses had available space but were reducing inventory in order to meet their own budget goals, while the main plant, keeping production rates up in order to retain its trained manufacturing personnel, was renting public warehouse space to hold the material the warehouses weren't ordering. This is certainly suboptimization at its worst.

This approach is usually defended by saying that the warehouse "buys" its inventory from the plant and that the warehouses are the plant's best customers. Unfortunately, very few companies would be in business very long if their best customers scheduled their manufacturing operations. This approach makes as much sense as eliminating the planning department and just having the shipping room supervisor (as the plant's best customer) walk into the factory once a week and tell them what is needed.

The distribution of warehouse inventory is therefore part of the responsibility of managing all the inventory that results from manufacturing. The plant's materials manager should assume the responsibility for distributing inventories to the warehouses and maintaining services at these warehouses. This is just a further extension of the responsibility for balancing the three conflicting objectives. Increases in levels of warehouse inventories must be known to the materials manager in order to plan for the manufacturing of this extra inventory. Plans for any decreases in inventory levels at the warehouses also affect the plant's production plan. Once these production levels have been set, it is necessary to have information on the inventory status of individual items fed back from the warehouses so that these items can be replenished as needed.

Establishing Warehouse Inventory Control

The successful control of warehouse inventories involves the following steps:

1. Integrate the responsibility for warehouse inventories under the same executive who is responsible for the inventories at the main plant and make sure that the management of these inventories also includes maintaining customer service and plant operating efficiency to avoid suboptimization.

2. Establish an economical replenishment period for sending shipments to each warehouse.

3. Set the warehouse inventory level and allow for any increases or decreases required when planning the production level at the plant.

4. Develop inventory targets for each specific item in the inventory.

5. Replenish the warehouse inventory as it is sold, taking into consideration efficient shipping quantities and minimum package quantities. This technique involves replacing approximately the same quantity of each item that was sold during the replenishment period, called the **sales replacement technique**. It insures that the level of warehouse inventories will not change but that the mix will respond to sales requirements.

Integrating Warehouse Inventory Control

The problems involved in setting up an integrated system for warehouse inventory control are usually more political and educational than technical. If the branch warehouse inventories come under the jurisdiction of a sales, marketing or distribution function, these people will usually argue vigorously against losing this control by stating:

1. "Home office people are not close enough to the specialized needs of our region." While usually grossly exaggerated, this problem is a real one and underscores the need for the branch warehouse personnel to be educated to assume their responsibilities for notifying the central inventory control function of special local situations.

2. "Red tape will keep us from servicing special requirements quickly. " This potential problem can be avoided by giving the local branch manager the authority to order any extra quantity of a standard item or any nonwarehouse stock item with the understanding that as long as such items are handled on an exception basis, the rule will be to ship first and ask questions later.

3. "The home office people will not give us a fair share of short-supply items." With most decentralized systems, the orders from branch warehouses are often very difficult to evaluate in trying to allocate scarce items and personnel at the main plant may have developed the attitude (usually partly justified) that the warehouses are ordering beyond their needs and taking stock needed for main plant customers. The challenge then is to develop an effective information system that will make it possible to distribute scarce items equitably among all customers served by the main plant and the warehouses and to hold the central inventory control personnel responsible for customer service at the branch warehouses as well as the main shipping warehouse. Distributing all stock status reports to each branch warehouse will also help by letting them see that scarce items are being distributed equitably.

The feedback of information from the branch warehouses can take many forms:

1. Branch warehouse sends in a copy of customer order (by mail, teletype, etc.) and it is posted against an inventory record for this warehouse maintained manually or by data processing equipment.

2. Branch warehouse uses electronic order processing equipment and data are transmitted periodically to the main office.

3. A summary of branch warehouse sales activity is sent in periodically to coincide with the shipping schedule. This summary can be manual, punched card, paper tape, magnetic tape, disks, etc.

One of the most effective techniques (though not always the most economical) is to continue to maintain inventory records in the branch warehouses and have them report periodically on the stock status of all items that are active during the review period. This approach has the advantage of keeping the responsibility for the records within the branches. It eliminates discussion about whether or not the records are correct and it gives the branch warehouse manager up-to-date stock status information with which to answer customer inquiries.

The rapid progress that has been made in reducing data transmission costs has made it practical to send information from the branches to the central control center daily or even more often. A fairly standard approach is to type the orders at the branches on a terminal for transmission by telephone line, and records are immediately updated at the central inventory. Whatever techniques are used, however, the key to success will always be in developing good working relationships between the main plant and the branch warehouses.

Establishing an Economical
Replenishment Period

One of the most important considerations in setting up a warehouse control system is the replenishment period. Trucking companies, railroads and even steamship lines have freight rate schedules based upon the amount of freight included in each shipment. Consequently, any warehouse replenishment system must plan to include in each shipment sufficient quantity to obtain the lowest possible freight rate that is consistent with maintaining reasonable inventory investment and good customer service.

Figure VII-2 shows the type of basic calculation involved in determining an economic warehouse-replenishment period, assuming some of each item is handled in each shipment. In this example, the annual forecast is $1,375,000 worth of material to be shipped to this particular warehouse. There is a cost associated with picking an item off the shelf in the storeroom at the main plant and putting it away on the shelf in the warehouse. This cost is fairly constant for a wide range of quantity involved since it requires a trip to the location where the item is stored, one shipping document, etc. It is similar to the setup cost that must be considered in calculating economic lot-sizes.

The average cycle inventory is also similar to the average cycle inventory that results from an economic lot-size. If a weekly shipping quantity of $27,500 were chosen, the annual order cost would be $2000 (50 shipments times $40 picking cost) and the average cycle inventory (that portion of the inventory that results from the lot-size—which can never be smaller than the usage during the replenishment period—would be one-half of the shipping quantity, or $13,750.

Consequently, the costs can be calculated for any proposed shipping frequency by considering

1. The order cost (order frequency times fixed order picking and put away cost)

Inventory carrying cost = 10%

Annual shipments forecast = $1,375,000

Fixed order picking and put-away cost = $40

Shipping frequency	Order frequency	Order cost	Shipping quantity	Average cycle inv.	Average* reserve stock inv.	Total average inv.	Inv. carrying cost	Annual freight cost	Total cost
Every week	50/yr	$2000	$27,500	$13,750	$50,000	$63,750	$6375	$25,000	$33,375
Every 2nd week	25/yr	$1000	$55,000	$27,500	$58,500	$86,000	$8600	$22,000	$31,600
Every 3rd week	17/yr	$680	$81,000	$40,500	$66,500	$107,000	$10,700	$20,000	$31,380
Every 4th week	13/yr	$520	$106,000	$53,000	$74,000	$127,000	$12,700	$19,000	$32,220

*Assuming that a three-week replenishment lead time plus 1-week review period (4-week total lead time) requires $50,000 reserve stock inventory and using Table in Fig. 5-9, to estimate added reserve required as longer replenishment periods increase total lead time.

Figure VII-2 ECONOMIC WAREHOUSE REPLENISHMENT PERIOD

2. The inventory carrying cost (one-half the shipping quantity plus the reserve stock times the inventory carrying cost expressed as a decimal fraction)

3. The annual freight cost (which will diminish as larger shipments are made)

4. The change in reserve stock required as total lead time changes due to the change in shipping interval

In this particular example, the lowest total cost would result when a shipping schedule was set up so that the warehouse was replenished every third week.

As stated earlier, this example assumes that each item on which there was sales activity is replenished in the following shipment and that there is a fairly uniform number of items in each shipment, so that a constant order cost is valid.

Economies can be realized by shipping low-value items less frequently and in larger quantities. In such a system, C items could be replenished in every third or fourth shipment, requiring less handling at both ends and resulting in fewer different items in each shipment.

The use of computer techniques makes it possible to accumulate warehouse requirements until a shipment totaling a truckload is required and then to dispatch this to the warehouse. In practice, many companies perfer to make their shipments on a regular schedule so that the storeroom, shipping room and warehouse can each schedule their work on an orderly basis and so that the warehouse will know when to expect shipments and advise customers of deliveries. This requires adjusting each total shipping quantity to meet a predetermined minimum (carload, truckload, etc.) quantity. Techniques for meeting this requirement are discussed in the following sections.

Setting Levels of Branch Warehouse Inventory

The principle of setting the level of inventory and selecting the mix according to the latest customer demand applies to levels of branch warehouse inventories as well as to those in the main plant. Control of individual items in inventory is usually based on target inventory levels. The construction of these targets is discussed in detail in Chapter 5 (periodic review systems) and further specific applications to branch warehouse inventory control are discussed below. The base inventory level for a branch warehouse is the same as that for a main plant finished-goods inventory—it is equal to approximately one-half the sum of the order quantities plus the reserve stocks for all items (not counting, of course, the material in transit to the warehouse).

Total inventory levels for branch warehouses can then be planned using the same general format as the production plan covered in Chapter 9. Production, however, will now be the amount shipped from the main plant while sales are, of course, the shipments to (or, preferably, orders received from) customers. The reason for making out a warehouse inventory plan is to make sure that the production plans at the factory include any increases or decreases in the total warehouse inventories so that the effects of these fluctuations can be reflected in the total production level.

In practice, for most fairly stable product lines, it is not necessary to make a detailed inventory plan for a branch warehouse, but it is imperative that production planning at the main plant include changes in the warehouse inventory levels. These changes can usually be kept to a minimum and, for most stable product lines, the only significant buildup in the branch warehouse inventory would be to anticipate the annual plant vacation shutdown or to prepare for a major sales promotion effort. Changes in the level of inventory for individual items would normally be accounted for as target inventory levels for each item are recalculated.

Establishing Target Inventory Levels

The target inventory level for each stock item is made up of three elements:

1. Anticipated demand during the lead time
2. Anticipated demand during the review period
3. Reserve stock

The construction of a simple target inventory level was discussed in detail in Chapter 5. Its use for warehouses is presented later.

Lead Time

The lead time for a branch warehouse consists of the total elapsed time from the moment that it is decided to place a stock replenishment order on the main plant until the stock has been received at the branch warehouse, put away, and is once again available to the customers. The total replenishment cycle includes

1. Time for making up, transmitting and processing the stock replenishment order.
2. Time for picking and packing the replenishment order at the main plant
3. Transit time from the main plant to the branch warehouse
4. Put-away time at the branch warehouse

Total replenishment lead time is worth investigating in some detail to find out what it is (as opposed to what some people think it should be). Information should also be gathered on the dependability of replenishment lead time. This is an area that normally receives very little consideration. It is not unusual for shipping rooms to use branch warehouse replenishment orders as fill-in work around shipments to regular customers. The variability in replenishment lead time and the total replenishment lead time should be reduced to the lowest possible levels because longer and more variable lead times require greater reserve stocks (forecast reliability decreases as the forecast period is extended).

If, for example, it is felt that the shipping room should handle branch warehouse replenishment orders on a fill-in basis, then the total extra warehouse inventory (over that required to maintain customer service) caused by the resulting increase in variability in lead time should be spelled out clearly by materials control personnel so that management is aware of the effects of this decision.

Review Period

For all practical purposes, the length of the review period is the same as that of the warehouse replenishment period and, as the former is increased, the total replenishment lead time is increased by the same amount. In determining an economical replenishment period (as described in an earlier section of this appendix it will be found that reserve stock requirements increase very substantially as the replenishment period is increased.

It might be argued (from a purely theoretical point of view) that as the review cycle increases, the order quantities become larger—thus giving fewer exposures to stockout and requiring less reserve stock (refer to Chapter 5 for the concept of exposures). There is no doubt that the minimum order quantities become larger as the replenishment period increases. For example, if the replenishment period were increased from 1 to 3 weeks, the smallest reasonable order quantity would be equivalent to a 3-week supply (the order quantity in a periodic review system is equivalent to the usage during the review period). In the case of a periodically replenished inventory, however, this is much more a theoretical than an actual consideration.

In Chapter 5, while discussing statistical measures of customer service, it was pointed out that counting stockouts alone neglects the *duration* of stockouts. In a continuous review system, the length of time that an item is out of stock is not likely to change as the order quantities are increased so that measuring service by the number of stockouts becomes an effective means of measuring relative performance. This is not true, however, in a periodic-review system, since lengthening the replenishment period not only makes the lot-sizes larger but also increases the potential duration of any stockout that occurs and a comparable measure of service no longer exists.

In practice, it is best to ignore the theoretical effect of the increased lot-sizes and reduced exposure to stockout that occurs when the replenishment period is increased. From the customers' point of view, service might be poorer because it will take longer to correct an out-of-stock situation with more time between factory shipments.

Reserve Stock

Reserve stock for individual items can be calculated using the same statistical techniques described in Chapter 5. With a computer, periodic updating of reserves is thoroughly practical. In many applications (particularly since warehouse inventory control can usually be improved drastically by integrating it with factory control) it is often worthwhile to start out with some fairly simple reserve stock calculations.

These calculations can be handled by sampling some representative items from each of the product groups, picking samples of A items, B items and C items. Order quantities frequently work out to be nearly equal and may then be standardized in terms of length of supply for all A items, all B items and all C items. For example, in a warehouse inventory that was being replenished every second week, it might be decided to order up to the target inventory level for any A or B item that was below target and to order any C item that was far enough below the target to be shipped in an economical quantity (usually a unit package). Since these order quantities are often similar (with a tendency for the C items to have the largest order quantities and the A items to have the smallest order quantities), it is sometimes satisfactory as a starting method without computing equipment to set reserve stocks by category. This might involve, for example, having a 3-week reserve stock on all A items, 4-week stock on B items, and 5-week stock on C items since the lower-volume items tend to have a greater variation in demand.

In many cases, it actually turns out to be fairly satisfactory to maintain the same level of reserve stock for all classes of items (since the A items, while having a more stable demand, also have a higher service requirement). Nevertheless, this conclusion should not be drawn automatically. Even where only manual techniques are available, an analysis of a sample of inventory items should be made and a series of simple rules should be established for determining reserve stocks rationally. Once the system is operative, further improvements can usually be made by doing a weekly or monthly statistical analysis of incoming business by item, recalculating the standard deviation of forecast error and computing the reserve stock requirements for each item according to this error.

Additional reserve stocks may be required if shipping lead times are unpredictable or if the shipping quantity is limited. For example, a company that uses its own truck to ship to its branch warehouses would normally ship only as much as that truck could hold to avoid using more expensive common carriers for small overages. If the total sales ran higher than anticipated for a number of weeks, there would be a chance of jeopardizing customer service seriously if only one truckload could be shipped during each replenishment period. This can be avoided by scheduling an extra common carrier shipment, by sending an extra shipment via the company truck between regular replenishment periods or by carrying extra stabilization stock in the warehouse such as would be carried to protect against variations in the total level of incoming business in conjunction with the production plan (see Chapter 9).

Order quantities in a warehouse replenishment system are basically a function of the replenishment period. Standard economic order quantity calculations should almost never be used for a branch warehouse. When the replenishment period has been determined, the minimum order quantity that will probably be used on the majority of items in inventory is automatically determined, since the order quantity can never be less than the average demand during the review period in a periodic review system. Moreover, the items being ordered from the main plant are usually in inventory, all items are included in one order and the ordering costs are usually very small. There will be no setup cost in the factory directly related to the number of warehouse replenishment orders, the total cost for picking an order will usually vary little with reasonably small changes in the number of pieces of items to be picked and the cost of putting items away in the warehouse varies little with the number of pieces of each item.

In general, then, the order quantity for all A items is usually made equivalent to the demand during the review period and each A item is simply ordered up to the target level and replenished in each shipment made to the warehouse. The C items, which also tend to be the slow-moving items, are usually replenished only in reasonable minimum shipping quantities (such as carton or pallet-load quantities). The B items are frequently treated like A items or some minimum ordering quantity is set for them in order to reduce the number of items that are picked each week. For example, it might be reasonable to set the minimum ordering quantity for a B item at a 4-week supply when the normal replenishment period is 2 weeks. This would mean then that A items were picked in the main plant warehouse to go with every shipment, that half of the B items would normally be picked one time and half the other, and that C items would be picked only when it was possible to ship a minimum economical shipping quantity.

While these are broad, common-sense rules for determining order quantities in a replenishment operation for a branch warehouse, there are occasional freight and handling economies available through shipping in pallet loads or other large unit loads that are practical only for the fast-moving items and that increase inventories. When studying such alternatives, it is important for the materials manager to be capable of showing the added inventory investment that will be required so that the actual economies involved in shipping in large quantities can be evaluated objectively.

The calculation of the target inventory for an individual inventory item is

$$T = \text{DLT} + \text{DRP} + R$$

where

$$T = \text{Target Order Level}$$
$$DLT = \text{Demand during replenishment lead time}$$
$$DRP = \text{Demand during review period}$$
$$R = \text{Reserve stock}$$

Data for item 114 are:

$$\text{Lead time} = 2 \text{ weeks}$$
$$\text{Review period} = 1 \text{ week}$$
$$\text{Reserve} = 1.5 \text{ weeks}$$
$$\text{Forecast} = 80 \text{ units per week}$$
$$T = 160 + 80 + 120 = 360 \text{ units}$$

Thus whenever a replenishment order is being prepared and the inventory for item 114 is under 360 units, the difference between the actual inventory level and the target will be ordered. The order quantity in a simple periodic review system is equal to the demand during the review period so the average order quantity for item 114 would be 80 units if actual incoming orders were as forecast.

There are circumstances in which it is desirable to have a minimum order quantity. If item 114 were shipped only in cartons of 144 units each, the target inventory would then be

$$T = \text{DLT} + \text{OQ} + R$$

where OQ is the minimum ordering quantity (greater than DRP). Then

$$T = 160 + 144 + 120 = 424 \text{ units}$$

This formula simply reflects the fact that when the minimum order quantity is greater than the demand during the review period the target inventory must be adjusted upward to reflect this. The new order quantity should be as close to a multiple of the usage during the replenishment period as possible so that, on the average, the inventory for this item would be replenished every second, third or fourth shipment to the warehouse.

The base inventory level for a branch warehouse can be calculated like any other base inventory level and, on the average, will be equal to the sum of one-half the order quantities plus the reserve stocks for all items. If the accounting records charge in-transit inventory to the branch warehouses, these will also have to be added to the base inventory levels.

The Sales Replacement Concept

The basic idea in setting up a warehouse replenishment system is to set the overall levels of inventory and keep them fairly constant and to replace what has been sold. This concept, called **sales replacement**, is utilized in practically every successful warehouse inventory replenishment system and usually takes the following form:

1. Target inventory levels are set for each item.
2. These target inventory levels determine the total base inventory level for the branch warehouse under consideration.
3. Periodically (usually coinciding with the replenishment cycle, although sometimes more frequently), either sales during the past replenishment period or the current inventory situation for each item is reported back to the main plant and all items are reordered up to their target inventory level and shipped to the branch warehouse.

The principal advantage of the sales replacement technique is that it stabilizes warehouse demand and keeps it from amplifying customer demand while, at the same time, it relays the actual requirements and the latest activity at the warehouse, so that this can be fed into the manufacturing control system of the main plant.

Some companies still use the cycle review system. Once every month or two, a physical inventory is taken and replacement stocks are then reordered from the main plant. This type of inventory replenishment system requires very high inventories and usually results in very poor service since it is slow to respond to change.

Fair Shares Distribution

Modern data transmission and low computer storage and calculating costs make it possible to refine the balancing of warehouse inventories in multiple locations. Centralized planning at the replenishment source keeps records of available inventory on each stocked unit and also of forecasts of customer demand at each location.

Production for warehouses and for those customers served by the plant directly is planned at a smooth rate. As each batch is completed, it is distributed to each warehouse to give each a **fair share**. This is defined by Robert G. Brown, a strong proponent of the technique, as the amount each warehouse needs, combined with present available inventories, to give it a time period equal to other locations before stockouts (*equal runout time*). The technique is quite similar to the major/minor setups method of distributing an economic order quantity among items in a family (see Chapter 3).

The calculated fair share is shipped to each warehouse when the quantity produced is adequate. When production is inadequate to cover all current needs, the decision on which warehouse gets how much must be made on the basis of giving the least worst customer service and keeping shipping costs low. Such a situation indicates a real capacity problem and this must be solved before any priority technique can work effectively.

Branch Warehouse Stock-Status Reports

Branch warehouse stock status reports can range from very simple manual reports to fairly sophisticated reports turned out by computers. Figure VII-3 shows a basic branch warehouse stock-status report. If the target inventory for each item on this report were equal to a 6-week's supply, the weekly averages could be multiplied by 6 to establish the individual target levels.

For the sake of this example, however, it has been assumed that there is a further complication. In this particular case, a company truck is used to make regular shipments to the branch warehouse, but it can hold only approximately 1000 units (this assumes that 1000 units usually comprise about the same volume and weight, which is often true for product families). Because of this limitation, each new order must total approximately 1000 units. The formula for determining the total target level in this case is shown on the bottom of Figure VII-3. This formula calculates the total weeks of supply of all inventories available including on hand, in transit, on order and the next complete shipment.

The determination of specific order quantities for each item involves first setting up a target level which should be the same number of weeks of supply as calculated for all items. Thus all items should run out of stock simultaneously if not replenished and a balanced inventory results. Figure VII-4 shows target-level inventories for each item and Figure VII-5 shows the new order for each, calculated by substracting the on hand, in transit and on order figures from the target level. Note that the total of new orders is approximately 1000 units.

					Week #22
Item	Weekly average (W. A.)	Minimum order quantity	On hand (O. H.)	In transit (I. T.)	On order with main plant (O. O.)
#112	200	50	740	200	---
#114	80	10	210	80	180
#116	20	--	90	20	---
#118	90	10	240	100	100
#120	300	50	670	700	200
#124	100	10	250	150	100
#126	150	10	590	100	---
#130	70	10	430	---	---
Totals	1010		3220	1350	580

$$\text{S.Q.} = \text{Weekly shipping quantity} = 1000 \text{ units}$$

$$\text{Total available} = (\text{O.H.} + \text{I.T.} + \text{O.O.} + \text{S.Q.}) \div \text{W.A.}$$

$$= \frac{3220 + 1350 + 580 + 1000}{1010}$$

$$= \frac{6150}{1010}$$

$$= 6.1 \text{ weeks supply}$$

Figure VII-3 BRANCH WAREHOUSE STOCK STATUS REPORT (ALL FIGURES IN UNITS)

					Week #22	
Item	Weekly average (W.A.)	Minimum order quantity	On hand (O.H.)	In transit (I.T.)	On order with main plant (O.O.)	Target level
#112	200	50	740	200	---	1220
#114	80	10	210	80	180	490
#116	20	--	90	20	---	120
#118	90	10	240	100	100	550
#120	300	50	670	700	200	1830
#124	100	10	250	150	100	610
#126	150	10	590	100	---	910
#130	70	10	430	---	---	430
Totals	1010		3220	1350	580	6160

Figure VII-4 BRANCH WAREHOUSE STOCK STATUS REPORT WITH TARGET LEVEL (ALL FIGURES IN UNITS)

Item	Weekly average (W.A.)	Minimum order quantity	On hand (O.H.)	In transit (I.T.)	On order with main plant (O.O.)	Target level	New order
						Week #22	
#112	200	50	740	200	---	1220	280
#114	80	10	210	80	180	490	20
#116	20	--	90	20	---	120	10
#118	90	10	240	100	100	550	110
#120	300	50	670	700	200	1830	260
#124	100	10	250	150	100	610	110
#126	150	10	590	100	---	910	220
#130	70	10	430	---	---	430	---
Totals 1010			3220	1350	580	6160	1010

Figure VII-5 BRANCH WAREHOUSE STOCK STATUS REPORT WITH NEW ORDER QUANTITIES (ALL FIGURES IN UNITS)

One of the important points to keep in mind if the total shipping quantity is limited is that the total inventory on hand will decrease if total sales exceed this shipping quantity. The ordering technique illustrated by Figures VII-3, VII-4 and VII-5 will only allocate this shipping quantity and will not protect against loss of customer service. It is necessary to carry some total reserve stock to guard against variations in demand when shipping restrictions exist. This situation was discussed in this appendix in the section, "Establishing Target Inventory Levels."

There are many other variations possible in branch warehouse stock status reports. One of the simplest approaches is to set an ordering target, usually in the form of a minimum weight which will meet an economical shipping quantity using common carriers. An order clerk then reviews the warehouse stock status of all items, orders those required and then compares the shipping weight of this order with the total shipping weight target. If enough are not ordered, a few items in adequate supply at the main plant are added to raise the total to the target level. The added items are those which would have been ordered in the next week or two anyway.

Most companies find that for many product families, average weights are satisfactory for such calculations. When a computer is available, of course, it is quite reasonable to calculate the total from the actual weight of each item on the proposed order. In fact, a computer can be programmed to reexamine the items in stock and order those that are closest to the target level in any week when the total weight is not reached with the regular order. A computer can also be used to calculate exponential smoothing forecasts for each item, readjust targets, calculate statistical reserve stocks to establish more accurate target levels and set up a replenishment system that will be practically automatic except, of course, for special programs or unusual conditions.

Practical Considerations

The following suggestions can help the practitioner solve warehousing problems:

1. When installing a computer system, particularly one with automatic replenishment, it is important to assign operating responsibility to one person other than the system's designer. There is a strong temptation for everyone involved to take a hands-off approach to the system. Consequently, inaccurate input or circumstances that were unforeseen when the computer system was programmed pass uncorrected until a disaster of major proportions occurs and the problems are then blamed on the computer system.

2. It is wise not to develop too-sophisticated a branch warehouse replenishment system at first. The important point in developing any system is to improve upon the present situation in the first steps as quickly as possible and then to refine the system. Inventory replenishment systems are frequently so crude that they can be improved substantially with very little sophistication. The practitioner will usually find that the present system can be improved readily without starting with a complex set of new techniques.

3. The most serious problem of all will be developing coordination between the main plant and the branch warehouses—this will be a difficult concept to sell. It is important not to oversell it, since even this most necessary step will not cure all the problems existing in any normal inventory control system. Present performance should be measured—the inventory turnover and the customer service being given at each branch warehouse with the present system—and then the improvement resulting from system changes can be shown clearly. Many of the personnel involved, particularly those not in favor of an integrated warehouse inventory replenishment system, will tend to remember the "good old days" when there was never anything out of stock and everything worked out beautifully! Performance measures provide objective comparisons and goals for everyone.

4. When developing good communications between the main plant and the branch warehouse after ordering targets have been calculated at the main plant, even if done using data processing equipment, the individual targets should be reviewed by the branch warehouse managers so that they have a feeling of having had a part in establishing these targets and, equally important, so that adjustments may be made to them for special circumstances in the territory covered.

5. The ideal branch warehouse stock status report should be made at the main plant using inventory figures submitted by the branch warehouses and should show on it the inventory stock status for the main plant as well as for all branch warehouses. This enables the order clerk to do an effective job of allocating items that are in scarce supply and will also be of great help when ordering to a minimum shipping weight target. For example, since the clerk can tell which items are and which are not available at the main plant, the order is not likely to include critical items that cannot be shipped and would therefore, cause the total order to fall below the weight target. A copy of this stock status report sent to the branch warehouse will show the branch warehouse manager the details of the order that will be shipped subsequently. It will also show the stock condition at the main plant to demonstrate that the branch warehouse is getting a fair share of the available inventory. This will help tremendously in developing trust and a better working relationship between the manager of the branch warehouse and the main plant.

6. A regular shipping schedule for the branch warehouses (particularly if there are many of them) should be established for the main plant shipping room and the performance of the main plant in meeting this shipping schedule, as well as in shipping customer orders, should be measured.

7. One of the frequent complaints heard from planning and control people is that things are beyond their control. Management decisions, for example, are made to increase the number of branch warehouses or to use a cheaper method of shipping that will increase the shipping lead time or will require shipping to the branches at less frequent intervals. Management personnel making this type of decision should be given information as to the effects likely to occur (increased inventory or poorer customer service that will completely or partially offset the advantages of reduced costs or increased sales). Far from being beyond the control of the planners, it is their responsibility to assist in formulating these decisions.

In the future, there will be many times in most companies when the management will have to determine whether or not to add warehouses, eliminate warehouses or use premium shipping methods such as air freight. There are many intangibles involved in this type of decision but the amount of added inventory investment and the probable changes in the level of customer service are not intangible. These should be pointed out clearly and objectively by the materials manager.

INDEX

433

‘